2008 | THE LITTLE DATA BOOK

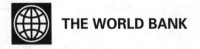

THE WORLD BANK

Copyright © 2008 by the International Bank for
Reconstruction and Development/THE WORLD BANK
1818 H Street, N.W.
Washington, D.C. 20433
U.S.A.

All rights reserved
Manufactured in the United States of America
First printing May 2008

ISBN: 978-0-8213-7400-9
E-ISBN: 9780821374283
DOI: 10.1596/978-0-8213-7400-9

The Little Data Book 2008 is a product of the Development Data Group
of the Development Economics Vice Presidency of the World Bank.

Editing, design, and layout by Communications Development Incorporated,
Washington, D.C. Cover design by Peter Grundy Art & Design, London, U.K.

Contents

Acknowledgments

The Little Data Book 2008 was prepared by a team led by David Cieslikowski, under the supervision of Eric Swanson, and comprising Awatif Abuzeid, Mehdi Akhlaghi, Azita Amjadi, Uranbileg Batjargal, Sebastien Dessus, Richard Fix, Masako Hiraga, Kiyomi Horiuchi, Soong Sup Lee, Ibrahim Levent, Raymond Muhula, Kyoko Okamoto, Saeed Ordoubadi, Sulekha Patel, Beatriz Prieto-Oramas, Changqing Sun, and K. M. Vijayalakshmi. The work was carried out under the management of Shaida Badiee.

Richard Fix, with the assistance of Azita Amjadi, Buyant Erdene Khaltarkhuu, Beatriz Prieto-Oramas, and William Prince, coordinated all stages of production. Meta de Coquereaumont, Christopher Trott, and Elaine Wilson of Communications Development Incorporated, provided design, editing, and layout. Staff from External Affairs oversaw publication and dissemination of the book.

Introduction

The Little Data Book 2008 is a pocket edition of *World Development Indicators 2008*. It is intended as a quick reference for users of the *World Development Indicators 2008* book and CD-ROM and *WDI Online,* our electronic subscription database. Together, they cover more than 800 indicators and span more than 40 years.

The 209 country tables in *The Little Data Book* present the latest available data for World Bank member countries and other economies with populations of more than 30,000. The 14 summary tables cover regional and income group aggregates.

For more information about these data or other World Bank data publications, visit our data Web site at www.worldbank.org/data, e-mail us at data@worldbank.org, call our data hotline 800 590 1906 or 202 473 7824, or fax us at 202 522 1498.

To order *World Development Indicators 2008* or the *World Development Indicators 2008* CD-ROM, visit the publications Web site at www.worldbank.org/publications, call 800 645 7247 or 703 661 1580, or fax 703 661 1501.

Data notes

The data in this book are for 1990, 2000, and 2006 or the most recent year unless otherwise noted in the *Glossary*.

- Growth rates are proportional changes from the previous year unless otherwise noted.

- Regional aggregates include data for low- and middle-income economies only.

- Figures in italics indicate data for years or periods other than those specified.

Symbols used:

..	indicates that data are not available or that aggregates cannot be calculated because of missing data
0 or 0.0	indicates zero or small enough that the number would round to zero at the displayed number of decimal places
$	indicates current U.S. dollars

Data are shown for economies with populations greater than 30,000 or for smaller economies if they are members of the World Bank. The term *country* (used interchangeably with *economy*) does not imply political independence or official recognition by the World Bank but refers to any economy for which the authorities report separate social or economic statistics.

The selection of indicators in these pages includes some of those being used to monitor progress towards the Millennium Development Goals. For more information about the eight goals—halving poverty and increasing well-being by 2015—please visit our Web site www.developmentgoals.org or see the other books in the *World Development Indicators 2008* series.

Regional tables

The country composition of regions is based on the World Bank's analytical regions and may differ from common geographic usage.

East Asia and Pacific

American Samoa, Cambodia, China, Fiji, Indonesia, Kiribati, Democratic Republic of Korea, Lao People's Democratic Republic, Malaysia, Marshall Islands, Federated States of Micronesia, Mongolia, Myanmar, Northern Mariana Islands, Palau, Papua New Guinea, Philippines, Samoa, Solomon Islands, Thailand, Timor-Leste, Tonga, Vanuatu, Vietnam

Europe and Central Asia

Albania, Armenia, Azerbaijan, Belarus, Bosnia and Herzegovina, Bulgaria, Croatia, Georgia, Hungary, Kazakhstan, Kyrgyz Republic, Latvia, Lithuania, Former Yugoslav Republic of Macedonia, Moldova, Montenegro, Poland, Romania, Russian Federation, Serbia, Slovak Republic, Tajikistan, Turkey, Turkmenistan, Ukraine, Uzbekistan

Latin America and the Caribbean

Argentina, Belize, Bolivia, Brazil, Chile, Colombia, Costa Rica, Cuba, Dominica, Dominican Republic, Ecuador, El Salvador, Grenada, Guatemala, Guyana, Haiti, Honduras, Jamaica, Mexico, Nicaragua, Panama, Paraguay, Peru, St. Kitts and Nevis, St. Lucia, St. Vincent and the Grenadines, Suriname, Uruguay, Bolivarian Republic of Venezuela

Middle East and North Africa

Algeria, Djibouti, Arab Republic of Egypt, Islamic Republic of Iran, Iraq, Jordan, Lebanon, Libya, Morocco, Oman, Syrian Arab Republic, Tunisia, West Bank and Gaza, Republic of Yemen

South Asia

Afghanistan, Bangladesh, Bhutan, India, Maldives, Nepal, Pakistan, Sri Lanka

Sub-Saharan Africa

Angola, Benin, Botswana, Burkina Faso, Burundi, Cameroon, Cape Verde, Central African Republic, Chad, Comoros, Democratic Republic of the Congo, Republic of Congo, Côte d'Ivoire, Equatorial Guinea, Eritrea, Ethiopia, Gabon, The Gambia, Ghana, Guinea, Guinea-Bissau, Kenya, Lesotho, Liberia, Madagascar, Malawi, Mali, Mauritania, Mauritius, Mayotte, Mozambique, Namibia, Niger, Nigeria, Rwanda, São Tomé and Principe, Senegal, Seychelles, Sierra Leone, Somalia, South Africa, Sudan, Swaziland, Tanzania, Togo, Uganda, Zambia, Zimbabwe

World

Population (millions)	6,538	Population growth (%)	1.2
Surface area (1,000 sq. km)	133,946	National poverty rate (% of pop.)	..
GNI ($ billions)	48,694.1	GNI per capita ($)	7,448
GNI, PPP ($ billions)	60,209.9	GNI per capita, PPP ($)	9,209

	1990	2000	2006
People			
Share of poorest 20% in nat'l consumption/income (%)	..	..	..
Life expectancy at birth (years)	65	67	68
Total fertility (births per woman)	3.1	2.7	2.5
Adolescent fertility (births per 1,000 women 15–19)	..	63	52
Contraceptive prevalence (% of married women 15–49)	57	..	60
Births attended by skilled health staff (% of total)	..	..	65
Under-five mortality rate (per 1,000)	92	84	73
Child malnutrition, underweight (% of under age 5)	..	..	24
Child immunization, measles (% of ages 12–23 mos.)	73	73	80
Primary completion rate, total (% of relevant age group)	79	83	86
Gross secondary enrollment, total (% of relevant age group)	..	60	65
Ratio of girls to boys in primary & secondary school (%)	86	92	95
HIV prevalence rate (% of population ages 15–49)	..	..	1.0
Environment			
Forests (1,000 sq. km)	40,679	397,922	39,426
Deforestation (average annual %, 1990–2005)			0.2
Freshwater use (% of internal resources)	..	9.1	..
Access to improved water source (% of total pop.)	76	81	83
Access to improved sanitation facilities (% of total pop.)	45	55	57
Energy use per capita (kilograms of oil equivalent)	1,682	1,672	1,796
Carbon dioxide emissions per capita (metric tons)	4.1	4.0	4.3
Electricity use per capita (kilowatt-hours)	2,118	2,389	2,678
Economy			
GDP ($ billions)	21,828.4	31,876.2	48,461.9
GDP growth (annual %)	2.9	4.1	3.8
GDP implicit price deflator (annual % growth)	8.2	4.8	5.7
Value added in agriculture (% of GDP)	5	4	3
Value added in industry (% of GDP)	33	29	28
Value added in services (% of GDP)	61	67	69
Exports of goods and services (% of GDP)	19	25	27
Imports of goods and services (% of GDP)	19	25	27
Gross capital formation (% of GDP)	23	22	22
Central government revenue (% of GDP)	..	26.1	27.0
Central government cash surplus/deficit (% of GDP)	..	–0.1	–1.2
States and markets			
Starting a business (days)			44
Stock market capitalization (% of GDP)	47.6	102.7	113.9
Military expenditures (% of GDP)	3.6	2.3	2.5
Fixed-line and mobile subscribers (per 100 people)	10	28	59
Internet users (per 100 people)	0.1	6.5	21.4
Paved roads (% of total)	36	36	..
High-technology exports (% of manufactured exports)	16	23	21
Global links			
Merchandise trade (% of GDP)	32.3	41.2	49.9
Net barter terms of trade (2000 = 100)	..	..	..
Total external debt ($ billions)	..	..	..
Short-term debt ($ billions)	..	..	..
Total debt service (% of exports)	..	..	..
Foreign direct investment, net inflows ($ billions)	205	1,518	1,352
Remittances received ($ billions)	69	132	297
Aid ($ billions)	59	58	105

East Asia & Pacific

Population (millions)	1,899	Population growth (%)	0.8
Surface area (1,000 sq. km)	16,300	National poverty rate (% of pop.)	..
GNI ($ billions)	3,524.7	GNI per capita ($)	1,856
GNI, PPP ($ billions)	8,277.0	GNI per capita, PPP ($)	4,359

	1990	2000	2006
People			
Share of poorest 20% in nat'l consumption/income (%)	..	..	..
Life expectancy at birth (years)	67	69	71
Total fertility (births per woman)	2.4	2.1	2.0
Adolescent fertility (births per 1,000 women 15–19)	..	18	16
Contraceptive prevalence (% of married women 15–49)	75	..	79
Births attended by skilled health staff (% of total)	47	..	87
Under-five mortality rate (per 1,000)	56	41	29
Child malnutrition, underweight (% of under age 5)	..	..	13
Child immunization, measles (% of ages 12–23 mos.)	90	83	89
Primary completion rate, total (% of relevant age group)	101	102	98
Gross secondary enrollment, total (% of relevant age group)	..	62	72
Ratio of girls to boys in primary & secondary school (%)	89	98	99
HIV prevalence rate (% of population ages 15–49)	..	..	0.2
Environment			
Forests (1,000 sq. km)	4,581	4,462	4,507
Deforestation (average annual %, 1990–2005)			0.1
Freshwater use (% of internal resources)	..	11.1	..
Access to improved water source (% of total pop.)	72	77	79
Access to improved sanitation facilities (% of total pop.)	30	47	51
Energy use per capita (kilograms of oil equivalent)	717	842	1,182
Carbon dioxide emissions per capita (metric tons)	1.9	2.4	3.3
Electricity use per capita (kilowatt-hours)	461	886	1,492
Economy			
GDP ($ billions)	667.5	1,719.1	3,616.7
GDP growth (annual %)	5.5	7.6	9.4
GDP implicit price deflator (annual % growth)	5.8	3.4	4.7
Value added in agriculture (% of GDP)	25	15	12
Value added in industry (% of GDP)	40	44	47
Value added in services (% of GDP)	35	41	41
Exports of goods and services (% of GDP)	24	36	47
Imports of goods and services (% of GDP)	23	32	40
Gross capital formation (% of GDP)	35	32	39
Central government revenue (% of GDP)	9.3	8.4	11.0
Central government cash surplus/deficit (% of GDP)	..	-2.6	-1.3
States and markets			
Starting a business (days)			47
Stock market capitalization (% of GDP)	16.4	47.2	85.1
Military expenditures (% of GDP)	2.5	1.7	1.8
Fixed-line and mobile subscribers (per 100 people)	1	15	58
Internet users (per 100 people)	0.0	1.9	11.1
Paved roads (% of total)	17	11	..
High-technology exports (% of manufactured exports)	11	31	33
Global links			
Merchandise trade (% of GDP)	47.1	59.7	75.7
Net barter terms of trade (2000 = 100)	..	..	..
Total external debt ($ billions)	234	498	660
Short-term debt ($ billions)	37	63	246
Total debt service (% of exports)	17.6	11.4	5.0
Foreign direct investment, net inflows ($ billions)	11	45	105
Remittances received ($ billions)	3.3	16.7	52.8
Aid ($ billions)	7.7	8.6	7.9

Europe & Central Asia

Population (millions)	461	Population growth (%)	0.1
Surface area (1,000 sq. km)	24,114	National poverty rate (% of pop.)	..
GNI ($ billions)	2,217.1	GNI per capita ($)	4,815
GNI, PPP ($ billions)	4,508.7	GNI per capita, PPP ($)	9,791

	1990	2000	2006
People			
Share of poorest 20% in nat'l consumption/income (%)	..	..	..
Life expectancy at birth (years)	69	69	69
Total fertility (births per woman)	2.3	1.6	1.6
Adolescent fertility (births per 1,000 women 15–19)		35	29
Contraceptive prevalence (% of married women 15–49)	46		63
Births attended by skilled health staff (% of total)	81	..	95
Under-five mortality rate (per 1,000)	49	36	26
Child malnutrition, underweight (% of under age 5)	..	..	..
Child immunization, measles (% of ages 12–23 mos.)	84	94	97
Primary completion rate, total (% of relevant age group)	93	95	95
Gross secondary enrollment, total (% of relevant age group)	84	88	89
Ratio of girls to boys in primary & secondary school (%)	98	97	96
HIV prevalence rate (% of population ages 15–49)	..	..	0.6
Environment			
Forests (1,000 sq. km)	8,845	8,865	8,869
Deforestation (average annual %, 1990–2005)			–0.02
Freshwater use (% of internal resources)	..	7.5	..
Access to improved water source (% of total pop.)	92	91	92
Access to improved sanitation facilities (% of total pop.)	84	85	85
Energy use per capita (kilograms of oil equivalent)	3,878	2,639	2,826
Carbon dioxide emissions per capita (metric tons)	10.3	6.7	7.1
Electricity use per capita (kilowatt-hours)	4,317	3,276	3,633
Economy			
GDP ($ billions)	1,076.2	901.8	2,499.4
GDP growth (annual %)	–1.9	6.7	6.8
GDP implicit price deflator (annual % growth)	13.6	12.9	8.4
Value added in agriculture (% of GDP)	16	10	7
Value added in industry (% of GDP)	42	32	33
Value added in services (% of GDP)	41	58	60
Exports of goods and services (% of GDP)	22	39	40
Imports of goods and services (% of GDP)	23	37	40
Gross capital formation (% of GDP)	27	22	23
Central government revenue (% of GDP)	..	..	31.5
Central government cash surplus/deficit (% of GDP)	..	..	1.8
States and markets			
Starting a business (days)			26
Stock market capitalization (% of GDP)	2.2	19.0	66.7
Military expenditures (% of GDP)	4.4	3.2	2.9
Fixed-line and mobile subscribers (per 100 people)	12	31	88
Internet users (per 100 people)	0.0	2.8	19.2
Paved roads (% of total)	77	74	..
High-technology exports (% of manufactured exports)	..	11	9
Global links			
Merchandise trade (% of GDP)	49.6	61.2	66.2
Net barter terms of trade (2000 = 100)	..	..	..
Total external debt ($ billions)	211	487	1,047
Short-term debt ($ billions)	37	77	222
Total debt service (% of exports)	..	19.0	20.0
Foreign direct investment, net inflows ($ billions)	3.3	24.8	124.6
Remittances received ($ billions)	3.2	13.1	35.4
Aid ($ billions)	3.5	10.3	6.2

Latin America & Caribbean

Population (millions)	556	Population growth (%)		1.3
Surface area (1,000 sq. km)	20,421	National poverty rate (% of pop.)		..
GNI ($ billions)	2,661.2	GNI per capita ($)		4,785
GNI, PPP ($ billions)	4,828.4	GNI per capita, PPP ($)		8,682

	1990	2000	2006
People			
Share of poorest 20% in nat'l consumption/income (%)	..	..	..
Life expectancy at birth (years)	68	72	73
Total fertility (births per woman)	3.2	2.7	2.4
Adolescent fertility (births per 1,000 women 15–19)	..	82	77
Contraceptive prevalence (% of married women 15–49)	57	..	69
Births attended by skilled health staff (% of total)	73	..	88
Under-five mortality rate (per 1,000)	55	35	26
Child malnutrition, underweight (% of under age 5)	..	..	5
Child immunization, measles (% of ages 12–23 mos.)	76	92	93
Primary completion rate, total (% of relevant age group)	82	97	99
Gross secondary enrollment, total (% of relevant age group)	51	83	89
Ratio of girls to boys in primary & secondary school (%)	99	101	101
HIV prevalence rate (% of population ages 15–49)	..	..	0.6
Environment			
Forests (1,000 sq. km)	9,834	9,385	9,147
Deforestation (average annual %, 1990–2005)			0.5
Freshwater use (% of internal resources)	..	2.0	..
Access to improved water source (% of total pop.)	83	89	91
Access to improved sanitation facilities (% of total pop.)	67	75	77
Energy use per capita (kilograms of oil equivalent)	1,039	1,150	1,198
Carbon dioxide emissions per capita (metric tons)	2.4	2.6	2.5
Electricity use per capita (kilowatt-hours)	1,188	1,580	1,715
Economy			
GDP ($ billions)	1,097.1	2,016.6	2,964.2
GDP growth (annual %)	0.3	3.9	5.5
GDP implicit price deflator (annual % growth)	23.8	6.6	6.8
Value added in agriculture (% of GDP)	9	6	6
Value added in industry (% of GDP)	36	30	31
Value added in services (% of GDP)	55	64	62
Exports of goods and services (% of GDP)	17	20	26
Imports of goods and services (% of GDP)	15	21	23
Gross capital formation (% of GDP)	19	20	21
Central government revenue (% of GDP)	19.5	18.4	..
Central government cash surplus/deficit (% of GDP)	-2.6	-1.3	..
States and markets			
Starting a business (days)			73
Stock market capitalization (% of GDP)	7.6	31.8	51.7
Military expenditures (% of GDP)	1.9	1.3	1.3
Fixed-line and mobile subscribers (per 100 people)	6	27	73
Internet users (per 100 people)	0.0	3.8	18.4
Paved roads (% of total)	22	24	..
High-technology exports (% of manufactured exports)	5	16	12
Global links			
Merchandise trade (% of GDP)	23.0	36.3	43.1
Net barter terms of trade (2000 = 100)	..	..	..
Total external debt ($ billions)	441	754	734
Short-term debt ($ billions)	73	111	106
Total debt service (% of exports)	23.9	39.0	23.0
Foreign direct investment, net inflows ($ billions)	8.1	79.5	70.5
Remittances received ($ billions)	5.7	20.0	56.9
Aid ($ billions)	5.1	4.8	6.9

Middle East & North Africa

Population (millions)	311	Population growth (%)	1.8
Surface area (1,000 sq. km)	9,087	National poverty rate (% of pop.)	
GNI ($ billions)	778.8	GNI per capita ($)	2,507
GNI, PPP ($ billions)	2,084.4	GNI per capita, PPP ($)	6,710

	1990	2000	2006
People			
Share of poorest 20% in nat'l consumption/income (%)	..	..	..
Life expectancy at birth (years)	64	68	70
Total fertility (births per woman)	4.8	3.2	2.9
Adolescent fertility (births per 1,000 women 15–19)	..	39	30
Contraceptive prevalence (% of married women 15–49)	41	..	60
Births attended by skilled health staff (% of total)	48	..	77
Under-five mortality rate (per 1,000)	77	51	42
Child malnutrition, underweight (% of under age 5)	..	..	..
Child immunization, measles (% of ages 12–23 mos.)	83	91	92
Primary completion rate, total (% of relevant age group)	77	82	91
Gross secondary enrollment, total (% of relevant age group)	..	68	74
Ratio of girls to boys in primary & secondary school (%)	82	90	94
HIV prevalence rate (% of population ages 15–49)	..	..	0.1
Environment			
Forests (1,000 sq. km)	200	208	211
Deforestation (average annual %, 1990–2005)			-0.4
Freshwater use (% of internal resources)	..	105.0	..
Access to improved water source (% of total pop.)	88	89	89
Access to improved sanitation facilities (% of total pop.)	70	76	76
Energy use per capita (kilograms of oil equivalent)	861	1,077	1,270
Carbon dioxide emissions per capita (metric tons)	2.5	3.6	3.9
Electricity use per capita (kilowatt-hours)	751	1,077	1,358
Economy			
GDP ($ billions)	276.9	451.4	734.4
GDP growth (annual %)	7.0	3.3	5.1
GDP implicit price deflator (annual % growth)	18.4	7.3	6.6
Value added in agriculture (% of GDP)	17	12	12
Value added in industry (% of GDP)	33	44	40
Value added in services (% of GDP)	50	44	48
Exports of goods and services (% of GDP)	24	28	38
Imports of goods and services (% of GDP)	34	26	35
Gross capital formation (% of GDP)	28	24	26
Central government revenue (% of GDP)	..	25.1	31.8
Central government cash surplus/deficit (% of GDP)	..	-0.4	1.0
States and markets			
Starting a business (days)			39
Stock market capitalization (% of GDP)	..	19.7	48.9
Military expenditures (% of GDP)	3.8	4.3	3.5
Fixed-line and mobile subscribers (per 100 people)	3	11	53
Internet users (per 100 people)	0.0	0.9	13.8
Paved roads (% of total)	70	63	70
High-technology exports (% of manufactured exports)	1	3	5
Global links			
Merchandise trade (% of GDP)	43.5	49.6	59.8
Net barter terms of trade (2000 = 100)	..	..	..
Total external debt ($ billions)	140	145	141
Short-term debt ($ billions)	20	21	24
Total debt service (% of exports)	20.6	12.7	10.4
Foreign direct investment, net inflows ($ billions)	0.7	4.8	27.5
Remittances received ($ billions)	11	13	27
Aid ($ billions)	10.4	4.5	16.8

South Asia

Population (millions)	1,499	Population growth (%)	1.6
Surface area (1,000 sq. km)	5,140	National poverty rate (% of pop.)	..
GNI ($ billions)	1,151.3	GNI per capita ($)	768
GNI, PPP ($ billions)	3,431.9	GNI per capita, PPP ($)	2,289

	1990	2000	2006
People			
Share of poorest 20% in nat'l consumption/income (%)	..	..	..
Life expectancy at birth (years)	59	63	64
Total fertility (births per woman)	4.1	3.3	2.8
Adolescent fertility (births per 1,000 women 15–19)	..	87	69
Contraceptive prevalence (% of married women 15–49)	40	..	53
Births attended by skilled health staff (% of total)	32	..	41
Under-five mortality rate (per 1,000)	123	96	83
Child malnutrition, underweight (% of under age 5)	..	..	41
Child immunization, measles (% of ages 12–23 mos.)	56	55	65
Primary completion rate, total (% of relevant age group)	62	69	80
Gross secondary enrollment, total (% of relevant age group)	38	44	49
Ratio of girls to boys in primary & secondary school (%)	70	80	90
HIV prevalence rate (% of population ages 15–49)	..	..	0.7
Environment			
Forests (1,000 sq. km)	789	807	801
Deforestation (average annual %, 1990–2005)			-0.1
Freshwater use (% of internal resources)	..	51.8	..
Access to improved water source (% of total pop.)	71	81	84
Access to improved sanitation facilities (% of total pop.)	17	32	37
Energy use per capita (kilograms of oil equivalent)	350	418	453
Carbon dioxide emissions per capita (metric tons)	0.7	1.0	1.0
Electricity use per capita (kilowatt-hours)	246	359	432
Economy			
GDP ($ billions)	402.5	608.2	1,146.7
GDP growth (annual %)	5.4	4.3	8.7
GDP implicit price deflator (annual % growth)	8.6	3.5	6.3
Value added in agriculture (% of GDP)	29	24	18
Value added in industry (% of GDP)	26	26	28
Value added in services (% of GDP)	45	50	54
Exports of goods and services (% of GDP)	9	14	22
Imports of goods and services (% of GDP)	12	16	26
Gross capital formation (% of GDP)	23	24	32
Central government revenue (% of GDP)	13.6	12.3	12.9
Central government cash surplus/deficit (% of GDP)	-3.4	-4.0	-3.1
States and markets			
Starting a business (days)			33
Stock market capitalization (% of GDP)	10.8	26.1	77.2
Military expenditures (% of GDP)	3.4	3.1	2.7
Fixed-line and mobile subscribers (per 100 people)	1	3	19
Internet users (per 100 people)	0.0	0.5	4.9
Paved roads (% of total)	38	31	57
High-technology exports (% of manufactured exports)	2	4	4
Global links			
Merchandise trade (% of GDP)	16.4	24.0	34.4
Net barter terms of trade (2000 = 100)	..	..	..
Total external debt ($ billions)	124	160	227
Short-term debt ($ billions)	12.3	6.1	15.4
Total debt service (% of exports)	27.5	14.6	7.5
Foreign direct investment, net inflows ($ billions)	0.5	4.4	22.9
Remittances received ($ billions)	5.6	17.2	39.8
Aid ($ billions)	6.0	4.2	9.3

Sub-Saharan Africa

Population (millions)	782	Population growth (%)	2.5
Surface area (1,000 sq. km)	24,270	National poverty rate (% of pop.)	..
GNI ($ billions)	647.9	GNI per capita ($)	829
GNI, PPP ($ billions)	1,314.3	GNI per capita, PPP ($)	1,681

	1990	2000	2006
People			
Share of poorest 20% in nat'l consumption/income (%)	..	..	..
Life expectancy at birth (years)	50	49	50
Total fertility (births per woman)	6.2	5.6	5.2
Adolescent fertility (births per 1,000 women 15–19)	..	146	122
Contraceptive prevalence (% of married women 15–49)	15	..	22
Births attended by skilled health staff (% of total)	44	..	45
Under-five mortality rate (per 1,000)	184	167	157
Child malnutrition, underweight (% of under age 5)	..	..	27
Child immunization, measles (% of ages 12–23 mos.)	57	55	71
Primary completion rate, total (% of relevant age group)	51	50	60
Gross secondary enrollment, total (% of relevant age group)	..	25	31
Ratio of girls to boys in primary & secondary school (%)	79	85	86
HIV prevalence rate (% of population ages 15–49)	..	..	5.8
Environment			
Forests (1,000 sq. km)	6,913	6,468	6,263
Deforestation (average annual %, 1990–2005)			0.7
Freshwater use (% of internal resources)	..	3.1	..
Access to improved water source (% of total pop.)	49	54	56
Access to improved sanitation facilities (% of total pop.)	31	35	37
Energy use per capita (kilograms of oil equivalent)	685	654	681
Carbon dioxide emissions per capita (metric tons)	0.9	0.9	0.9
Electricity use per capita (kilowatt-hours)	511	490	542
Economy			
GDP ($ billions)	297.6	342.6	712.7
GDP growth (annual %)	1.1	3.5	5.6
GDP implicit price deflator (annual % growth)	8.7	6.1	7.1
Value added in agriculture (% of GDP)	20	18	15
Value added in industry (% of GDP)	34	32	30
Value added in services (% of GDP)	47	50	55
Exports of goods and services (% of GDP)	26	33	35
Imports of goods and services (% of GDP)	26	31	36
Gross capital formation (% of GDP)	17	18	21
Central government revenue (% of GDP)	..	..	..
Central government cash surplus/deficit (% of GDP)	..	..	..
States and markets			
Starting a business (days)			56
Stock market capitalization (% of GDP)	52.2	89.9	159.9
Military expenditures (% of GDP)	3.1	1.7	1.3
Fixed-line and mobile subscribers (per 100 people)	1	3	15
Internet users (per 100 people)	0.0	0.5	3.8
Paved roads (% of total)	16	12	..
High-technology exports (% of manufactured exports)	..	4	..
Global links			
Merchandise trade (% of GDP)	42.5	51.7	60.8
Net barter terms of trade (2000 = 100)	..	..	..
Total external debt ($ billions)	177	212	174
Short-term debt ($ billions)	21	32	43
Total debt service (% of exports)	13.6	11.4	8.3
Foreign direct investment, net inflows ($ billions)	1.2	6.8	17.1
Remittances received ($ billions)	1.9	4.6	10.3
Aid ($ billions)	18	13	41

Income group tables

For operational and analytical purposes the World Bank's main criterion for classifying economies is gross national income (GNI) per capita. Every economy in *The Little Data Book* is classified as low income, middle income, or high income. Low- and middle-income economies are sometimes referred to as developing economies. The use of the term is convenient; it is not intended to imply that all economies in the group are experiencing similar development or that other economies have reached a preferred or final stage of development. Classification by income does not necessarily reflect development status.

Low-income economies are those with a GNI per capita of $905 or less in 2006.

Middle-income economies are those with a GNI per capita of more than $905 but less than $11,116. Lower-middle-income and upper-middle-income economies are separated at a GNI per capita of $3,595.

High-income economies are those with a GNI per capita of $11,116 or more.

Euro area includes the member states of the Economic and Monetary Union of the European Union that have adopted the euro as their currency: Austria, Belgium, Cyprus, Finland, France, Germany, Greece, Ireland, Italy, Luxembourg, Malta, Netherlands, Portugal, Slovenia, and Spain.

Low income

Population (millions)	2,420	Population growth (%)		1.8
Surface area (1,000 sq. km)	29,220	National poverty rate (% of pop.)		..
GNI ($ billions)	1,570.8	GNI per capita ($)		649
GNI, PPP ($ billions)	4,500.6	GNI per capita, PPP ($)		1,860

	1990	2000	2006
People			
Share of poorest 20% in nat'l consumption/income (%)	..	..	..
Life expectancy at birth (years)	57	59	60
Total fertility (births per woman)	4.7	3.9	3.5
Adolescent fertility (births per 1,000 women 15–19)	..	102	82
Contraceptive prevalence (% of married women 15–49)	33	..	44
Births attended by skilled health staff (% of total)	..	..	43
Under-five mortality rate (per 1,000)	143	123	112
Child malnutrition, underweight (% of under age 5)	..	..	35
Child immunization, measles (% of ages 12–23 mos.)	58	57	69
Primary completion rate, total (% of relevant age group)	57	64	73
Gross secondary enrollment, total (% of relevant age group)	..	39	45
Ratio of girls to boys in primary & secondary school (%)	73	82	89
HIV prevalence rate (% of population ages 15–49)	..	..	1.7
Environment			
Forests (1,000 sq. km)	7,392	6,940	6,714
Deforestation (average annual %, 1990–2005)			0.6
Freshwater use (% of internal resources)	..	18.9	..
Access to improved water source (% of total pop.)	64	72	75
Access to improved sanitation facilities (% of total pop.)	21	33	38
Energy use per capita (kilograms of oil equivalent)	426	454	486
Carbon dioxide emissions per capita (metric tons)	0.8	0.8	0.9
Electricity use per capita (kilowatt-hours)	265	325	391
Economy			
GDP ($ billions)	591.4	843.2	1,618.7
GDP growth (annual %)	4.5	4.0	8.0
GDP implicit price deflator (annual % growth)	9.3	6.1	7.3
Value added in agriculture (% of GDP)	31	26	20
Value added in industry (% of GDP)	26	26	28
Value added in services (% of GDP)	43	47	52
Exports of goods and services (% of GDP)	13	19	27
Imports of goods and services (% of GDP)	16	21	30
Gross capital formation (% of GDP)	21	23	30
Central government revenue (% of GDP)	13.5	12.2	12.9
Central government cash surplus/deficit (% of GDP)	-3.4	-3.7	-2.6
States and markets			
Starting a business (days)			54
Stock market capitalization (% of GDP)	10.5	23.9	67.0
Military expenditures (% of GDP)	3.2	2.8	2.4
Fixed-line and mobile subscribers (per 100 people)	1	2	17
Internet users (per 100 people)	0.0	0.3	4.2
Paved roads (% of total)	16	12	..
High-technology exports (% of manufactured exports)	2	4	6
Global links			
Merchandise trade (% of GDP)	23.8	32.4	44.1
Net barter terms of trade (2000 = 100)	..	..	..
Total external debt ($ billions)	310	346	375
Short-term debt ($ billions)	33	26	42
Total debt service (% of exports)	23.8	12.8	6.6
Foreign direct investment, net inflows ($ billions)	2.3	10.2	41.7
Remittances received ($ billions)	7.7	21.8	55.2
Aid ($ billions)	22	19	48

Middle income

Population (millions)	3,088	Population growth (%)	0.8
Surface area (1,000 sq. km)	70,112	National poverty rate (% of pop.)	..
GNI ($ billions)	9,426.9	GNI per capita ($)	3,053
GNI, PPP ($ billions)	19,920.3	GNI per capita, PPP ($)	6,451

	1990	2000	2006
People			
Share of poorest 20% in nat'l consumption/income (%)	..	..	..
Life expectancy at birth (years)	68	69	71
Total fertility (births per woman)	2.7	2.2	2.1
Adolescent fertility (births per 1,000 women 15–19)	..	38	32
Contraceptive prevalence (% of married women 15–49)	68	45	75
Births attended by skilled health staff (% of total)	53	..	88
Under-five mortality rate (per 1,000)	56	42	33
Child malnutrition, underweight (% of under age 5)	..	..	9
Child immunization, measles (% of ages 12–23 mos.)	86	86	91
Primary completion rate, total (% of relevant age group)	93	96	97
Gross secondary enrollment, total (% of relevant age group)	..	71	78
Ratio of girls to boys in primary & secondary school (%)	91	98	99
HIV prevalence rate (% of population ages 15–49)	..	..	0.7
Environment			
Forests (1,000 sq. km)	23,770	23,255	23,086
Deforestation (average annual %, 1990–2005)			0.2
Freshwater use (% of internal resources)	..	6.3	..
Access to improved water source (% of total pop.)	78	83	84
Access to improved sanitation facilities (% of total pop.)	47	60	62
Energy use per capita (kilograms of oil equivalent)	1,346	1,231	1,486
Carbon dioxide emissions per capita (metric tons)	3.6	3.3	4.0
Electricity use per capita (kilowatt-hours)	1,310	1,464	1,928
Economy			
GDP ($ billions)	3,217.2	5,194.6	10,059.2
GDP growth (annual %)	1.4	5.5	7.2
GDP implicit price deflator (annual % growth)	13.2	6.6	6.0
Value added in agriculture (% of GDP)	16	10	8
Value added in industry (% of GDP)	38	36	37
Value added in services (% of GDP)	46	54	54
Exports of goods and services (% of GDP)	21	30	36
Imports of goods and services (% of GDP)	20	28	33
Gross capital formation (% of GDP)	26	24	27
Central government revenue (% of GDP)	..	15.5	..
Central government cash surplus/deficit (% of GDP)	..	..	..
States and markets			
Starting a business (days)			48
Stock market capitalization (% of GDP)	18.6	37.2	74.2
Military expenditures (% of GDP)	4.8	2.0	2.0
Fixed-line and mobile subscribers (per 100 people)	4	20	66
Internet users (per 100 people)	0.0	2.4	14.1
Paved roads (% of total)	49	44	..
High-technology exports (% of manufactured exports)	3	20	20
Global links			
Merchandise trade (% of GDP)	34.4	49.6	61.8
Net barter terms of trade (2000 = 100)	..	..	..
Total external debt ($ billions)	1,017	1,910	2,609
Short-term debt ($ billions)	168	284	616
Total debt service (% of exports)	19.6	21.0	13.4
Foreign direct investment, net inflows ($ billions)	22	155	326
Remittances received ($ billions)	23	63	167
Aid ($ billions)	27	24	35

Lower middle income

Population (millions)	2,276	Population growth (%)		0.9
Surface area (1,000 sq. km)	28,646	National poverty rate (% of pop.)		..
GNI ($ billions)	4,639.8	GNI per capita ($)		2,038
GNI, PPP ($ billions)	11,152.3	GNI per capita, PPP ($)		4,899

	1990	2000	2006
People			
Share of poorest 20% in nat'l consumption/income (%)	..	..	..
Life expectancy at birth (years)	67	69	71
Total fertility (births per woman)	2.6	2.2	2.1
Adolescent fertility (births per 1,000 women 15–19)	..	29	24
Contraceptive prevalence (% of married women 15–49)	73	..	76
Births attended by skilled health staff (% of total)	50	..	86
Under-five mortality rate (per 1,000)	60	45	36
Child malnutrition, underweight (% of under age 5)	..	..	11
Child immunization, measles (% of ages 12–23 mos.)	88	84	90
Primary completion rate, total (% of relevant age group)	95	96	97
Gross secondary enrollment, total (% of relevant age group)	..	65	73
Ratio of girls to boys in primary & secondary school (%)	89	98	98
HIV prevalence rate (% of population ages 15–49)	..	..	0.3
Environment			
Forests (1,000 sq. km)	7,550	7,384	7,413
Deforestation (average annual %, 1990–2005)			0.1
Freshwater use (% of internal resources)	..	7.3	..
Access to improved water source (% of total pop.)	74	80	81
Access to improved sanitation facilities (% of total pop.)	37	53	55
Energy use per capita (kilograms of oil equivalent)	894	913	1,216
Carbon dioxide emissions per capita (metric tons)	2.3	2.6	3.4
Electricity use per capita (kilowatt-hours)	672	968	1,502
Economy			
GDP ($ billions)	1,113.0	2,311.4	4,735.7
GDP growth (annual %)	3.8	6.3	8.8
GDP implicit price deflator (annual % growth)	11.8	6.6	6.0
Value added in agriculture (% of GDP)	23	14	12
Value added in industry (% of GDP)	38	42	44
Value added in services (% of GDP)	39	43	45
Exports of goods and services (% of GDP)	22	30	40
Imports of goods and services (% of GDP)	23	29	36
Gross capital formation (% of GDP)	32	29	35
Central government revenue (% of GDP)	10.4	12.1	16.0
Central government cash surplus/deficit (% of GDP)	..	-2.6	-0.9
States and markets			
Starting a business (days)			53
Stock market capitalization (% of GDP)	8.7	35.8	74.5
Military expenditures (% of GDP)	2.7	2.1	2.0
Fixed-line and mobile subscribers (per 100 people)	2	15	60
Internet users (per 100 people)	0.0	1.6	11.4
Paved roads (% of total)	50	49	66
High-technology exports (% of manufactured exports)	3	20	24
Global links			
Merchandise trade (% of GDP)	40.2	51.0	66.5
Net barter terms of trade (2000 = 100)	..	..	..
Total external debt ($ billions)	427	731	921
Short-term debt ($ billions)	67	95	293
Total debt service (% of exports)	20.1	13.5	7.0
Foreign direct investment, net inflows ($ billions)	11	54	142
Remittances received ($ billions)	14	40	103
Aid ($ billions)	21	16	28

Upper middle income

Population (millions)	811	Population growth (%)	0.8
Surface area (1,000 sq. km)	41,466	National poverty rate (% of pop.)	..
GNI ($ billions)	4,797.3	GNI per capita ($)	5,913
GNI, PPP ($ billions)	8,825.8	GNI per capita, PPP ($)	10,879

	1990	2000	2006
People			
Share of poorest 20% in nat'l consumption/income (%)	..	..	..
Life expectancy at birth (years)	69	69	70
Total fertility (births per woman)	2.7	2.2	2.0
Adolescent fertility (births per 1,000 women 15–19)	..	60	56
Contraceptive prevalence (% of married women 15–49)	51	..	..
Births attended by skilled health staff (% of total)	..	..	94
Under-five mortality rate (per 1,000)	47	33	26
Child malnutrition, underweight (% of under age 5)	..	..	..
Child immunization, measles (% of ages 12–23 mos.)	80	93	94
Primary completion rate, total (% of relevant age group)	88	98	99
Gross secondary enrollment, total (% of relevant age group)	67	88	92
Ratio of girls to boys in primary & secondary school (%)	99	100	100
HIV prevalence rate (% of population ages 15–49)	..	..	1.7
Environment			
Forests (1,000 sq. km)	16,220	15,871	15,673
Deforestation (average annual %, 1990–2005)			0.2
Freshwater use (% of internal resources)	..	4.0	..
Access to improved water source (% of total pop.)	88	91	93
Access to improved sanitation facilities (% of total pop.)	77	81	81
Energy use per capita (kilograms of oil equivalent)	2,586	2,123	2,248
Carbon dioxide emissions per capita (metric tons)	6.9	5.4	5.6
Electricity use per capita (kilowatt-hours)	3,057	2,855	3,131
Economy			
GDP ($ billions)	2,100.1	2,883.4	5,324.6
GDP growth (annual %)	0.0	4.9	5.7
GDP implicit price deflator (annual % growth)	15.4	6.7	6.1
Value added in agriculture (% of GDP)	10	6	6
Value added in industry (% of GDP)	39	31	32
Value added in services (% of GDP)	51	63	62
Exports of goods and services (% of GDP)	20	29	33
Imports of goods and services (% of GDP)	19	28	30
Gross capital formation (% of GDP)	22	21	21
Central government revenue (% of GDP)	..	..	..
Central government cash surplus/deficit (% of GDP)	..	..	..
States and markets			
Starting a business (days)			41
Stock market capitalization (% of GDP)	22.7	38.3	74.0
Military expenditures (% of GDP)	6.0	2.0	2.0
Fixed-line and mobile subscribers (per 100 people)	10	33	88
Internet users (per 100 people)	0.0	4.7	22.2
Paved roads (% of total)	36	34	..
High-technology exports (% of manufactured exports)	6	20	16
Global links			
Merchandise trade (% of GDP)	30.4	48.6	57.6
Net barter terms of trade (2000 = 100)	..	..	..
Total external debt ($ billions)	590	1,179	1,688
Short-term debt ($ billions)	101	189	324
Total debt service (% of exports)	19.0	27.3	20.1
Foreign direct investment, net inflows ($ billions)	11	101	184
Remittances received ($ billions)	9.6	22.7	64.1
Aid ($ billions)	5.7	7.5	5.7

Low and middle income

Population (millions)	5,507	Population growth (%)	1.3
Surface area (1,000 sq. km)	99,332	National poverty rate (% of pop.)	..
GNI ($ billions)	10,997.7	GNI per capita ($)	1,997
GNI, PPP ($ billions)	24,430.5	GNI per capita, PPP ($)	4,436

	1990	2000	2006
People			
Share of poorest 20% in nat'l consumption/income (%)	..	..	..
Life expectancy at birth (years)	63	65	66
Total fertility (births per woman)	3.4	2.9	2.7
Adolescent fertility (births per 1,000 women 15–19)		68	56
Contraceptive prevalence (% of married women 15–49)	54	..	60
Births attended by skilled health staff (% of total)	..	..	62
Under-five mortality rate (per 1,000)	101	87	79
Child malnutrition, underweight (% of under age 5)	..	..	25
Child immunization, measles (% of ages 12–23 mos.)	72	71	79
Primary completion rate, total (% of relevant age group)	78	81	85
Gross secondary enrollment, total (% of relevant age group)	..	56	61
Ratio of girls to boys in primary & secondary school (%)	84	91	94
HIV prevalence rate (% of population ages 15–49)	..	..	1.1
Environment			
Forests (1,000 sq. km)	31,161	30,194	29,799
Deforestation (average annual %, 1990–2005)			0.3
Freshwater use (% of internal resources)	..	8.8	..
Access to improved water source (% of total pop.)	72	78	80
Access to improved sanitation facilities (% of total pop.)	36	49	51
Energy use per capita (kilograms of oil equivalent)	993	918	1,071
Carbon dioxide emissions per capita (metric tons)	2.4	2.3	2.6
Electricity use per capita (kilowatt-hours)	910	1,004	1,290
Economy			
GDP ($ billions)	3,809.5	6,038.4	11,678.6
GDP growth (annual %)	1.8	5.3	7.3
GDP implicit price deflator (annual % growth)	10.9	6.3	6.8
Value added in agriculture (% of GDP)	18	12	10
Value added in industry (% of GDP)	37	35	36
Value added in services (% of GDP)	46	53	54
Exports of goods and services (% of GDP)	20	28	35
Imports of goods and services (% of GDP)	20	27	33
Gross capital formation (% of GDP)	26	24	27
Central government revenue (% of GDP)	..	15.0	..
Central government cash surplus/deficit (% of GDP)	..	..	..
States and markets			
Starting a business (days)			50
Stock market capitalization (% of GDP)	18.1	35.6	73.3
Military expenditures (% of GDP)	4.6	2.1	2.1
Fixed-line and mobile subscribers (per 100 people)	3	13	44
Internet users (per 100 people)	0.0	1.6	8.0
Paved roads (% of total)	24	27	..
High-technology exports (% of manufactured exports)	7	18	20
Global links			
Merchandise trade (% of GDP)	32.5	47.3	59.4
Net barter terms of trade (2000 = 100)	..	..	..
Total external debt ($ billions)	1,327	2,256	2,984
Short-term debt ($ billions)	200	310	658
Total debt service (% of exports)	20.1	20.2	12.6
Foreign direct investment, net inflows ($ billions)	24	165	367
Remittances received ($ billions)	31	85	222
Aid ($ billions)	57	55	105

Euro area

Population (millions)	317	Population growth (%)	0.5
Surface area (1,000 sq. km)	2,536	National poverty rate (% of pop.)	..
GNI ($ billions)	10,864.1	GNI per capita ($)	34,307
GNI, PPP ($ billions)	9,874.1	GNI per capita, PPP ($)	31,818

	1990	2000	2006
People			
Share of poorest 20% in nat'l consumption/income (%)	..	..	..
Life expectancy at birth (years)	76	78	80
Total fertility (births per woman)	1.5	1.5	1.5
Adolescent fertility (births per 1,000 women 15–19)	..	..	..
Contraceptive prevalence (% of married women 15–49)	..	..	..
Births attended by skilled health staff (% of total)	..	..	..
Under-five mortality rate (per 1,000)	9	6	4
Child malnutrition, underweight (% of under age 5)	..	..	..
Child immunization, measles (% of ages 12–23 mos.)	74	87	91
Primary completion rate, total (% of relevant age group)	100	..	..
Gross secondary enrollment, total (% of relevant age group)	..	..	..
Ratio of girls to boys in primary & secondary school (%)	101	..	..
HIV prevalence rate (% of population ages 15–49)	..	..	0.3
Environment			
Forests (1,000 sq. km)	824	889	916
Deforestation (average annual %, 1990–2005)			−0.7
Freshwater use (% of internal resources)	..	22.3	..
Access to improved water source (% of total pop.)	100	100	100
Access to improved sanitation facilities (% of total pop.)	100	100	100
Energy use per capita (kilograms of oil equivalent)	3,562	3,846	3,961
Carbon dioxide emissions per capita (metric tons)	8.4	8.0	8.2
Electricity use per capita (kilowatt-hours)	5,361	6,410	6,926
Economy			
GDP ($ billions)	5,684.6	6,244.9	10,636.4
GDP growth (annual %)	3.6	3.9	2.7
GDP implicit price deflator (annual % growth)	3.3	3.0	2.3
Value added in agriculture (% of GDP)	3	2	2
Value added in industry (% of GDP)	32	28	27
Value added in services (% of GDP)	64	70	72
Exports of goods and services (% of GDP)	27	37	40
Imports of goods and services (% of GDP)	28	36	38
Gross capital formation (% of GDP)	23	22	21
Central government revenue (% of GDP)	..	36.2	35.5
Central government cash surplus/deficit (% of GDP)	..	0.1	−1.3
States and markets			
Starting a business (days)			22
Stock market capitalization (% of GDP)	21.1	87.0	81.2
Military expenditures (% of GDP)	2.5	1.8	1.6
Fixed-line and mobile subscribers (per 100 people)	41	115	153
Internet users (per 100 people)	0.1	23.0	47.9
Paved roads (% of total)	93	99	..
High-technology exports (% of manufactured exports)	12	19	16
Global links			
Merchandise trade (% of GDP)	43.9	60.7	65.2
Net barter terms of trade (2000 = 100)	..	..	..
Total external debt ($ billions)	..	..	..
Short-term debt ($ billions)	..	..	..
Total debt service (% of exports)	..	..	..
Foreign direct investment, net inflows ($ billions)	61	635	400
Remittances received ($ billions)	28	33	50
Aid ($ billions)	..	..	..

High income

Population (millions)	1,031	Population growth (%)	0.7
Surface area (1,000 sq. km)	34,614	National poverty rate (% of pop.)	..
GNI ($ billions)	37,731.7	GNI per capita ($)	36,608
GNI, PPP ($ billions)	36,005.0	GNI per capita, PPP ($)	34,933

	1990	2000	2006
People			
Share of poorest 20% in nat'l consumption/income (%)	..	..	..
Life expectancy at birth (years)	76	78	79
Total fertility (births per woman)	1.8	1.7	1.7
Adolescent fertility (births per 1,000 women 15–19)	..	23	22
Contraceptive prevalence (% of married women 15–49)	71	..	..
Births attended by skilled health staff (% of total)	..	..	99
Under-five mortality rate (per 1,000)	12	7	7
Child malnutrition, underweight (% of under age 5)	..	..	..
Child immunization, measles (% of ages 12–23 mos.)	83	91	93
Primary completion rate, total (% of relevant age group)	..	98	97
Gross secondary enrollment, total (% of relevant age group)	..	101	101
Ratio of girls to boys in primary & secondary school (%)	100	100	100
HIV prevalence rate (% of population ages 15–49)	..	..	0.4
Environment			
Forests (1,000 sq. km)	9,492	9,571	9,600
Deforestation (average annual %, 1990–2005)			–0.1
Freshwater use (% of internal resources)	..	10.2	..
Access to improved water source (% of total pop.)	100	99	99
Access to improved sanitation facilities (% of total pop.)	100	100	100
Energy use per capita (kilograms of oil equivalent)	4,841	5,414	5,498
Carbon dioxide emissions per capita (metric tons)	11.9	13.1	13.2
Electricity use per capita (kilowatt-hours)	7,662	9,265	9,760
Economy			
GDP ($ billions)	18,017.3	25,839.9	36,794.5
GDP growth (annual %)	3.1	3.8	2.9
GDP implicit price deflator (annual % growth)	4.3	3.0	2.3
Value added in agriculture (% of GDP)	3	2	2
Value added in industry (% of GDP)	32	28	26
Value added in services (% of GDP)	65	70	72
Exports of goods and services (% of GDP)	19	24	26
Imports of goods and services (% of GDP)	19	24	26
Gross capital formation (% of GDP)	23	22	21
Central government revenue (% of GDP)	..	27.6	27.2
Central government cash surplus/deficit (% of GDP)	..	0.2	–1.3
States and markets			
Starting a business (days)			22
Stock market capitalization (% of GDP)	51.1	117.3	126.1
Military expenditures (% of GDP)	3.4	2.3	2.6
Fixed-line and mobile subscribers (per 100 people)	45	109	143
Internet users (per 100 people)	0.3	31.6	59.3
Paved roads (% of total)	79	93	91
High-technology exports (% of manufactured exports)	17	24	21
Global links			
Merchandise trade (% of GDP)	32.2	39.8	46.9
Net barter terms of trade (2000 = 100)	..	..	..
Total external debt ($ billions)	..	..	..
Short-term debt ($ billions)	..	..	..
Total debt service (% of exports)	..	..	..
Foreign direct investment, net inflows ($ billions)	181	1,353	985
Remittances received ($ billions)	37	47	75
Aid ($ billions)	2.5	2.3	0.0

Country tables

China

Unless otherwise noted, data for China do not include data for Hong Kong, China; Macao, China, and Taiwan, China.

Serbia and Montenegro

Montenegro declared independence from Serbia and Montenegro on June 3, 2006. Where available, data for each country are shown separately. However, some indicators for Serbia prior to 2006 include data for Montenegro. Moreover, data for most indicators from 1999 onward for Serbia exclude data for Kosovo and Metohija.

Afghanistan

South Asia			Low income

Population (millions)	..	Population growth (%)	..
Surface area (1,000 sq. km)	652	National poverty rate (% of pop.)	..
GNI ($ billions)	8.1	GNI per capita ($)	..
GNI, PPP ($ billions)	23.9	GNI per capita, PPP ($)	..

	1990	2000	2006
People			
Share of poorest 20% in nat'l consumption/income (%)	..	..	..
Life expectancy at birth (years)	..	..	..
Total fertility (births per woman)	..	..	..
Adolescent fertility (births per 1,000 women 15–19)	..	..	..
Contraceptive prevalence (% of married women 15–49)	..	..	..
Births attended by skilled health staff (% of total)	..	..	..
Under-five mortality rate (per 1,000)	..	..	..
Child malnutrition, underweight (% of under age 5)	..	..	..
Child immunization, measles (% of ages 12–23 mos.)	..	..	..
Primary completion rate, total (% of relevant age group)	..	..	..
Gross secondary enrollment, total (% of relevant age group)	..	..	..
Ratio of girls to boys in primary & secondary school (%)	..	..	..
HIV prevalence rate (% of population ages 15–49)	..	..	..
Environment			
Forests (1,000 sq. km)	13.1	10.2	8.7
Deforestation (average annual %, 1990–2005)			2.7
Freshwater use (% of internal resources)	..	42.3	..
Access to improved water source (% of total pop.)	..	..	..
Access to improved sanitation facilities (% of total pop.)	..	..	..
Energy use per capita (kilograms of oil equivalent)	..	..	..
Carbon dioxide emissions per capita (metric tons)	..	..	..
Electricity use per capita (kilowatt-hours)	..	..	..
Economy			
GDP ($ millions)	..	2,462	8,399
GDP growth (annual %)	..	..	5.3
GDP implicit price deflator (annual % growth)	..	..	9.7
Value added in agriculture (% of GDP)	..	50	36
Value added in industry (% of GDP)	..	20	24
Value added in services (% of GDP)	..	30	39
Exports of goods and services (% of GDP)	..	33	12
Imports of goods and services (% of GDP)	..	66	56
Gross capital formation (% of GDP)	..	28	25
Central government revenue (% of GDP)	..	..	7.4
Central government cash surplus/deficit (% of GDP)	..	..	–1.7
States and markets			
Starting a business (days)			9
Stock market capitalization (% of GDP)	..	..	..
Military expenditures (% of GDP)	..	..	9.9
Fixed-line and mobile subscribers (per 100 people)	..	..	..
Internet users (per 100 people)	..	..	..
Paved roads (% of total)	13	13	24
High-technology exports (% of manufactured exports)	..	..	..
Global links			
Merchandise trade (% of GDP)	..	73.0	40.4
Net barter terms of trade (2000 = 100)	..	..	..
Total external debt ($ billions)	..	..	1.8
Short-term debt ($ millions)	..	..	10.5
Total debt service (% of exports)	..	..	..
Foreign direct investment, net inflows ($ billions)	..	..	..
Remittances received ($ billions)	..	..	..
Aid ($ billions)	0.1	0.1	3.0

Albania

Europe & Central Asia		Lower middle income	
Population (millions)	3.2	Population growth (%)	0.6
Surface area (1,000 sq. km)	29	National poverty rate (% of pop.)	25
GNI ($ billions)	9.3	GNI per capita ($)	2,930
GNI, PPP ($ billions)	19.0	GNI per capita, PPP ($)	6,000

	1990	2000	2006
People			
Share of poorest 20% in nat'l consumption/income (%)	..	9.0	8.2
Life expectancy at birth (years)	72	75	76
Total fertility (births per woman)	2.9	2.3	1.4
Adolescent fertility (births per 1,000 women 15–19)	..	16	16
Contraceptive prevalence (% of married women 15–49)	..	58	60
Births attended by skilled health staff (% of total)	..	99	100
Under-five mortality rate (per 1,000)	45	25	17
Child malnutrition, underweight (% of under age 5)	..	17.0	..
Child immunization, measles (% of ages 12–23 mos.)	88	95	97
Primary completion rate, total (% of relevant age group)	..	95	96
Gross secondary enrollment, total (% of relevant age group)	78	70	77
Ratio of girls to boys in primary & secondary school (%)	96	99	97
HIV prevalence rate (% of population ages 15–49)	..	..	0.2
Environment			
Forests (1,000 sq. km)	7.9	7.7	7.9
Deforestation (average annual %, 1990–2005)			-0.04
Freshwater use (% of internal resources)	..	6.4	..
Access to improved water source (% of total pop.)	96	96	96
Access to improved sanitation facilities (% of total pop.)	..	90	91
Energy use per capita (kilograms of oil equivalent)	809	591	762
Carbon dioxide emissions per capita (metric tons)	2.2	0.7	1.2
Electricity use per capita (kilowatt-hours)	522	1,191	1,167
Economy			
GDP ($ billions)	2.1	3.7	9.1
GDP growth (annual %)	-9.6	7.3	5.0
GDP implicit price deflator (annual % growth)	-0.5	4.3	2.0
Value added in agriculture (% of GDP)	36	29	23
Value added in industry (% of GDP)	48	19	22
Value added in services (% of GDP)	16	52	56
Exports of goods and services (% of GDP)	15	19	25
Imports of goods and services (% of GDP)	23	37	49
Gross capital formation (% of GDP)	29	25	25
Central government revenue (% of GDP)	..	23.4	23.6
Central government cash surplus/deficit (% of GDP)	..	-6.7	-3.0
States and markets			
Starting a business (days)			36
Stock market capitalization (% of GDP)	..	..	..
Military expenditures (% of GDP)	5.9	1.2	1.6
Fixed-line and mobile subscribers (per 100 people)	1	6	60
Internet users (per 100 people)	0.0	0.1	14.9
Paved roads (% of total)	..	39	..
High-technology exports (% of manufactured exports)	..	1	13
Global links			
Merchandise trade (% of GDP)	29.0	36.6	42.3
Net barter terms of trade (2000 = 100)	..	..	..
Total external debt ($ billions)	0.5	1.1	2.3
Short-term debt ($ millions)	425	37	575
Total debt service (% of exports)	4.3	2.0	3.5
Foreign direct investment, net inflows ($ millions)	20	143	325
Remittances received ($ billions)	0.0	0.6	1.4
Aid ($ millions)	11	317	321

Algeria

Middle East & North Africa		Lower middle income	
Population (millions)	33	Population growth (%)	1.5
Surface area (1,000 sq. km)	2,382	National poverty rate (% of pop.)	..
GNI ($ billions)	101.2	GNI per capita ($)	3,030
GNI, PPP ($ billions)	198.0	GNI per capita, PPP ($)	5,940

	1990	2000	2006
People			
Share of poorest 20% in nat'l consumption/income (%)	6.5	..	..
Life expectancy at birth (years)	67	70	72
Total fertility (births per woman)	4.6	2.7	2.4
Adolescent fertility (births per 1,000 women 15–19)	..	10	8
Contraceptive prevalence (% of married women 15–49)	47	64	61
Births attended by skilled health staff (% of total)	77	92	95
Under-five mortality rate (per 1,000)	69	44	38
Child malnutrition, underweight (% of under age 5)	..	5.4	..
Child immunization, measles (% of ages 12–23 mos.)	83	80	91
Primary completion rate, total (% of relevant age group)	81	83	85
Gross secondary enrollment, total (% of relevant age group)	60	75	83
Ratio of girls to boys in primary & secondary school (%)	83	98	99
HIV prevalence rate (% of population ages 15–49)	..	..	0.1
Environment			
Forests (1,000 sq. km)	18	21	23
Deforestation (average annual %, 1990–2005)			-1.6
Freshwater use (% of internal resources)	..	54.2	..
Access to improved water source (% of total pop.)	94	89	85
Access to improved sanitation facilities (% of total pop.)	88	91	92
Energy use per capita (kilograms of oil equivalent)	944	959	1,058
Carbon dioxide emissions per capita (metric tons)	3.0	6.4	6.0
Electricity use per capita (kilowatt-hours)	542	695	899
Economy			
GDP ($ billions)	62.0	54.8	114.7
GDP growth (annual %)	0.8	2.2	3.0
GDP implicit price deflator (annual % growth)	30.3	24.6	9.1
Value added in agriculture (% of GDP)	11	9	8
Value added in industry (% of GDP)	48	59	61
Value added in services (% of GDP)	40	33	30
Exports of goods and services (% of GDP)	23	41	48
Imports of goods and services (% of GDP)	25	21	24
Gross capital formation (% of GDP)	29	25	30
Central government revenue (% of GDP)	..	38.3	43.1
Central government cash surplus/deficit (% of GDP)	..	9.7	13.8
States and markets			
Starting a business (days)			24
Stock market capitalization (% of GDP)	..	..	..
Military expenditures (% of GDP)	1.5	3.4	2.7
Fixed-line and mobile subscribers (per 100 people)	3	6	71
Internet users (per 100 people)	0.0	0.5	7.4
Paved roads (% of total)	67	69	70
High-technology exports (% of manufactured exports)	0	4	2
Global links			
Merchandise trade (% of GDP)	36.6	56.9	66.3
Net barter terms of trade (2000 = 100)	74	100	179
Total external debt ($ billions)	28.1	25.3	5.6
Short-term debt ($ millions)	791	222	541
Total debt service (% of exports)	63.4	..	..
Foreign direct investment, net inflows ($ billions)	0.0	0.4	1.8
Remittances received ($ billions)	0.4	0.8	2.5
Aid ($ millions)	132	201	209

American Samoa

East Asia & Pacific   **Upper middle income**

Population (thousands)	60	Population growth (%)	2.2
Surface area (sq. km)	200	National poverty rate (% of pop.)	..
GNI ($ billions)	..	GNI per capita ($)	..
GNI, PPP ($ billions)	..	GNI per capita, PPP ($)	..

	1990	2000	2006
People			
Share of poorest 20% in nat'l consumption/income (%)	..		..
Life expectancy at birth (years)	..	..	..
Total fertility (births per woman)	..	..	..
Adolescent fertility (births per 1,000 women 15–19)	..	..	..
Contraceptive prevalence (% of married women 15–49)	..	..	..
Births attended by skilled health staff (% of total)	..	100	..
Under-five mortality rate (per 1,000)	..	..	..
Child malnutrition, underweight (% of under age 5)	..	..	..
Child immunization, measles (% of ages 12–23 mos.)	..	..	..
Primary completion rate, total (% of relevant age group)	..	..	..
Gross secondary enrollment, total (% of relevant age group)	..	..	..
Ratio of girls to boys in primary & secondary school (%)	..	..	..
HIV prevalence rate (% of population ages 15–49)	..	..	..
Environment			
Forests (sq. km)	180	180	180
Deforestation (average annual %, 1990–2005)			0.00
Freshwater use (% of internal resources)	..	..	..
Access to improved water source (% of total pop.)	..	..	..
Access to improved sanitation facilities (% of total pop.)	..	..	..
Energy use per capita (kilograms of oil equivalent)	..	..	..
Carbon dioxide emissions per capita (metric tons)	..	..	..
Electricity use per capita (kilowatt-hours)	..	..	..
Economy			
GDP ($ billions)	..	..	..
GDP growth (annual %)	..	..	..
GDP implicit price deflator (annual % growth)	..	..	..
Value added in agriculture (% of GDP)	..	..	..
Value added in industry (% of GDP)	..	..	..
Value added in services (% of GDP)	..	..	..
Exports of goods and services (% of GDP)	..	..	..
Imports of goods and services (% of GDP)	..	..	..
Gross capital formation (% of GDP)	..	..	..
Central government revenue (% of GDP)	..	..	..
Central government cash surplus/deficit (% of GDP)	..	..	..
States and markets			
Starting a business (days)			..
Stock market capitalization (% of GDP)	..	..	..
Military expenditures (% of GDP)	..	..	..
Fixed-line and mobile subscribers (per 100 people)	..	..	22
Internet users (per 100 people)	..	..	..
Paved roads (% of total)	..	..	..
High-technology exports (% of manufactured exports)	..	..	..
Global links			
Merchandise trade (% of GDP)	..	..	..
Net barter terms of trade (2000 = 100)	..	..	..
Total external debt ($ billions)	..	..	..
Short-term debt ($ billions)	..	..	..
Total debt service (% of exports)	..	..	..
Foreign direct investment, net inflows ($ billions)	..	..	..
Remittances received ($ billions)	..	..	..
Aid ($ billions)	..	..	..

Andorra

High income

Population (thousands)	67	Population growth (%)		1.1
Surface area (sq. km)	470	National poverty rate (% of pop.)		..
GNI ($ billions)	..	GNI per capita ($)		..
GNI, PPP ($ billions)	..	GNI per capita, PPP ($)		..

	1990	2000	2006
People			
Share of poorest 20% in nat'l consumption/income (%)	..	..	..
Life expectancy at birth (years)	..	..	..
Total fertility (births per woman)	..	..	..
Adolescent fertility (births per 1,000 women 15–19)		..	..
Contraceptive prevalence (% of married women 15–49)	..	..	..
Births attended by skilled health staff (% of total)	..	..	..
Under-five mortality rate (per 1,000)	6	4	3
Child malnutrition, underweight (% of under age 5)		..	..
Child immunization, measles (% of ages 12–23 mos.)	..	97	91
Primary completion rate, total (% of relevant age group)	..	100	103
Gross secondary enrollment, total (% of relevant age group)	..	80	85
Ratio of girls to boys in primary & secondary school (%)	..	101	102
HIV prevalence rate (% of population ages 15–49)	..	..	..
Environment			
Forests (sq. km)	160	160	160
Deforestation (average annual %, 1990–2005)			0.00
Freshwater use (% of internal resources)	..	..	..
Access to improved water source (% of total pop.)	100	100	100
Access to improved sanitation facilities (% of total pop.)	100	100	100
Energy use per capita (kilograms of oil equivalent)	..	..	..
Carbon dioxide emissions per capita (metric tons)	..	..	..
Electricity use per capita (kilowatt-hours)	..	..	..
Economy			
GDP ($ billions)	..	..	..
GDP growth (annual %)	..	..	..
GDP implicit price deflator (annual % growth)	..	..	..
Value added in agriculture (% of GDP)	..	..	..
Value added in industry (% of GDP)	..	..	..
Value added in services (% of GDP)	..	..	..
Exports of goods and services (% of GDP)	..	..	..
Imports of goods and services (% of GDP)	..	..	..
Gross capital formation (% of GDP)	..	..	..
Central government revenue (% of GDP)	..	..	..
Central government cash surplus/deficit (% of GDP)	..	..	..
States and markets			
Starting a business (days)			..
Stock market capitalization (% of GDP)	..	..	..
Military expenditures (% of GDP)	..	..	..
Fixed-line and mobile subscribers (per 100 people)	..	..	151
Internet users (per 100 people)	..	..	33.1
Paved roads (% of total)	..	..	..
High-technology exports (% of manufactured exports)	..	11	27
Global links			
Merchandise trade (% of GDP)	..	..	..
Net barter terms of trade (2000 = 100)	..	..	..
Total external debt ($ billions)	..	..	..
Short-term debt ($ billions)	..	..	..
Total debt service (% of exports)	..	..	..
Foreign direct investment, net inflows ($ billions)	..	..	..
Remittances received ($ billions)	..	..	..
Aid ($ billions)	..	..	..

Angola

Lower middle income

Population (millions)	17	Population growth (%)		2.8
Surface area (1,000 sq. km)	1,247	National poverty rate (% of pop.)		..
GNI ($ billions)	32.6	GNI per capita ($)		1,970
GNI, PPP ($ billions)	64.5	GNI per capita, PPP ($)		3,890

	1990	2000	2006
People			
Share of poorest 20% in nat'l consumption/income (%)	..	..	..
Life expectancy at birth (years)	40	41	42
Total fertility (births per woman)	7.1	6.8	6.5
Adolescent fertility (births per 1,000 women 15–19)	..	144	139
Contraceptive prevalence (% of married women 15–49)	..	6	..
Births attended by skilled health staff (% of total)	..	47	..
Under-five mortality rate (per 1,000)	260	260	260
Child malnutrition, underweight (% of under age 5)	..	27.5	..
Child immunization, measles (% of ages 12–23 mos.)	38	41	48
Primary completion rate, total (% of relevant age group)	35	..	..
Gross secondary enrollment, total (% of relevant age group)	11	15	..
Ratio of girls to boys in primary & secondary school (%)	..	85	..
HIV prevalence rate (% of population ages 15–49)	..	..	3.7
Environment			
Forests (1,000 sq. km)	610	597	591
Deforestation (average annual %, 1990–2005)			0.2
Freshwater use (% of internal resources)	..	0.2	..
Access to improved water source (% of total pop.)	36	46	53
Access to improved sanitation facilities (% of total pop.)	29	30	31
Energy use per capita (kilograms of oil equivalent)	597	569	615
Carbon dioxide emissions per capita (metric tons)	0.4	0.5	0.5
Electricity use per capita (kilowatt-hours)	60	89	141
Economy			
GDP ($ billions)	10.3	9.1	45.2
GDP growth (annual %)	-0.3	3.0	18.6
GDP implicit price deflator (annual % growth)	10.9	418.2	14.7
Value added in agriculture (% of GDP)	18	6	9
Value added in industry (% of GDP)	41	72	70
Value added in services (% of GDP)	41	22	21
Exports of goods and services (% of GDP)	39	90	74
Imports of goods and services (% of GDP)	21	63	38
Gross capital formation (% of GDP)	12	15	14
Central government revenue (% of GDP)	..	..	..
Central government cash surplus/deficit (% of GDP)	..	..	..
States and markets			
Starting a business (days)			119
Stock market capitalization (% of GDP)	..	..	..
Military expenditures (% of GDP)	7.8	2.2	5.4
Fixed-line and mobile subscribers (per 100 people)	1	1	14
Internet users (per 100 people)	0.0	0.1	0.5
Paved roads (% of total)	..	10	..
High-technology exports (% of manufactured exports)	..	..	..
Global links			
Merchandise trade (% of GDP)	53.5	120.1	103.2
Net barter terms of trade (2000 = 100)	94	100	197
Total external debt ($ billions)	8.6	9.4	9.6
Short-term debt ($ billions)	1.0	1.3	2.2
Total debt service (% of exports)	8.1	20.7	12.8
Foreign direct investment, net inflows ($ millions)	-335	879	-38
Remittances received ($ billions)	..	..	..
Aid ($ millions)	266	302	171

Antigua and Barbuda

		High income
Population (thousands)	84	
Surface area (sq. km)	440	
GNI ($ millions)	929	
GNI, PPP ($ billions)	1.3	

		High income
Population growth (%)		1.3
National poverty rate (% of pop.)		..
GNI per capita ($)		11,050
GNI per capita, PPP ($)		15,130

	1990	2000	2006
People			
Share of poorest 20% in nat'l consumption/income (%)	..	..	..
Life expectancy at birth (years)	74	75	..
Total fertility (births per woman)	1.7	1.7	..
Adolescent fertility (births per 1,000 women 15–19)	..	..	..
Contraceptive prevalence (% of married women 15–49)	53	53	..
Births attended by skilled health staff (% of total)	..	100	100
Under-five mortality rate (per 1,000)	..	15	11
Child malnutrition, underweight (% of under age 5)	..	..	..
Child immunization, measles (% of ages 12–23 mos.)	89	95	99
Primary completion rate, total (% of relevant age group)	..	..	..
Gross secondary enrollment, total (% of relevant age group)	..	..	..
Ratio of girls to boys in primary & secondary school (%)	..	..	..
HIV prevalence rate (% of population ages 15–49)	..	..	..
Environment			
Forests (sq. km)	90	90	90
Deforestation (average annual %, 1990–2005)			0.00
Freshwater use (% of internal resources)	..	..	..
Access to improved water source (% of total pop.)	..	92	91
Access to improved sanitation facilities (% of total pop.)	..	95	95
Energy use per capita (kilograms of oil equivalent)	..	..	..
Carbon dioxide emissions per capita (metric tons)	4.9	4.6	5.1
Electricity use per capita (kilowatt-hours)	..	..	..
Economy			
GDP ($ millions)	392	665	998
GDP growth (annual %)	2.5	3.3	11.5
GDP implicit price deflator (annual % growth)	2.3	–1.2	2.8
Value added in agriculture (% of GDP)	4	4	4
Value added in industry (% of GDP)	20	20	23
Value added in services (% of GDP)	76	76	74
Exports of goods and services (% of GDP)	89	70	60
Imports of goods and services (% of GDP)	87	75	71
Gross capital formation (% of GDP)	32	48	59
Central government revenue (% of GDP)	..	..	..
Central government cash surplus/deficit (% of GDP)	..	..	..
States and markets			
Starting a business (days)			21
Stock market capitalization (% of GDP)	..	..	..
Military expenditures (% of GDP)	..	..	..
Fixed-line and mobile subscribers (per 100 people)	26	79	169
Internet users (per 100 people)	0.0	6.5	38.1
Paved roads (% of total)	..	33	..
High-technology exports (% of manufactured exports)	..	0	1
Global links			
Merchandise trade (% of GDP)	70.5	69.0	65.6
Net barter terms of trade (2000 = 100)	..	..	..
Total external debt ($ billions)	..	..	..
Short-term debt ($ billions)	..	..	..
Total debt service (% of exports)	..	..	..
Foreign direct investment, net inflows ($ millions)	61	43	116
Remittances received ($ millions)	13	10	10
Aid ($ millions)	4.6	9.8	3.3

Argentina

Latin America & Caribbean		Upper middle income		
Population (millions)	39	Population growth (%)		1.0
Surface area (1,000 sq. km)	2,780	National poverty rate (% of pop.)		..
GNI ($ billions)	201.3	GNI per capita ($)		5,150
GNI, PPP ($ billions)	456.8	GNI per capita, PPP ($)		11,670

	1990	2000	2006
People			
Share of poorest 20% in nat'l consumption/income (%)	4.6	3.2	3.1
Life expectancy at birth (years)	72	74	75
Total fertility (births per woman)	3.0	2.5	2.3
Adolescent fertility (births per 1,000 women 15–19)	..	64	58
Contraceptive prevalence (% of married women 15–49)	..	..	..
Births attended by skilled health staff (% of total)	96	98	99
Under-five mortality rate (per 1,000)	29	19	16
Child malnutrition, underweight (% of under age 5)	..	..	2.3
Child immunization, measles (% of ages 12–23 mos.)	93	91	97
Primary completion rate, total (% of relevant age group)	..	99	99
Gross secondary enrollment, total (% of relevant age group)	72	97	86
Ratio of girls to boys in primary & secondary school (%)	..	103	104
HIV prevalence rate (% of population ages 15–49)	..	..	0.6
Environment			
Forests (1,000 sq. km)	353	338	330
Deforestation (average annual %, 1990–2005)			0.4
Freshwater use (% of internal resources)	..	10.6	..
Access to improved water source (% of total pop.)	94	96	96
Access to improved sanitation facilities (% of total pop.)	81	89	91
Energy use per capita (kilograms of oil equivalent)	1,415	1,679	1,644
Carbon dioxide emissions per capita (metric tons)	3.4	3.7	3.7
Electricity use per capita (kilowatt-hours)	1,305	2,087	2,418
Economy			
GDP ($ billions)	141.4	284.2	214.2
GDP growth (annual %)	-2.4	-0.8	8.5
GDP implicit price deflator (annual % growth)	2,076.8	1.0	13.5
Value added in agriculture (% of GDP)	8	5	8
Value added in industry (% of GDP)	36	28	36
Value added in services (% of GDP)	56	67	56
Exports of goods and services (% of GDP)	10	11	25
Imports of goods and services (% of GDP)	5	12	19
Gross capital formation (% of GDP)	14	16	24
Central government revenue (% of GDP)	..	14.1	18.1
Central government cash surplus/deficit (% of GDP)	..	-5.7	-0.5
States and markets			
Starting a business (days)			31
Stock market capitalization (% of GDP)	2.3	58.4	37.2
Military expenditures (% of GDP)	1.2	1.3	0.9
Fixed-line and mobile subscribers (per 100 people)	9	39	105
Internet users (per 100 people)	0.0	7.0	20.9
Paved roads (% of total)	29	29	..
High-technology exports (% of manufactured exports)	0	9	7
Global links			
Merchandise trade (% of GDP)	11.6	18.1	37.7
Net barter terms of trade (2000 = 100)	64	100	113
Total external debt ($ billions)	62	144	122
Short-term debt ($ billions)	10	28	35
Total debt service (% of exports)	37.0	69.6	31.6
Foreign direct investment, net inflows ($ billions)	1.8	10.4	4.8
Remittances received ($ millions)	15	86	541
Aid ($ millions)	169	53	114

Armenia

Europe & Central Asia		Lower middle income	
Population (millions)	3.0	Population growth (%)	-0.3
Surface area (1,000 sq. km)	30	National poverty rate (% of pop.)	51
GNI ($ billions)	5.8	GNI per capita ($)	1,920
GNI, PPP ($ billions)	14.9	GNI per capita, PPP ($)	4,950

	1990	2000	2006
People			
Share of poorest 20% in nat'l consumption/income (%)	..	7.6	..
Life expectancy at birth (years)	68	71	72
Total fertility (births per woman)	2.5	1.5	1.3
Adolescent fertility (births per 1,000 women 15–19)	..	40	30
Contraceptive prevalence (% of married women 15–49)	..	61	53
Births attended by skilled health staff (% of total)	..	97	98
Under-five mortality rate (per 1,000)	56	36	24
Child malnutrition, underweight (% of under age 5)	..	2.7	4.2
Child immunization, measles (% of ages 12–23 mos.)	93	92	92
Primary completion rate, total (% of relevant age group)	..	77	91
Gross secondary enrollment, total (% of relevant age group)	..	86	90
Ratio of girls to boys in primary & secondary school (%)	..	103	104
HIV prevalence rate (% of population ages 15–49)	..	..	0.1
Environment			
Forests (1,000 sq. km)	3.5	3.1	2.8
Deforestation (average annual %, 1990–2005)			1.3
Freshwater use (% of internal resources)	..	32.4	..
Access to improved water source (% of total pop.)	..	92	92
Access to improved sanitation facilities (% of total pop.)	..	84	83
Energy use per capita (kilograms of oil equivalent)	2,240	672	848
Carbon dioxide emissions per capita (metric tons)	1.2	1.1	1.2
Electricity use per capita (kilowatt-hours)	2,718	1,292	1,503
Economy			
GDP ($ billions)	2.3	1.9	6.4
GDP growth (annual %)	-11.7	5.9	13.3
GDP implicit price deflator (annual % growth)	79.4	-1.4	4.6
Value added in agriculture (% of GDP)	17	26	20
Value added in industry (% of GDP)	52	35	44
Value added in services (% of GDP)	31	39	37
Exports of goods and services (% of GDP)	35	23	22
Imports of goods and services (% of GDP)	46	51	36
Gross capital formation (% of GDP)	47	19	34
Central government revenue (% of GDP)	..	..	18.8
Central government cash surplus/deficit (% of GDP)	..	..	-0.3
States and markets			
Starting a business (days)			18
Stock market capitalization (% of GDP)	..	0.1	0.9
Military expenditures (% of GDP)	2.1	3.6	2.8
Fixed-line and mobile subscribers (per 100 people)	16	18	30
Internet users (per 100 people)	0.0	1.3	5.7
Paved roads (% of total)	99	97	90
High-technology exports (% of manufactured exports)	..	5	1
Global links			
Merchandise trade (% of GDP)	..	61.5	50.1
Net barter terms of trade (2000 = 100)	..	..	..
Total external debt ($ billions)	..	0.9	2.1
Short-term debt ($ millions)	..	44.4	297.9
Total debt service (% of exports)	..	8.2	7.6
Foreign direct investment, net inflows ($ billions)	1.8	0.1	0.3
Remittances received ($ billions)	..	0.1	1.2
Aid ($ millions)	2.7	215.9	213.3

Aruba

Population (thousands)	101	Population growth (%)		0.9
Surface area (sq. km)	180	National poverty rate (% of pop.)		..
GNI ($ billions)	..	GNI per capita ($)		..
GNI, PPP ($ billions)	..	GNI per capita, PPP ($)		..

	1990	2000	2006
People			
Share of poorest 20% in nat'l consumption/income (%)	..	..	..
Life expectancy at birth (years)	..	..	..
Total fertility (births per woman)	..	..	..
Adolescent fertility (births per 1,000 women 15–19)	..	31	24
Contraceptive prevalence (% of married women 15–49)	..	..	..
Births attended by skilled health staff (% of total)	..	96	..
Under-five mortality rate (per 1,000)	..	..	..
Child malnutrition, underweight (% of under age 5)	..	..	..
Child immunization, measles (% of ages 12–23 mos.)	..	..	..
Primary completion rate, total (% of relevant age group)	..	97	98
Gross secondary enrollment, total (% of relevant age group)	..	100	100
Ratio of girls to boys in primary & secondary school (%)	..	99	100
HIV prevalence rate (% of population ages 15–49)	..	..	..
Environment			
Forests (1,000 sq. km)	..	..	..
Deforestation (average annual %, 1990–2005)			..
Freshwater use (% of internal resources)	..	..	
Access to improved water source (% of total pop.)	100	100	100
Access to improved sanitation facilities (% of total pop.)	..	..	..
Energy use per capita (kilograms of oil equivalent)	..	..	..
Carbon dioxide emissions per capita (metric tons)	..	..	21.8
Electricity use per capita (kilowatt-hours)	..	..	..
Economy			
GDP ($ millions)	872.1	1,858.7	..
GDP growth (annual %)	12.0	3.7	..
GDP implicit price deflator (annual % growth)	5.7	4.0	..
Value added in agriculture (% of GDP)	..	..	..
Value added in industry (% of GDP)	..	..	..
Value added in services (% of GDP)	..	..	..
Exports of goods and services (% of GDP)	101	70	..
Imports of goods and services (% of GDP)	161	91	..
Gross capital formation (% of GDP)	..	..	..
Central government revenue (% of GDP)	..	..	..
Central government cash surplus/deficit (% of GDP)	..	..	..
States and markets			
Starting a business (days)			..
Stock market capitalization (% of GDP)	..	..	..
Military expenditures (% of GDP)	..	..	..
Fixed-line and mobile subscribers (per 100 people)	..	..	146
Internet users (per 100 people)	..	..	23.9
Paved roads (% of total)	..	..	..
High-technology exports (% of manufactured exports)	0	0	4
Global links			
Merchandise trade (% of GDP)	58.1	54.2	..
Net barter terms of trade (2000 = 100)	..	100	166
Total external debt ($ billions)	..	..	..
Short-term debt ($ billions)	..	..	..
Total debt service (% of exports)	..	..	..
Foreign direct investment, net inflows ($ millions)	131	-120	326
Remittances received ($ millions)	3.0	8.0	18.2
Aid ($ millions)	30	12	-11

Australia

Population (millions)	21	Population growth (%)	1.5
Surface area (1,000 sq. km)	7,741	National poverty rate (% of pop.)	..
GNI ($ billions)	742.3	GNI per capita ($)	35,860
GNI, PPP ($ billions)	702.5	GNI per capita, PPP ($)	33,940

	1990	2000	2006
People			
Share of poorest 20% in nat'l consumption/income (%)	..	..	..
Life expectancy at birth (years)	77	79	81
Total fertility (births per woman)	1.9	1.8	1.8
Adolescent fertility (births per 1,000 women 15–19)	..	18	15
Contraceptive prevalence (% of married women 15–49)	..	..	..
Births attended by skilled health staff (% of total)	100	99	..
Under-five mortality rate (per 1,000)	10	6	6
Child malnutrition, underweight (% of under age 5)	..	..	..
Child immunization, measles (% of ages 12–23 mos.)	86	91	94
Primary completion rate, total (% of relevant age group)	..	..	..
Gross secondary enrollment, total (% of relevant age group)	83	162	149
Ratio of girls to boys in primary & secondary school (%)	101	100	97
HIV prevalence rate (% of population ages 15–49)	..	..	0.1
Environment			
Forests (1,000 sq. km)	1,679	1,646	1,637
Deforestation (average annual %, 1990–2005)			0.2
Freshwater use (% of internal resources)	..	4.9	..
Access to improved water source (% of total pop.)	100	100	100
Access to improved sanitation facilities (% of total pop.)	100	100	100
Energy use per capita (kilograms of oil equivalent)	5,130	5,769	5,978
Carbon dioxide emissions per capita (metric tons)	16.3	17.6	16.2
Electricity use per capita (kilowatt-hours)	8,456	10,055	11,481
Economy			
GDP ($ billions)	319.1	399.6	780.5
GDP growth (annual %)	-0.6	1.9	2.5
GDP implicit price deflator (annual % growth)	3.6	4.8	4.6
Value added in agriculture (% of GDP)	4	4	3
Value added in industry (% of GDP)	30	26	28
Value added in services (% of GDP)	66	70	69
Exports of goods and services (% of GDP)	16	23	20
Imports of goods and services (% of GDP)	16	22	22
Gross capital formation (% of GDP)	23	22	27
Central government revenue (% of GDP)	..	24.9	26.0
Central government cash surplus/deficit (% of GDP)	..	1.9	1.7
States and markets			
Starting a business (days)			2
Stock market capitalization (% of GDP)	34.2	93.3	140.4
Military expenditures (% of GDP)	2.0	1.7	1.8
Fixed-line and mobile subscribers (per 100 people)	47	97	143
Internet users (per 100 people)	0.6	34.5	73.9
Paved roads (% of total)	35	39	..
High-technology exports (% of manufactured exports)	8	15	12
Global links			
Merchandise trade (% of GDP)	25.6	33.9	33.6
Net barter terms of trade (2000 = 100)	116	100	146
Total external debt ($ billions)	..	..	..
Short-term debt ($ billions)	..	..	..
Total debt service (% of exports)	..	..	..
Foreign direct investment, net inflows ($ billions)	8.1	13.6	26.6
Remittances received ($ billions)	2.4	1.9	3.1
Aid ($ billions)	..	..	..

Austria

Population (millions)	8.3	Population growth (%)	0.6
Surface area (1,000 sq. km)	84	National poverty rate (% of pop.)	..
GNI ($ billions)	329.2	GNI per capita ($)	39,750
GNI, PPP ($ billions)	298.4	GNI per capita, PPP ($)	36,040

	1990	2000	2006
People			
Share of poorest 20% in nat'l consumption/income (%)	..	8.6	..
Life expectancy at birth (years)	76	78	80
Total fertility (births per woman)	1.5	1.4	1.4
Adolescent fertility (births per 1,000 women 15–19)	..	14	12
Contraceptive prevalence (% of married women 15–49)	..	..	..
Births attended by skilled health staff (% of total)	..	..	..
Under-five mortality rate (per 1,000)	10	6	5
Child malnutrition, underweight (% of under age 5)	..	..	..
Child immunization, measles (% of ages 12–23 mos.)	60	75	80
Primary completion rate, total (% of relevant age group)	..	103	103
Gross secondary enrollment, total (% of relevant age group)	102	99	102
Ratio of girls to boys in primary & secondary school (%)	95	97	97
HIV prevalence rate (% of population ages 15–49)	..	..	0.3
Environment			
Forests (1,000 sq. km)	38	38	39
Deforestation (average annual %, 1990–2005)			–0.2
Freshwater use (% of internal resources)	..	3.8	..
Access to improved water source (% of total pop.)	100	100	100
Access to improved sanitation facilities (% of total pop.)	100	100	100
Energy use per capita (kilograms of oil equivalent)	3,251	3,624	4,174
Carbon dioxide emissions per capita (metric tons)	7.5	7.6	8.5
Electricity use per capita (kilowatt-hours)	6,078	7,107	7,889
Economy			
GDP ($ billions)	165.0	193.8	322.0
GDP growth (annual %)	4.6	3.4	3.1
GDP implicit price deflator (annual % growth)	3.0	1.8	1.6
Value added in agriculture (% of GDP)	4	2	2
Value added in industry (% of GDP)	32	31	31
Value added in services (% of GDP)	64	67	67
Exports of goods and services (% of GDP)	38	45	58
Imports of goods and services (% of GDP)	37	44	52
Gross capital formation (% of GDP)	24	23	21
Central government revenue (% of GDP)	..	38.2	39.8
Central government cash surplus/deficit (% of GDP)	..	–1.9	–1.6
States and markets			
Starting a business (days)			28
Stock market capitalization (% of GDP)	7.0	15.4	59.4
Military expenditures (% of GDP)	1.2	1.0	0.8
Fixed-line and mobile subscribers (per 100 people)	43	126	155
Internet users (per 100 people)	0.1	33.7	50.7
Paved roads (% of total)	100	100	..
High-technology exports (% of manufactured exports)	8	14	13
Global links			
Merchandise trade (% of GDP)	54.8	72.3	87.2
Net barter terms of trade (2000 = 100)	..	..	..
Total external debt ($ billions)	..	..	..
Short-term debt ($ billions)	..	..	..
Total debt service (% of exports)	..	..	..
Foreign direct investment, net inflows ($ billions)	0.7	8.5	0.2
Remittances received ($ billions)	0.6	1.4	2.0
Aid ($ billions)	..	..	..

Azerbaijan

Europe & Central Asia		Lower middle income	
Population (millions)	8.5	Population growth (%)	1.1
Surface area (1,000 sq. km)	87	National poverty rate (% of pop.)	50
GNI ($ billions)	15.6	GNI per capita ($)	1,840
GNI, PPP ($ billions)	46.1	GNI per capita, PPP ($)	5,430

	1990	2000	2006
People			
Share of poorest 20% in nat'l consumption/income (%)	..	7.4	..
Life expectancy at birth (years)	71	72	72
Total fertility (births per woman)	2.7	2.1	2.3
Adolescent fertility (births per 1,000 women 15–19)	..	34	29
Contraceptive prevalence (% of married women 15–49)	..	55	..
Births attended by skilled health staff (% of total)	..	84	100
Under-five mortality rate (per 1,000)	105	93	88
Child malnutrition, underweight (% of under age 5)	..	14.0	..
Child immunization, measles (% of ages 12–23 mos.)	66	99	96
Primary completion rate, total (% of relevant age group)	..	89	92
Gross secondary enrollment, total (% of relevant age group)	88	75	83
Ratio of girls to boys in primary & secondary school (%)	100	100	96
HIV prevalence rate (% of population ages 15–49)	..	..	0.1
Environment			
Forests (1,000 sq. km)	9.4	9.4	9.4
Deforestation (average annual %, 1990–2005)			0.00
Freshwater use (% of internal resources)	..	213.0	..
Access to improved water source (% of total pop.)	68	75	77
Access to improved sanitation facilities (% of total pop.)	..	55	54
Energy use per capita (kilograms of oil equivalent)	3,637	1,430	1,649
Carbon dioxide emissions per capita (metric tons)	7.5	3.8	3.8
Electricity use per capita (kilowatt-hours)	2,584	2,040	2,407
Economy			
GDP ($ billions)	8.9	5.3	19.9
GDP growth (annual %)	-11.7	11.1	34.5
GDP implicit price deflator (annual % growth)	83.5	12.5	5.3
Value added in agriculture (% of GDP)	29	17	7
Value added in industry (% of GDP)	33	45	70
Value added in services (% of GDP)	38	38	22
Exports of goods and services (% of GDP)	44	39	70
Imports of goods and services (% of GDP)	39	38	41
Gross capital formation (% of GDP)	27	21	32
Central government revenue (% of GDP)	..	17.6	..
Central government cash surplus/deficit (% of GDP)	..	-4.7	..
States and markets			
Starting a business (days)			30
Stock market capitalization (% of GDP)	..	0.1	..
Military expenditures (% of GDP)	2.5	2.3	3.3
Fixed-line and mobile subscribers (per 100 people)	9	15	53
Internet users (per 100 people)	0.0	0.1	9.8
Paved roads (% of total)	..	92	49
High-technology exports (% of manufactured exports)	..	4	2
Global links			
Merchandise trade (% of GDP)	..	55.3	58.6
Net barter terms of trade (2000 = 100)	..	..	..
Total external debt ($ billions)	..	1.3	1.9
Short-term debt ($ millions)	..	156.2	302.0
Total debt service (% of exports)	..	5.8	1.6
Foreign direct investment, net inflows ($ millions)	3.9	129.9	-584.0
Remittances received ($ millions)	..	57.0	812.5
Aid ($ millions)	0.3	139.1	205.7

Bahamas, The

Population (thousands)	327	Population growth (%)		1.2
Surface area (1,000 sq. km)	14	National poverty rate (% of pop.)		..
GNI ($ billions)	..	GNI per capita ($)		..
GNI, PPP ($ billions)	..	GNI per capita, PPP ($)		..

	1990	2000	2006
People			
Share of poorest 20% in nat'l consumption/income (%)	..	..	..
Life expectancy at birth (years)	70	70	73
Total fertility (births per woman)	2.6	2.2	2.0
Adolescent fertility (births per 1,000 women 15–19)	..	59	54
Contraceptive prevalence (% of married women 15–49)	62	..	..
Births attended by skilled health staff (% of total)	99	99	99
Under-five mortality rate (per 1,000)	29	19	14
Child malnutrition, underweight (% of under age 5)	..	..	..
Child immunization, measles (% of ages 12–23 mos.)	86	93	88
Primary completion rate, total (% of relevant age group)	..	83	95
Gross secondary enrollment, total (% of relevant age group)	..	80	91
Ratio of girls to boys in primary & secondary school (%)	..	97	100
HIV prevalence rate (% of population ages 15–49)	..	..	3.3
Environment			
Forests (1,000 sq. km)	5.2	5.2	5.2
Deforestation (average annual %, 1990–2005)			0.00
Freshwater use (% of internal resources)	..	..	
Access to improved water source (% of total pop.)	..	97	97
Access to improved sanitation facilities (% of total pop.)	100	100	100
Energy use per capita (kilograms of oil equivalent)	..	..	..
Carbon dioxide emissions per capita (metric tons)	7.6	5.9	6.3
Electricity use per capita (kilowatt-hours)	..	..	..
Economy			
GDP ($ billions)	3.1	5.0	..
GDP growth (annual %)	1.1	5.0	..
GDP implicit price deflator (annual % growth)	3.2	4.2	..
Value added in agriculture (% of GDP)	..	..	..
Value added in industry (% of GDP)	..	..	..
Value added in services (% of GDP)	..	..	..
Exports of goods and services (% of GDP)	..	..	..
Imports of goods and services (% of GDP)	..	..	..
Gross capital formation (% of GDP)	..	..	..
Central government revenue (% of GDP)	16.0	18.7	18.3
Central government cash surplus/deficit (% of GDP)	-1.9	0.4	-1.8
States and markets			
Starting a business (days)			..
Stock market capitalization (% of GDP)			
Military expenditures (% of GDP)	0.8	0.6	0.7
Fixed-line and mobile subscribers (per 100 people)	28	48	112
Internet users (per 100 people)	0.0	4.3	31.9
Paved roads (% of total)	52	57	..
High-technology exports (% of manufactured exports)	0	7	..
Global links			
Merchandise trade (% of GDP)	89.8	53.0	..
Net barter terms of trade (2000 = 100)	..	..	..
Total external debt ($ billions)	..	..	..
Short-term debt ($ billions)	..	..	..
Total debt service (% of exports)	..	..	..
Foreign direct investment, net inflows ($ millions)	-17	250	706
Remittances received ($ billions)	..	..	..
Aid ($ millions)	3.2	5.5	4.8

Bahrain

			High income
Population (thousands)	739	Population growth (%)	1.9
Surface area (sq. km)	710	National poverty rate (% of pop.)	..
GNI ($ billions)	14.0	GNI per capita ($)	19,350
GNI, PPP ($ billions)	24.9	GNI per capita, PPP ($)	34,310

	1990	2000	2006
People			
Share of poorest 20% in nat'l consumption/income (%)	..	..	..
Life expectancy at birth (years)	72	75	76
Total fertility (births per woman)	3.6	2.6	2.3
Adolescent fertility (births per 1,000 women 15–19)	..	20	17
Contraceptive prevalence (% of married women 15–49)	53	..	..
Births attended by skilled health staff (% of total)	94	..	99
Under-five mortality rate (per 1,000)	19	12	10
Child malnutrition, underweight (% of under age 5)	..	..	..
Child immunization, measles (% of ages 12–23 mos.)	87	98	99
Primary completion rate, total (% of relevant age group)	97	98	105
Gross secondary enrollment, total (% of relevant age group)	100	97	101
Ratio of girls to boys in primary & secondary school (%)	101	104	102
HIV prevalence rate (% of population ages 15–49)	..	..	0.2
Environment			
Forests (1,000 sq. km)	..	..	..
Deforestation (average annual %, 1990–2005)			..
Freshwater use (% of internal resources)		..	..
Access to improved water source (% of total pop.)	..	..	..
Access to improved sanitation facilities (% of total pop.)	..	..	..
Energy use per capita (kilograms of oil equivalent)	9,796	9,591	11,214
Carbon dioxide emissions per capita (metric tons)	23.7	28.7	23.8
Electricity use per capita (kilowatt-hours)	6,573	8,830	11,401
Economy			
GDP ($ billions)	4.2	8.0	16.0
GDP growth (annual %)	4.4	5.3	7.8
GDP implicit price deflator (annual % growth)	4.8	14.3	33.1
Value added in agriculture (% of GDP)	1	..	..
Value added in industry (% of GDP)	46	..	..
Value added in services (% of GDP)	53	..	..
Exports of goods and services (% of GDP)	116	89	73
Imports of goods and services (% of GDP)	95	64	54
Gross capital formation (% of GDP)	16	10	16
Central government revenue (% of GDP)	27.1	32.9	27.0
Central government cash surplus/deficit (% of GDP)	-2.3	8.5	6.3
States and markets			
Starting a business (days)			..
Stock market capitalization (% of GDP)	..	83.1	108.3
Military expenditures (% of GDP)	5.1	4.0	3.0
Fixed-line and mobile subscribers (per 100 people)	20	58	148
Internet users (per 100 people)	0.0	6.2	21.3
Paved roads (% of total)	75	78	..
High-technology exports (% of manufactured exports)	0	0	0
Global links			
Merchandise trade (% of GDP)	176.7	135.8	112.0
Net barter terms of trade (2000 = 100)	..	100	132
Total external debt ($ billions)	..	..	..
Short-term debt ($ billions)	..	..	..
Total debt service (% of exports)	..	..	..
Foreign direct investment, net inflows ($ billions)	-0.2	0.4	2.9
Remittances received ($ billions)	..	..	..
Aid ($ millions)	137	49	57

Bangladesh

Population (millions)	156	Population growth (%)	1.8
Surface area (1,000 sq. km)	144	National poverty rate (% of pop.)	50
GNI ($ billions)	70.5	GNI per capita ($)	450
GNI, PPP ($ billions)	191.9	GNI per capita, PPP ($)	1,230

	1990	2000	2006
People			
Share of poorest 20% in nat'l consumption/income (%)	9.4	8.7	8.8
Life expectancy at birth (years)	55	61	64
Total fertility (births per woman)	4.3	3.3	2.9
Adolescent fertility (births per 1,000 women 15-19)	..	150	129
Contraceptive prevalence (% of married women 15-49)	40	54	58
Births attended by skilled health staff (% of total)	..	12	20
Under-five mortality rate (per 1,000)	149	92	69
Child malnutrition, underweight (% of under age 5)	..	..	39.2
Child immunization, measles (% of ages 12-23 mos.)	65	76	81
Primary completion rate, total (% of relevant age group)	49	77	72
Gross secondary enrollment, total (% of relevant age group)	..	46	44
Ratio of girls to boys in primary & secondary school (%)	..	102	103
HIV prevalence rate (% of population ages 15-49)	..	..	0.1
Environment			
Forests (1,000 sq. km)	8.8	8.8	8.7
Deforestation (average annual %, 1990-2005)			0.1
Freshwater use (% of internal resources)	..	75.6	..
Access to improved water source (% of total pop.)	72	74	74
Access to improved sanitation facilities (% of total pop.)	20	33	39
Energy use per capita (kilograms of oil equivalent)	113	134	158
Carbon dioxide emissions per capita (metric tons)	0.1	0.2	0.2
Electricity use per capita (kilowatt-hours)	45	96	136
Economy			
GDP ($ billions)	30.1	47.1	61.9
GDP growth (annual %)	5.9	5.9	6.6
GDP implicit price deflator (annual % growth)	6.3	1.9	5.2
Value added in agriculture (% of GDP)	30	26	20
Value added in industry (% of GDP)	21	25	28
Value added in services (% of GDP)	48	49	52
Exports of goods and services (% of GDP)	6	14	19
Imports of goods and services (% of GDP)	14	19	25
Gross capital formation (% of GDP)	17	23	25
Central government revenue (% of GDP)	..	9.8	10.0
Central government cash surplus/deficit (% of GDP)	..	-0.7	-0.7
States and markets			
Starting a business (days)			74
Stock market capitalization (% of GDP)	1.1	2.5	5.8
Military expenditures (% of GDP)	1.1	1.4	1.1
Fixed-line and mobile subscribers (per 100 people)	0	1	13
Internet users (per 100 people)	0.0	0.1	0.3
Paved roads (% of total)	7	10	..
High-technology exports (% of manufactured exports)	0	0	0
Global links			
Merchandise trade (% of GDP)	17.6	32.4	45.1
Net barter terms of trade (2000 = 100)	117	100	73
Total external debt ($ billions)	12	16	21
Short-term debt ($ billions)	0.2	0.3	1.2
Total debt service (% of exports)	25.8	8.6	3.7
Foreign direct investment, net inflows ($ millions)	3.2	280.4	697.2
Remittances received ($ billions)	0.8	2.0	5.4
Aid ($ billions)	2.1	1.2	1.2

Barbados

High income

Population (thousands)	293	Population growth (%)		0.3
Surface area (sq. km)	430	National poverty rate (% of pop.)		..
GNI ($ billions)	..	GNI per capita ($)		..
GNI, PPP ($ billions)	4.4	GNI per capita, PPP ($)		15,150

	1990	2000	2006
People			
Share of poorest 20% in nat'l consumption/income (%)	..	..	..
Life expectancy at birth (years)	74	75	77
Total fertility (births per woman)	1.7	1.5	1.5
Adolescent fertility (births per 1,000 women 15–19)	..	43	42
Contraceptive prevalence (% of married women 15–49)	55	..	..
Births attended by skilled health staff (% of total)	..	98	100
Under-five mortality rate (per 1,000)	17	13	12
Child malnutrition, underweight (% of under age 5)	..	..	..
Child immunization, measles (% of ages 12–23 mos.)	87	94	92
Primary completion rate, total (% of relevant age group)	..	93	96
Gross secondary enrollment, total (% of relevant age group)	..	96	102
Ratio of girls to boys in primary & secondary school (%)	..	101	101
HIV prevalence rate (% of population ages 15–49)	..	..	1.5
Environment			
Forests (sq. km)	20	20	20
Deforestation (average annual %, 1990–2005)			0.00
Freshwater use (% of internal resources)	..	90.0	..
Access to improved water source (% of total pop.)	100	100	100
Access to improved sanitation facilities (% of total pop.)	100	100	100
Energy use per capita (kilograms of oil equivalent)	..	..	..
Carbon dioxide emissions per capita (metric tons)	4.0	4.1	4.4
Electricity use per capita (kilowatt-hours)	..	..	..
Economy			
GDP ($ billions)	1.7	2.5	3.4
GDP growth (annual %)	-4.8	2.3	..
GDP implicit price deflator (annual % growth)	5.5	0.8	..
Value added in agriculture (% of GDP)	7	4	4
Value added in industry (% of GDP)	20	16	18
Value added in services (% of GDP)	73	79	78
Exports of goods and services (% of GDP)	49	50	54
Imports of goods and services (% of GDP)	52	57	63
Gross capital formation (% of GDP)	19	19	24
Central government revenue (% of GDP)	..	..	43.9
Central government cash surplus/deficit (% of GDP)	..	..	3.7
States and markets			
Starting a business (days)			..
Stock market capitalization (% of GDP)	16.5	66.4	144.4
Military expenditures (% of GDP)	0.8	0.9	0.8
Fixed-line and mobile subscribers (per 100 people)	27	53	117
Internet users (per 100 people)	0.0	3.5	54.8
Paved roads (% of total)	87	99	100
High-technology exports (% of manufactured exports)	0	23	17
Global links			
Merchandise trade (% of GDP)	53.8	56.1	57.5
Net barter terms of trade (2000 = 100)	..	100	115
Total external debt ($ billions)	..	..	..
Short-term debt ($ billions)	..	..	..
Total debt service (% of exports)	..	..	..
Foreign direct investment, net inflows ($ millions)	11	19	62
Remittances received ($ millions)	38	102	140
Aid ($ millions)	2.6	0.2	-0.6

Belarus

Europe & Central Asia		Lower middle income	
Population (millions)	9.7	Population growth (%)	-0.4
Surface area (1,000 sq. km)	208	National poverty rate (% of pop.)	19
GNI ($ billions)	33.8	GNI per capita ($)	3,470
GNI, PPP ($ billions)	94.4	GNI per capita, PPP ($)	9,700

	1990	2000	2006
People			
Share of poorest 20% in nat'l consumption/income (%)	10.4	8.5	8.8
Life expectancy at birth (years)	71	68	69
Total fertility (births per woman)	1.9	1.3	1.3
Adolescent fertility (births per 1,000 women 15–19)	..	28	22
Contraceptive prevalence (% of married women 15–49)	..	..	73
Births attended by skilled health staff (% of total)	..	100	100
Under-five mortality rate (per 1,000)	24	17	13
Child malnutrition, underweight (% of under age 5)	..	..	..
Child immunization, measles (% of ages 12–23 mos.)	94	98	97
Primary completion rate, total (% of relevant age group)	82	102	95
Gross secondary enrollment, total (% of relevant age group)	93	87	96
Ratio of girls to boys in primary & secondary school (%)	..	102	101
HIV prevalence rate (% of population ages 15–49)	..	..	0.3
Environment			
Forests (1,000 sq. km)	74	78	79
Deforestation (average annual %, 1990–2005)			-0.5
Freshwater use (% of internal resources)	..	7.5	..
Access to improved water source (% of total pop.)	100	100	100
Access to improved sanitation facilities (% of total pop.)	..	83	84
Energy use per capita (kilograms of oil equivalent)	4,139	2,459	2,720
Carbon dioxide emissions per capita (metric tons)	10.6	5.9	6.6
Electricity use per capita (kilowatt-hours)	3,401	2,989	3,209
Economy			
GDP ($ billions)	17.4	12.7	36.9
GDP growth (annual %)	-1.2	5.8	9.9
GDP implicit price deflator (annual % growth)	103.6	185.3	10.8
Value added in agriculture (% of GDP)	24	14	9
Value added in industry (% of GDP)	47	39	42
Value added in services (% of GDP)	29	47	49
Exports of goods and services (% of GDP)	46	69	60
Imports of goods and services (% of GDP)	44	72	64
Gross capital formation (% of GDP)	27	25	30
Central government revenue (% of GDP)	31.5	28.7	36.0
Central government cash surplus/deficit (% of GDP)	-4.8	0.1	1.4
States and markets			
Starting a business (days)			48
Stock market capitalization (% of GDP)	..	..	..
Military expenditures (% of GDP)	1.5	1.3	1.7
Fixed-line and mobile subscribers (per 100 people)	15	28	96
Internet users (per 100 people)	0.0	1.9	56.3
Paved roads (% of total)	96	96	89
High-technology exports (% of manufactured exports)	..	4	3
Global links			
Merchandise trade (% of GDP)	..	125.4	113.8
Net barter terms of trade (2000 = 100)	..	..	..
Total external debt ($ billions)	..	2.1	6.1
Short-term debt ($ billions)	..	1.2	4.4
Total debt service (% of exports)	..	4.8	3.3
Foreign direct investment, net inflows ($ millions)	7.0	118.8	354.0
Remittances received ($ millions)	..	139.0	334.2
Aid ($ millions)	187	40	73

Belgium

High income

Population (millions)	11	Population growth (%)		0.6
Surface area (1,000 sq. km)	31	National poverty rate (% of pop.)		..
GNI ($ billions)	405.4	GNI per capita ($)		38,460
GNI, PPP ($ billions)	356.9	GNI per capita, PPP ($)		33,860

	1990	2000	2006
People			
Share of poorest 20% in nat'l consumption/income (%)	..	8.5	..
Life expectancy at birth (years)	76	78	79
Total fertility (births per woman)	1.6	1.7	1.7
Adolescent fertility (births per 1,000 women 15–19)	..	9	7
Contraceptive prevalence (% of married women 15–49)	78	..	..
Births attended by skilled health staff (% of total)	..	99	..
Under-five mortality rate (per 1,000)	10	6	4
Child malnutrition, underweight (% of under age 5)	..	..	..
Child immunization, measles (% of ages 12–23 mos.)	85	82	88
Primary completion rate, total (% of relevant age group)	79	..	..
Gross secondary enrollment, total (% of relevant age group)	101	146	109
Ratio of girls to boys in primary & secondary school (%)	101	106	98
HIV prevalence rate (% of population ages 15–49)	..	..	0.3
Environment			
Forests (1,000 sq. km)	6.8	6.7	6.7
Deforestation (average annual %, 1990–2005)			0.1
Freshwater use (% of internal resources)	..	..	..
Access to improved water source (% of total pop.)	..	..	..
Access to improved sanitation facilities (% of total pop.)	..	..	..
Energy use per capita (kilograms of oil equivalent)	4,932	5,763	5,407
Carbon dioxide emissions per capita (metric tons)	10.1	10.0	9.7
Electricity use per capita (kilowatt-hours)	6,380	8,247	8,510
Economy			
GDP ($ billions)	202.7	231.9	394.0
GDP growth (annual %)	3.1	3.7	3.2
GDP implicit price deflator (annual % growth)	2.8	1.8	2.0
Value added in agriculture (% of GDP)	2	1	1
Value added in industry (% of GDP)	31	27	24
Value added in services (% of GDP)	67	72	75
Exports of goods and services (% of GDP)	69	85	88
Imports of goods and services (% of GDP)	68	82	85
Gross capital formation (% of GDP)	22	22	22
Central government revenue (% of GDP)	..	42.9	41.2
Central government cash surplus/deficit (% of GDP)	..	0.1	0.3
States and markets			
Starting a business (days)			4
Stock market capitalization (% of GDP)	32.3	78.7	100.6
Military expenditures (% of GDP)	2.3	1.4	1.1
Fixed-line and mobile subscribers (per 100 people)	40	104	136
Internet users (per 100 people)	0.0	29.3	45.8
Paved roads (% of total)	81	78	78
High-technology exports (% of manufactured exports)	..	9	8
Global links			
Merchandise trade (% of GDP)	117.1	157.8	183.5
Net barter terms of trade (2000 = 100)	..	100	99
Total external debt ($ billions)	..	..	..
Short-term debt ($ billions)	..	..	..
Total debt service (% of exports)	..	..	..
Foreign direct investment, net inflows ($ billions)	8.0	214.9	62.0
Remittances received ($ billions)	3.6	4.0	7.5
Aid ($ billions)	..	..	..

Belize

Latin America & Caribbean		Upper middle income	
Population (thousands)	298	Population growth (%)	2.0
Surface area (1,000 sq. km)	23	National poverty rate (% of pop.)	..
GNI ($ billions)	1.1	GNI per capita ($)	3,740
GNI, PPP ($ billions)	2.1	GNI per capita, PPP ($)	7,080

	1990	2000	2006
People			
Share of poorest 20% in nat'l consumption/income (%)	..	..	..
Life expectancy at birth (years)	72	72	72
Total fertility (births per woman)	4.5	3.4	2.9
Adolescent fertility (births per 1,000 women 15–19)	..	97	81
Contraceptive prevalence (% of married women 15–49)	47	56	..
Births attended by skilled health staff (% of total)	77	83	89
Under-five mortality rate (per 1,000)	43	23	16
Child malnutrition, underweight (% of under age 5)	..	..	..
Child immunization, measles (% of ages 12–23 mos.)	86	95	99
Primary completion rate, total (% of relevant age group)	92	99	104
Gross secondary enrollment, total (% of relevant age group)	44	68	79
Ratio of girls to boys in primary & secondary school (%)	100	99	100
HIV prevalence rate (% of population ages 15–49)	..	..	2.5
Environment			
Forests (1,000 sq. km)	17	17	17
Deforestation (average annual %, 1990–2005)			0.00
Freshwater use (% of internal resources)	..	0.9	..
Access to improved water source (% of total pop.)	..	90	91
Access to improved sanitation facilities (% of total pop.)	..	47	47
Energy use per capita (kilograms of oil equivalent)	..	..	..
Carbon dioxide emissions per capita (metric tons)	1.6	2.8	2.8
Electricity use per capita (kilowatt-hours)	..	..	..
Economy			
GDP ($ millions)	413	832	1,214
GDP growth (annual %)	10.6	12.2	5.6
GDP implicit price deflator (annual % growth)	2.8	1.2	3.1
Value added in agriculture (% of GDP)	20	17	14
Value added in industry (% of GDP)	22	21	21
Value added in services (% of GDP)	58	62	65
Exports of goods and services (% of GDP)	62	53	64
Imports of goods and services (% of GDP)	60	73	62
Gross capital formation (% of GDP)	27	33	19
Central government revenue (% of GDP)	25.4	..	..
Central government cash surplus/deficit (% of GDP)	-0.6	..	..
States and markets			
Starting a business (days)			44
Stock market capitalization (% of GDP)	..	..	..
Military expenditures (% of GDP)	1.2	..	..
Fixed-line and mobile subscribers (per 100 people)	9	21	51
Internet users (per 100 people)	0.0	6.0	11.4
Paved roads (% of total)	..	17	..
High-technology exports (% of manufactured exports)	0	0	10
Global links			
Merchandise trade (% of GDP)	83.3	89.2	77.6
Net barter terms of trade (2000 = 100)	..	100	94
Total external debt ($ billions)	0.1	0.6	1.0
Short-term debt ($ millions)	6.1	50.0	6.6
Total debt service (% of exports)	6.8	16.4	15.9
Foreign direct investment, net inflows ($ millions)	17	23	73
Remittances received ($ millions)	18	22	65
Aid ($ millions)	30.3	14.7	7.6

Benin

Sub-Saharan Africa		Low income
Population (millions)	8.8	Population growth (%)	3.1
Surface area (1,000 sq. km)	113	National poverty rate (% of pop.)	..
GNI ($ billions)	4.7	GNI per capita ($)	530
GNI, PPP ($ billions)	10.9	GNI per capita, PPP ($)	1,250

	1990	2000	2006
People			
Share of poorest 20% in nat'l consumption/income (%)	..	..	..
Life expectancy at birth (years)	53	54	56
Total fertility (births per woman)	6.7	6.0	5.5
Adolescent fertility (births per 1,000 women 15–19)	..	142	123
Contraceptive prevalence (% of married women 15–49)	..	19	17
Births attended by skilled health staff (% of total)	..	66	79
Under-five mortality rate (per 1,000)	185	160	148
Child malnutrition, underweight (% of under age 5)	..	21.5	..
Child immunization, measles (% of ages 12–23 mos.)	79	68	89
Primary completion rate, total (% of relevant age group)	18	35	65
Gross secondary enrollment, total (% of relevant age group)	10	20	32
Ratio of girls to boys in primary & secondary school (%)	49	64	73
HIV prevalence rate (% of population ages 15–49)	..	..	1.8
Environment			
Forests (1,000 sq. km)	33	27	24
Deforestation (average annual %, 1990–2005)			2.3
Freshwater use (% of internal resources)	..	1.3	..
Access to improved water source (% of total pop.)	63	65	67
Access to improved sanitation facilities (% of total pop.)	12	26	33
Energy use per capita (kilograms of oil equivalent)	324	277	304
Carbon dioxide emissions per capita (metric tons)	0.1	0.2	0.3
Electricity use per capita (kilowatt-hours)	34	55	69
Economy			
GDP ($ billions)	1.8	2.3	4.8
GDP growth (annual %)	3.2	5.8	4.1
GDP implicit price deflator (annual % growth)	1.6	3.2	6.1
Value added in agriculture (% of GDP)	36	37	32
Value added in industry (% of GDP)	13	14	13
Value added in services (% of GDP)	51	50	54
Exports of goods and services (% of GDP)	14	15	13
Imports of goods and services (% of GDP)	26	28	26
Gross capital formation (% of GDP)	14	19	20
Central government revenue (% of GDP)	..	16.5	16.7
Central government cash surplus/deficit (% of GDP)	..	0.7	0.2
States and markets			
Starting a business (days)			31
Stock market capitalization (% of GDP)	..	..	..
Military expenditures (% of GDP)	..	..	..
Fixed-line and mobile subscribers (per 100 people)	0	1	13
Internet users (per 100 people)	0.0	0.2	8.0
Paved roads (% of total)	20	20	10
High-technology exports (% of manufactured exports)	0	0	0
Global links			
Merchandise trade (% of GDP)	30.0	44.6	32.5
Net barter terms of trade (2000 = 100)	107	100	81
Total external debt ($ billions)	1.3	1.6	0.8
Short-term debt ($ millions)	55	65	39
Total debt service (% of exports)	8.2	11.9	7.4
Foreign direct investment, net inflows ($ millions)	62	60	63
Remittances received ($ millions)	101	87	173
Aid ($ millions)	267	238	375

Bermuda

Population (thousands)	64	Population growth (%)	0.4
Surface area (sq. km)	50	National poverty rate (% of pop.)	..
GNI ($ billions)	..	GNI per capita ($)	..
GNI, PPP ($ billions)	..	GNI per capita, PPP ($)	..

	1990	2000	2006
People			
Share of poorest 20% in nat'l consumption/income (%)	..	..	..
Life expectancy at birth (years)	74	78	79
Total fertility (births per woman)	..	1.7	1.8
Adolescent fertility (births per 1,000 women 15–19)	..	..	..
Contraceptive prevalence (% of married women 15–49)	..	..	..
Births attended by skilled health staff (% of total)	..	..	..
Under-five mortality rate (per 1,000)	..	..	..
Child malnutrition, underweight (% of under age 5)	..	..	..
Child immunization, measles (% of ages 12–23 mos.)	..	..	..
Primary completion rate, total (% of relevant age group)	..	104	96
Gross secondary enrollment, total (% of relevant age group)	..	87	84
Ratio of girls to boys in primary & secondary school (%)	..	101	95
HIV prevalence rate (% of population ages 15–49)	..	..	..
Environment			
Forests (sq. km)	10	10	10
Deforestation (average annual %, 1990–2005)			0.00
Freshwater use (% of internal resources)	..	..	..
Access to improved water source (% of total pop.)	..	..	..
Access to improved sanitation facilities (% of total pop.)	..	..	..
Energy use per capita (kilograms of oil equivalent)	..	..	..
Carbon dioxide emissions per capita (metric tons)	9.7	8.0	8.7
Electricity use per capita (kilowatt-hours)	..	..	..
Economy			
GDP ($ billions)	1.6	..	..
GDP growth (annual %)	0.0	..	..
GDP implicit price deflator (annual % growth)	6.0	..	..
Value added in agriculture (% of GDP)	..	..	..
Value added in industry (% of GDP)	..	..	..
Value added in services (% of GDP)	..	..	..
Exports of goods and services (% of GDP)	..	..	..
Imports of goods and services (% of GDP)	..	..	..
Gross capital formation (% of GDP)	..	..	..
Central government revenue (% of GDP)	..	..	..
Central government cash surplus/deficit (% of GDP)	..	..	..
States and markets			
Starting a business (days)			..
Stock market capitalization (% of GDP)	..	..	..
Military expenditures (% of GDP)	..	..	..
Fixed-line and mobile subscribers (per 100 people)	64	111	185
Internet users (per 100 people)	0.0	43.5	66.1
Paved roads (% of total)	..	..	..
High-technology exports (% of manufactured exports)	..	..	..
Global links			
Merchandise trade (% of GDP)	41.1	..	..
Net barter terms of trade (2000 = 100)	..	..	..
Total external debt ($ billions)	..	..	..
Short-term debt ($ billions)	..	..	..
Total debt service (% of exports)	..	..	..
Foreign direct investment, net inflows ($ billions)	..	..	..
Remittances received ($ billions)	..	..	..
Aid ($ millions)	42.2	0.1	0.1

Bhutan

South Asia   **Lower middle income**

Population (thousands)	649	Population growth (%)	1.8
Surface area (1,000 sq. km)	47	National poverty rate (% of pop.)	..
GNI ($ millions)	928	GNI per capita ($)	1,430
GNI, PPP ($ billions)	2.6	GNI per capita, PPP ($)	4,000

	1990	2000	2006
People			
Share of poorest 20% in nat'l consumption/income (%)	..	..	..
Life expectancy at birth (years)	53	62	65
Total fertility (births per woman)	5.7	3.4	2.3
Adolescent fertility (births per 1,000 women 15-19)	..	60	40
Contraceptive prevalence (% of married women 15-49)	..	31	..
Births attended by skilled health staff (% of total)	..	24	51
Under-five mortality rate (per 1,000)	166	100	70
Child malnutrition, underweight (% of under age 5)	..	14.1	..
Child immunization, measles (% of ages 12-23 mos.)	93	76	90
Primary completion rate, total (% of relevant age group)	..	52	73
Gross secondary enrollment, total (% of relevant age group)	..	42	49
Ratio of girls to boys in primary & secondary school (%)	..	86	95
HIV prevalence rate (% of population ages 15-49)	..	..	0.1
Environment			
Forests (1,000 sq. km)	30	31	32
Deforestation (average annual %, 1990-2005)			-0.3
Freshwater use (% of internal resources)	..	0.4	..
Access to improved water source (% of total pop.)	..	62	62
Access to improved sanitation facilities (% of total pop.)	..	70	70
Energy use per capita (kilograms of oil equivalent)	..	..	..
Carbon dioxide emissions per capita (metric tons)	0.2	0.7	0.7
Electricity use per capita (kilowatt-hours)	..	..	..
Economy			
GDP ($ millions)	304	448	942
GDP growth (annual %)	10.7	7.2	8.5
GDP implicit price deflator (annual % growth)	5.9	2.3	4.4
Value added in agriculture (% of GDP)	36	28	22
Value added in industry (% of GDP)	25	35	38
Value added in services (% of GDP)	39	36	40
Exports of goods and services (% of GDP)	26	29	32
Imports of goods and services (% of GDP)	30	47	45
Gross capital formation (% of GDP)	30	47	55
Central government revenue (% of GDP)	16.8	22.4	15.5
Central government cash surplus/deficit (% of GDP)	-5.8	-2.4	2.0
States and markets			
Starting a business (days)			48
Stock market capitalization (% of GDP)	..	8.9	..
Military expenditures (% of GDP)	..	..	..
Fixed-line and mobile subscribers (per 100 people)	0	3	18
Internet users (per 100 people)	0.0	0.4	4.6
Paved roads (% of total)	77	..	..
High-technology exports (% of manufactured exports)	0	0	..
Global links			
Merchandise trade (% of GDP)	49.7	62.2	71.1
Net barter terms of trade (2000 = 100)	..	..	..
Total external debt ($ millions)	84	204	713
Short-term debt ($ millions)	3.3	1.5	16.0
Total debt service (% of exports)	..	..	..
Foreign direct investment, net inflows ($ millions)	1.6	-0.1	6.1
Remittances received ($ billions)	..	..	..
Aid ($ millions)	46	53	94

Bolivia

Latin America & Caribbean   **Lower middle income**

Population (millions)	9.4	Population growth (%)	1.9
Surface area (1,000 sq. km)	1,099	National poverty rate (% of pop.)	65
GNI ($ billions)	10.3	GNI per capita ($)	1,100
GNI, PPP ($ billions)	35.6	GNI per capita, PPP ($)	3,810

	1990	2000	2006
People			
Share of poorest 20% in nat'l consumption/income (%)	5.5	1.5	..
Life expectancy at birth (years)	59	63	65
Total fertility (births per woman)	4.9	4.1	3.6
Adolescent fertility (births per 1,000 women 15–19)	..	85	79
Contraceptive prevalence (% of married women 15–49)	30	53	..
Births attended by skilled health staff (% of total)	43	69	..
Under-five mortality rate (per 1,000)	125	84	61
Child malnutrition, underweight (% of under age 5)	8.9	5.9	5.9
Child immunization, measles (% of ages 12–23 mos.)	53	79	81
Primary completion rate, total (% of relevant age group)	..	99	101
Gross secondary enrollment, total (% of relevant age group)	..	80	82
Ratio of girls to boys in primary & secondary school (%)	..	98	98
HIV prevalence rate (% of population ages 15–49)	..	..	0.1
Environment			
Forests (1,000 sq. km)	628	601	587
Deforestation (average annual %, 1990–2005)			0.4
Freshwater use (% of internal resources)	..	0.5	..
Access to improved water source (% of total pop.)	72	82	85
Access to improved sanitation facilities (% of total pop.)	33	43	46
Energy use per capita (kilograms of oil equivalent)	416	594	578
Carbon dioxide emissions per capita (metric tons)	0.8	1.0	0.8
Electricity use per capita (kilowatt-hours)	274	421	479
Economy			
GDP ($ billions)	4.9	8.4	11.2
GDP growth (annual %)	4.6	2.5	4.6
GDP implicit price deflator (annual % growth)	16.3	5.2	12.2
Value added in agriculture (% of GDP)	17	15	14
Value added in industry (% of GDP)	35	30	34
Value added in services (% of GDP)	48	55	52
Exports of goods and services (% of GDP)	23	18	42
Imports of goods and services (% of GDP)	24	27	33
Gross capital formation (% of GDP)	13	18	12
Central government revenue (% of GDP)	..	18.4	23.8
Central government cash surplus/deficit (% of GDP)	..	-8.7	12.5
States and markets			
Starting a business (days)			50
Stock market capitalization (% of GDP)	..	20.7	19.9
Military expenditures (% of GDP)	2.3	1.7	1.5
Fixed-line and mobile subscribers (per 100 people)	3	13	36
Internet users (per 100 people)	0.0	1.4	6.2
Paved roads (% of total)	4	7	7
High-technology exports (% of manufactured exports)	0	40	4
Global links			
Merchandise trade (% of GDP)	33.1	36.4	59.9
Net barter terms of trade (2000 = 100)	102	100	135
Total external debt ($ billions)	4.3	5.8	5.3
Short-term debt ($ millions)	154	402	220
Total debt service (% of exports)	38.6	37.1	8.5
Foreign direct investment, net inflows ($ millions)	27	736	240
Remittances received ($ millions)	5.0	127.0	611.9
Aid ($ millions)	545	472	581

Bosnia and Herzegovina

Europe & Central Asia		Lower middle income	
Population (millions)	3.9	Population growth (%)	0.3
Surface area (1,000 sq. km)	51	National poverty rate (% of pop.)	20
GNI ($ billions)	12.7	GNI per capita ($)	3,230
GNI, PPP ($ billions)	26.6	GNI per capita, PPP ($)	6,780

	1990	2000	2006
People			
Share of poorest 20% in nat'l consumption/income (%)	..	..	7.0
Life expectancy at birth (years)	72	74	75
Total fertility (births per woman)	1.7	1.4	1.2
Adolescent fertility (births per 1,000 women 15–19)	..	26	21
Contraceptive prevalence (% of married women 15–49)	..	48	36
Births attended by skilled health staff (% of total)	97	100	100
Under-five mortality rate (per 1,000)	22	17	15
Child malnutrition, underweight (% of under age 5)	..	4.2	..
Child immunization, measles (% of ages 12–23 mos.)	52	80	90
Primary completion rate, total (% of relevant age group)	..	..	..
Gross secondary enrollment, total (% of relevant age group)	..	..	..
Ratio of girls to boys in primary & secondary school (%)	..	..	..
HIV prevalence rate (% of population ages 15–49)	..	..	0.1
Environment			
Forests (1,000 sq. km)	22	22	22
Deforestation (average annual %, 1990–2005)			0.1
Freshwater use (% of internal resources)	..	..	
Access to improved water source (% of total pop.)	97	97	97
Access to improved sanitation facilities (% of total pop.)	..	95	95
Energy use per capita (kilograms of oil equivalent)	1,633	1,061	1,268
Carbon dioxide emissions per capita (metric tons)	1.6	6.1	4.0
Electricity use per capita (kilowatt-hours)	3,043	2,011	2,316
Economy			
GDP ($ millions)	..	5,338	12,255
GDP growth (annual %)	..	5.5	6.0
GDP implicit price deflator (annual % growth)	..	18.1	6.5
Value added in agriculture (% of GDP)	..	11	10
Value added in industry (% of GDP)	..	24	25
Value added in services (% of GDP)	..	65	65
Exports of goods and services (% of GDP)	..	30	25
Imports of goods and services (% of GDP)	..	78	47
Gross capital formation (% of GDP)	..	21	16
Central government revenue (% of GDP)	..	..	39.8
Central government cash surplus/deficit (% of GDP)	..	..	2.9
States and markets			
Starting a business (days)			54
Stock market capitalization (% of GDP)	..	..	..
Military expenditures (% of GDP)	..	3.6	1.6
Fixed-line and mobile subscribers (per 100 people)	15	23	73
Internet users (per 100 people)	0.0	1.1	24.2
Paved roads (% of total)	54	52	52
High-technology exports (% of manufactured exports)	..	..	3
Global links			
Merchandise trade (% of GDP)	..	78.2	86.6
Net barter terms of trade (2000 = 100)	..	..	..
Total external debt ($ billions)	..	2.8	5.7
Short-term debt ($ billions)	..	0.0	1.1
Total debt service (% of exports)	..	9.9	8.7
Foreign direct investment, net inflows ($ millions)	..	146.1	423.5
Remittances received ($ billions)	..	1.6	2.1
Aid ($ millions)	9.7	736.9	494.4

Botswana

Population (millions)	1.9	Population growth (%)		1.2
Surface area (1,000 sq. km)	582	National poverty rate (% of pop.)		..
GNI ($ billions)	10.4	GNI per capita ($)		5,570
GNI, PPP ($ billions)	21.8	GNI per capita, PPP ($)		11,730

	1990	2000	2006
People			
Share of poorest 20% in nat'l consumption/income (%)	..	..	..
Life expectancy at birth (years)	63	49	50
Total fertility (births per woman)	4.6	3.4	3.0
Adolescent fertility (births per 1,000 women 15–19)	..	66	54
Contraceptive prevalence (% of married women 15–49)	33	44	..
Births attended by skilled health staff (% of total)	77	94	..
Under-five mortality rate (per 1,000)	58	101	124
Child malnutrition, underweight (% of under age 5)	..	10.7	..
Child immunization, measles (% of ages 12–23 mos.)	87	90	90
Primary completion rate, total (% of relevant age group)	76	90	95
Gross secondary enrollment, total (% of relevant age group)	48	75	75
Ratio of girls to boys in primary & secondary school (%)	109	102	100
HIV prevalence rate (% of population ages 15–49)	..	..	24.1
Environment			
Forests (1,000 sq. km)	137	125	119
Deforestation (average annual %, 1990–2005)			0.9
Freshwater use (% of internal resources)	..	8.1	..
Access to improved water source (% of total pop.)	93	95	95
Access to improved sanitation facilities (% of total pop.)	38	41	42
Energy use per capita (kilograms of oil equivalent)	930	1,065	1,032
Carbon dioxide emissions per capita (metric tons)	1.6	2.5	2.4
Electricity use per capita (kilowatt-hours)	724	921	1,406
Economy			
GDP ($ billions)	3.8	6.2	10.6
GDP growth (annual %)	6.8	8.2	2.1
GDP implicit price deflator (annual % growth)	6.3	12.0	13.5
Value added in agriculture (% of GDP)	5	2	2
Value added in industry (% of GDP)	61	59	53
Value added in services (% of GDP)	34	39	45
Exports of goods and services (% of GDP)	55	53	55
Imports of goods and services (% of GDP)	50	34	29
Gross capital formation (% of GDP)	37	36	26
Central government revenue (% of GDP)	50.8	..	..
Central government cash surplus/deficit (% of GDP)	19.1	..	..
States and markets			
Starting a business (days)			108
Stock market capitalization (% of GDP)	6.6	15.8	37.2
Military expenditures (% of GDP)	4.1	3.0	3.0
Fixed-line and mobile subscribers (per 100 people)	2	21	60
Internet users (per 100 people)	0.0	2.9	3.3
Paved roads (% of total)	32	35	33
High-technology exports (% of manufactured exports)	..	0	..
Global links			
Merchandise trade (% of GDP)	98.4	77.0	73.9
Net barter terms of trade (2000 = 100)	98	100	94
Total external debt ($ millions)	553	453	408
Short-term debt ($ millions)	5.8	15.0	24.0
Total debt service (% of exports)	4.3	2.0	0.9
Foreign direct investment, net inflows ($ millions)	96	57	486
Remittances received ($ millions)	86	26	117
Aid ($ millions)	145	31	65

Brazil

Latin America & Caribbean		Upper middle income	
Population (millions)	189	Population growth (%)	1.3
Surface area (1,000 sq. km)	8,515	National poverty rate (% of pop.)	22
GNI ($ billions)	892.6	GNI per capita ($)	4,710
GNI, PPP ($ billions)	1,647.5	GNI per capita, PPP ($)	8,700

	1990	2000	2006
People			
Share of poorest 20% in nat'l consumption/income (%)	2.3	2.5	2.9
Life expectancy at birth (years)	67	70	72
Total fertility (births per woman)	2.8	2.4	2.3
Adolescent fertility (births per 1,000 women 15–19)	..	90	89
Contraceptive prevalence (% of married women 15–49)	59	..	..
Births attended by skilled health staff (% of total)	72	96	..
Under-five mortality rate (per 1,000)	57	30	20
Child malnutrition, underweight (% of under age 5)	..	..	..
Child immunization, measles (% of ages 12–23 mos.)	78	99	99
Primary completion rate, total (% of relevant age group)	..	108	105
Gross secondary enrollment, total (% of relevant age group)	40	104	106
Ratio of girls to boys in primary & secondary school (%)	..	103	102
HIV prevalence rate (% of population ages 15–49)	..	..	0.5
Environment			
Forests (1,000 sq. km)	5,200	4,932	4,777
Deforestation (average annual %, 1990–2005)			0.6
Freshwater use (% of internal resources)	..	1.1	..
Access to improved water source (% of total pop.)	83	89	90
Access to improved sanitation facilities (% of total pop.)	71	74	75
Energy use per capita (kilograms of oil equivalent)	896	1,066	1,122
Carbon dioxide emissions per capita (metric tons)	1.4	1.9	1.8
Electricity use per capita (kilowatt-hours)	1,456	1,894	2,008
Economy			
GDP ($ billions)	462.0	644.5	1,067.5
GDP growth (annual %)	-4.3	4.3	3.7
GDP implicit price deflator (annual % growth)	2,735.5	6.2	4.3
Value added in agriculture (% of GDP)	8	6	5
Value added in industry (% of GDP)	39	28	31
Value added in services (% of GDP)	53	67	64
Exports of goods and services (% of GDP)	8	10	15
Imports of goods and services (% of GDP)	7	12	12
Gross capital formation (% of GDP)	20	18	17
Central government revenue (% of GDP)	22.8	22.6	..
Central government cash surplus/deficit (% of GDP)	-3.4	-0.8	..
States and markets			
Starting a business (days)			152
Stock market capitalization (% of GDP)	3.6	35.1	66.6
Military expenditures (% of GDP)	2.6	1.6	1.5
Fixed-line and mobile subscribers (per 100 people)	6	31	73
Internet users (per 100 people)	0.0	2.9	22.5
Paved roads (% of total)	10	6	..
High-technology exports (% of manufactured exports)	7	19	12
Global links			
Merchandise trade (% of GDP)	11.7	17.7	21.9
Net barter terms of trade (2000 = 100)	66	100	104
Total external debt ($ billions)	120	242	194
Short-term debt ($ billions)	24	31	20
Total debt service (% of exports)	22.1	93.5	37.3
Foreign direct investment, net inflows ($ billions)	1.0	32.8	18.8
Remittances received ($ billions)	0.6	1.6	4.3
Aid ($ millions)	151	232	82

Brunei Darussalam

High income

Population (thousands)	382	Population growth (%)	2.1
Surface area (1,000 sq. km)	5.8	National poverty rate (% of pop.)	..
GNI ($ billions)	10.3	GNI per capita ($)	26,930
GNI, PPP ($ billions)	19.1	GNI per capita, PPP ($)	49.900

	1990	2000	2006
People			
Share of poorest 20% in nat'l consumption/income (%)	..	..	..
Life expectancy at birth (years)	74	76	77
Total fertility (births per woman)	3.2	2.6	2.3
Adolescent fertility (births per 1,000 women 15–19)	..	32	28
Contraceptive prevalence (% of married women 15–49)	..	..	..
Births attended by skilled health staff (% of total)	..	100	100
Under-five mortality rate (per 1,000)	11	9	9
Child malnutrition, underweight (% of under age 5)	..	..	..
Child immunization, measles (% of ages 12–23 mos.)	99	99	97
Primary completion rate, total (% of relevant age group)	100	122	107
Gross secondary enrollment, total (% of relevant age group)	77	85	98
Ratio of girls to boys in primary & secondary school (%)	100	102	102
HIV prevalence rate (% of population ages 15–49)	..	..	0.1
Environment			
Forests (1,000 sq. km)	3.1	2.9	2.8
Deforestation (average annual %, 1990–2005)			0.8
Freshwater use (% of internal resources)	..	..	
Access to improved water source (% of total pop.)	..	..	99
Access to improved sanitation facilities (% of total pop.)	..	..	
Energy use per capita (kilograms of oil equivalent)	7,070	7,623	7,065
Carbon dioxide emissions per capita (metric tons)	22.6	25.5	24.1
Electricity use per capita (kilowatt-hours)	4,354	7,539	7,498
Economy			
GDP ($ billions)	3.5	6.0	11.6
GDP growth (annual %)	1.1	2.8	5.1
GDP implicit price deflator (annual % growth)	8.4	29.0	10.1
Value added in agriculture (% of GDP)	1	1	1
Value added in industry (% of GDP)	62	64	73
Value added in services (% of GDP)	37	35	26
Exports of goods and services (% of GDP)	62	67	71
Imports of goods and services (% of GDP)	37	36	25
Gross capital formation (% of GDP)	19	13	10
Central government revenue (% of GDP)	..	..	..
Central government cash surplus/deficit (% of GDP)	..	..	..
States and markets			
Starting a business (days)			116
Stock market capitalization (% of GDP)	..	..	
Military expenditures (% of GDP)	6.6	4.1	2.4
Fixed-line and mobile subscribers (per 100 people)	14	53	87
Internet users (per 100 people)	0.0	9.0	43.3
Paved roads (% of total)	31	35	77
High-technology exports (% of manufactured exports)	0	0	6
Global links			
Merchandise trade (% of GDP)	91.3	83.5	81.6
Net barter terms of trade (2000 = 100)	..	100	179
Total external debt ($ billions)	..	..	..
Short-term debt ($ billions)	..	..	..
Total debt service (% of exports)	..	..	..
Foreign direct investment, net inflows ($ billions)	..	..	..
Remittances received ($ billions)	..	..	..
Aid ($ millions)	3.9	0.6	0.8

Bulgaria

Europe & Central Asia		Upper middle income	

Population (millions)	7.7	Population growth (%)	-0.6
Surface area (1,000 sq. km)	111	National poverty rate (% of pop.)	13
GNI ($ billions)	30.7	GNI per capita ($)	3,990
GNI, PPP ($ billions)	79.0	GNI per capita, PPP ($)	10,270

	1990	2000	2006
People			
Share of poorest 20% in nat'l consumption/income (%)	8.3	6.5	..
Life expectancy at birth (years)	72	72	73
Total fertility (births per woman)	1.8	1.3	1.4
Adolescent fertility (births per 1,000 women 15–19)	..	45	41
Contraceptive prevalence (% of married women 15–49)	..	..	..
Births attended by skilled health staff (% of total)	..	99	99
Under-five mortality rate (per 1,000)	19	16	14
Child malnutrition, underweight (% of under age 5)	..	..	1.6
Child immunization, measles (% of ages 12–23 mos.)	99	89	96
Primary completion rate, total (% of relevant age group)	102	99	99
Gross secondary enrollment, total (% of relevant age group)	75	92	105
Ratio of girls to boys in primary & secondary school (%)	99	98	97
HIV prevalence rate (% of population ages 15–49)	..	..	0.1
Environment			
Forests (1,000 sq. km)	33	34	36
Deforestation (average annual %, 1990–2005)			-0.6
Freshwater use (% of internal resources)	..	50.0	..
Access to improved water source (% of total pop.)	99	99	99
Access to improved sanitation facilities (% of total pop.)	99	99	99
Energy use per capita (kilograms of oil equivalent)	3,306	2,322	2,592
Carbon dioxide emissions per capita (metric tons)	8.6	5.3	5.5
Electricity use per capita (kilowatt-hours)	4,759	3,724	4,121
Economy			
GDP ($ billions)	20.7	12.6	31.5
GDP growth (annual %)	-9.1	5.4	6.1
GDP implicit price deflator (annual % growth)	26.2	6.7	8.1
Value added in agriculture (% of GDP)	17	14	9
Value added in industry (% of GDP)	49	31	31
Value added in services (% of GDP)	34	55	60
Exports of goods and services (% of GDP)	33	56	64
Imports of goods and services (% of GDP)	37	61	83
Gross capital formation (% of GDP)	26	18	32
Central government revenue (% of GDP)	47.1	33.7	36.8
Central government cash surplus/deficit (% of GDP)	-5.0	-0.4	3.4
States and markets			
Starting a business (days)			32
Stock market capitalization (% of GDP)	..	4.9	32.8
Military expenditures (% of GDP)	3.5	2.5	2.3
Fixed-line and mobile subscribers (per 100 people)	25	45	138
Internet users (per 100 people)	0.0	5.3	24.3
Paved roads (% of total)	92	92	99
High-technology exports (% of manufactured exports)	..	3	6
Global links			
Merchandise trade (% of GDP)	48.9	89.8	121.3
Net barter terms of trade (2000 = 100)	..	..	..
Total external debt ($ billions)	11	11	21
Short-term debt ($ billions)	1.1	1.5	8.0
Total debt service (% of exports)	19.4	17.7	12.4
Foreign direct investment, net inflows ($ billions)	0.0	1.0	5.2
Remittances received ($ billions)	..	0.1	1.7
Aid ($ millions)	14	311	..

Burkina Faso

Low income

Population (millions)	14	Population growth (%)	3.0
Surface area (1,000 sq. km)	274	National poverty rate (% of pop.)	46
GNI ($ billions)	6.2	GNI per capita ($)	440
GNI, PPP ($ billions)	16.2	GNI per capita, PPP ($)	1,130

	1990	2000	2006
People			
Share of poorest 20% in nat'l consumption/income (%)	..	5.9	..
Life expectancy at birth (years)	50	50	52
Total fertility (births per woman)	7.3	6.5	6.1
Adolescent fertility (births per 1,000 women 15–19)	..	145	129
Contraceptive prevalence (% of married women 15–49)	..	13	17
Births attended by skilled health staff (% of total)	..	31	54
Under-five mortality rate (per 1,000)	206	194	204
Child malnutrition, underweight (% of under age 5)	..	..	..
Child immunization, measles (% of ages 12–23 mos.)	79	59	88
Primary completion rate, total (% of relevant age group)	20	25	31
Gross secondary enrollment, total (% of relevant age group)	7	10	15
Ratio of girls to boys in primary & secondary school (%)	62	70	80
HIV prevalence rate (% of population ages 15–49)	..	..	2.0
Environment			
Forests (1,000 sq. km)	72	69	68
Deforestation (average annual %, 1990–2005)			0.3
Freshwater use (% of internal resources)	..	6.4	..
Access to improved water source (% of total pop.)	38	54	61
Access to improved sanitation facilities (% of total pop.)	7	11	13
Energy use per capita (kilograms of oil equivalent)	..	..	..
Carbon dioxide emissions per capita (metric tons)	0.1	0.1	0.1
Electricity use per capita (kilowatt-hours)	..	..	..
Economy			
GDP ($ billions)	3.1	2.6	6.2
GDP growth (annual %)	-0.6	1.8	6.4
GDP implicit price deflator (annual % growth)	1.8	-1.7	2.5
Value added in agriculture (% of GDP)	28	27	33
Value added in industry (% of GDP)	20	23	22
Value added in services (% of GDP)	49	44	45
Exports of goods and services (% of GDP)	11	9	11
Imports of goods and services (% of GDP)	24	25	25
Gross capital formation (% of GDP)	19	17	17
Central government revenue (% of GDP)	..	..	12.1
Central government cash surplus/deficit (% of GDP)	..	..	-5.7
States and markets			
Starting a business (days)			18
Stock market capitalization (% of GDP)	..	..	..
Military expenditures (% of GDP)	2.7	1.4	1.4
Fixed-line and mobile subscribers (per 100 people)	0	1	8
Internet users (per 100 people)	0.0	0.1	0.6
Paved roads (% of total)	17	16	4
High-technology exports (% of manufactured exports)	..	3	10
Global links			
Merchandise trade (% of GDP)	22.2	31.4	30.6
Net barter terms of trade (2000 = 100)	119	100	90
Total external debt ($ billions)	0.8	1.4	1.1
Short-term debt ($ millions)	84	84	85
Total debt service (% of exports)	6.8	14.9	..
Foreign direct investment, net inflows ($ millions)	0.5	23.2	25.9
Remittances received ($ millions)	140	67	50
Aid ($ millions)	327	335	871

Burundi

Sub-Saharan Africa   **Low income**

Population (millions)	8.2	Population growth (%)	3.9
Surface area (1,000 sq. km)	28	National poverty rate (% of pop.)	..
GNI ($ millions)	815	GNI per capita ($)	100
GNI, PPP ($ billions)	2.6	GNI per capita, PPP ($)	320

	1990	2000	2006
People			
Share of poorest 20% in nat'l consumption/income (%)	7.9	5.1	..
Life expectancy at birth (years)	46	46	49
Total fertility (births per woman)	6.8	6.8	6.8
Adolescent fertility (births per 1,000 women 15–19)	..	55	55
Contraceptive prevalence (% of married women 15–49)	..	16	9
Births attended by skilled health staff (% of total)	..	25	34
Under-five mortality rate (per 1,000)	190	181	181
Child malnutrition, underweight (% of under age 5)	..	38.9	..
Child immunization, measles (% of ages 12–23 mos.)	74	75	75
Primary completion rate, total (% of relevant age group)	41	25	36
Gross secondary enrollment, total (% of relevant age group)	5	..	14
Ratio of girls to boys in primary & secondary school (%)	82	..	89
HIV prevalence rate (% of population ages 15–49)	..	..	3.3
Environment			
Forests (1,000 sq. km)	2.9	2.0	1.5
Deforestation (average annual %, 1990–2005)			4.2
Freshwater use (% of internal resources)	..	2.9	..
Access to improved water source (% of total pop.)	69	77	79
Access to improved sanitation facilities (% of total pop.)	44	38	36
Energy use per capita (kilograms of oil equivalent)	..	..	..
Carbon dioxide emissions per capita (metric tons)	0.03	0.04	0.03
Electricity use per capita (kilowatt-hours)	..	..	..
Economy			
GDP ($ billions)	1.1	0.7	0.9
GDP growth (annual %)	3.5	-0.9	5.1
GDP implicit price deflator (annual % growth)	6.0	13.2	2.6
Value added in agriculture (% of GDP)	56	40	35
Value added in industry (% of GDP)	19	19	20
Value added in services (% of GDP)	25	41	45
Exports of goods and services (% of GDP)	8	8	11
Imports of goods and services (% of GDP)	28	20	48
Gross capital formation (% of GDP)	15	6	17
Central government revenue (% of GDP)	18.2	15.8	..
Central government cash surplus/deficit (% of GDP)	-2.3	-2.4	..
States and markets			
Starting a business (days)			43
Stock market capitalization (% of GDP)	..	..	..
Military expenditures (% of GDP)	3.5	6.0	5.5
Fixed-line and mobile subscribers (per 100 people)	0	1	2
Internet users (per 100 people)	0.0	0.1	0.7
Paved roads (% of total)	..	7	10
High-technology exports (% of manufactured exports)	..	0	4
Global links			
Merchandise trade (% of GDP)	27.0	27.9	54.2
Net barter terms of trade (2000 = 100)	128	100	126
Total external debt ($ billions)	0.9	1.1	1.4
Short-term debt ($ millions)	13	65	38
Total debt service (% of exports)	43.4	39.4	40.4
Foreign direct investment, net inflows ($ millions)	1.3	11.7	0.0
Remittances received ($ millions)	..	..	0.1
Aid ($ millions)	263	93	415

Cambodia

Population (millions)	14	Population growth (%)		1.7
Surface area (1,000 sq. km)	181	National poverty rate (% of pop.)		35
GNI ($ billions)	7.0	GNI per capita ($)		490
GNI, PPP ($ billions)	22.1	GNI per capita, PPP ($)		1,550

	1990	2000	2006
People			
Share of poorest 20% in nat'l consumption/income (%)	..	..	6.8
Life expectancy at birth (years)	55	56	59
Total fertility (births per woman)	5.7	4.0	3.3
Adolescent fertility (births per 1,000 women 15–19)	..	53	43
Contraceptive prevalence (% of married women 15–49)	..	24	40
Births attended by skilled health staff (% of total)	..	32	44
Under-five mortality rate (per 1,000)	116	104	82
Child malnutrition, underweight (% of under age 5)	..	39.5	28.4
Child immunization, measles (% of ages 12–23 mos.)	34	65	78
Primary completion rate, total (% of relevant age group)	..	47	87
Gross secondary enrollment, total (% of relevant age group)	25	18	38
Ratio of girls to boys in primary & secondary school (%)	73	82	89
HIV prevalence rate (% of population ages 15–49)	..	..	1.6
Environment			
Forests (1,000 sq. km)	129	115	104
Deforestation (average annual %, 1990–2005)			1.4
Freshwater use (% of internal resources)	..	3.4	..
Access to improved water source (% of total pop.)	..	35	41
Access to improved sanitation facilities (% of total pop.)	..	16	17
Energy use per capita (kilograms of oil equivalent)	..	..	..
Carbon dioxide emissions per capita (metric tons)	0.05	0.04	0.04
Electricity use per capita (kilowatt-hours)	..	..	..
Economy			
GDP ($ billions)	1.1	3.7	7.3
GDP growth (annual %)	..	8.8	10.8
GDP implicit price deflator (annual % growth)	..	-3.2	4.7
Value added in agriculture (% of GDP)	..	36	30
Value added in industry (% of GDP)	..	22	26
Value added in services (% of GDP)	..	42	44
Exports of goods and services (% of GDP)	6	50	69
Imports of goods and services (% of GDP)	13	62	76
Gross capital formation (% of GDP)	8	18	21
Central government revenue (% of GDP)	..	10.3	9.8
Central government cash surplus/deficit (% of GDP)	..	-3.4	-1.7
States and markets			
Starting a business (days)			86
Stock market capitalization (% of GDP)	..	..	..
Military expenditures (% of GDP)	3.1	3.2	1.7
Fixed-line and mobile subscribers (per 100 people)	0	1	8
Internet users (per 100 people)	0.0	0.0	0.3
Paved roads (% of total)	8	16	6
High-technology exports (% of manufactured exports)	..	0	0
Global links			
Merchandise trade (% of GDP)	22.4	91.1	119.9
Net barter terms of trade (2000 = 100)	..	100	89
Total external debt ($ billions)	1.8	2.6	3.5
Short-term debt ($ millions)	136	227	209
Total debt service (% of exports)	4.0	1.6	0.6
Foreign direct investment, net inflows ($ millions)	33	149	483
Remittances received ($ millions)	9.0	121.0	297.4
Aid ($ millions)	41	396	529

Cameroon

Sub-Saharan Africa		Lower middle income

Population (millions)	18	Population growth (%)	2.1
Surface area (1,000 sq. km)	475	National poverty rate (% of pop.)	40
GNI ($ billions)	18.1	GNI per capita ($)	990
GNI, PPP ($ billions)	37.4	GNI per capita, PPP ($)	2,060

	1990	2000	2006
People			
Share of poorest 20% in nat'l consumption/income (%)	..	5.6	..
Life expectancy at birth (years)	55	51	50
Total fertility (births per woman)	5.9	5.0	4.4
Adolescent fertility (births per 1,000 women 15–19)	..	139	122
Contraceptive prevalence (% of married women 15–49)	16	26	29
Births attended by skilled health staff (% of total)	58	60	63
Under-five mortality rate (per 1,000)	139	151	149
Child malnutrition, underweight (% of under age 5)	..	..	15.1
Child immunization, measles (% of ages 12–23 mos.)	56	49	73
Primary completion rate, total (% of relevant age group)	57	50	58
Gross secondary enrollment, total (% of relevant age group)	26	27	41
Ratio of girls to boys in primary & secondary school (%)	83	85	84
HIV prevalence rate (% of population ages 15–49)	..	..	5.4
Environment			
Forests (1,000 sq. km)	245	223	212
Deforestation (average annual %, 1990–2005)			1.0
Freshwater use (% of internal resources)	..	0.4	..
Access to improved water source (% of total pop.)	50	61	66
Access to improved sanitation facilities (% of total pop.)	48	50	51
Energy use per capita (kilograms of oil equivalent)	411	400	392
Carbon dioxide emissions per capita (metric tons)	0.1	0.2	0.2
Electricity use per capita (kilowatt-hours)	192	171	196
Economy			
GDP ($ billions)	11.2	10.1	18.3
GDP growth (annual %)	-6.1	4.2	3.8
GDP implicit price deflator (annual % growth)	1.6	2.8	3.7
Value added in agriculture (% of GDP)	25	22	20
Value added in industry (% of GDP)	29	36	33
Value added in services (% of GDP)	46	42	47
Exports of goods and services (% of GDP)	20	23	26
Imports of goods and services (% of GDP)	17	20	27
Gross capital formation (% of GDP)	18	17	18
Central government revenue (% of GDP)	14.3	14.1	..
Central government cash surplus/deficit (% of GDP)	-5.6	0.1	..
States and markets			
Starting a business (days)			37
Stock market capitalization (% of GDP)	..	..	..
Military expenditures (% of GDP)	1.5	1.3	1.4
Fixed-line and mobile subscribers (per 100 people)	0	1	13
Internet users (per 100 people)	0.0	0.3	2.0
Paved roads (% of total)	11	8	10
High-technology exports (% of manufactured exports)	3	1	3
Global links			
Merchandise trade (% of GDP)	30.5	33.0	35.8
Net barter terms of trade (2000 = 100)	81	100	136
Total external debt ($ billions)	6.4	10.1	3.2
Short-term debt ($ billions)	0.9	1.2	0.6
Total debt service (% of exports)	20.2	21.3	15.9
Foreign direct investment, net inflows ($ millions)	-113	159	309
Remittances received ($ millions)	23	11	103
Aid ($ billions)	0.4	0.4	1.7

Canada

Population (millions)	33	Population growth (%)		1.0
Surface area (1,000 sq. km)	9,985	National poverty rate (% of pop.)		..
GNI ($ billions)	1,196.6	GNI per capita ($)		36,650
GNI, PPP ($ billions)	1,184.4	GNI per capita, PPP ($)		36,280

	1990	2000	2006
People			
Share of poorest 20% in nat'l consumption/income (%)	..	7.2	..
Life expectancy at birth (years)	77	79	80
Total fertility (births per woman)	1.8	1.5	1.5
Adolescent fertility (births per 1,000 women 15–19)	..	16	14
Contraceptive prevalence (% of married women 15–49)	..	..	..
Births attended by skilled health staff (% of total)	..	98	100
Under-five mortality rate (per 1,000)	8	7	6
Child malnutrition, underweight (% of under age 5)	..	..	..
Child immunization, measles (% of ages 12–23 mos.)	89	95	94
Primary completion rate, total (% of relevant age group)	..	..	..
Gross secondary enrollment, total (% of relevant age group)	101	107	117
Ratio of girls to boys in primary & secondary school (%)	99	100	98
HIV prevalence rate (% of population ages 15–49)	..	..	0.3
Environment			
Forests (1,000 sq. km)	3,101	3,101	3,101
Deforestation (average annual %, 1990–2005)			0.00
Freshwater use (% of internal resources)	..	1.6	..
Access to improved water source (% of total pop.)	100	100	100
Access to improved sanitation facilities (% of total pop.)	100	100	100
Energy use per capita (kilograms of oil equivalent)	7,535	8,098	8,417
Carbon dioxide emissions per capita (metric tons)	15.0	19.0	20.0
Electricity use per capita (kilowatt-hours)	16,106	16,986	17,285
Economy			
GDP ($ billions)	582.7	724.9	1,271.6
GDP growth (annual %)	0.2	5.2	2.8
GDP implicit price deflator (annual % growth)	3.2	4.1	2.3
Value added in agriculture (% of GDP)	3	2	..
Value added in industry (% of GDP)	31	33	..
Value added in services (% of GDP)	66	65	..
Exports of goods and services (% of GDP)	26	46	38
Imports of goods and services (% of GDP)	26	40	34
Gross capital formation (% of GDP)	21	20	22
Central government revenue (% of GDP)	21.2	20.9	19.5
Central government cash surplus/deficit (% of GDP)	-4.5	1.4	1.5
States and markets			
Starting a business (days)			3
Stock market capitalization (% of GDP)	41.5	116.1	133.7
Military expenditures (% of GDP)	2.0	1.1	1.2
Fixed-line and mobile subscribers (per 100 people)	57	96	117
Internet users (per 100 people)	0.4	42.2	68.1
Paved roads (% of total)	35	..	40
High-technology exports (% of manufactured exports)	14	19	15
Global links			
Merchandise trade (% of GDP)	43.1	71.9	58.8
Net barter terms of trade (2000 = 100)	103	100	116
Total external debt ($ billions)	..	..	..
Short-term debt ($ billions)	..	..	..
Total debt service (% of exports)	..	..	..
Foreign direct investment, net inflows ($ billions)	7.6	66.1	69.1
Remittances received ($ billions)	..	..	..
Aid ($ billions)	..	..	..

Cape Verde

Sub-Saharan Africa   **Lower middle income**

Population (thousands)	519	Population growth (%)	2.3
Surface area (1,000 sq. km)	4.0	National poverty rate (% of pop.)	..
GNI ($ billions)	1.1	GNI per capita ($)	2,130
GNI, PPP ($ billions)	1.3	GNI per capita, PPP ($)	2,590

	1990	2000	2006
People			
Share of poorest 20% in nat'l consumption/income (%)	..	4.4	..
Life expectancy at birth (years)	65	69	71
Total fertility (births per woman)	5.4	3.9	3.4
Adolescent fertility (births per 1,000 women 15–19)	..	97	85
Contraceptive prevalence (% of married women 15–49)	..	53	..
Births attended by skilled health staff (% of total)	..	89	..
Under-five mortality rate (per 1,000)	60	42	34
Child malnutrition, underweight (% of under age 5)	..	..	..
Child immunization, measles (% of ages 12–23 mos.)	79	80	65
Primary completion rate, total (% of relevant age group)	51	102	92
Gross secondary enrollment, total (% of relevant age group)	21	63	80
Ratio of girls to boys in primary & secondary school (%)	..	99	99
HIV prevalence rate (% of population ages 15–49)	..	..	..
Environment			
Forests (sq. km)	580	820	840
Deforestation (average annual %, 1990–2005)			-2.5
Freshwater use (% of internal resources)	..	7.3	..
Access to improved water source (% of total pop.)	..	80	80
Access to improved sanitation facilities (% of total pop.)	..	41	43
Energy use per capita (kilograms of oil equivalent)	..	..	..
Carbon dioxide emissions per capita (metric tons)	0.2	0.4	0.6
Electricity use per capita (kilowatt-hours)	..	..	..
Economy			
GDP ($ millions)	339	531	1,144
GDP growth (annual %)	0.7	6.6	6.1
GDP implicit price deflator (annual % growth)	2.3	-1.2	7.0
Value added in agriculture (% of GDP)	14	12	9
Value added in industry (% of GDP)	21	18	17
Value added in services (% of GDP)	64	70	74
Exports of goods and services (% of GDP)	13	28	20
Imports of goods and services (% of GDP)	44	61	55
Gross capital formation (% of GDP)	23	20	39
Central government revenue (% of GDP)	..	..	..
Central government cash surplus/deficit (% of GDP)	..	..	..
States and markets			
Starting a business (days)			52
Stock market capitalization (% of GDP)	..	..	..
Military expenditures (% of GDP)	1.7	1.3	0.7
Fixed-line and mobile subscribers (per 100 people)	2	17	35
Internet users (per 100 people)	0.0	1.8	5.7
Paved roads (% of total)	78	69	..
High-technology exports (% of manufactured exports)	..	1	0
Global links			
Merchandise trade (% of GDP)	41.9	45.4	49.2
Net barter terms of trade (2000 = 100)	100	100	114
Total external debt ($ millions)	134	326	601
Short-term debt ($ millions)	4.7	12.6	57.6
Total debt service (% of exports)	4.8	6.8	4.7
Foreign direct investment, net inflows ($ millions)	0.3	33.4	122.6
Remittances received ($ millions)	59	87	137
Aid ($ millions)	105	94	138

Cayman Islands

High income

Population (thousands)	46	Population growth (%)	2.2
Surface area (sq. km)	260	National poverty rate (% of pop.)	..
GNI ($ billions)	..	GNI per capita ($)	..
GNI, PPP ($ billions)	..	GNI per capita, PPP ($)	..

	1990	2000	2006
People			
Share of poorest 20% in nat'l consumption/income (%)	..	..	..
Life expectancy at birth (years)	..	..	..
Total fertility (births per woman)	..	..	..
Adolescent fertility (births per 1,000 women 15-19)	..	..	..
Contraceptive prevalence (% of married women 15-49)	..	..	..
Births attended by skilled health staff (% of total)	..	..	100
Under-five mortality rate (per 1,000)	..	..	..
Child malnutrition, underweight (% of under age 5)	..	..	..
Child immunization, measles (% of ages 12-23 mos.)	..	..	..
Primary completion rate, total (% of relevant age group)	..	102	85
Gross secondary enrollment, total (% of relevant age group)	..	96	88
Ratio of girls to boys in primary & secondary school (%)	..	99	100
HIV prevalence rate (% of population ages 15-49)	..	..	..
Environment			
Forests (sq. km)	120	120	120
Deforestation (average annual %, 1990-2005)			0.00
Freshwater use (% of internal resources)		..	..
Access to improved water source (% of total pop.)	..	..	..
Access to improved sanitation facilities (% of total pop.)	..	..	..
Energy use per capita (kilograms of oil equivalent)	..	..	..
Carbon dioxide emissions per capita (metric tons)	..	..	7.1
Electricity use per capita (kilowatt-hours)	..	..	..
Economy			
GDP ($ billions)	..	..	..
GDP growth (annual %)	..	..	..
GDP implicit price deflator (annual % growth)	..	..	..
Value added in agriculture (% of GDP)	..	..	..
Value added in industry (% of GDP)	..	..	..
Value added in services (% of GDP)	..	..	..
Exports of goods and services (% of GDP)	..	..	..
Imports of goods and services (% of GDP)	..	..	..
Gross capital formation (% of GDP)	..	..	..
Central government revenue (% of GDP)	..	..	..
Central government cash surplus/deficit (% of GDP)	..	..	..
States and markets			
Starting a business (days)			..
Stock market capitalization (% of GDP)	..	..	..
Military expenditures (% of GDP)	..	..	..
Fixed-line and mobile subscribers (per 100 people)	..	..	..
Internet users (per 100 people)	..	..	45.7
Paved roads (% of total)	..	..	..
High-technology exports (% of manufactured exports)	..	..	..
Global links			
Merchandise trade (% of GDP)	..	..	..
Net barter terms of trade (2000 = 100)	..	..	..
Total external debt ($ billions)	..	..	..
Short-term debt ($ billions)	..	..	..
Total debt service (% of exports)	..	..	..
Foreign direct investment, net inflows ($ billions)	..	..	..
Remittances received ($ billions)	..	..	..
Aid ($ millions)	3.0	-3.6	0.4

Central African Republic

Sub-Saharan Africa		Low income

Population (millions)	4.3	Population growth (%)	1.7
Surface area (1,000 sq. km)	623	National poverty rate (% of pop.)	..
GNI ($ billions)	1.5	GNI per capita ($)	350
GNI, PPP ($ billions)	2.9	GNI per capita, PPP ($)	690

	1990	2000	2006
People			
Share of poorest 20% in nat'l consumption/income (%)	..	..	..
Life expectancy at birth (years)	50	44	44
Total fertility (births per woman)	5.6	5.1	4.7
Adolescent fertility (births per 1,000 women 15–19)	..	140	119
Contraceptive prevalence (% of married women 15–49)	..	28	19
Births attended by skilled health staff (% of total)	..	44	53
Under-five mortality rate (per 1,000)	173	186	175
Child malnutrition, underweight (% of under age 5)	..	21.8	..
Child immunization, measles (% of ages 12–23 mos.)	83	36	35
Primary completion rate, total (% of relevant age group)	29	..	24
Gross secondary enrollment, total (% of relevant age group)	11	12	..
Ratio of girls to boys in primary & secondary school (%)	60	..	..
HIV prevalence rate (% of population ages 15–49)	..	..	10.7
Environment			
Forests (1,000 sq. km)	232	229	228
Deforestation (average annual %, 1990–2005)			0.1
Freshwater use (% of internal resources)	..	0.0	
Access to improved water source (% of total pop.)	52	70	75
Access to improved sanitation facilities (% of total pop.)	23	26	27
Energy use per capita (kilograms of oil equivalent)	..	..	..
Carbon dioxide emissions per capita (metric tons)	0.1	0.1	0.1
Electricity use per capita (kilowatt-hours)	..	..	..
Economy			
GDP ($ billions)	1.5	1.0	1.5
GDP growth (annual %)	-2.1	2.3	4.1
GDP implicit price deflator (annual % growth)	2.3	3.2	3.8
Value added in agriculture (% of GDP)	48	53	56
Value added in industry (% of GDP)	20	16	15
Value added in services (% of GDP)	33	31	29
Exports of goods and services (% of GDP)	15	20	14
Imports of goods and services (% of GDP)	28	24	22
Gross capital formation (% of GDP)	12	10	9
Central government revenue (% of GDP)	..	..	8.1
Central government cash surplus/deficit (% of GDP)	..	..	-0.5
States and markets			
Starting a business (days)			14
Stock market capitalization (% of GDP)	..	..	..
Military expenditures (% of GDP)	1.5	1.0	1.1
Fixed-line and mobile subscribers (per 100 people)	0	0	3
Internet users (per 100 people)	0.0	0.1	0.3
Paved roads (% of total)	..	3	..
High-technology exports (% of manufactured exports)	0	0	0
Global links			
Merchandise trade (% of GDP)	18.4	29.0	24.1
Net barter terms of trade (2000 = 100)	238	100	90
Total external debt ($ billions)	0.7	0.9	1.0
Short-term debt ($ millions)	38	41	115
Total debt service (% of exports)	13.2	..	..
Foreign direct investment, net inflows ($ millions)	0.7	0.9	24.3
Remittances received ($ billions)	..	..	..
Aid ($ millions)	249	75	134

Chad

Sub-Saharan Africa			Low income	
Population (millions)	10	Population growth (%)		3.1
Surface area (1,000 sq. km)	1,284	National poverty rate (% of pop.)		..
GNI ($ billions)	4.7	GNI per capita ($)		450
GNI, PPP ($ billions)	12.3	GNI per capita, PPP ($)		1,170

	1990	2000	2006
People			
Share of poorest 20% in nat'l consumption/income (%)	..	..	..
Life expectancy at birth (years)	51	51	51
Total fertility (births per woman)	6.7	6.6	6.3
Adolescent fertility (births per 1,000 women 15–19)	..	191	169
Contraceptive prevalence (% of married women 15–49)	..	8	3
Births attended by skilled health staff (% of total)	..	16	14
Under-five mortality rate (per 1,000)	201	205	209
Child malnutrition, underweight (% of under age 5)	..	29.4	33.9
Child immunization, measles (% of ages 12–23 mos.)	32	28	23
Primary completion rate, total (% of relevant age group)	17	22	31
Gross secondary enrollment, total (% of relevant age group)	7	11	15
Ratio of girls to boys in primary & secondary school (%)	42	56	61
HIV prevalence rate (% of population ages 15–49)	..	..	3.5
Environment			
Forests (1,000 sq. km)	131	123	119
Deforestation (average annual %, 1990–2005)			0.6
Freshwater use (% of internal resources)	..	1.5	..
Access to improved water source (% of total pop.)	19	35	42
Access to improved sanitation facilities (% of total pop.)	7	8	9
Energy use per capita (kilograms of oil equivalent)	..	..	..
Carbon dioxide emissions per capita (metric tons)	0.02	0.01	0.01
Electricity use per capita (kilowatt-hours)	..	..	..
Economy			
GDP ($ billions)	1.7	1.4	6.5
GDP growth (annual %)	-4.2	-0.9	0.5
GDP implicit price deflator (annual % growth)	8.0	5.3	9.7
Value added in agriculture (% of GDP)	29	42	21
Value added in industry (% of GDP)	18	11	55
Value added in services (% of GDP)	53	46	25
Exports of goods and services (% of GDP)	13	17	59
Imports of goods and services (% of GDP)	28	35	38
Gross capital formation (% of GDP)	7	23	22
Central government revenue (% of GDP)	..	..	..
Central government cash surplus/deficit (% of GDP)	..	..	..
States and markets			
Starting a business (days)			75
Stock market capitalization (% of GDP)	..	..	..
Military expenditures (% of GDP)	..	1.9	0.9
Fixed-line and mobile subscribers (per 100 people)	0	0	5
Internet users (per 100 people)	0.0	0.0	0.6
Paved roads (% of total)	1	1	..
High-technology exports (% of manufactured exports)	..	..	..
Global links			
Merchandise trade (% of GDP)	27.2	36.1	76.4
Net barter terms of trade (2000 = 100)			..
Total external debt ($ billions)	0.5	1.1	1.8
Short-term debt ($ millions)	30	29	18
Total debt service (% of exports)	4.4	..	..
Foreign direct investment, net inflows ($ millions)	9.4	114.8	700.0
Remittances received ($ millions)	1.0	..	..
Aid ($ millions)	311	130	284

Channel Islands

Population (thousands)	149	Population growth (%)		0.2
Surface area (sq. km)	190	National poverty rate (% of pop.)		..
GNI ($ billions)	..	GNI per capita ($)		..
GNI, PPP ($ billions)	..	GNI per capita, PPP ($)		..

	1990	2000	2006
People			
Share of poorest 20% in nat'l consumption/income (%)	..	..	..
Life expectancy at birth (years)	76	78	79
Total fertility (births per woman)	1.5	1.4	1.4
Adolescent fertility (births per 1,000 women 15–19)	..	13	10
Contraceptive prevalence (% of married women 15–49)	..	..	..
Births attended by skilled health staff (% of total)	..	..	..
Under-five mortality rate (per 1,000)	..	..	..
Child malnutrition, underweight (% of under age 5)	..	..	..
Child immunization, measles (% of ages 12–23 mos.)	..	..	..
Primary completion rate, total (% of relevant age group)	..	..	..
Gross secondary enrollment, total (% of relevant age group)	..	..	..
Ratio of girls to boys in primary & secondary school (%)	..	..	..
HIV prevalence rate (% of population ages 15–49)	..	..	..
Environment			
Forests (sq. km)	10	10	10
Deforestation (average annual %, 1990–2005)			0.00
Freshwater use (% of internal resources)	..	..	
Access to improved water source (% of total pop.)	..	..	..
Access to improved sanitation facilities (% of total pop.)	..	..	..
Energy use per capita (kilograms of oil equivalent)	..	..	..
Carbon dioxide emissions per capita (metric tons)	..	..	..
Electricity use per capita (kilowatt-hours)	..	..	..
Economy			
GDP ($ billions)	..	..	..
GDP growth (annual %)	..	..	..
GDP implicit price deflator (annual % growth)	..	..	..
Value added in agriculture (% of GDP)	..	..	..
Value added in industry (% of GDP)	..	..	..
Value added in services (% of GDP)	..	..	..
Exports of goods and services (% of GDP)	..	..	..
Imports of goods and services (% of GDP)	..	..	..
Gross capital formation (% of GDP)	..	..	..
Central government revenue (% of GDP)	..	..	..
Central government cash surplus/deficit (% of GDP)	..	..	..
States and markets			
Starting a business (days)			..
Stock market capitalization (% of GDP)	..	..	..
Military expenditures (% of GDP)	..	..	..
Fixed-line and mobile subscribers (per 100 people)	..	..	..
Internet users (per 100 people)	..	..	..
Paved roads (% of total)	..	..	..
High-technology exports (% of manufactured exports)	..	..	..
Global links			
Merchandise trade (% of GDP)	..	..	..
Net barter terms of trade (2000 = 100)	..	..	..
Total external debt ($ billions)	..	..	..
Short-term debt ($ billions)	..	..	..
Total debt service (% of exports)	..	..	..
Foreign direct investment, net inflows ($ billions)	..	..	..
Remittances received ($ billions)	..	..	..
Aid ($ billions)	..	..	..

Chile

Latin America & Caribbean		**Upper middle income**	
Population (millions)	16	Population growth (%)	0.8
Surface area (1,000 sq. km)	757	National poverty rate (% of pop.)	..
GNI ($ billions)	111.9	GNI per capita ($)	6,810
GNI, PPP ($ billions)	185.6	GNI per capita, PPP ($)	11,300

	1990	2000	2006
People			
Share of poorest 20% in nat'l consumption/income (%)	3.4	3.5	..
Life expectancy at birth (years)	74	77	78
Total fertility (births per woman)	2.6	2.1	2.0
Adolescent fertility (births per 1,000 women 15–19)	..	64	60
Contraceptive prevalence (% of married women 15–49)	56	..	..
Births attended by skilled health staff (% of total)	..	100	100
Under-five mortality rate (per 1,000)	21	11	9
Child malnutrition, underweight (% of under age 5)	..	..	..
Child immunization, measles (% of ages 12–23 mos.)	97	97	91
Primary completion rate, total (% of relevant age group)	..	98	123
Gross secondary enrollment, total (% of relevant age group)	73	83	91
Ratio of girls to boys in primary & secondary school (%)	100	100	98
HIV prevalence rate (% of population ages 15–49)	..	..	0.3
Environment			
Forests (1,000 sq. km)	153	158	161
Deforestation (average annual %, 1990–2005)			-0.4
Freshwater use (% of internal resources)	..	1.4	..
Access to improved water source (% of total pop.)	90	94	95
Access to improved sanitation facilities (% of total pop.)	84	90	91
Energy use per capita (kilograms of oil equivalent)	1,067	1,684	1,815
Carbon dioxide emissions per capita (metric tons)	2.7	3.9	3.9
Electricity use per capita (kilowatt-hours)	1,247	2,488	3,074
Economy			
GDP ($ billions)	31.6	75.8	145.8
GDP growth (annual %)	3.7	4.5	4.0
GDP implicit price deflator (annual % growth)	22.5	4.6	11.7
Value added in agriculture (% of GDP)	9	6	4
Value added in industry (% of GDP)	41	38	48
Value added in services (% of GDP)	50	55	48
Exports of goods and services (% of GDP)	34	32	45
Imports of goods and services (% of GDP)	31	30	31
Gross capital formation (% of GDP)	25	22	20
Central government revenue (% of GDP)	..	21.6	25.9
Central government cash surplus/deficit (% of GDP)	..	-0.7	7.7
States and markets			
Starting a business (days)			27
Stock market capitalization (% of GDP)	43.1	79.7	119.7
Military expenditures (% of GDP)	4.2	3.7	3.6
Fixed-line and mobile subscribers (per 100 people)	7	43	96
Internet users (per 100 people)	0.0	16.5	25.3
Paved roads (% of total)	14	18	..
High-technology exports (% of manufactured exports)	5	3	7
Global links			
Merchandise trade (% of GDP)	51.1	49.8	66.2
Net barter terms of trade (2000 = 100)	114	100	184
Total external debt ($ billions)	19	37	48
Short-term debt ($ billions)	3.4	6.2	9.4
Total debt service (% of exports)	25.9	24.8	20.0
Foreign direct investment, net inflows ($ billions)	0.7	4.9	8.0
Remittances received ($ millions)	1.0	13.0	2.5
Aid ($ millions)	104	49	83

China

Lower middle income

Population (millions)	1,312	Population growth (%)	0.6
Surface area (1,000 sq. km)	9,598	National poverty rate (% of pop.)	..
GNI ($ billions)	2,621.0	GNI per capita ($)	2,000
GNI, PPP ($ billions)	6,119.9	GNI per capita, PPP ($)	4,660

	1990	2000	2006
People			
Share of poorest 20% in nat'l consumption/income (%)	..	..	4.3
Life expectancy at birth (years)	69	70	72
Total fertility (births per woman)	2.1	1.9	1.8
Adolescent fertility (births per 1,000 women 15–19)	..	4	7
Contraceptive prevalence (% of married women 15–49)	85	87	..
Births attended by skilled health staff (% of total)	50	97	98
Under-five mortality rate (per 1,000)	45	37	24
Child malnutrition, underweight (% of under age 5)	..	6.8	..
Child immunization, measles (% of ages 12–23 mos.)	98	85	93
Primary completion rate, total (% of relevant age group)	101	..	..
Gross secondary enrollment, total (% of relevant age group)	49	63	76
Ratio of girls to boys in primary & secondary school (%)	87	99	100
HIV prevalence rate (% of population ages 15–49)	..	..	0.1
Environment			
Forests (1,000 sq. km)	1,571	1,770	1,973
Deforestation (average annual %, 1990–2005)			–1.5
Freshwater use (% of internal resources)	..	22.4	..
Access to improved water source (% of total pop.)	70	76	77
Access to improved sanitation facilities (% of total pop.)	23	41	44
Energy use per capita (kilograms of oil equivalent)	760	875	1,316
Carbon dioxide emissions per capita (metric tons)	2.1	2.6	3.9
Electricity use per capita (kilowatt-hours)	511	993	1,781
Economy			
GDP ($ billions)	354.6	1,198.5	2,644.7
GDP growth (annual %)	3.8	8.4	10.7
GDP implicit price deflator (annual % growth)	5.7	2.1	3.6
Value added in agriculture (% of GDP)	27	15	12
Value added in industry (% of GDP)	42	46	48
Value added in services (% of GDP)	31	39	40
Exports of goods and services (% of GDP)	19	23	40
Imports of goods and services (% of GDP)	16	21	32
Gross capital formation (% of GDP)	36	35	45
Central government revenue (% of GDP)	6.3	7.1	9.6
Central government cash surplus/deficit (% of GDP)	..	–2.6	–1.6
States and markets			
Starting a business (days)			35
Stock market capitalization (% of GDP)	0.5	48.5	91.7
Military expenditures (% of GDP) [See note in *Glossary*.]	2.7	1.8	1.9
Fixed-line and mobile subscribers (per 100 people)	1	18	63
Internet users (per 100 people)	0.0	1.8	10.4
Paved roads (% of total)	..	78	82
High-technology exports (% of manufactured exports)	0	19	30
Global links			
Merchandise trade (% of GDP)	32.5	39.6	66.6
Net barter terms of trade (2000 = 100)	102	100	82
Total external debt ($ billions)	55	146	323
Short-term debt ($ billions)	9.3	13.1	173.4
Total debt service (% of exports)	11.7	9.3	2.5
Foreign direct investment, net inflows ($ billions)	3.5	38.4	78.1
Remittances received ($ billions)	0.2	6.2	23.3
Aid ($ billions)	2.0	1.7	1.2

Colombia

Latin America & Caribbean		Lower middle income

Population (millions)	46	Population growth (%)		1.4
Surface area (1,000 sq. km)	1,142	National poverty rate (% of pop.)		..
GNI ($ billions)	142.0	GNI per capita ($)		3,120
GNI, PPP ($ billions)	279.2	GNI per capita, PPP ($)		6,130

	1990	2000	2006
People			
Share of poorest 20% in nat'l consumption/income (%)	3.4	2.6	2.9
Life expectancy at birth (years)	68	71	73
Total fertility (births per woman)	3.0	2.6	2.3
Adolescent fertility (births per 1,000 women 15–19)	..	79	67
Contraceptive prevalence (% of married women 15–49)	66	77	78
Births attended by skilled health staff (% of total)	82	86	96
Under-five mortality rate (per 1,000)	35	26	21
Child malnutrition, underweight (% of under age 5)	..	4.9	5.1
Child immunization, measles (% of ages 12–23 mos.)	82	75	88
Primary completion rate, total (% of relevant age group)	67	92	105
Gross secondary enrollment, total (% of relevant age group)	50	69	82
Ratio of girls to boys in primary & secondary school (%)	108	104	104
HIV prevalence rate (% of population ages 15–49)	..	..	0.6
Environment			
Forests (1,000 sq. km)	614	610	607
Deforestation (average annual %, 1990–2005)			0.1
Freshwater use (% of internal resources)	..	0.5	..
Access to improved water source (% of total pop.)	92	92	93
Access to improved sanitation facilities (% of total pop.)	82	85	86
Energy use per capita (kilograms of oil equivalent)	710	658	636
Carbon dioxide emissions per capita (metric tons)	1.7	1.4	1.2
Electricity use per capita (kilowatt-hours)	827	838	890
Economy			
GDP ($ billions)	40.3	83.8	153.4
GDP growth (annual %)	6.0	2.9	6.8
GDP implicit price deflator (annual % growth)	26.1	12.1	5.4
Value added in agriculture (% of GDP)	17	13	12
Value added in industry (% of GDP)	38	30	36
Value added in services (% of GDP)	45	57	52
Exports of goods and services (% of GDP)	21	22	22
Imports of goods and services (% of GDP)	15	19	25
Gross capital formation (% of GDP)	19	14	24
Central government revenue (% of GDP)	..	18.2	26.0
Central government cash surplus/deficit (% of GDP)	..	-7.0	-3.9
States and markets			
Starting a business (days)			42
Stock market capitalization (% of GDP)	3.5	11.4	36.6
Military expenditures (% of GDP)	2.2	3.4	3.5
Fixed-line and mobile subscribers (per 100 people)	7	23	83
Internet users (per 100 people)	0.0	2.1	14.7
Paved roads (% of total)	12	14	..
High-technology exports (% of manufactured exports)	0	8	4
Global links			
Merchandise trade (% of GDP)	30.7	29.3	32.9
Net barter terms of trade (2000 = 100)	81	100	115
Total external debt ($ billions)	17	34	40
Short-term debt ($ billions)	1.4	2.9	4.8
Total debt service (% of exports)	40.9	27.7	31.3
Foreign direct investment, net inflows ($ billions)	0.5	2.4	6.5
Remittances received ($ billions)	0.5	1.6	3.9
Aid ($ millions)	89	187	988

Comoros

Sub-Saharan Africa | **Low income**

Population (thousands)	614	Population growth (%)	2.2
Surface area (1,000 sq. km)	1.9	National poverty rate (% of pop.)	..
GNI ($ millions)	406	GNI per capita ($)	660
GNI, PPP ($ millions)	698	GNI per capita, PPP ($)	1,140

	1990	2000	2006
People			
Share of poorest 20% in nat'l consumption/income (%)	..	..	..
Life expectancy at birth (years)	56	61	63
Total fertility (births per woman)	5.8	4.3	4.0
Adolescent fertility (births per 1,000 women 15–19)	..	62	51
Contraceptive prevalence (% of married women 15–49)	..	26	..
Births attended by skilled health staff (% of total)	..	62	..
Under-five mortality rate (per 1,000)	120	84	68
Child malnutrition, underweight (% of under age 5)	..	25.0	..
Child immunization, measles (% of ages 12–23 mos.)	87	70	66
Primary completion rate, total (% of relevant age group)	32	48	50
Gross secondary enrollment, total (% of relevant age group)	18	24	35
Ratio of girls to boys in primary & secondary school (%)	71	84	84
HIV prevalence rate (% of population ages 15–49)	..	..	0.1
Environment			
Forests (sq. km)	120	80	50
Deforestation (average annual %, 1990–2005)			5.7
Freshwater use (% of internal resources)	..	0.8	..
Access to improved water source (% of total pop.)	93	88	86
Access to improved sanitation facilities (% of total pop.)	32	34	33
Energy use per capita (kilograms of oil equivalent)	..	..	..
Carbon dioxide emissions per capita (metric tons)	0.2	0.2	0.1
Electricity use per capita (kilowatt-hours)	..	..	..
Economy			
GDP ($ millions)	250	202	403
GDP growth (annual %)	5.1	0.9	0.5
GDP implicit price deflator (annual % growth)	2.2	3.8	2.7
Value added in agriculture (% of GDP)	41	49	45
Value added in industry (% of GDP)	8	12	12
Value added in services (% of GDP)	50	40	38
Exports of goods and services (% of GDP)	14	17	12
Imports of goods and services (% of GDP)	37	33	36
Gross capital formation (% of GDP)	20	10	10
Central government revenue (% of GDP)	..	..	..
Central government cash surplus/deficit (% of GDP)	..	..	..
States and markets			
Starting a business (days)			23
Stock market capitalization (% of GDP)	..	..	..
Military expenditures (% of GDP)	..	..	..
Fixed-line and mobile subscribers (per 100 people)	1	1	5
Internet users (per 100 people)	0.0	0.3	3.4
Paved roads (% of total)	69	77	..
High-technology exports (% of manufactured exports)	..	1	..
Global links			
Merchandise trade (% of GDP)	28.0	28.2	30.0
Net barter terms of trade (2000 = 100)	..	..	..
Total external debt ($ millions)	188	237	282
Short-term debt ($ millions)	12	28	22
Total debt service (% of exports)	2.3	..	..
Foreign direct investment, net inflows ($ millions)	0.4	0.1	0.8
Remittances received ($ millions)	10	12	12
Aid ($ millions)	45	19	30

Congo, Dem. Rep.

Sub-Saharan Africa   **Low income**

Population (millions)	61	Population growth (%)		3.2
Surface area (1,000 sq. km)	2,345	National poverty rate (% of pop.)		..
GNI ($ billions)	7.7	GNI per capita ($)		130
GNI, PPP ($ billions)	16.2	GNI per capita, PPP ($)		270

	1990	2000	2006
People			
Share of poorest 20% in nat'l consumption/income (%)	..	..	..
Life expectancy at birth (years)	46	44	46
Total fertility (births per woman)	6.7	6.7	6.3
Adolescent fertility (births per 1,000 women 15–19)	..	230	224
Contraceptive prevalence (% of married women 15–49)	8	31	..
Births attended by skilled health staff (% of total)	..	61	..
Under-five mortality rate (per 1,000)	205	205	205
Child malnutrition, underweight (% of under age 5)	..	33.6	..
Child immunization, measles (% of ages 12–23 mos.)	38	46	73
Primary completion rate, total (% of relevant age group)	46	39	..
Gross secondary enrollment, total (% of relevant age group)	..	18	..
Ratio of girls to boys in primary & secondary school (%)	..	73	..
HIV prevalence rate (% of population ages 15–49)	..	..	3.2
Environment			
Forests (1,000 sq. km)	1,405	1,352	1,336
Deforestation (average annual %, 1990–2005)			0.3
Freshwater use (% of internal resources)	..	0.0	..
Access to improved water source (% of total pop.)	43	45	46
Access to improved sanitation facilities (% of total pop.)	16	25	30
Energy use per capita (kilograms of oil equivalent)	314	291	289
Carbon dioxide emissions per capita (metric tons)	0.10	0.03	0.04
Electricity use per capita (kilowatt-hours)	119	89	91
Economy			
GDP ($ billions)	9.3	4.3	8.5
GDP growth (annual %)	-6.6	-6.9	5.1
GDP implicit price deflator (annual % growth)	109.0	515.8	13.1
Value added in agriculture (% of GDP)	31	50	46
Value added in industry (% of GDP)	29	20	28
Value added in services (% of GDP)	40	30	27
Exports of goods and services (% of GDP)	30	22	29
Imports of goods and services (% of GDP)	29	21	41
Gross capital formation (% of GDP)	9	3	16
Central government revenue (% of GDP)	10.1	3.7	..
Central government cash surplus/deficit (% of GDP)	-6.5	-4.0	..
States and markets			
Starting a business (days)			155
Stock market capitalization (% of GDP)	..	..	..
Military expenditures (% of GDP)	..	1.0	0.0
Fixed-line and mobile subscribers (per 100 people)	0	0	7
Internet users (per 100 people)	0.0	0.0	0.3
Paved roads (% of total)	..	..	2
High-technology exports (% of manufactured exports)	..	..	..
Global links			
Merchandise trade (% of GDP)	43.5	35.3	59.7
Net barter terms of trade (2000 = 100)	86	100	126
Total external debt ($ billions)	10	12	11
Short-term debt ($ billions)	0.7	3.4	0.5
Total debt service (% of exports)	..	..	..
Foreign direct investment, net inflows ($ millions)	23	166	180
Remittances received ($ billions)	..	..	..
Aid ($ billions)	0.9	0.2	2.1

Congo, Rep.

Sub-Saharan Africa   **Lower middle income**

Population (millions)	3.7	Population growth (%)	2.2
Surface area (1,000 sq. km)	342	National poverty rate (% of pop.)	..
GNI ($ billions)	3.8	GNI per capita ($)	1,050
GNI, PPP ($ billions)	8.7	GNI per capita, PPP ($)	2,420

	1990	2000	2006
People			
Share of poorest 20% in nat'l consumption/income (%)	..	..	..
Life expectancy at birth (years)	57	53	55
Total fertility (births per woman)	5.3	4.8	4.6
Adolescent fertility (births per 1,000 women 15–19)	..	128	118
Contraceptive prevalence (% of married women 15–49)	..	..	44
Births attended by skilled health staff (% of total)	..	..	86
Under-five mortality rate (per 1,000)	103	117	126
Child malnutrition, underweight (% of under age 5)	..	..	11.8
Child immunization, measles (% of ages 12–23 mos.)	75	34	66
Primary completion rate, total (% of relevant age group)	59	55	73
Gross secondary enrollment, total (% of relevant age group)	46	34	43
Ratio of girls to boys in primary & secondary school (%)	85	84	90
HIV prevalence rate (% of population ages 15–49)	..	..	5.3
Environment			
Forests (1,000 sq. km)	227	226	225
Deforestation (average annual %, 1990–2005)			0.1
Freshwater use (% of internal resources)	..	0.0	..
Access to improved water source (% of total pop.)	..	57	58
Access to improved sanitation facilities (% of total pop.)	..	27	27
Energy use per capita (kilograms of oil equivalent)	436	265	332
Carbon dioxide emissions per capita (metric tons)	0.5	0.7	1.0
Electricity use per capita (kilowatt-hours)	169	119	160
Economy			
GDP ($ billions)	2.8	3.2	7.4
GDP growth (annual %)	1.0	7.6	6.4
GDP implicit price deflator (annual % growth)	-1.0	47.0	15.2
Value added in agriculture (% of GDP)	13	5	4
Value added in industry (% of GDP)	41	72	73
Value added in services (% of GDP)	46	23	22
Exports of goods and services (% of GDP)	54	80	91
Imports of goods and services (% of GDP)	46	44	46
Gross capital formation (% of GDP)	16	23	24
Central government revenue (% of GDP)	..	32.3	..
Central government cash surplus/deficit (% of GDP)	..	-1.3	..
States and markets			
Starting a business (days)			37
Stock market capitalization (% of GDP)	..	..	..
Military expenditures (% of GDP)	..	1.4	1.1
Fixed-line and mobile subscribers (per 100 people)	1	3	14
Internet users (per 100 people)	0.0	0.0	1.9
Paved roads (% of total)	10	10	5
High-technology exports (% of manufactured exports)	..	..	..
Global links			
Merchandise trade (% of GDP)	57.2	91.7	109.7
Net barter terms of trade (2000 = 100)	63	100	184
Total external debt ($ billions)	4.9	4.9	6.1
Short-term debt ($ billions)	0.7	1.1	0.8
Total debt service (% of exports)	35.3	1.6	2.4
Foreign direct investment, net inflows ($ millions)	-14	166	344
Remittances received ($ millions)	4.0	10.0	11.4
Aid ($ millions)	217	33	254

Costa Rica

Latin America & Caribbean		Upper middle income	
Population (millions)	4.4	Population growth (%)	1.6
Surface area (1,000 sq. km)	51	National poverty rate (% of pop.)	24
GNI ($ billions)	21.9	GNI per capita ($)	4,980
GNI, PPP ($ billions)	40.6	GNI per capita, PPP ($)	9,220

	1990	2000	2006
People			
Share of poorest 20% in nat'l consumption/income (%)	4.0	4.1	4.1
Life expectancy at birth (years)	76	78	79
Total fertility (births per woman)	3.1	2.4	2.1
Adolescent fertility (births per 1,000 women 15–19)	..	81	73
Contraceptive prevalence (% of married women 15–49)	..	80	96
Births attended by skilled health staff (% of total)	98	98	99
Under-five mortality rate (per 1,000)	18	14	12
Child malnutrition, underweight (% of under age 5)	..	..	..
Child immunization, measles (% of ages 12–23 mos.)	90	82	89
Primary completion rate, total (% of relevant age group)	75	87	89
Gross secondary enrollment, total (% of relevant age group)	45	61	86
Ratio of girls to boys in primary & secondary school (%)	101	101	102
HIV prevalence rate (% of population ages 15–49)	..	..	0.3
Environment			
Forests (1,000 sq. km)	26	24	24
Deforestation (average annual %, 1990–2005)			0.5
Freshwater use (% of internal resources)	..	2.4	..
Access to improved water source (% of total pop.)	..	97	97
Access to improved sanitation facilities (% of total pop.)	..	92	92
Energy use per capita (kilograms of oil equivalent)	658	842	883
Carbon dioxide emissions per capita (metric tons)	0.9	1.4	1.5
Electricity use per capita (kilowatt-hours)	1,087	1,518	1,719
Economy			
GDP ($ billions)	7.4	15.9	22.2
GDP growth (annual %)	3.9	1.8	8.2
GDP implicit price deflator (annual % growth)	17.1	7.0	10.1
Value added in agriculture (% of GDP)	12	9	9
Value added in industry (% of GDP)	30	32	29
Value added in services (% of GDP)	58	58	62
Exports of goods and services (% of GDP)	30	49	50
Imports of goods and services (% of GDP)	36	46	56
Gross capital formation (% of GDP)	18	17	27
Central government revenue (% of GDP)	..	..	24.1
Central government cash surplus/deficit (% of GDP)	..	..	1.2
States and markets			
Starting a business (days)			77
Stock market capitalization (% of GDP)	5.5	18.3	8.7
Military expenditures (% of GDP)	..	..	..
Fixed-line and mobile subscribers (per 100 people)	9	28	64
Internet users (per 100 people)	0.0	5.8	27.6
Paved roads (% of total)	15	22	24
High-technology exports (% of manufactured exports)	0	52	45
Global links			
Merchandise trade (% of GDP)	46.4	76.7	88.8
Net barter terms of trade (2000 = 100)	75	100	86
Total external debt ($ billions)	3.8	4.5	6.8
Short-term debt ($ billions)	0.4	1.0	2.3
Total debt service (% of exports)	23.9	8.0	5.0
Foreign direct investment, net inflows ($ billions)	0.2	0.4	1.5
Remittances received ($ millions)	12	136	513
Aid ($ millions)	227	11	24

Côte d'Ivoire

Sub-Saharan Africa		Low income	
Population (millions)	19	Population growth (%)	1.8
Surface area (1,000 sq. km)	322	National poverty rate (% of pop.)	..
GNI ($ billions)	16.6	GNI per capita ($)	880
GNI, PPP ($ billions)	29.8	GNI per capita, PPP ($)	1,580

	1990	2000	2006
People			
Share of poorest 20% in nat'l consumption/income (%)	6.7	5.2	..
Life expectancy at birth (years)	53	47	48
Total fertility (births per woman)	6.5	5.3	4.6
Adolescent fertility (births per 1,000 women 15–19)	..	143	112
Contraceptive prevalence (% of married women 15–49)	..	15	13
Births attended by skilled health staff (% of total)	..	63	57
Under-five mortality rate (per 1,000)	153	136	127
Child malnutrition, underweight (% of under age 5)	..	18.2	..
Child immunization, measles (% of ages 12–23 mos.)	56	73	73
Primary completion rate, total (% of relevant age group)	41	39	43
Gross secondary enrollment, total (% of relevant age group)	21	22	..
Ratio of girls to boys in primary & secondary school (%)	65	69	..
HIV prevalence rate (% of population ages 15–49)	..	..	7.1
Environment			
Forests (1,000 sq. km)	102	103	104
Deforestation (average annual %, 1990–2005)			-0.1
Freshwater use (% of internal resources)	..	1.2	..
Access to improved water source (% of total pop.)	69	83	84
Access to improved sanitation facilities (% of total pop.)	21	33	37
Energy use per capita (kilograms of oil equivalent)	345	402	422
Carbon dioxide emissions per capita (metric tons)	0.4	0.3	0.3
Electricity use per capita (kilowatt-hours)	150	168	170
Economy			
GDP ($ billions)	10.8	10.4	17.6
GDP growth (annual %)	-1.1	-3.7	0.9
GDP implicit price deflator (annual % growth)	-4.5	-0.4	5.6
Value added in agriculture (% of GDP)	32	24	23
Value added in industry (% of GDP)	23	25	26
Value added in services (% of GDP)	44	51	51
Exports of goods and services (% of GDP)	32	40	51
Imports of goods and services (% of GDP)	27	33	41
Gross capital formation (% of GDP)	7	11	10
Central government revenue (% of GDP)	..	16.7	17.4
Central government cash surplus/deficit (% of GDP)	..	2.8	-1.4
States and markets			
Starting a business (days)			40
Stock market capitalization (% of GDP)	5.1	11.4	23.7
Military expenditures (% of GDP)	1.3	..	..
Fixed-line and mobile subscribers (per 100 people)	1	4	23
Internet users (per 100 people)	0.0	0.2	1.6
Paved roads (% of total)	9	10	8
High-technology exports (% of manufactured exports)	..	2	42
Global links			
Merchandise trade (% of GDP)	47.9	64.1	78.2
Net barter terms of trade (2000 = 100)	143	100	135
Total external debt ($ billions)	17	12	14
Short-term debt ($ billions)	3.6	1.0	2.0
Total debt service (% of exports)	35.4	22.6	1.4
Foreign direct investment, net inflows ($ millions)	48	235	315
Remittances received ($ millions)	44	119	164
Aid ($ millions)	686	351	251

Croatia

     Upper middle income

Population (millions)	4.4	Population growth (%)	0.0
Surface area (1,000 sq. km)	57	National poverty rate (% of pop.)	..
GNI ($ billions)	41.3	GNI per capita ($)	9,310
GNI, PPP ($ billions)	61.5	GNI per capita, PPP ($)	13,850

	1990	2000	2006
People			
Share of poorest 20% in nat'l consumption/income (%)	10.3	8.3	8.8
Life expectancy at birth (years)	72	73	76
Total fertility (births per woman)	1.6	1.4	1.4
Adolescent fertility (births per 1,000 women 15–19)	..	16	13
Contraceptive prevalence (% of married women 15–49)	..	69	..
Births attended by skilled health staff (% of total)	100	100	100
Under-five mortality rate (per 1,000)	12	8	6
Child malnutrition, underweight (% of under age 5)	..	..	..
Child immunization, measles (% of ages 12–23 mos.)	90	93	96
Primary completion rate, total (% of relevant age group)	..	92	92
Gross secondary enrollment, total (% of relevant age group)	76	85	89
Ratio of girls to boys in primary & secondary school (%)	102	101	..
HIV prevalence rate (% of population ages 15–49)	..	..	0.1
Environment			
Forests (1,000 sq. km)	21	21	21
Deforestation (average annual %, 1990–2005)			-0.1
Freshwater use (% of internal resources)	..	..	..
Access to improved water source (% of total pop.)	100	100	100
Access to improved sanitation facilities (% of total pop.)	100	100	100
Energy use per capita (kilograms of oil equivalent)	1,897	1,727	2,000
Carbon dioxide emissions per capita (metric tons)	5.1	4.6	5.3
Electricity use per capita (kilowatt-hours)	2,991	2,792	3,475
Economy			
GDP ($ billions)	24.8	18.4	42.9
GDP growth (annual %)	-21.1	2.9	4.8
GDP implicit price deflator (annual % growth)	99.3	4.7	3.4
Value added in agriculture (% of GDP)	11	9	7
Value added in industry (% of GDP)	36	30	32
Value added in services (% of GDP)	53	61	61
Exports of goods and services (% of GDP)	78	47	48
Imports of goods and services (% of GDP)	86	52	57
Gross capital formation (% of GDP)	14	20	33
Central government revenue (% of GDP)	33.0	41.7	40.0
Central government cash surplus/deficit (% of GDP)	-4.6	-6.2	-1.8
States and markets			
Starting a business (days)			40
Stock market capitalization (% of GDP)	..	14.9	67.6
Military expenditures (% of GDP)	7.4	3.0	1.6
Fixed-line and mobile subscribers (per 100 people)	17	61	142
Internet users (per 100 people)	0.0	6.6	35.5
Paved roads (% of total)	..	85	89
High-technology exports (% of manufactured exports)	5	8	10
Global links			
Merchandise trade (% of GDP)	88.8	66.9	74.2
Net barter terms of trade (2000 = 100)	..	..	..
Total external debt ($ billions)	..	12.4	37.5
Short-term debt ($ billions)	..	0.9	5.6
Total debt service (% of exports)	..	31.9	33.1
Foreign direct investment, net inflows ($ billions)	..	1.1	3.4
Remittances received ($ billions)	..	0.6	1.2
Aid ($ millions)	0.0	65.6	200.0

Cuba

Latin America & Caribbean		Lower middle income	
Population (millions)	11	Population growth (%)	0.1
Surface area (1,000 sq. km)	111	National poverty rate (% of pop.)	..
GNI ($ billions)	..	GNI per capita ($)	..
GNI, PPP ($ billions)	..	GNI per capita, PPP ($)	..

	1990	2000	2006
People			
Share of poorest 20% in nat'l consumption/income (%)	..	..	..
Life expectancy at birth (years)	75	77	78
Total fertility (births per woman)	1.7	1.6	1.5
Adolescent fertility (births per 1,000 women 15–19)	..	57	48
Contraceptive prevalence (% of married women 15–49)	..	73	73
Births attended by skilled health staff (% of total)	..	100	100
Under-five mortality rate (per 1,000)	13	9	7
Child malnutrition, underweight (% of under age 5)	..	..	..
Child immunization, measles (% of ages 12–23 mos.)	94	94	96
Primary completion rate, total (% of relevant age group)	92	104	92
Gross secondary enrollment, total (% of relevant age group)	94	79	94
Ratio of girls to boys in primary & secondary school (%)	106	100	100
HIV prevalence rate (% of population ages 15–49)	..	..	0.1
Environment			
Forests (1,000 sq. km)	21	24	27
Deforestation (average annual %, 1990–2005)			-1.9
Freshwater use (% of internal resources)	..	21.5	..
Access to improved water source (% of total pop.)	..	91	91
Access to improved sanitation facilities (% of total pop.)	98	98	98
Energy use per capita (kilograms of oil equivalent)	1,587	1,032	906
Carbon dioxide emissions per capita (metric tons)	3.0	2.3	2.3
Electricity use per capita (kilowatt-hours)	1,212	1,136	1,152
Economy			
GDP ($ billions)	..	..	..
GDP growth (annual %)	..	5.6	5.4
GDP implicit price deflator (annual % growth)	..	21.3	0.9
Value added in agriculture (% of GDP)	..	6	..
Value added in industry (% of GDP)	..	47	..
Value added in services (% of GDP)	..	46	..
Exports of goods and services (% of GDP)	..	16	..
Imports of goods and services (% of GDP)	..	19	..
Gross capital formation (% of GDP)	..	9	..
Central government revenue (% of GDP)	..	..	..
Central government cash surplus/deficit (% of GDP)	..	..	..
States and markets			
Starting a business (days)			..
Stock market capitalization (% of GDP)	..	..	..
Military expenditures (% of GDP)	..	..	..
Fixed-line and mobile subscribers (per 100 people)	3	4	10
Internet users (per 100 people)	0.0	0.5	2.1
Paved roads (% of total)	51	49	..
High-technology exports (% of manufactured exports)	..	21	12
Global links			
Merchandise trade (% of GDP)	..	..	..
Net barter terms of trade (2000 = 100)	..	100	149
Total external debt ($ billions)	..	..	..
Short-term debt ($ billions)	..	..	..
Total debt service (% of exports)	..	..	..
Foreign direct investment, net inflows ($ billions)	..	..	..
Remittances received ($ billions)	..	..	..
Aid ($ millions)	52	44	78

Cyprus

High income

Population (thousands)	771	Population growth (%)		1.8
Surface area (1,000 sq. km)	9.3	National poverty rate (% of pop.)		..
GNI ($ billions)	17.9	GNI per capita ($)		23,270
GNI, PPP ($ billions)	19.3	GNI per capita, PPP ($)		25,060

	1990	2000	2006
People			
Share of poorest 20% in nat'l consumption/income (%)	..	..	..
Life expectancy at birth (years)	76	78	79
Total fertility (births per woman)	2.4	1.6	1.4
Adolescent fertility (births per 1,000 women 15–19)	..	10	8
Contraceptive prevalence (% of married women 15–49)	..	..	..
Births attended by skilled health staff (% of total)	..	..	..
Under-five mortality rate (per 1,000)	12	6	4
Child malnutrition, underweight (% of under age 5)	..	..	..
Child immunization, measles (% of ages 12–23 mos.)	77	86	87
Primary completion rate, total (% of relevant age group)	83	98	100
Gross secondary enrollment, total (% of relevant age group)	72	92	97
Ratio of girls to boys in primary & secondary school (%)	100	102	101
HIV prevalence rate (% of population ages 15–49)	..	..	0.2
Environment			
Forests (1,000 sq. km)	1.6	1.7	1.7
Deforestation (average annual %, 1990–2005)			-0.5
Freshwater use (% of internal resources)	..	30.0	..
Access to improved water source (% of total pop.)	100	100	100
Access to improved sanitation facilities (% of total pop.)	100	100	100
Energy use per capita (kilograms of oil equivalent)	2,792	3,500	3,368
Carbon dioxide emissions per capita (metric tons)	8.0	9.3	9.1
Electricity use per capita (kilowatt-hours)	3,213	4,585	5,560
Economy			
GDP ($ billions)	5.6	9.3	18.4
GDP growth (annual %)	7.4	5.0	4.0
GDP implicit price deflator (annual % growth)	5.4	3.8	2.8
Value added in agriculture (% of GDP)	7	..	..
Value added in industry (% of GDP)	26	..	..
Value added in services (% of GDP)	67	..	..
Exports of goods and services (% of GDP)	52	42	..
Imports of goods and services (% of GDP)	57	46	..
Gross capital formation (% of GDP)	27	18	..
Central government revenue (% of GDP)	..	36.5	42.7
Central government cash surplus/deficit (% of GDP)	..	-2.2	-1.1
States and markets			
Starting a business (days)			..
Stock market capitalization (% of GDP)	22.2	46.7	86.5
Military expenditures (% of GDP)	5.0	2.0	1.4
Fixed-line and mobile subscribers (per 100 people)	43	95	154
Internet users (per 100 people)	0.0	17.3	46.2
Paved roads (% of total)	60	61	63
High-technology exports (% of manufactured exports)	6	2	24
Global links			
Merchandise trade (% of GDP)	62.9	51.5	45.0
Net barter terms of trade (2000 = 100)	..	..	..
Total external debt ($ billions)	..	..	..
Short-term debt ($ billions)	..	..	..
Total debt service (% of exports)	..	..	..
Foreign direct investment, net inflows ($ billions)	0.1	0.9	1.5
Remittances received ($ millions)	79	64	172
Aid ($ millions)	38	54	60

Czech Republic

High income

Population (millions)	10	Population growth (%)	0.4
Surface area (1,000 sq. km)	79	National poverty rate (% of pop.)	..
GNI ($ billions)	131.4	GNI per capita ($)	12,790
GNI, PPP ($ billions)	214.9	GNI per capita, PPP ($)	20,920

	1990	2000	2006
People			
Share of poorest 20% in nat'l consumption/income (%)	11.9	..	..
Life expectancy at birth (years)	71	75	76
Total fertility (births per woman)	1.9	1.1	1.3
Adolescent fertility (births per 1,000 women 15–19)	..	14	11
Contraceptive prevalence (% of married women 15–49)	78	..	..
Births attended by skilled health staff (% of total)	..	100	100
Under-five mortality rate (per 1,000)	13	5	4
Child malnutrition, underweight (% of under age 5)	..	2.1	..
Child immunization, measles (% of ages 12–23 mos.)	..	98	97
Primary completion rate, total (% of relevant age group)	..	100	102
Gross secondary enrollment, total (% of relevant age group)	91	88	96
Ratio of girls to boys in primary & secondary school (%)	98	101	101
HIV prevalence rate (% of population ages 15–49)	..	..	0.1
Environment			
Forests (1,000 sq. km)	26	26	26
Deforestation (average annual %, 1990–2005)			-0.05
Freshwater use (% of internal resources)	..	19.5	..
Access to improved water source (% of total pop.)	100	100	100
Access to improved sanitation facilities (% of total pop.)	99	98	98
Energy use per capita (kilograms of oil equivalent)	4,728	3,932	4,417
Carbon dioxide emissions per capita (metric tons)	15.6	11.6	11.5
Electricity use per capita (kilowatt-hours)	5,584	5,694	6,343
Economy			
GDP ($ billions)	34.9	56.7	143.0
GDP growth (annual %)	-11.6	3.6	6.1
GDP implicit price deflator (annual % growth)	36.2	1.5	2.0
Value added in agriculture (% of GDP)	6	4	3
Value added in industry (% of GDP)	49	38	39
Value added in services (% of GDP)	45	58	58
Exports of goods and services (% of GDP)	45	63	76
Imports of goods and services (% of GDP)	43	66	73
Gross capital formation (% of GDP)	25	29	27
Central government revenue (% of GDP)	..	30.5	30.6
Central government cash surplus/deficit (% of GDP)	..	-3.6	-4.3
States and markets			
Starting a business (days)			17
Stock market capitalization (% of GDP)	..	19.4	34.0
Military expenditures (% of GDP)	..	2.0	1.7
Fixed-line and mobile subscribers (per 100 people)	16	80	147
Internet users (per 100 people)	0.0	9.7	34.5
Paved roads (% of total)	100	100	100
High-technology exports (% of manufactured exports)	..	8	14
Global links			
Merchandise trade (% of GDP)	83.6	107.7	131.7
Net barter terms of trade (2000 = 100)	..	..	..
Total external debt ($ billions)	..	..	..
Short-term debt ($ billions)	..	..	..
Total debt service (% of exports)	..	..	..
Foreign direct investment, net inflows ($ billions)	..	5.0	6.0
Remittances received ($ billions)	..	0.3	1.2
Aid ($ millions)	14	438	..

Denmark

Population (millions)	5.4	Population growth (%)	0.4
Surface area (1,000 sq. km)	43	National poverty rate (% of pop.)	..
GNI ($ billions)	283.3	GNI per capita ($)	52,110
GNI, PPP ($ billions)	196.7	GNI per capita, PPP ($)	36,190

	1990	2000	2006
People			
Share of poorest 20% in nat'l consumption/income (%)	..	..	..
Life expectancy at birth (years)	75	77	78
Total fertility (births per woman)	1.7	1.8	1.9
Adolescent fertility (births per 1,000 women 15–19)	..	7	6
Contraceptive prevalence (% of married women 15–49)	78	..	..
Births attended by skilled health staff (% of total)	..	..	..
Under-five mortality rate (per 1,000)	9	6	5
Child malnutrition, underweight (% of under age 5)	..	..	..
Child immunization, measles (% of ages 12–23 mos.)	84	99	99
Primary completion rate, total (% of relevant age group)	95	101	99
Gross secondary enrollment, total (% of relevant age group)	109	127	124
Ratio of girls to boys in primary & secondary school (%)	101	102	102
HIV prevalence rate (% of population ages 15–49)	..	..	0.2
Environment			
Forests (1,000 sq. km)	4.5	4.9	5.0
Deforestation (average annual %, 1990–2005)			–0.8
Freshwater use (% of internal resources)	..	21.2	..
Access to improved water source (% of total pop.)	100	100	100
Access to improved sanitation facilities (% of total pop.)	..	..	..
Energy use per capita (kilograms of oil equivalent)	3,482	3,627	3,621
Carbon dioxide emissions per capita (metric tons)	9.7	8.7	9.8
Electricity use per capita (kilowatt-hours)	5,945	6,484	6,663
Economy			
GDP ($ billions)	135.8	160.1	275.4
GDP growth (annual %)	1.5	3.5	3.2
GDP implicit price deflator (annual % growth)	3.0	3.0	2.2
Value added in agriculture (% of GDP)	4	3	2
Value added in industry (% of GDP)	26	27	26
Value added in services (% of GDP)	70	71	72
Exports of goods and services (% of GDP)	37	47	52
Imports of goods and services (% of GDP)	33	41	49
Gross capital formation (% of GDP)	20	21	23
Central government revenue (% of GDP)	..	36.5	36.0
Central government cash surplus/deficit (% of GDP)	..	1.7	5.1
States and markets			
Starting a business (days)			6
Stock market capitalization (% of GDP)	28.8	67.3	83.9
Military expenditures (% of GDP)	2.0	1.5	1.4
Fixed-line and mobile subscribers (per 100 people)	60	135	164
Internet users (per 100 people)	0.1	39.2	58.3
Paved roads (% of total)	100	100	100
High-technology exports (% of manufactured exports)	15	21	20
Global links			
Merchandise trade (% of GDP)	51.7	60.5	65.0
Net barter terms of trade (2000 = 100)	102	100	105
Total external debt ($ billions)	..	..	..
Short-term debt ($ billions)	..	..	..
Total debt service (% of exports)	..	..	..
Foreign direct investment, net inflows ($ billions)	1.1	36.0	3.3
Remittances received ($ millions)	464	667	869
Aid ($ billions)	..	..	..

Djibouti

Middle East & North Africa		Lower middle income	
Population (thousands)	819	Population growth (%)	1.8
Surface area (1,000 sq. km)	23	National poverty rate (% of pop.)	..
GNI ($ millions)	864	GNI per capita ($)	1,060
GNI, PPP ($ billions)	1.8	GNI per capita, PPP ($)	2,180

	1990	2000	2006
People			
Share of poorest 20% in nat'l consumption/income (%)	..	..	..
Life expectancy at birth (years)	51	53	54
Total fertility (births per woman)	6.1	4.8	4.1
Adolescent fertility (births per 1,000 women 15–19)	..	30	24
Contraceptive prevalence (% of married women 15–49)	..	9	18
Births attended by skilled health staff (% of total)	..	..	..
Under-five mortality rate (per 1,000)	175	147	130
Child malnutrition, underweight (% of under age 5)	..	..	..
Child immunization, measles (% of ages 12–23 mos.)	85	50	67
Primary completion rate, total (% of relevant age group)	32	28	35
Gross secondary enrollment, total (% of relevant age group)	11	14	22
Ratio of girls to boys in primary & secondary school (%)	71	71	76
HIV prevalence rate (% of population ages 15–49)	..	..	3.1
Environment			
Forests (sq. km)	60	60	60
Deforestation (average annual %, 1990–2005)			0.00
Freshwater use (% of internal resources)	..	6.3	..
Access to improved water source (% of total pop.)	72	73	73
Access to improved sanitation facilities (% of total pop.)	79	81	82
Energy use per capita (kilograms of oil equivalent)	..	..	..
Carbon dioxide emissions per capita (metric tons)	0.6	0.5	0.5
Electricity use per capita (kilowatt-hours)	..	..	..
Economy			
GDP ($ millions)	452	551	769
GDP growth (annual %)	-4.3	0.4	4.9
GDP implicit price deflator (annual % growth)	6.8	2.4	3.5
Value added in agriculture (% of GDP)	3	4	4
Value added in industry (% of GDP)	22	15	16
Value added in services (% of GDP)	75	81	80
Exports of goods and services (% of GDP)	54	35	40
Imports of goods and services (% of GDP)	78	50	57
Gross capital formation (% of GDP)	14	9	30
Central government revenue (% of GDP)	..	..	..
Central government cash surplus/deficit (% of GDP)	..	..	..
States and markets			
Starting a business (days)			37
Stock market capitalization (% of GDP)	..	..	..
Military expenditures (% of GDP)	5.9	4.1	..
Fixed-line and mobile subscribers (per 100 people)	1	1	7
Internet users (per 100 people)	0.0	0.2	1.3
Paved roads (% of total)	13	45	..
High-technology exports (% of manufactured exports)	..	..	..
Global links			
Merchandise trade (% of GDP)	53.1	43.2	51.5
Net barter terms of trade (2000 = 100)	..	..	..
Total external debt ($ millions)	205	262	464
Short-term debt ($ millions)	50	11	19
Total debt service (% of exports)	5.6	6.2	6.4
Foreign direct investment, net inflows ($ millions)	2.3	3.3	108.3
Remittances received ($ millions)	13.0	..	28.5
Aid ($ millions)	194	71	117

Dominica

Latin America & Caribbean		Upper middle income	
Population (thousands)	72	Population growth (%)	0.5
Surface area (sq. km)	750	National poverty rate (% of pop.)	..
GNI ($ millions)	300	GNI per capita ($)	4,160
GNI, PPP ($ millions)	566	GNI per capita, PPP ($)	7,870

	1990	2000	2006
People			
Share of poorest 20% in nat'l consumption/income (%)	..	..	..
Life expectancy at birth (years)	73	76	..
Total fertility (births per woman)	2.7	1.9	..
Adolescent fertility (births per 1,000 women 15–19)	..	..	..
Contraceptive prevalence (% of married women 15–49)	..	50	..
Births attended by skilled health staff (% of total)	..	100	100
Under-five mortality rate (per 1,000)	17	17	15
Child malnutrition, underweight (% of under age 5)	..	..	..
Child immunization, measles (% of ages 12–23 mos.)	88	99	99
Primary completion rate, total (% of relevant age group)	..	94	96
Gross secondary enrollment, total (% of relevant age group)	..	95	106
Ratio of girls to boys in primary & secondary school (%)	..	103	101
HIV prevalence rate (% of population ages 15–49)	..	..	..
Environment			
Forests (sq. km)	500	470	460
Deforestation (average annual %, 1990–2005)			0.6
Freshwater use (% of internal resources)	..	..	
Access to improved water source (% of total pop.)	..	97	97
Access to improved sanitation facilities (% of total pop.)	..	82	84
Energy use per capita (kilograms of oil equivalent)	..	..	..
Carbon dioxide emissions per capita (metric tons)	0.8	1.4	1.5
Electricity use per capita (kilowatt-hours)	..	..	..
Economy			
GDP ($ millions)	166	271	319
GDP growth (annual %)	5.3	0.7	4.0
GDP implicit price deflator (annual % growth)	3.0	0.6	2.0
Value added in agriculture (% of GDP)	25	18	19
Value added in industry (% of GDP)	19	23	24
Value added in services (% of GDP)	56	58	58
Exports of goods and services (% of GDP)	55	53	42
Imports of goods and services (% of GDP)	81	68	65
Gross capital formation (% of GDP)	41	28	29
Central government revenue (% of GDP)	..	..	..
Central government cash surplus/deficit (% of GDP)	..	..	..
States and markets			
Starting a business (days)			19
Stock market capitalization (% of GDP)	..	..	..
Military expenditures (% of GDP)	..	..	..
Fixed-line and mobile subscribers (per 100 people)	16	34	88
Internet users (per 100 people)	0.0	8.4	36.1
Paved roads (% of total)	46	50	..
High-technology exports (% of manufactured exports)	0	7	8
Global links			
Merchandise trade (% of GDP)	104.0	74.1	64.0
Net barter terms of trade (2000 = 100)	..	..	..
Total external debt ($ millions)	88	167	269
Short-term debt ($ millions)	2.0	19.0	22.0
Total debt service (% of exports)	5.6	7.4	14.1
Foreign direct investment, net inflows ($ millions)	13	18	34
Remittances received ($ millions)	14.0	3.0	4.6
Aid ($ millions)	20	15	19

Dominican Republic

Latin America & Caribbean		Lower middle income	
Population (millions)	9.6	Population growth (%)	1.5
Surface area (1,000 sq. km)	49	National poverty rate (% of pop.)	42
GNI ($ billions)	28.0	GNI per capita ($)	2,910
GNI, PPP ($ billions)	53.3	GNI per capita, PPP ($)	5,550

	1990	2000	2006
People			
Share of poorest 20% in nat'l consumption/income (%)	4.3	3.5	4.1
Life expectancy at birth (years)	68	71	72
Total fertility (births per woman)	3.3	3.0	2.8
Adolescent fertility (births per 1,000 women 15–19)	..	114	109
Contraceptive prevalence (% of married women 15–49)	56	65	61
Births attended by skilled health staff (% of total)	93	98	96
Under-five mortality rate (per 1,000)	65	40	29
Child malnutrition, underweight (% of under age 5)	8.4	3.5	..
Child immunization, measles (% of ages 12–23 mos.)	96	88	99
Primary completion rate, total (% of relevant age group)	..	80	83
Gross secondary enrollment, total (% of relevant age group)	..	61	69
Ratio of girls to boys in primary & secondary school (%)	..	104	104
HIV prevalence rate (% of population ages 15–49)	..	1.0	1.1
Environment			
Forests (1,000 sq. km)	14	14	14
Deforestation (average annual %, 1990–2005)			0.00
Freshwater use (% of internal resources)	..	16.1	..
Access to improved water source (% of total pop.)	84	92	95
Access to improved sanitation facilities (% of total pop.)	52	71	78
Energy use per capita (kilograms of oil equivalent)	567	892	777
Carbon dioxide emissions per capita (metric tons)	1.3	2.3	2.1
Electricity use per capita (kilowatt-hours)	383	716	1,000
Economy			
GDP ($ billions)	7.1	19.8	31.8
GDP growth (annual %)	-5.5	8.1	10.7
GDP implicit price deflator (annual % growth)	50.5	7.7	7.6
Value added in agriculture (% of GDP)	13	11	12
Value added in industry (% of GDP)	31	34	26
Value added in services (% of GDP)	55	55	62
Exports of goods and services (% of GDP)	34	45	33
Imports of goods and services (% of GDP)	44	55	40
Gross capital formation (% of GDP)	25	24	20
Central government revenue (% of GDP)	..	..	17.9
Central government cash surplus/deficit (% of GDP)	..	..	-1.2
States and markets			
Starting a business (days)			22
Stock market capitalization (% of GDP)	..	0.8	..
Military expenditures (% of GDP)	0.6	0.9	0.5
Fixed-line and mobile subscribers (per 100 people)	5	18	57
Internet users (per 100 people)	0.0	3.7	20.8
Paved roads (% of total)	45	49	..
High-technology exports (% of manufactured exports)	0	1	..
Global links			
Merchandise trade (% of GDP)	73.2	77.0	55.4
Net barter terms of trade (2000 = 100)	96	100	95
Total external debt ($ billions)	4.4	4.5	8.9
Short-term debt ($ billions)	0.8	1.2	1.5
Total debt service (% of exports)	10.4	4.8	9.6
Foreign direct investment, net inflows ($ billions)	0.1	1.0	1.2
Remittances received ($ billions)	0.3	1.8	3.0
Aid ($ millions)	102	56	53

Ecuador

Latin America & Caribbean		Lower middle income	

Population (millions)	13	Population growth (%)	1.1
Surface area (1,000 sq. km)	284	National poverty rate (% of pop.)	..
GNI ($ billions)	38.5	GNI per capita ($)	2,910
GNI, PPP ($ billions)	89.9	GNI per capita, PPP ($)	6,810

	1990	2000	2006
People			
Share of poorest 20% in nat'l consumption/income (%)	..	3.3	..
Life expectancy at birth (years)	69	73	75
Total fertility (births per woman)	3.6	2.9	2.6
Adolescent fertility (births per 1,000 women 15–19)	..	85	83
Contraceptive prevalence (% of married women 15–49)	53	66	73
Births attended by skilled health staff (% of total)	..	99	75
Under-five mortality rate (per 1,000)	57	32	24
Child malnutrition, underweight (% of under age 5)	..	..	6.2
Child immunization, measles (% of ages 12–23 mos.)	60	84	97
Primary completion rate, total (% of relevant age group)	..	98	106
Gross secondary enrollment, total (% of relevant age group)	55	57	65
Ratio of girls to boys in primary & secondary school (%)	..	100	100
HIV prevalence rate (% of population ages 15–49)	..	..	0.3
Environment			
Forests (1,000 sq. km)	138	118	109
Deforestation (average annual %, 1990–2005)			1.6
Freshwater use (% of internal resources)	..	3.9	..
Access to improved water source (% of total pop.)	73	88	94
Access to improved sanitation facilities (% of total pop.)	63	82	89
Energy use per capita (kilograms of oil equivalent)	597	674	799
Carbon dioxide emissions per capita (metric tons)	1.6	1.7	2.3
Electricity use per capita (kilowatt-hours)	479	654	714
Economy			
GDP ($ billions)	10.4	15.9	41.4
GDP growth (annual %)	2.7	2.8	3.9
GDP implicit price deflator (annual % growth)	5.9	-7.0	7.2
Value added in agriculture (% of GDP)	13	11	7
Value added in industry (% of GDP)	38	35	35
Value added in services (% of GDP)	49	55	59
Exports of goods and services (% of GDP)	33	37	34
Imports of goods and services (% of GDP)	32	31	33
Gross capital formation (% of GDP)	21	20	23
Central government revenue (% of GDP)	14.4	..	..
Central government cash surplus/deficit (% of GDP)	2.9	..	..
States and markets			
Starting a business (days)			65
Stock market capitalization (% of GDP)	0.6	4.4	9.8
Military expenditures (% of GDP)	2.0	1.7	2.3
Fixed-line and mobile subscribers (per 100 people)	5	14	78
Internet users (per 100 people)	0.0	1.5	11.7
Paved roads (% of total)	13	19	15
High-technology exports (% of manufactured exports)	0	6	8
Global links			
Merchandise trade (% of GDP)	44.2	54.2	59.7
Net barter terms of trade (2000 = 100)	114	100	110
Total external debt ($ billions)	12	14	17
Short-term debt ($ billions)	1.8	0.8	1.4
Total debt service (% of exports)	32.5	26.0	24.1
Foreign direct investment, net inflows ($ millions)	126	720	271
Remittances received ($ billions)	0.1	1.3	2.9
Aid ($ millions)	159	146	189

Egypt, Arab Rep.

Middle East & North Africa		Lower middle income	

Population (millions)	74	Population growth (%)	1.8
Surface area (1,000 sq. km)	1,001	National poverty rate (% of pop.)	17
GNI ($ billions)	100.9	GNI per capita ($)	1,360
GNI, PPP ($ billions)	366.5	GNI per capita, PPP ($)	4,940

	1990	2000	2006
People			
Share of poorest 20% in nat'l consumption/income (%)	8.6	8.6	8.9
Life expectancy at birth (years)	62	69	71
Total fertility (births per woman)	4.3	3.3	2.9
Adolescent fertility (births per 1,000 women 15–19)	..	51	41
Contraceptive prevalence (% of married women 15–49)	47	56	59
Births attended by skilled health staff (% of total)	37	61	74
Under-five mortality rate (per 1,000)	91	51	35
Child malnutrition, underweight (% of under age 5)	..	..	5.4
Child immunization, measles (% of ages 12–23 mos.)	86	98	98
Primary completion rate, total (% of relevant age group)	..	98	98
Gross secondary enrollment, total (% of relevant age group)	71	85	86
Ratio of girls to boys in primary & secondary school (%)	81	92	93
HIV prevalence rate (% of population ages 15–49)	..	..	0.1
Environment			
Forests (sq. km)	440	590	670
Deforestation (average annual %, 1990–2005)			-2.8
Freshwater use (% of internal resources)	..	3,794.4	..
Access to improved water source (% of total pop.)	94	97	98
Access to improved sanitation facilities (% of total pop.)	54	65	70
Energy use per capita (kilograms of oil equivalent)	578	683	841
Carbon dioxide emissions per capita (metric tons)	1.4	2.1	2.2
Electricity use per capita (kilowatt-hours)	690	1,011	1,245
Economy			
GDP ($ billions)	43.1	99.8	107.5
GDP growth (annual %)	5.7	5.4	6.8
GDP implicit price deflator (annual % growth)	18.4	4.9	7.4
Value added in agriculture (% of GDP)	19	17	14
Value added in industry (% of GDP)	29	33	38
Value added in services (% of GDP)	52	50	48
Exports of goods and services (% of GDP)	20	16	30
Imports of goods and services (% of GDP)	33	23	32
Gross capital formation (% of GDP)	29	20	19
Central government revenue (% of GDP)	17.7	21.3	24.1
Central government cash surplus/deficit (% of GDP)	-3.9	-3.3	-5.8
States and markets			
Starting a business (days)			9
Stock market capitalization (% of GDP)	4.1	28.8	87.0
Military expenditures (% of GDP)	4.7	3.2	2.7
Fixed-line and mobile subscribers (per 100 people)	3	10	39
Internet users (per 100 people)	0.0	0.7	8.1
Paved roads (% of total)	72	78	81
High-technology exports (% of manufactured exports)	0	0	1
Global links			
Merchandise trade (% of GDP)	36.8	18.7	31.9
Net barter terms of trade (2000 = 100)	101	100	127
Total external debt ($ billions)	33	29	29
Short-term debt ($ billions)	4.5	4.1	1.6
Total debt service (% of exports)	20.4	8.5	4.9
Foreign direct investment, net inflows ($ billions)	0.7	1.2	10.0
Remittances received ($ billions)	4.3	2.9	5.3
Aid ($ billions)	5.4	1.3	0.9

El Salvador

Latin America & Caribbean		Lower middle income	
Population (millions)	6.8	Population growth (%)	1.4
Surface area (1,000 sq. km)	21	National poverty rate (% of pop.)	37
GNI ($ billions)	18.1	GNI per capita ($)	2,680
GNI, PPP ($ billions)	37.9	GNI per capita, PPP ($)	5,610

	1990	2000	2006
People			
Share of poorest 20% in nat'l consumption/income (%)	2.4	2.8	..
Life expectancy at birth (years)	66	70	72
Total fertility (births per woman)	3.7	3.0	2.7
Adolescent fertility (births per 1,000 women 15–19)	..	90	82
Contraceptive prevalence (% of married women 15–49)	47	60	..
Births attended by skilled health staff (% of total)	52	..	..
Under-five mortality rate (per 1,000)	60	35	25
Child malnutrition, underweight (% of under age 5)	..	..	..
Child immunization, measles (% of ages 12-23 mos.)	98	97	98
Primary completion rate, total (% of relevant age group)	58	88	88
Gross secondary enrollment, total (% of relevant age group)	25	54	64
Ratio of girls to boys in primary & secondary school (%)	102	96	99
HIV prevalence rate (% of population ages 15–49)	..	..	0.9
Environment			
Forests (1,000 sq. km)	3.8	3.2	3.0
Deforestation (average annual %, 1990–2005)			1.5
Freshwater use (% of internal resources)	..	7.2	..
Access to improved water source (% of total pop.)	67	80	84
Access to improved sanitation facilities (% of total pop.)	51	61	62
Energy use per capita (kilograms of oil equivalent)	496	658	694
Carbon dioxide emissions per capita (metric tons)	0.5	0.9	0.9
Electricity use per capita (kilowatt-hours)	368	653	666
Economy			
GDP ($ billions)	4.8	13.1	18.7
GDP growth (annual %)	4.8	2.2	4.2
GDP implicit price deflator (annual % growth)	4.7	3.2	4.9
Value added in agriculture (% of GDP)	17	10	11
Value added in industry (% of GDP)	27	32	29
Value added in services (% of GDP)	55	58	60
Exports of goods and services (% of GDP)	19	27	27
Imports of goods and services (% of GDP)	31	42	47
Gross capital formation (% of GDP)	14	17	16
Central government revenue (% of GDP)	..	16.0	17.2
Central government cash surplus/deficit (% of GDP)	..	-4.7	-3.2
States and markets			
Starting a business (days)			26
Stock market capitalization (% of GDP)	..	15.5	29.3
Military expenditures (% of GDP)	2.3	0.9	0.6
Fixed-line and mobile subscribers (per 100 people)	2	22	72
Internet users (per 100 people)	0.0	1.1	9.6
Paved roads (% of total)	14	20	..
High-technology exports (% of manufactured exports)	0	6	3
Global links			
Merchandise trade (% of GDP)	38.4	60.1	59.7
Net barter terms of trade (2000 = 100)	84	100	95
Total external debt ($ billions)	2.1	4.5	9.1
Short-term debt ($ billions)	0.2	1.6	1.2
Total debt service (% of exports)	15.3	6.6	13.1
Foreign direct investment, net inflows ($ millions)	1.9	173.4	203.6
Remittances received ($ billions)	0.4	1.8	3.3
Aid ($ millions)	347	180	157

Equatorial Guinea

Sub-Saharan Africa		Upper middle income	
Population (thousands)	496	Population growth (%)	2.4
Surface area (1,000 sq. km)	28	National poverty rate (% of pop.)	..
GNI ($ billions)	4.2	GNI per capita ($)	8,510
GNI, PPP ($ billions)	8.2	GNI per capita, PPP ($)	16,620

	1990	2000	2006
People			
Share of poorest 20% in nat'l consumption/income (%)	..	..	..
Life expectancy at birth (years)	47	49	51
Total fertility (births per woman)	5.9	5.7	5.4
Adolescent fertility (births per 1,000 women 15–19)	..	131	124
Contraceptive prevalence (% of married women 15–49)	..	..	..
Births attended by skilled health staff (% of total)	..	65	..
Under-five mortality rate (per 1,000)	170	200	206
Child malnutrition, underweight (% of under age 5)	..	15.7	..
Child immunization, measles (% of ages 12–23 mos.)	88	51	51
Primary completion rate, total (% of relevant age group)	..	56	58
Gross secondary enrollment, total (% of relevant age group)	..	33	..
Ratio of girls to boys in primary & secondary school (%)	..	86	..
HIV prevalence rate (% of population ages 15–49)	..	..	3.2
Environment			
Forests (1,000 sq. km)	19	17	16
Deforestation (average annual %, 1990–2005)			0.9
Freshwater use (% of internal resources)	..	0.4	..
Access to improved water source (% of total pop.)	..	43	43
Access to improved sanitation facilities (% of total pop.)	..	52	53
Energy use per capita (kilograms of oil equivalent)	..	..	..
Carbon dioxide emissions per capita (metric tons)	0.3	0.6	11.5
Electricity use per capita (kilowatt-hours)	..	..	..
Economy			
GDP ($ millions)	132	1,254	8,565
GDP growth (annual %)	3.3	13.5	-5.6
GDP implicit price deflator (annual % growth)	-2.5	46.6	19.4
Value added in agriculture (% of GDP)	62	10	3
Value added in industry (% of GDP)	11	86	94
Value added in services (% of GDP)	28	4	3
Exports of goods and services (% of GDP)	32	99	95
Imports of goods and services (% of GDP)	70	85	50
Gross capital formation (% of GDP)	17	61	42
Central government revenue (% of GDP)	..	..	..
Central government cash surplus/deficit (% of GDP)	..	..	..
States and markets			
Starting a business (days)			136
Stock market capitalization (% of GDP)	..	..	..
Military expenditures (% of GDP)	..	..	..
Fixed-line and mobile subscribers (per 100 people)	0	3	22
Internet users (per 100 people)	0.0	0.2	1.6
Paved roads (% of total)	..	..	..
High-technology exports (% of manufactured exports)	..	..	..
Global links			
Merchandise trade (% of GDP)	95.3	123.4	129.6
Net barter terms of trade (2000 = 100)	38	100	176
Total external debt ($ millions)	241	248	278
Short-term debt ($ millions)	26	44	54
Total debt service (% of exports)	12.1	..	..
Foreign direct investment, net inflows ($ billions)	0.0	0.1	1.7
Remittances received ($ millions)	1.0	..	..
Aid ($ millions)	60	21	27

Eritrea

Sub-Saharan Africa				Low income

Population (millions)	4.7	Population growth (%)		3.6
Surface area (1,000 sq. km)	118	National poverty rate (% of pop.)		..
GNI ($ millions)	888	GNI per capita ($)		190
GNI, PPP ($ billions)	3.2	GNI per capita, PPP ($)		680

	1990	2000	2006
People			
Share of poorest 20% in nat'l consumption/income (%)	..	..	..
Life expectancy at birth (years)	49	54	57
Total fertility (births per woman)	6.2	5.7	5.1
Adolescent fertility (births per 1,000 women 15–19)	..	92	75
Contraceptive prevalence (% of married women 15–49)	..	8	..
Births attended by skilled health staff (% of total)	..	28	..
Under-five mortality rate (per 1,000)	147	97	74
Child malnutrition, underweight (% of under age 5)	..	34.5	..
Child immunization, measles (% of ages 12–23 mos.)	18	86	95
Primary completion rate, total (% of relevant age group)	..	36	48
Gross secondary enrollment, total (% of relevant age group)	..	25	31
Ratio of girls to boys in primary & secondary school (%)	..	77	72
HIV prevalence rate (% of population ages 15–49)	..	..	2.4
Environment			
Forests (1,000 sq. km)	16	16	16
Deforestation (average annual %, 1990–2005)			0.3
Freshwater use (% of internal resources)	..	10.7	..
Access to improved water source (% of total pop.)	43	54	60
Access to improved sanitation facilities (% of total pop.)	7	8	9
Energy use per capita (kilograms of oil equivalent)	..	..	..
Carbon dioxide emissions per capita (metric tons)	..	0.2	0.2
Electricity use per capita (kilowatt-hours)	..	..	..
Economy			
GDP ($ millions)	477	634	1,085
GDP growth (annual %)	..	-13.1	-1.0
GDP implicit price deflator (annual % growth)	..	25.0	12.0
Value added in agriculture (% of GDP)	31	15	17
Value added in industry (% of GDP)	12	23	23
Value added in services (% of GDP)	57	62	60
Exports of goods and services (% of GDP)	11	15	8
Imports of goods and services (% of GDP)	45	82	50
Gross capital formation (% of GDP)	8	32	19
Central government revenue (% of GDP)		..	..
Central government cash surplus/deficit (% of GDP)	..	..	..
States and markets			
Starting a business (days)			84
Stock market capitalization (% of GDP)	..	..	..
Military expenditures (% of GDP)	..	36.4	..
Fixed-line and mobile subscribers (per 100 people)	0	1	2
Internet users (per 100 people)	0.0	0.1	2.1
Paved roads (% of total)	19	22	..
High-technology exports (% of manufactured exports)	..	0	..
Global links			
Merchandise trade (% of GDP)	77.0	80.2	50.7
Net barter terms of trade (2000 = 100)	..	..	..
Total external debt ($ millions)	..	311.1	799.9
Short-term debt ($ millions)	..	13.1	18.6
Total debt service (% of exports)	..	3.1	..
Foreign direct investment, net inflows ($ millions)	..	27.9	3.7
Remittances received ($ millions)	..	3.0	..
Aid ($ millions)	..	175.8	129.1

Estonia

Population (millions)	1.3	Population growth (%)	-0.3
Surface area (1,000 sq. km)	45	National poverty rate (% of pop.)	..
GNI ($ billions)	15.3	GNI per capita ($)	11,400
GNI, PPP ($ billions)	24.3	GNI per capita, PPP ($)	18,090

	1990	2000	2006
People			
Share of poorest 20% in nat'l consumption/income (%)	9.9	6.6	6.8
Life expectancy at birth (years)	69	71	73
Total fertility (births per woman)	2.0	1.3	1.5
Adolescent fertility (births per 1,000 women 15–19)	..	26	22
Contraceptive prevalence (% of married women 15–49)	..	..	..
Births attended by skilled health staff (% of total)	..	100	100
Under-five mortality rate (per 1,000)	16	11	7
Child malnutrition, underweight (% of under age 5)	..	..	..
Child immunization, measles (% of ages 12–23 mos.)	..	93	96
Primary completion rate, total (% of relevant age group)	..	91	106
Gross secondary enrollment, total (% of relevant age group)	100	92	100
Ratio of girls to boys in primary & secondary school (%)	103	100	100
HIV prevalence rate (% of population ages 15–49)	..	..	1.3
Environment			
Forests (1,000 sq. km)	22	22	23
Deforestation (average annual %, 1990–2005)		.	-0.4
Freshwater use (% of internal resources)	..	1.2	..
Access to improved water source (% of total pop.)	100	100	100
Access to improved sanitation facilities (% of total pop.)	97	97	97
Energy use per capita (kilograms of oil equivalent)	6,107	3,307	3,786
Carbon dioxide emissions per capita (metric tons)	18.1	11.7	14.0
Electricity use per capita (kilowatt-hours)	5,757	4,632	5,567
Economy			
GDP ($ billions)	5.0	5.6	16.4
GDP growth (annual %)	-7.1	7.9	11.4
GDP implicit price deflator (annual % growth)	33.7	8.3	6.1
Value added in agriculture (% of GDP)	17	5	3
Value added in industry (% of GDP)	50	28	29
Value added in services (% of GDP)	34	67	68
Exports of goods and services (% of GDP)	60	85	80
Imports of goods and services (% of GDP)	54	89	90
Gross capital formation (% of GDP)	30	29	38
Central government revenue (% of GDP)	..	31.3	31.8
Central government cash surplus/deficit (% of GDP)	..	0.2	3.6
States and markets			
Starting a business (days)			7
Stock market capitalization (% of GDP)	..	32.8	36.3
Military expenditures (% of GDP)	0.5	1.4	1.4
Fixed-line and mobile subscribers (per 100 people)	20	79	164
Internet users (per 100 people)	0.0	28.6	56.6
Paved roads (% of total)	52	20	23
High-technology exports (% of manufactured exports)	..	30	13
Global links			
Merchandise trade (% of GDP)	..	157.9	138.6
Net barter terms of trade (2000 = 100)	..	..	..
Total external debt ($ billions)	..	..	..
Short-term debt ($ billions)	..	..	..
Total debt service (% of exports)	..	..	..
Foreign direct investment, net inflows ($ billions)	0.1	0.4	1.6
Remittances received ($ millions)	..	3.0	401.9
Aid ($ millions)	15	64	..

Ethiopia

Sub-Saharan Africa		Low income	
Population (millions)	77	Population growth (%)	2.6
Surface area (1,000 sq. km)	1,104	National poverty rate (% of pop.)	44
GNI ($ billions)	12.9	GNI per capita ($)	170
GNI, PPP ($ billions)	49.0	GNI per capita, PPP ($)	630

	1990	2000	2006
People			
Share of poorest 20% in nat'l consumption/income (%)	..	9.1	..
Life expectancy at birth (years)	48	50	52
Total fertility (births per woman)	6.8	6.0	5.3
Adolescent fertility (births per 1,000 women 15–19)	..	114	97
Contraceptive prevalence (% of married women 15–49)	4	8	15
Births attended by skilled health staff (% of total)	..	6	6
Under-five mortality rate (per 1,000)	204	151	123
Child malnutrition, underweight (% of under age 5)	..	42.0	34.6
Child immunization, measles (% of ages 12–23 mos.)	38	52	63
Primary completion rate, total (% of relevant age group)	26	22	49
Gross secondary enrollment, total (% of relevant age group)	13	13	27
Ratio of girls to boys in primary & secondary school (%)	68	65	81
HIV prevalence rate (% of population ages 15–49)	..	..	1.4
Environment			
Forests (1,000 sq. km)	151	137	130
Deforestation (average annual %, 1990–2005)			1.0
Freshwater use (% of internal resources)	..	4.6	..
Access to improved water source (% of total pop.)	23	22	22
Access to improved sanitation facilities (% of total pop.)	3	8	13
Energy use per capita (kilograms of oil equivalent)	296	284	288
Carbon dioxide emissions per capita (metric tons)	0.1	0.1	0.1
Electricity use per capita (kilowatt-hours)	21	23	34
Economy			
GDP ($ billions)	12.1	7.9	13.3
GDP growth (annual %)	2.7	5.9	9.0
GDP implicit price deflator (annual % growth)	3.3	6.0	7.8
Value added in agriculture (% of GDP)	54	47	47
Value added in industry (% of GDP)	11	13	13
Value added in services (% of GDP)	35	40	39
Exports of goods and services (% of GDP)	6	12	16
Imports of goods and services (% of GDP)	9	25	42
Gross capital formation (% of GDP)	13	19	20
Central government revenue (% of GDP)	..	15.0	..
Central government cash surplus/deficit (% of GDP)	..	–7.9	..
States and markets			
Starting a business (days)			16
Stock market capitalization (% of GDP)	..	..	..
Military expenditures (% of GDP)	6.5	7.9	2.6
Fixed-line and mobile subscribers (per 100 people)	0	0	2
Internet users (per 100 people)	0.0	0.0	0.2
Paved roads (% of total)	15	12	13
High-technology exports (% of manufactured exports)	..	0	..
Global links			
Merchandise trade (% of GDP)	11.4	22.1	42.1
Net barter terms of trade (2000 = 100)	..	100	99
Total external debt ($ billions)	8.6	5.5	2.3
Short-term debt ($ millions)	145	79	114
Total debt service (% of exports)	39.0	12.9	6.8
Foreign direct investment, net inflows ($ millions)	12	135	364
Remittances received ($ millions)	5.0	53.0	172.0
Aid ($ billions)	1.0	0.7	1.9

Faeroe Islands

High income

Population (thousands)	48	Population growth (%)		0.0
Surface area (1,000 sq. km)	1.4	National poverty rate (% of pop.)		..
GNI ($ billions)	..	GNI per capita ($)		..
GNI, PPP ($ billions)	..	GNI per capita, PPP ($)		..

	1990	2000	2006
People			
Share of poorest 20% in nat'l consumption/income (%)	..	..	..
Life expectancy at birth (years)	..	..	79
Total fertility (births per woman)	..	..	..
Adolescent fertility (births per 1,000 women 15-19)	..	..	..
Contraceptive prevalence (% of married women 15-49)	..	..	..
Births attended by skilled health staff (% of total)	..	..	..
Under-five mortality rate (per 1,000)	..	..	..
Child malnutrition, underweight (% of under age 5)	..	..	..
Child immunization, measles (% of ages 12-23 mos.)	..	..	..
Primary completion rate, total (% of relevant age group)	..	..	..
Gross secondary enrollment, total (% of relevant age group)	..	..	..
Ratio of girls to boys in primary & secondary school (%)	..	..	..
HIV prevalence rate (% of population ages 15-49)	..	..	..
Environment			
Forests (1,000 sq. km)	..	..	..
Deforestation (average annual %, 1990-2005)			..
Freshwater use (% of internal resources)	..	..	..
Access to improved water source (% of total pop.)	..	..	..
Access to improved sanitation facilities (% of total pop.)	..	..	..
Energy use per capita (kilograms of oil equivalent)	..	..	..
Carbon dioxide emissions per capita (metric tons)	..	..	13.7
Electricity use per capita (kilowatt-hours)	..	..	..
Economy			
GDP ($ billions)	..	..	..
GDP growth (annual %)	..	..	..
GDP implicit price deflator (annual % growth)	..	..	..
Value added in agriculture (% of GDP)	..	..	..
Value added in industry (% of GDP)	..	..	..
Value added in services (% of GDP)	..	..	..
Exports of goods and services (% of GDP)	..	..	..
Imports of goods and services (% of GDP)	..	..	..
Gross capital formation (% of GDP)	..	..	..
Central government revenue (% of GDP)	..	..	..
Central government cash surplus/deficit (% of GDP)	..	..	..
States and markets			
Starting a business (days)			..
Stock market capitalization (% of GDP)	..	..	..
Military expenditures (% of GDP)	..	..	..
Fixed-line and mobile subscribers (per 100 people)	..	..	151
Internet users (per 100 people)	..	..	70.5
Paved roads (% of total)	..	..	..
High-technology exports (% of manufactured exports)	0	0	1
Global links			
Merchandise trade (% of GDP)	..	..	..
Net barter terms of trade (2000 = 100)	..	..	..
Total external debt ($ billions)	..	..	..
Short-term debt ($ billions)	..	..	..
Total debt service (% of exports)	..	..	..
Foreign direct investment, net inflows ($ billions)	..	..	..
Remittances received ($ billions)	..	..	..
Aid ($ billions)	..	..	..

Fiji

East Asia & Pacific   **Lower middle income**

Population (thousands)	833	Population growth (%)	0.6
Surface area (1,000 sq. km)	18	National poverty rate (% of pop.)	..
GNI ($ billions)	3.1	GNI per capita ($)	3,720
GNI, PPP ($ billions)	3.7	GNI per capita, PPP ($)	4,450

	1990	2000	2006
People			
Share of poorest 20% in nat'l consumption/income (%)	..	..	..
Life expectancy at birth (years)	67	67	69
Total fertility (births per woman)	3.4	3.1	2.8
Adolescent fertility (births per 1,000 women 15–19)	..	46	34
Contraceptive prevalence (% of married women 15–49)	..	44	..
Births attended by skilled health staff (% of total)	..	99	..
Under-five mortality rate (per 1,000)	22	18	18
Child malnutrition, underweight (% of under age 5)	..	..	..
Child immunization, measles (% of ages 12–23 mos.)	84	85	99
Primary completion rate, total (% of relevant age group)	..	100	98
Gross secondary enrollment, total (% of relevant age group)	64	80	86
Ratio of girls to boys in primary & secondary school (%)	98	103	102
HIV prevalence rate (% of population ages 15–49)	..	..	0.1
Environment			
Forests (1,000 sq. km)	9.8	10.0	10.0
Deforestation (average annual %, 1990–2005)			−0.1
Freshwater use (% of internal resources)	..	0.0	..
Access to improved water source (% of total pop.)	..	47	47
Access to improved sanitation facilities (% of total pop.)	68	71	72
Energy use per capita (kilograms of oil equivalent)	..	..	..
Carbon dioxide emissions per capita (metric tons)	1.1	1.1	1.3
Electricity use per capita (kilowatt-hours)	..	..	..
Economy			
GDP ($ billions)	1.3	1.7	3.1
GDP growth (annual %)	7.4	−1.7	3.6
GDP implicit price deflator (annual % growth)	2.8	−4.5	3.4
Value added in agriculture (% of GDP)	20	17	15
Value added in industry (% of GDP)	24	22	26
Value added in services (% of GDP)	56	61	59
Exports of goods and services (% of GDP)	62	65	55
Imports of goods and services (% of GDP)	67	70	73
Gross capital formation (% of GDP)	14	17	19
Central government revenue (% of GDP)	26.8	..	25.2
Central government cash surplus/deficit (% of GDP)	0.9	..	−2.9
States and markets			
Starting a business (days)			46
Stock market capitalization (% of GDP)	..	14.5	20.3
Military expenditures (% of GDP)	2.3	2.0	1.2
Fixed-line and mobile subscribers (per 100 people)	6	18	38
Internet users (per 100 people)	0.0	1.5	9.6
Paved roads (% of total)	45	49	..
High-technology exports (% of manufactured exports)	12	0	2
Global links			
Merchandise trade (% of GDP)	93.6	83.9	79.1
Net barter terms of trade (2000 = 100)	142	100	103
Total external debt ($ millions)	403	134	237
Short-term debt ($ millions)	12	16	111
Total debt service (% of exports)	12.0	2.8	1.0
Foreign direct investment, net inflows ($ millions)	91.9	−1.7	157.1
Remittances received ($ millions)	22	24	165
Aid ($ millions)	50	29	56

Finland

High income

Population (millions)	5.3	Population growth (%)	0.4
Surface area (1,000 sq. km)	338	National poverty rate (% of pop.)	..
GNI ($ billions)	217.8	GNI per capita ($)	41,360
GNI, PPP ($ billions)	174.7	GNI per capita, PPP ($)	33,170

	1990	2000	2006
People			
Share of poorest 20% in nat'l consumption/income (%)	..	9.6	..
Life expectancy at birth (years)	75	78	79
Total fertility (births per woman)	1.8	1.7	1.8
Adolescent fertility (births per 1,000 women 15–19)	..	10	10
Contraceptive prevalence (% of married women 15–49)	77	..	..
Births attended by skilled health staff (% of total)	..	100	..
Under-five mortality rate (per 1,000)	7	4	4
Child malnutrition, underweight (% of under age 5)	..	..	..
Child immunization, measles (% of ages 12–23 mos.)	97	96	97
Primary completion rate, total (% of relevant age group)	102	97	100
Gross secondary enrollment, total (% of relevant age group)	116	124	111
Ratio of girls to boys in primary & secondary school (%)	109	105	102
HIV prevalence rate (% of population ages 15–49)	..	..	0.1
Environment			
Forests (1,000 sq. km)	222	225	225
Deforestation (average annual %, 1990–2005)			-0.1
Freshwater use (% of internal resources)	..	2.3	..
Access to improved water source (% of total pop.)	100	100	100
Access to improved sanitation facilities (% of total pop.)	100	100	100
Energy use per capita (kilograms of oil equivalent)	5,851	6,371	6,664
Carbon dioxide emissions per capita (metric tons)	10.3	10.0	12.6
Electricity use per capita (kilowatt-hours)	12,487	15,286	16,120
Economy			
GDP ($ billions)	139.6	121.9	210.7
GDP growth (annual %)	0.1	5.0	5.5
GDP implicit price deflator (annual % growth)	5.8	2.6	1.3
Value added in agriculture (% of GDP)	6	4	3
Value added in industry (% of GDP)	33	34	32
Value added in services (% of GDP)	60	63	65
Exports of goods and services (% of GDP)	23	44	44
Imports of goods and services (% of GDP)	24	33	38
Gross capital formation (% of GDP)	29	20	21
Central government revenue (% of GDP)	..	40.9	38.3
Central government cash surplus/deficit (% of GDP)	..	6.8	3.9
States and markets			
Starting a business (days)			14
Stock market capitalization (% of GDP)	16.3	241.0	126.0
Military expenditures (% of GDP)	1.5	1.3	1.4
Fixed-line and mobile subscribers (per 100 people)	59	127	144
Internet users (per 100 people)	0.4	37.2	55.5
Paved roads (% of total)	61	62	65
High-technology exports (% of manufactured exports)	8	27	22
Global links			
Merchandise trade (% of GDP)	38.4	66.1	69.3
Net barter terms of trade (2000 = 100)	..	..	..
Total external debt ($ billions)	..	..	..
Short-term debt ($ billions)	..	..	..
Total debt service (% of exports)	..	..	..
Foreign direct investment, net inflows ($ billions)	0.8	9.1	5.3
Remittances received ($ millions)	63	473	698
Aid ($ billions)	..	..	..

France

High income

Population (millions)	61	Population growth (%)	0.6
Surface area (1,000 sq. km)	552	National poverty rate (% of pop.)	..
GNI ($ billions)	2,306.7	GNI per capita ($)	36,560
GNI, PPP ($ billions)	1,974.9	GNI per capita, PPP ($)	32,240

	1990	2000	2006
People			
Share of poorest 20% in nat'l consumption/income (%)	..	..	..
Life expectancy at birth (years)	77	79	81
Total fertility (births per woman)	1.8	1.9	2.0
Adolescent fertility (births per 1,000 women 15–19)	..	8	7
Contraceptive prevalence (% of married women 15–49)	81	..	..
Births attended by skilled health staff (% of total)	..	..	..
Under-five mortality rate (per 1,000)	9	6	4
Child malnutrition, underweight (% of under age 5)	..	..	..
Child immunization, measles (% of ages 12–23 mos.)	71	84	87
Primary completion rate, total (% of relevant age group)	99	99	..
Gross secondary enrollment, total (% of relevant age group)	98	110	114
Ratio of girls to boys in primary & secondary school (%)	102	100	100
HIV prevalence rate (% of population ages 15–49)	..	..	0.4
Environment			
Forests (1,000 sq. km)	145	154	156
Deforestation (average annual %, 1990–2005)			-0.5
Freshwater use (% of internal resources)	..	22.4	..
Access to improved water source (% of total pop.)	100	100	100
Access to improved sanitation facilities (% of total pop.)	..	..	..
Energy use per capita (kilograms of oil equivalent)	4,015	4,387	4,534
Carbon dioxide emissions per capita (metric tons)	6.4	6.1	6.2
Electricity use per capita (kilowatt-hours)	6,127	7,486	7,938
Economy			
GDP ($ billions)	1,244.5	1,328.0	2,248.1
GDP growth (annual %)	2.6	3.9	2.0
GDP implicit price deflator (annual % growth)	2.6	1.4	2.3
Value added in agriculture (% of GDP)	4	3	2
Value added in industry (% of GDP)	27	23	21
Value added in services (% of GDP)	70	74	77
Exports of goods and services (% of GDP)	21	29	27
Imports of goods and services (% of GDP)	23	28	28
Gross capital formation (% of GDP)	23	20	21
Central government revenue (% of GDP)	..	42.8	43.0
Central government cash surplus/deficit (% of GDP)	..	-1.7	-2.3
States and markets			
Starting a business (days)			7
Stock market capitalization (% of GDP)	25.2	108.9	108.0
Military expenditures (% of GDP)	3.4	2.5	2.4
Fixed-line and mobile subscribers (per 100 people)	50	107	140
Internet users (per 100 people)	0.1	14.4	49.1
Paved roads (% of total)	..	100	100
High-technology exports (% of manufactured exports)	16	24	21
Global links			
Merchandise trade (% of GDP)	36.2	50.2	45.6
Net barter terms of trade (2000 = 100)	103	100	102
Total external debt ($ billions)	..	..	..
Short-term debt ($ billions)	..	..	..
Total debt service (% of exports)	..	..	..
Foreign direct investment, net inflows ($ billions)	13	42	81
Remittances received ($ billions)	4.0	8.6	12.5
Aid ($ billions)	..	..	..

French Polynesia

Population (thousands)	259	Population growth (%)	1.4
Surface area (1,000 sq. km)	4.0	National poverty rate (% of pop.)	..
GNI ($ billions)	..	GNI per capita ($)	..
GNI, PPP ($ billions)	..	GNI per capita, PPP ($)	..

	1990	2000	2006
People			
Share of poorest 20% in nat'l consumption/income (%)	..	..	..
Life expectancy at birth (years)	70	73	74
Total fertility (births per woman)	3.3	2.5	2.3
Adolescent fertility (births per 1,000 women 15–19)	..	49	36
Contraceptive prevalence (% of married women 15–49)	..	..	..
Births attended by skilled health staff (% of total)	..	99	..
Under-five mortality rate (per 1,000)	..	..	..
Child malnutrition, underweight (% of under age 5)	..	..	..
Child immunization, measles (% of ages 12–23 mos.)	..	..	..
Primary completion rate, total (% of relevant age group)	..	..	..
Gross secondary enrollment, total (% of relevant age group)	..	..	..
Ratio of girls to boys in primary & secondary school (%)	..	..	..
HIV prevalence rate (% of population ages 15–49)	..	..	..
Environment			
Forests (1,000 sq. km)	1.1	1.1	1.1
Deforestation (average annual %, 1990–2005)			0.00
Freshwater use (% of internal resources)		..	..
Access to improved water source (% of total pop.)	100	100	100
Access to improved sanitation facilities (% of total pop.)	98	98	98
Energy use per capita (kilograms of oil equivalent)		..	..
Carbon dioxide emissions per capita (metric tons)	3.1	2.7	2.7
Electricity use per capita (kilowatt-hours)	..	..	..
Economy			
GDP ($ billions)	3.2	3.4	..
GDP growth (annual %)	2.2	4.0	..
GDP implicit price deflator (annual % growth)	0.8	1.0	..
Value added in agriculture (% of GDP)	1	5	..
Value added in industry (% of GDP)	..	..	..
Value added in services (% of GDP)	..	..	..
Exports of goods and services (% of GDP)	1	5	..
Imports of goods and services (% of GDP)	28	24	..
Gross capital formation (% of GDP)	..	..	..
Central government revenue (% of GDP)	..	..	..
Central government cash surplus/deficit (% of GDP)	..	..	..
States and markets			
Starting a business (days)			..
Stock market capitalization (% of GDP)	..	..	..
Military expenditures (% of GDP)	..		
Fixed-line and mobile subscribers (per 100 people)	20	40	79
Internet users (per 100 people)	0.0	6.4	25.1
Paved roads (% of total)	..	..	..
High-technology exports (% of manufactured exports)	0	11	12
Global links			
Merchandise trade (% of GDP)	32.7	34.6	..
Net barter terms of trade (2000 = 100)	..	100	86
Total external debt ($ billions)	..	..	..
Short-term debt ($ billions)	..	..	..
Total debt service (% of exports)	..	..	..
Foreign direct investment, net inflows ($ millions)	..	10.9	30.7
Remittances received ($ millions)	..	..	600.7
Aid ($ millions)	260	403	580

Gabon

Sub-Saharan Africa		Upper middle income	
Population (millions)	1.3	Population growth (%)	1.5
Surface area (1,000 sq. km)	268	National poverty rate (% of pop.)	..
GNI ($ billions)	7.0	GNI per capita ($)	5,360
GNI, PPP ($ billions)	14.7	GNI per capita, PPP ($)	11,180

	1990	2000	2006
People			
Share of poorest 20% in nat'l consumption/income (%)	..	..	..
Life expectancy at birth (years)	61	58	57
Total fertility (births per woman)	4.7	3.6	3.1
Adolescent fertility (births per 1,000 women 15–19)	..	103	85
Contraceptive prevalence (% of married women 15–49)	..	33	..
Births attended by skilled health staff (% of total)	..	86	..
Under-five mortality rate (per 1,000)	92	91	91
Child malnutrition, underweight (% of under age 5)	..	8.8	..
Child immunization, measles (% of ages 12–23 mos.)	76	55	55
Primary completion rate, total (% of relevant age group)	58	76	..
Gross secondary enrollment, total (% of relevant age group)	..	49	..
Ratio of girls to boys in primary & secondary school (%)	..	96	..
HIV prevalence rate (% of population ages 15–49)	..	..	7.9
Environment			
Forests (1,000 sq. km)	219	218	218
Deforestation (average annual %, 1990–2005)			0.05
Freshwater use (% of internal resources)	..	0.1	..
Access to improved water source (% of total pop.)	..	86	88
Access to improved sanitation facilities (% of total pop.)	..	36	36
Energy use per capita (kilograms of oil equivalent)	1,354	1,304	1,333
Carbon dioxide emissions per capita (metric tons)	6.5	1.2	1.1
Electricity use per capita (kilowatt-hours)	951	914	999
Economy			
GDP ($ billions)	6.0	5.1	9.5
GDP growth (annual %)	5.2	-1.9	1.2
GDP implicit price deflator (annual % growth)	15.4	28.1	7.9
Value added in agriculture (% of GDP)	7	6	5
Value added in industry (% of GDP)	43	56	61
Value added in services (% of GDP)	50	38	34
Exports of goods and services (% of GDP)	46	69	65
Imports of goods and services (% of GDP)	31	33	24
Gross capital formation (% of GDP)	22	22	23
Central government revenue (% of GDP)	..	..	..
Central government cash surplus/deficit (% of GDP)	..	..	..
States and markets			
Starting a business (days)			58
Stock market capitalization (% of GDP)	..	..	..
Military expenditures (% of GDP)	..	1.8	1.2
Fixed-line and mobile subscribers (per 100 people)	2	13	61
Internet users (per 100 people)	0.0	1.3	6.2
Paved roads (% of total)	8	10	10
High-technology exports (% of manufactured exports)	..	7	32
Global links			
Merchandise trade (% of GDP)	52.5	71.0	76.8
Net barter terms of trade (2000 = 100)	157	100	179
Total external debt ($ billions)	4.0	3.9	4.4
Short-term debt ($ millions)	693	377	434
Total debt service (% of exports)	6.4	9.9	5.3
Foreign direct investment, net inflows ($ millions)	73	-43	268
Remittances received ($ millions)	..	6.0	6.9
Aid ($ millions)	131	12	31

Gambia, The

Sub-Saharan Africa   **Low income**

Population (millions)	1.7	Population growth (%)		2.8
Surface area (1,000 sq. km)	11	National poverty rate (% of pop.)		61
GNI ($ millions)	488	GNI per capita ($)		290
GNI, PPP ($ billions)	1.8	GNI per capita, PPP ($)		1,110

	1990	2000	2006
People			
Share of poorest 20% in nat'l consumption/income (%)	4.4	4.0	..
Life expectancy at birth (years)	51	57	59
Total fertility (births per woman)	6.0	5.3	4.8
Adolescent fertility (births per 1,000 women 15–19)	..	120	106
Contraceptive prevalence (% of married women 15–49)	12	10	..
Births attended by skilled health staff (% of total)	44	55	57
Under-five mortality rate (per 1,000)	153	132	113
Child malnutrition, underweight (% of under age 5)	..	15.4	..
Child immunization, measles (% of ages 12-23 mos.)	86	85	95
Primary completion rate, total (% of relevant age group)	44	53	63
Gross secondary enrollment, total (% of relevant age group)	17	33	45
Ratio of girls to boys in primary & secondary school (%)	66	82	102
HIV prevalence rate (% of population ages 15–49)	..	..	2.4
Environment			
Forests (1,000 sq. km)	4.4	4.6	4.7
Deforestation (average annual %, 1990–2005)			-0.4
Freshwater use (% of internal resources)	..	1.0	
Access to improved water source (% of total pop.)	..	82	82
Access to improved sanitation facilities (% of total pop.)	..	53	53
Energy use per capita (kilograms of oil equivalent)	..	..	..
Carbon dioxide emissions per capita (metric tons)	0.2	0.2	0.2
Electricity use per capita (kilowatt-hours)	..	..	..
Economy			
GDP ($ millions)	317	421	511
GDP growth (annual %)	3.6	5.5	4.5
GDP implicit price deflator (annual % growth)	12.0	3.7	4.1
Value added in agriculture (% of GDP)	29	36	33
Value added in industry (% of GDP)	13	13	13
Value added in services (% of GDP)	58	51	54
Exports of goods and services (% of GDP)	60	48	45
Imports of goods and services (% of GDP)	72	57	65
Gross capital formation (% of GDP)	22	17	24
Central government revenue (% of GDP)	19.4	..	..
Central government cash surplus/deficit (% of GDP)	0.1	..	..
States and markets			
Starting a business (days)			32
Stock market capitalization (% of GDP)	..	..	..
Military expenditures (% of GDP)	1.1	0.8	0.5
Fixed-line and mobile subscribers (per 100 people)	1	3	27
Internet users (per 100 people)	0.0	0.9	3.6
Paved roads (% of total)	32	35	19
High-technology exports (% of manufactured exports)	..	3	1
Global links			
Merchandise trade (% of GDP)	69.1	48.0	51.9
Net barter terms of trade (2000 = 100)	100	100	80
Total external debt ($ millions)	369	483	725
Short-term debt ($ millions)	16	27	18
Total debt service (% of exports)	22.2	..	12.4
Foreign direct investment, net inflows ($ millions)	14	44	82
Remittances received ($ millions)	10	14	64
Aid ($ millions)	97	49	74

Georgia

Europe & Central Asia **Lower middle income**

Population (millions)	4.4	Population growth (%)	-0.9
Surface area (1,000 sq. km)	70	National poverty rate (% of pop.)	55
GNI ($ billions)	7.0	GNI per capita ($)	1,580
GNI, PPP ($ billions)	17.2	GNI per capita, PPP ($)	3,880

	1990	2000	2006
People			
Share of poorest 20% in nat'l consumption/income (%)	..	5.9	5.4
Life expectancy at birth (years)	70	70	71
Total fertility (births per woman)	2.1	1.5	1.4
Adolescent fertility (births per 1,000 women 15–19)	..	43	31
Contraceptive prevalence (% of married women 15–49)	..	41	47
Births attended by skilled health staff (% of total)	..	96	92
Under-five mortality rate (per 1,000)	46	37	32
Child malnutrition, underweight (% of under age 5)	..	..	..
Child immunization, measles (% of ages 12–23 mos.)	16	73	95
Primary completion rate, total (% of relevant age group)	..	101	85
Gross secondary enrollment, total (% of relevant age group)	95	79	85
Ratio of girls to boys in primary & secondary school (%)	98	99	103
HIV prevalence rate (% of population ages 15–49)	..	..	0.2
Environment			
Forests (1,000 sq. km)	28	28	28
Deforestation (average annual %, 1990–2005)			0.00
Freshwater use (% of internal resources)	..	6.2	..
Access to improved water source (% of total pop.)	80	81	82
Access to improved sanitation facilities (% of total pop.)	97	95	94
Energy use per capita (kilograms of oil equivalent)	2,259	613	718
Carbon dioxide emissions per capita (metric tons)	3.2	1.0	0.9
Electricity use per capita (kilowatt-hours)	2,673	1,360	1,672
Economy			
GDP ($ billions)	7.7	3.1	7.7
GDP growth (annual %)	-14.8	1.8	9.4
GDP implicit price deflator (annual % growth)	22.4	4.7	8.4
Value added in agriculture (% of GDP)	32	22	13
Value added in industry (% of GDP)	33	22	25
Value added in services (% of GDP)	35	56	62
Exports of goods and services (% of GDP)	40	23	33
Imports of goods and services (% of GDP)	46	40	57
Gross capital formation (% of GDP)	31	27	27
Central government revenue (% of GDP)	..	10.4	22.5
Central government cash surplus/deficit (% of GDP)	..	-1.6	1.6
States and markets			
Starting a business (days)			11
Stock market capitalization (% of GDP)	..	0.8	8.6
Military expenditures (% of GDP)	..	0.6	3.1
Fixed-line and mobile subscribers (per 100 people)	10	15	51
Internet users (per 100 people)	0.0	0.5	7.5
Paved roads (% of total)	94	93	39
High-technology exports (% of manufactured exports)	..	11	16
Global links			
Merchandise trade (% of GDP)	..	33.8	60.3
Net barter terms of trade (2000 = 100)	..	..	..
Total external debt ($ billions)	0.1	1.6	2.0
Short-term debt ($ millions)	0.0	43.7	111.4
Total debt service (% of exports)	..	12.5	8.8
Foreign direct investment, net inflows ($ billions)	..	0.1	1.1
Remittances received ($ millions)	..	274.0	485.3
Aid ($ millions)	0.2	169.4	360.6

Germany

Population (millions)	82	Population growth (%)		-0.1
Surface area (1,000 sq. km)	357	National poverty rate (% of pop.)		..
GNI ($ billions)	3,032.6	GNI per capita ($)		36,810
GNI, PPP ($ billions)	2,692.3	GNI per capita, PPP ($)		32,680

	1990	2000	2006
People			
Share of poorest 20% in nat'l consumption/income (%)	..	8.5	..
Life expectancy at birth (years)	75	78	79
Total fertility (births per woman)	1.5	1.4	1.3
Adolescent fertility (births per 1,000 women 15–19)	..	12	10
Contraceptive prevalence (% of married women 15–49)	75	..	..
Births attended by skilled health staff (% of total)	..	..	100
Under-five mortality rate (per 1,000)	9	5	4
Child malnutrition, underweight (% of under age 5)	..	..	..
Child immunization, measles (% of ages 12–23 mos.)	75	93	94
Primary completion rate, total (% of relevant age group)	..	105	95
Gross secondary enrollment, total (% of relevant age group)	98	98	100
Ratio of girls to boys in primary & secondary school (%)	99	99	99
HIV prevalence rate (% of population ages 15–49)	..	..	0.1
Environment			
Forests (1,000 sq. km)	107	111	111
Deforestation (average annual %, 1990–2005)			-0.2
Freshwater use (% of internal resources)	..	44.0	..
Access to improved water source (% of total pop.)	100	100	100
Access to improved sanitation facilities (% of total pop.)	100	100	100
Energy use per capita (kilograms of oil equivalent)	4,485	4,180	4,180
Carbon dioxide emissions per capita (metric tons)	12.3	9.7	9.8
Electricity use per capita (kilowatt-hours)	6,640	6,680	7,111
Economy			
GDP ($ billions)	1,714.5	1,900.2	2,896.9
GDP growth (annual %)	5.3	3.2	2.8
GDP implicit price deflator (annual % growth)	3.4	-0.7	0.3
Value added in agriculture (% of GDP)	1	1	1
Value added in industry (% of GDP)	37	30	30
Value added in services (% of GDP)	61	68	69
Exports of goods and services (% of GDP)	25	33	45
Imports of goods and services (% of GDP)	25	33	40
Gross capital formation (% of GDP)	23	22	18
Central government revenue (% of GDP)	..	30.3	28.9
Central government cash surplus/deficit (% of GDP)	..	1.4	-1.4
States and markets			
Starting a business (days)			18
Stock market capitalization (% of GDP)	20.7	66.8	56.5
Military expenditures (% of GDP)	2.5	1.5	1.3
Fixed-line and mobile subscribers (per 100 people)	40	120	168
Internet users (per 100 people)	0.1	30.2	46.9
Paved roads (% of total)	99	..	..
High-technology exports (% of manufactured exports)	11	18	17
Global links			
Merchandise trade (% of GDP)	45.3	55.2	69.8
Net barter terms of trade (2000 = 100)	110	100	97
Total external debt ($ billions)	..	..	..
Short-term debt ($ billions)	..	..	..
Total debt service (% of exports)	..	..	..
Foreign direct investment, net inflows ($ billions)	3.0	210.1	43.4
Remittances received ($ billions)	4.9	3.6	6.7
Aid ($ billions)	..	..	..

Ghana

Sub-Saharan Africa		Low income	
Population (millions)	23	Population growth (%)	2.1
Surface area (1,000 sq. km)	239	National poverty rate (% of pop.)	29
GNI ($ billions)	11.8	GNI per capita ($)	510
GNI, PPP ($ billions)	28.4	GNI per capita, PPP ($)	1,240

	1990	2000	2006
People			
Share of poorest 20% in nat'l consumption/income (%)	6.7	5.6	..
Life expectancy at birth (years)	57	58	60
Total fertility (births per woman)	5.7	4.6	3.9
Adolescent fertility (births per 1,000 women 15–19)	..	77	58
Contraceptive prevalence (% of married women 15–49)	13	22	17
Births attended by skilled health staff (% of total)	40	44	50
Under-five mortality rate (per 1,000)	120	113	120
Child malnutrition, underweight (% of under age 5)	..	..	..
Child immunization, measles (% of ages 12–23 mos.)	61	84	85
Primary completion rate, total (% of relevant age group)	61	62	71
Gross secondary enrollment, total (% of relevant age group)	34	38	46
Ratio of girls to boys in primary & secondary school (%)	79	89	94
HIV prevalence rate (% of population ages 15–49)	..	..	2.3
Environment			
Forests (1,000 sq. km)	74	61	55
Deforestation (average annual %, 1990–2005)			2.0
Freshwater use (% of internal resources)	..	3.2	..
Access to improved water source (% of total pop.)	55	70	75
Access to improved sanitation facilities (% of total pop.)	15	18	18
Energy use per capita (kilograms of oil equivalent)	343	392	397
Carbon dioxide emissions per capita (metric tons)	0.2	0.3	0.3
Electricity use per capita (kilowatt-hours)	291	302	266
Economy			
GDP ($ billions)	5.9	5.0	12.9
GDP growth (annual %)	3.3	3.7	6.2
GDP implicit price deflator (annual % growth)	31.2	27.2	14.6
Value added in agriculture (% of GDP)	45	35	37
Value added in industry (% of GDP)	17	25	25
Value added in services (% of GDP)	38	39	37
Exports of goods and services (% of GDP)	17	49	39
Imports of goods and services (% of GDP)	26	67	64
Gross capital formation (% of GDP)	14	24	32
Central government revenue (% of GDP)	12.5	18.1	23.8
Central government cash surplus/deficit (% of GDP)	..	−6.5	−2.9
States and markets			
Starting a business (days)			42
Stock market capitalization (% of GDP)	1.2	10.1	25.0
Military expenditures (% of GDP)	0.5	1.0	0.7
Fixed-line and mobile subscribers (per 100 people)	0	2	24
Internet users (per 100 people)	0.0	0.1	2.7
Paved roads (% of total)	20	30	..
High-technology exports (% of manufactured exports)	2	2	0
Global links			
Merchandise trade (% of GDP)	35.7	93.3	71.3
Net barter terms of trade (2000 = 100)	100	100	132
Total external debt ($ billions)	3.7	6.1	3.2
Short-term debt ($ billions)	0.3	0.6	1.1
Total debt service (% of exports)	38.1	15.6	4.9
Foreign direct investment, net inflows ($ millions)	15	166	435
Remittances received ($ millions)	6.0	32.0	105.3
Aid ($ billions)	0.6	0.6	1.2

Greece

Population (millions)	11	Population growth (%)			0.4
Surface area (1,000 sq. km)	132	National poverty rate (% of pop.)			..
GNI ($ billions)	305.3	GNI per capita ($)			27,390
GNI, PPP ($ billions)	344.1	GNI per capita, PPP ($)			30,870

	1990	2000	2006
People			
Share of poorest 20% in nat'l consumption/income (%)	..	6.7	..
Life expectancy at birth (years)	77	78	79
Total fertility (births per woman)	1.4	1.3	1.4
Adolescent fertility (births per 1,000 women 15–19)	..	11	9
Contraceptive prevalence (% of married women 15–49)	..	..	..
Births attended by skilled health staff (% of total)	..	..	..
Under-five mortality rate (per 1,000)	11	7	4
Child malnutrition, underweight (% of under age 5)	..	..	..
Child immunization, measles (% of ages 12–23 mos.)	76	88	88
Primary completion rate, total (% of relevant age group)	99	..	100
Gross secondary enrollment, total (% of relevant age group)	94	89	102
Ratio of girls to boys in primary & secondary school (%)	99	103	99
HIV prevalence rate (% of population ages 15–49)	..	..	0.2
Environment			
Forests (1,000 sq. km)	33	36	38
Deforestation (average annual %, 1990–2005)			-0.9
Freshwater use (% of internal resources)	..	13.4	..
Access to improved water source (% of total pop.)	..	..	..
Access to improved sanitation facilities (% of total pop.)	..	..	..
Energy use per capita (kilograms of oil equivalent)	2,183	2,548	2,790
Carbon dioxide emissions per capita (metric tons)	7.1	8.3	8.7
Electricity use per capita (kilowatt-hours)	3,233	4,539	5,242
Economy			
GDP ($ billions)	108.1	144.2	308.4
GDP growth (annual %)	0.0	4.5	4.3
GDP implicit price deflator (annual % growth)	20.7	3.4	3.3
Value added in agriculture (% of GDP)	8	6	3
Value added in industry (% of GDP)	26	21	21
Value added in services (% of GDP)	66	73	76
Exports of goods and services (% of GDP)	15	22	19
Imports of goods and services (% of GDP)	25	33	27
Gross capital formation (% of GDP)	23	25	26
Central government revenue (% of GDP)	..	36.2	33.6
Central government cash surplus/deficit (% of GDP)	..	-3.2	-4.5
States and markets			
Starting a business (days)			38
Stock market capitalization (% of GDP)	14.1	76.9	67.5
Military expenditures (% of GDP)	3.6	3.8	3.2
Fixed-line and mobile subscribers (per 100 people)	39	106	155
Internet users (per 100 people)	0.0	9.2	18.4
Paved roads (% of total)	92	92	..
High-technology exports (% of manufactured exports)	2	13	11
Global links			
Merchandise trade (% of GDP)	25.8	31.4	27.3
Net barter terms of trade (2000 = 100)	103	100	..
Total external debt ($ billions)	..	..	..
Short-term debt ($ billions)	..	..	..
Total debt service (% of exports)	..	..	..
Foreign direct investment, net inflows ($ billions)	1.0	1.1	5.4
Remittances received ($ billions)	1.8	2.2	1.5
Aid ($ billions)	..	..	..

Greenland

High income

Population (thousands)	57	Population growth (%)		−0.3
Surface area (1,000 sq. km)	410	National poverty rate (% of pop.)		..
GNI ($ billions)	..	GNI per capita ($)		..
GNI, PPP ($ billions)	..	GNI per capita, PPP ($)		..

	1990	2000	2006
People			
Share of poorest 20% in nat'l consumption/income (%)	..	..	..
Life expectancy at birth (years)	65	66	..
Total fertility (births per woman)	2.4	2.3	..
Adolescent fertility (births per 1,000 women 15-19)		..	..
Contraceptive prevalence (% of married women 15-49)	..	..	..
Births attended by skilled health staff (% of total)	..	..	..
Under-five mortality rate (per 1,000)	..	..	..
Child malnutrition, underweight (% of under age 5)	..	..	..
Child immunization, measles (% of ages 12-23 mos.)	..	..	..
Primary completion rate, total (% of relevant age group)	..	..	..
Gross secondary enrollment, total (% of relevant age group)	..	..	..
Ratio of girls to boys in primary & secondary school (%)	..	..	..
HIV prevalence rate (% of population ages 15-49)	..	..	..
Environment			
Forests (1,000 sq. km)		..	..
Deforestation (average annual %, 1990-2005)			..
Freshwater use (% of internal resources)	..	..	..
Access to improved water source (% of total pop.)	..	..	..
Access to improved sanitation facilities (% of total pop.)	..	..	..
Energy use per capita (kilograms of oil equivalent)	..	..	..
Carbon dioxide emissions per capita (metric tons)	9.9	9.9	*10.0*
Electricity use per capita (kilowatt-hours)	..	..	..
Economy			
GDP ($ billions)	..	..	..
GDP growth (annual %)	..	..	..
GDP implicit price deflator (annual % growth)	..	..	..
Value added in agriculture (% of GDP)	..	..	..
Value added in industry (% of GDP)	..	..	..
Value added in services (% of GDP)	..	..	..
Exports of goods and services (% of GDP)	..	..	..
Imports of goods and services (% of GDP)	..	..	..
Gross capital formation (% of GDP)	..	..	..
Central government revenue (% of GDP)	..	..	..
Central government cash surplus/deficit (% of GDP)	..	..	..
States and markets			
Starting a business (days)			..
Stock market capitalization (% of GDP)	..	..	..
Military expenditures (% of GDP)			
Fixed-line and mobile subscribers (per 100 people)	30	75	..
Internet users (per 100 people)	0.0	31.7	66.8
Paved roads (% of total)	..	..	..
High-technology exports (% of manufactured exports)	10	30	..
Global links			
Merchandise trade (% of GDP)	..	..	..
Net barter terms of trade (2000 = 100)	..	..	..
Total external debt ($ billions)	..	..	..
Short-term debt ($ billions)	..	..	..
Total debt service (% of exports)	..	..	..
Foreign direct investment, net inflows ($ billions)	..	..	..
Remittances received ($ billions)	..	..	..
Aid ($ billions)	..	..	..

Grenada

Latin America & Caribbean		Upper middle income	
Population (thousands)	108	Population growth (%)	1.5
Surface area (sq. km)	340	National poverty rate (% of pop.)	..
GNI ($ millions)	495	GNI per capita ($)	4,650
GNI, PPP ($ millions)	934	GNI per capita, PPP ($)	8,770

	1990	2000	2006
People			
Share of poorest 20% in nat'l consumption/income (%)	..	..	..
Life expectancy at birth (years)	..	72	..
Total fertility (births per woman)	..	3.2	2.4
Adolescent fertility (births per 1,000 women 15–19)	..	55	44
Contraceptive prevalence (% of married women 15–49)	54	54	54
Births attended by skilled health staff (% of total)	..	100	100
Under-five mortality rate (per 1,000)	37	26	20
Child malnutrition, underweight (% of under age 5)	..	..	..
Child immunization, measles (% of ages 12–23 mos.)	85	92	98
Primary completion rate, total (% of relevant age group)	..	74	93
Gross secondary enrollment, total (% of relevant age group)	100	108	100
Ratio of girls to boys in primary & secondary school (%)	94	96	99
HIV prevalence rate (% of population ages 15–49)	..	..	..
Environment			
Forests (sq. km)	40	40	40
Deforestation (average annual %, 1990–2005)			0.00
Freshwater use (% of internal resources)	..	..	..
Access to improved water source (% of total pop.)	..	95	95
Access to improved sanitation facilities (% of total pop.)	97	96	96
Energy use per capita (kilograms of oil equivalent)	..	..	..
Carbon dioxide emissions per capita (metric tons)	1.3	2.0	2.0
Electricity use per capita (kilowatt-hours)	..	..	..
Economy			
GDP ($ millions)	221	410	525
GDP growth (annual %)	5.2	7.6	0.7
GDP implicit price deflator (annual % growth)	-1.4	0.3	2.6
Value added in agriculture (% of GDP)	13	8	7
Value added in industry (% of GDP)	18	24	29
Value added in services (% of GDP)	69	68	64
Exports of goods and services (% of GDP)	42	58	33
Imports of goods and services (% of GDP)	63	76	76
Gross capital formation (% of GDP)	38	44	63
Central government revenue (% of GDP)	..	..	..
Central government cash surplus/deficit (% of GDP)	..	..	..
States and markets			
Starting a business (days)			20
Stock market capitalization (% of GDP)	..	..	..
Military expenditures (% of GDP)	..	..	..
Fixed-line and mobile subscribers (per 100 people)	16	35	68
Internet users (per 100 people)	0.0	4.1	..
Paved roads (% of total)	55	61	..
High-technology exports (% of manufactured exports)	0	30	0
Global links			
Merchandise trade (% of GDP)	59.7	70.1	58.1
Net barter terms of trade (2000 = 100)	..	100	90
Total external debt ($ millions)	111	201	492
Short-term debt ($ millions)	13	22	35
Total debt service (% of exports)	3.1	6.0	6.5
Foreign direct investment, net inflows ($ millions)	13	37	119
Remittances received ($ millions)	18	22	25
Aid ($ millions)	14	17	27

Guam

Population (thousands)	171	Population growth (%)	1.5
Surface area (sq. km)	540	National poverty rate (% of pop.)	..
GNI ($ billions)	..	GNI per capita ($)	..
GNI, PPP ($ billions)	..	GNI per capita, PPP ($)	..

	1990	2000	2006
People			
Share of poorest 20% in nat'l consumption/income (%)	..	..	..
Life expectancy at birth (years)	72	74	75
Total fertility (births per woman)	3.1	2.8	2.6
Adolescent fertility (births per 1,000 women 15–19)	..	64	52
Contraceptive prevalence (% of married women 15–49)	..	..	..
Births attended by skilled health staff (% of total)	..	99	..
Under-five mortality rate (per 1,000)	..	..	..
Child malnutrition, underweight (% of under age 5)	..	..	..
Child immunization, measles (% of ages 12–23 mos.)	..	..	..
Primary completion rate, total (% of relevant age group)	..	..	..
Gross secondary enrollment, total (% of relevant age group)	..	..	..
Ratio of girls to boys in primary & secondary school (%)	..	..	..
HIV prevalence rate (% of population ages 15–49)	..	..	..
Environment			
Forests (sq. km)	260	260	260
Deforestation (average annual %, 1990–2005)			0.00
Freshwater use (% of internal resources)	..	..	
Access to improved water source (% of total pop.)	100	100	100
Access to improved sanitation facilities (% of total pop.)	99	99	99
Energy use per capita (kilograms of oil equivalent)	..	..	..
Carbon dioxide emissions per capita (metric tons)	16.93	26.23	..
Electricity use per capita (kilowatt-hours)	..	..	..
Economy			
GDP ($ billions)	..	..	..
GDP growth (annual %)	..	..	..
GDP implicit price deflator (annual % growth)	..	..	..
Value added in agriculture (% of GDP)	..	..	..
Value added in industry (% of GDP)	..	..	..
Value added in services (% of GDP)	..	..	..
Exports of goods and services (% of GDP)	..	..	..
Imports of goods and services (% of GDP)	..	..	..
Gross capital formation (% of GDP)	..	..	..
Central government revenue (% of GDP)	..	..	..
Central government cash surplus/deficit (% of GDP)	..	..	..
States and markets			
Starting a business (days)			..
Stock market capitalization (% of GDP)	..	..	..
Military expenditures (% of GDP)	..	..	..
Fixed-line and mobile subscribers (per 100 people)	29	65	..
Internet users (per 100 people)	0.0	16.1	38.6
Paved roads (% of total)	..	..	..
High-technology exports (% of manufactured exports)	..	..	..
Global links			
Merchandise trade (% of GDP)	..	..	..
Net barter terms of trade (2000 = 100)	..	..	..
Total external debt ($ billions)	..	..	..
Short-term debt ($ billions)	..	..	..
Total debt service (% of exports)	..	..	..
Foreign direct investment, net inflows ($ billions)	..	..	..
Remittances received ($ billions)	..	..	..
Aid ($ billions)	..	..	..

Guatemala

Latin America & Caribbean		Lower middle income	
Population (millions)	13	Population growth (%)	2.5
Surface area (1,000 sq. km)	109	National poverty rate (% of pop.)	56
GNI ($ billions)	33.7	GNI per capita ($)	2,590
GNI, PPP ($ billions)	66.7	GNI per capita, PPP ($)	5,120

	1990	2000	2006
People			
Share of poorest 20% in nat'l consumption/income (%)	2.2	3.5	3.9
Life expectancy at birth (years)	63	68	70
Total fertility (births per woman)	5.6	4.8	4.2
Adolescent fertility (births per 1,000 women 15–19)	..	118	109
Contraceptive prevalence (% of married women 15–49)	..	43	..
Births attended by skilled health staff (% of total)	..	41	..
Under-five mortality rate (per 1,000)	82	53	41
Child malnutrition, underweight (% of under age 5)	..	17.7	..
Child immunization, measles (% of ages 12–23 mos.)	68	88	95
Primary completion rate, total (% of relevant age group)	..	58	77
Gross secondary enrollment, total (% of relevant age group)	23	38	53
Ratio of girls to boys in primary & secondary school (%)	..	89	92
HIV prevalence rate (% of population ages 15–49)	..	..	0.9
Environment			
Forests (1,000 sq. km)	47	42	39
Deforestation (average annual %, 1990–2005)			1.2
Freshwater use (% of internal resources)	..	1.8	..
Access to improved water source (% of total pop.)	79	91	95
Access to improved sanitation facilities (% of total pop.)	58	78	86
Energy use per capita (kilograms of oil equivalent)	503	636	628
Carbon dioxide emissions per capita (metric tons)	0.6	0.9	1.0
Electricity use per capita (kilowatt-hours)	223	343	522
Economy			
GDP ($ billions)	7.7	19.3	35.3
GDP growth (annual %)	3.1	3.6	4.5
GDP implicit price deflator (annual % growth)	40.5	6.8	6.3
Value added in agriculture (% of GDP)	26	23	22
Value added in industry (% of GDP)	20	20	19
Value added in services (% of GDP)	54	57	59
Exports of goods and services (% of GDP)	21	20	16
Imports of goods and services (% of GDP)	25	29	31
Gross capital formation (% of GDP)	14	18	19
Central government revenue (% of GDP)	7.9	10.2	10.7
Central government cash surplus/deficit (% of GDP)	–1.9	–1.8	–1.7
States and markets			
Starting a business (days)			26
Stock market capitalization (% of GDP)	..	1.2	..
Military expenditures (% of GDP)	1.5	0.8	0.4
Fixed-line and mobile subscribers (per 100 people)	2	14	65
Internet users (per 100 people)	0.0	0.7	10.1
Paved roads (% of total)	25	35	..
High-technology exports (% of manufactured exports)	0	8	3
Global links			
Merchandise trade (% of GDP)	36.8	38.8	50.8
Net barter terms of trade (2000 = 100)	115	100	90
Total external debt ($ billions)	2.8	3.9	5.5
Short-term debt ($ billions)	0.4	1.2	1.5
Total debt service (% of exports)	13.6	8.4	4.8
Foreign direct investment, net inflows ($ millions)	48	230	354
Remittances received ($ billions)	0.1	0.6	3.6
Aid ($ millions)	201	263	487

Guinea

Population (millions)	9.2	Population growth (%)	2.0
Surface area (1,000 sq. km)	246	National poverty rate (% of pop.)	..
GNI ($ billions)	3.7	GNI per capita ($)	400
GNI, PPP ($ billions)	10.4	GNI per capita, PPP ($)	1,130

	1990	2000	2006
People			
Share of poorest 20% in nat'l consumption/income (%)	..	..	..
Life expectancy at birth (years)	47	53	56
Total fertility (births per woman)	6.6	6.0	5.5
Adolescent fertility (births per 1,000 women 15-19)	..	173	153
Contraceptive prevalence (% of married women 15-49)	..	6	9
Births attended by skilled health staff (% of total)	31	35	38
Under-five mortality rate (per 1,000)	235	184	161
Child malnutrition, underweight (% of under age 5)	..	21.2	22.5
Child immunization, measles (% of ages 12-23 mos.)	35	42	67
Primary completion rate, total (% of relevant age group)	19	33	64
Gross secondary enrollment, total (% of relevant age group)	10	17	35
Ratio of girls to boys in primary & secondary school (%)	45	61	74
HIV prevalence rate (% of population ages 15-49)	..	..	1.5
Environment			
Forests (1,000 sq. km)	74	69	67
Deforestation (average annual %, 1990-2005)			0.6
Freshwater use (% of internal resources)	..	0.7	..
Access to improved water source (% of total pop.)	44	49	50
Access to improved sanitation facilities (% of total pop.)	14	17	18
Energy use per capita (kilograms of oil equivalent)	..	..	..
Carbon dioxide emissions per capita (metric tons)	0.2	0.2	0.2
Electricity use per capita (kilowatt-hours)	..	..	..
Economy			
GDP ($ billions)	2.7	3.1	3.3
GDP growth (annual %)	4.3	1.9	2.8
GDP implicit price deflator (annual % growth)	17.3	11.1	38.4
Value added in agriculture (% of GDP)	24	20	13
Value added in industry (% of GDP)	33	33	37
Value added in services (% of GDP)	43	47	50
Exports of goods and services (% of GDP)	31	24	32
Imports of goods and services (% of GDP)	33	28	35
Gross capital formation (% of GDP)	25	20	13
Central government revenue (% of GDP)	..	12.0	..
Central government cash surplus/deficit (% of GDP)	..	-2.4	..
States and markets			
Starting a business (days)			41
Stock market capitalization (% of GDP)	..	..	..
Military expenditures (% of GDP)	2.4	1.5	2.0
Fixed-line and mobile subscribers (per 100 people)	0	1	2
Internet users (per 100 people)	0.0	0.1	0.5
Paved roads (% of total)	15	17	..
High-technology exports (% of manufactured exports)	..	0	..
Global links			
Merchandise trade (% of GDP)	52.3	41.1	57.3
Net barter terms of trade (2000 = 100)	122	100	204
Total external debt ($ billions)	2.5	3.4	3.3
Short-term debt ($ millions)	172	335	229
Total debt service (% of exports)	20.0	20.4	19.9
Foreign direct investment, net inflows ($ millions)	17.9	9.9	108.0
Remittances received ($ millions)	27.0	1.0	42.0
Aid ($ millions)	292	153	164

Guinea-Bissau

Sub-Saharan Africa | | **Low income**

Population (millions)	1.6	Population growth (%)	3.0
Surface area (1,000 sq. km)	36	National poverty rate (% of pop.)	66
GNI ($ millions)	307	GNI per capita ($)	190
GNI, PPP ($ millions)	761	GNI per capita, PPP ($)	460

	1990	2000	2006
People			
Share of poorest 20% in nat'l consumption/income (%)	..	..	..
Life expectancy at birth (years)	42	45	46
Total fertility (births per woman)	7.1	7.1	7.1
Adolescent fertility (births per 1,000 women 15–19)	..	197	190
Contraceptive prevalence (% of married women 15–49)	..	8	10
Births attended by skilled health staff (% of total)	..	35	39
Under-five mortality rate (per 1,000)	240	218	200
Child malnutrition, underweight (% of under age 5)	..	21.9	..
Child immunization, measles (% of ages 12–23 mos.)	53	59	60
Primary completion rate, total (% of relevant age group)	..	27	..
Gross secondary enrollment, total (% of relevant age group)	..	18	..
Ratio of girls to boys in primary & secondary school (%)	..	65	..
HIV prevalence rate (% of population ages 15–49)	..	..	3.8
Environment			
Forests (1,000 sq. km)	22	21	21
Deforestation (average annual %, 1990–2005)			0.4
Freshwater use (% of internal resources)	..	1.1	..
Access to improved water source (% of total pop.)	..	58	59
Access to improved sanitation facilities (% of total pop.)	..	34	35
Energy use per capita (kilograms of oil equivalent)	..	..	..
Carbon dioxide emissions per capita (metric tons)	0.2	0.2	0.2
Electricity use per capita (kilowatt-hours)	..	..	..
Economy			
GDP ($ millions)	244	215	304
GDP growth (annual %)	6.1	7.5	4.2
GDP implicit price deflator (annual % growth)	30.2	3.3	-3.8
Value added in agriculture (% of GDP)	61	56	62
Value added in industry (% of GDP)	19	13	11
Value added in services (% of GDP)	21	31	27
Exports of goods and services (% of GDP)	10	32	42
Imports of goods and services (% of GDP)	37	52	53
Gross capital formation (% of GDP)	30	11	17
Central government revenue (% of GDP)	..	..	..
Central government cash surplus/deficit (% of GDP)	..	..	..
States and markets			
Starting a business (days)			233
Stock market capitalization (% of GDP)	..	..	..
Military expenditures (% of GDP)	2.1	4.4	4.0
Fixed-line and mobile subscribers (per 100 people)	1	1	7
Internet users (per 100 people)	0.0	0.2	2.2
Paved roads (% of total)	8	28	..
High-technology exports (% of manufactured exports)	..	..	..
Global links			
Merchandise trade (% of GDP)	43.0	56.2	60.8
Net barter terms of trade (2000 = 100)	..	..	..
Total external debt ($ millions)	692	804	711
Short-term debt ($ millions)	56.5	64.2	8.1
Total debt service (% of exports)	31.1	30.1	40.2
Foreign direct investment, net inflows ($ millions)	2.0	0.7	42.0
Remittances received ($ millions)	1.0	2.0	28.0
Aid ($ millions)	126	80	82

Guyana

Latin America & Caribbean　　　　　　　　**Lower middle income**

Population (thousands)	739	Population growth (%)	-0.1
Surface area (1,000 sq. km)	215	National poverty rate (% of pop.)	..
GNI ($ millions)	849	GNI per capita ($)	1,150
GNI, PPP ($ billions)	2.5	GNI per capita, PPP ($)	3,410

	1990	2000	2006
People			
Share of poorest 20% in nat'l consumption/income (%)	..	4.5	..
Life expectancy at birth (years)	62	63	66
Total fertility (births per woman)	2.6	2.5	2.4
Adolescent fertility (births per 1,000 women 15–19)	..	74	64
Contraceptive prevalence (% of married women 15–49)	31	37	35
Births attended by skilled health staff (% of total)	..	86	..
Under-five mortality rate (per 1,000)	88	70	62
Child malnutrition, underweight (% of under age 5)	..	11.9	..
Child immunization, measles (% of ages 12–23 mos.)	73	86	90
Primary completion rate, total (% of relevant age group)	90	114	123
Gross secondary enrollment, total (% of relevant age group)	79	90	105
Ratio of girls to boys in primary & secondary school (%)	101	99	98
HIV prevalence rate (% of population ages 15–49)	..	..	2.4
Environment			
Forests (1,000 sq. km)	151	151	151
Deforestation (average annual %, 1990–2005)			0.00
Freshwater use (% of internal resources)	..	0.7	..
Access to improved water source (% of total pop.)	..	83	83
Access to improved sanitation facilities (% of total pop.)	..	69	70
Energy use per capita (kilograms of oil equivalent)	..	..	..
Carbon dioxide emissions per capita (metric tons)	1.5	2.1	2.0
Electricity use per capita (kilowatt-hours)	..	..	..
Economy			
GDP ($ millions)	397	713	896
GDP growth (annual %)	-3.0	-1.4	4.8
GDP implicit price deflator (annual % growth)	56.4	6.6	7.9
Value added in agriculture (% of GDP)	38	31	31
Value added in industry (% of GDP)	25	29	25
Value added in services (% of GDP)	37	40	44
Exports of goods and services (% of GDP)	63	96	88
Imports of goods and services (% of GDP)	80	111	124
Gross capital formation (% of GDP)	31	24	26
Central government revenue (% of GDP)	..	..	..
Central government cash surplus/deficit (% of GDP)	..	..	..
States and markets			
Starting a business (days)			44
Stock market capitalization (% of GDP)	..	..	20.9
Military expenditures (% of GDP)	0.9	..	..
Fixed-line and mobile subscribers (per 100 people)	2	15	53
Internet users (per 100 people)	0.0	6.8	21.6
Paved roads (% of total)	7	7	..
High-technology exports (% of manufactured exports)	..	2	0
Global links			
Merchandise trade (% of GDP)	143.2	150.3	165.8
Net barter terms of trade (2000 = 100)	..	100	105
Total external debt ($ billions)	2.0	1.4	1.2
Short-term debt ($ millions)	75	119	162
Total debt service (% of exports)	20.7	9.7	3.4
Foreign direct investment, net inflows ($ millions)	7.9	67.1	102.4
Remittances received ($ millions)	0.0	27.0	218.1
Aid ($ millions)	168	107	173

Haiti

Latin America & Caribbean		Low income	
Population (millions)	9.4	Population growth (%)	1.6
Surface area (1,000 sq. km)	28	National poverty rate (% of pop.)	..
GNI ($ billions)	4.0	GNI per capita ($)	430
GNI, PPP ($ billions)	10.1	GNI per capita, PPP ($)	1,070

	1990	2000	2006
People			
Share of poorest 20% in nat'l consumption/income (%)	..	2.4	..
Life expectancy at birth (years)	55	58	60
Total fertility (births per woman)	5.4	4.2	3.6
Adolescent fertility (births per 1,000 women 15-19)	..	56	48
Contraceptive prevalence (% of married women 15-49)	10	28	32
Births attended by skilled health staff (% of total)	23	24	26
Under-five mortality rate (per 1,000)	152	109	80
Child malnutrition, underweight (% of under age 5)	..	13.9	18.9
Child immunization, measles (% of ages 12-23 mos.)	31	55	58
Primary completion rate, total (% of relevant age group)	28	..	..
Gross secondary enrollment, total (% of relevant age group)	21	..	..
Ratio of girls to boys in primary & secondary school (%)	94	..	..
HIV prevalence rate (% of population ages 15-49)	..	..	2.2
Environment			
Forests (1,000 sq. km)	1.2	1.1	1.1
Deforestation (average annual %, 1990-2005)			0.7
Freshwater use (% of internal resources)	..	7.6	..
Access to improved water source (% of total pop.)	47	54	54
Access to improved sanitation facilities (% of total pop.)	24	28	30
Energy use per capita (kilograms of oil equivalent)	223	238	269
Carbon dioxide emissions per capita (metric tons)	0.1	0.2	0.2
Electricity use per capita (kilowatt-hours)	58	35	37
Economy			
GDP ($ billions)	2.9	3.8	5.0
GDP growth (annual %)	-0.1	0.4	2.3
GDP implicit price deflator (annual % growth)	14.1	13.5	12.7
Value added in agriculture (% of GDP)	..	28	..
Value added in industry (% of GDP)	..	17	..
Value added in services (% of GDP)	..	55	..
Exports of goods and services (% of GDP)	18	12	14
Imports of goods and services (% of GDP)	20	32	43
Gross capital formation (% of GDP)	13	26	29
Central government revenue (% of GDP)	..	..	..
Central government cash surplus/deficit (% of GDP)	..	..	..
States and markets			
Starting a business (days)			202
Stock market capitalization (% of GDP)	..	..	..
Military expenditures (% of GDP)	..	..	..
Fixed-line and mobile subscribers (per 100 people)	1	1	7
Internet users (per 100 people)	0.0	0.2	6.9
Paved roads (% of total)	22	24	..
High-technology exports (% of manufactured exports)	14	..	..
Global links			
Merchandise trade (% of GDP)	17.2	35.2	44.5
Net barter terms of trade (2000 = 100)	132	100	89
Total external debt ($ billions)	0.9	1.0	1.2
Short-term debt ($ millions)	101	90	123
Total debt service (% of exports)	11.1	3.8	3.2
Foreign direct investment, net inflows ($ millions)	8.0	13.3	160.0
Remittances received ($ billions)	0.1	0.6	1.1
Aid ($ millions)	167	208	581

Honduras

Latin America & Caribbean | **Lower middle income**

Population (millions)	7.0	Population growth (%)	2.0
Surface area (1,000 sq. km)	112	National poverty rate (% of pop.)	51
GNI ($ billions)	8.8	GNI per capita ($)	1,270
GNI, PPP ($ billions)	23.9	GNI per capita, PPP ($)	3,420

	1990	2000	2006
People			
Share of poorest 20% in nat'l consumption/income (%)	2.8	3.3	..
Life expectancy at birth (years)	66	68	70
Total fertility (births per woman)	5.1	4.0	3.4
Adolescent fertility (births per 1,000 women 15–19)	..	107	95
Contraceptive prevalence (% of married women 15–49)	47	62	65
Births attended by skilled health staff (% of total)	45	56	67
Under-five mortality rate (per 1,000)	58	40	27
Child malnutrition, underweight (% of under age 5)	..	12.5	8.6
Child immunization, measles (% of ages 12–23 mos.)	90	98	91
Primary completion rate, total (% of relevant age group)	64	..	89
Gross secondary enrollment, total (% of relevant age group)	33	..	76
Ratio of girls to boys in primary & secondary school (%)	106	..	109
HIV prevalence rate (% of population ages 15–49)	..	..	1.5
Environment			
Forests (1,000 sq. km)	74	54	46
Deforestation (average annual %, 1990–2005)			3.0
Freshwater use (% of internal resources)	..	0.9	..
Access to improved water source (% of total pop.)	84	87	87
Access to improved sanitation facilities (% of total pop.)	50	65	69
Energy use per capita (kilograms of oil equivalent)	494	486	566
Carbon dioxide emissions per capita (metric tons)	0.5	0.8	1.1
Electricity use per capita (kilowatt-hours)	373	519	626
Economy			
GDP ($ billions)	3.0	6.0	9.2
GDP growth (annual %)	0.1	5.7	6.0
GDP implicit price deflator (annual % growth)	21.2	9.7	5.1
Value added in agriculture (% of GDP)	22	16	14
Value added in industry (% of GDP)	26	32	31
Value added in services (% of GDP)	51	52	55
Exports of goods and services (% of GDP)	37	41	41
Imports of goods and services (% of GDP)	40	55	66
Gross capital formation (% of GDP)	23	31	33
Central government revenue (% of GDP)	..	..	19.4
Central government cash surplus/deficit (% of GDP)	..	..	-1.3
States and markets			
Starting a business (days)			21
Stock market capitalization (% of GDP)	1.3	8.8	..
Military expenditures (% of GDP)	..	0.6	0.6
Fixed-line and mobile subscribers (per 100 people)	2	7	42
Internet users (per 100 people)	0.0	1.2	4.8
Paved roads (% of total)	21	20	..
High-technology exports (% of manufactured exports)	0	0	1
Global links			
Merchandise trade (% of GDP)	57.9	70.9	79.6
Net barter terms of trade (2000 = 100)	78	100	83
Total external debt ($ billions)	3.7	5.4	4.1
Short-term debt ($ millions)	199	374	533
Total debt service (% of exports)	35.3	12.9	5.1
Foreign direct investment, net inflows ($ millions)	44	282	385
Remittances received ($ billions)	0.1	0.4	2.4
Aid ($ millions)	448	449	587

Hong Kong, China

High income

Population (millions)	6.9	Population growth (%)	0.6
Surface area (1,000 sq. km)	1.1	National poverty rate (% of pop.)	..
GNI ($ billions)	199.1	GNI per capita ($)	29,040
GNI, PPP ($ billions)	268.8	GNI per capita, PPP ($)	39,200

	1990	2000	2006
People			
Share of poorest 20% in nat'l consumption/income (%)	..	..	..
Life expectancy at birth (years)	77	81	82
Total fertility (births per woman)	1.3	1.0	1.0
Adolescent fertility (births per 1,000 women 15–19)	..	6	5
Contraceptive prevalence (% of married women 15–49)	86	..	..
Births attended by skilled health staff (% of total)	..	100	100
Under-five mortality rate (per 1,000)	..	..	..
Child malnutrition, underweight (% of under age 5)	..	..	..
Child immunization, measles (% of ages 12–23 mos.)	..	..	..
Primary completion rate, total (% of relevant age group)	102	108	..
Gross secondary enrollment, total (% of relevant age group)	80	81	85
Ratio of girls to boys in primary & secondary school (%)	103	96	..
HIV prevalence rate (% of population ages 15–49)	..	..	..
Environment			
Forests (1,000 sq. km)	..	..	..
Deforestation (average annual %, 1990–2005)	..	..	..
Freshwater use (% of internal resources)	..	..	..
Access to improved water source (% of total pop.)	..	..	..
Access to improved sanitation facilities (% of total pop.)	..	..	..
Energy use per capita (kilograms of oil equivalent)	1,869	2,385	2,653
Carbon dioxide emissions per capita (metric tons)	4.6	5.8	5.5
Electricity use per capita (kilowatt-hours)	4,178	5,447	5,878
Economy			
GDP ($ billions)	76.9	169.1	189.8
GDP growth (annual %)	1.9	10.2	6.8
GDP implicit price deflator (annual % growth)	9.6	–5.6	–0.1
Value added in agriculture (% of GDP)	0	0	0
Value added in industry (% of GDP)	24	13	9
Value added in services (% of GDP)	75	87	91
Exports of goods and services (% of GDP)	131	143	205
Imports of goods and services (% of GDP)	122	139	194
Gross capital formation (% of GDP)	27	27	21
Central government revenue (% of GDP)	..	..	..
Central government cash surplus/deficit (% of GDP)	..	..	..
States and markets			
Starting a business (days)			11
Stock market capitalization (% of GDP)	108.5	368.6	903.6
Military expenditures (% of GDP)	..	..	..
Fixed-line and mobile subscribers (per 100 people)	46	141	193
Internet users (per 100 people)	0.0	27.8	55.0
Paved roads (% of total)	100	100	100
High-technology exports (% of manufactured exports)	0	23	11
Global links			
Merchandise trade (% of GDP)	217.4	246.4	346.9
Net barter terms of trade (2000 = 100)	100	100	97
Total external debt ($ billions)	..	..	..
Short-term debt ($ billions)	..	..	..
Total debt service (% of exports)	..	..	..
Foreign direct investment, net inflows ($ billions)	..	61.9	42.9
Remittances received ($ millions)	..	136.0	297.0
Aid ($ millions)	38.2	4.3	..

Hungary

Europe & Central Asia **Upper middle income**

Population (millions)	10	Population growth (%)	-0.2
Surface area (1,000 sq. km)	93	National poverty rate (% of pop.)	..
GNI ($ billions)	109.5	GNI per capita ($)	10,870
GNI, PPP ($ billions)	170.8	GNI per capita, PPP ($)	16,970

	1990	2000	2006
People			
Share of poorest 20% in nat'l consumption/income (%)	10.4	9.5	8.6
Life expectancy at birth (years)	69	71	73
Total fertility (births per woman)	1.8	1.3	1.4
Adolescent fertility (births per 1,000 women 15–19)	..	23	20
Contraceptive prevalence (% of married women 15–49)	..	..	..
Births attended by skilled health staff (% of total)	..	100	100
Under-five mortality rate (per 1,000)	17	9	7
Child malnutrition, underweight (% of under age 5)	2.3	..	..
Child immunization, measles (% of ages 12–23 mos.)	99	99	99
Primary completion rate, total (% of relevant age group)	89	98	94
Gross secondary enrollment, total (% of relevant age group)	79	96	96
Ratio of girls to boys in primary & secondary school (%)	100	100	99
HIV prevalence rate (% of population ages 15–49)	..	..	0.1
Environment			
Forests (1,000 sq. km)	18	19	20
Deforestation (average annual %, 1990–2005)			-0.6
Freshwater use (% of internal resources)	..	127.3	..
Access to improved water source (% of total pop.)	99	99	99
Access to improved sanitation facilities (% of total pop.)	..	95	95
Energy use per capita (kilograms of oil equivalent)	2,753	2,450	2,752
Carbon dioxide emissions per capita (metric tons)	5.8	5.3	5.7
Electricity use per capita (kilowatt-hours)	3,427	3,309	3,771
Economy			
GDP ($ billions)	33.1	47.9	112.9
GDP growth (annual %)	-3.5	5.2	3.9
GDP implicit price deflator (annual % growth)	25.7	12.9	3.7
Value added in agriculture (% of GDP)	15	5	4
Value added in industry (% of GDP)	39	32	30
Value added in services (% of GDP)	46	62	66
Exports of goods and services (% of GDP)	31	72	78
Imports of goods and services (% of GDP)	29	76	77
Gross capital formation (% of GDP)	25	30	25
Central government revenue (% of GDP)	..	37.5	35.8
Central government cash surplus/deficit (% of GDP)	..	-2.7	-8.6
States and markets			
Starting a business (days)			16
Stock market capitalization (% of GDP)	1.5	25.1	37.1
Military expenditures (% of GDP)	2.8	1.7	1.2
Fixed-line and mobile subscribers (per 100 people)	10	67	132
Internet users (per 100 people)	0.0	7.0	34.8
Paved roads (% of total)	44	44	..
High-technology exports (% of manufactured exports)	0	26	24
Global links			
Merchandise trade (% of GDP)	61.5	125.9	134.1
Net barter terms of trade (2000 = 100)	111	100	96
Total external debt ($ billions)	21	30	108
Short-term debt ($ billions)	2.9	4.2	15.0
Total debt service (% of exports)	34.3	22.1	33.1
Foreign direct investment, net inflows ($ billions)	0.6	2.8	6.1
Remittances received ($ millions)	..	281.0	363.0
Aid ($ millions)	67	252	..

Iceland

High income

Population (thousands)	302	Population growth (%)	1.7
Surface area (1,000 sq. km)	103	National poverty rate (% of pop.)	..
GNI ($ billions)	15.1	GNI per capita ($)	49,960
GNI, PPP ($ billions)	10.2	GNI per capita, PPP ($)	33,740

	1990	2000	2006
People			
Share of poorest 20% in nat'l consumption/income (%)	..	..	..
Life expectancy at birth (years)	77	79	81
Total fertility (births per woman)	2.3	2.1	2.1
Adolescent fertility (births per 1,000 women 15–19)	..	20	15
Contraceptive prevalence (% of married women 15–49)	..	..	..
Births attended by skilled health staff (% of total)	..	..	..
Under-five mortality rate (per 1,000)	7	3	3
Child malnutrition, underweight (% of under age 5)	..	..	..
Child immunization, measles (% of ages 12–23 mos.)	99	91	95
Primary completion rate, total (% of relevant age group)	..	98	99
Gross secondary enrollment, total (% of relevant age group)	100	108	109
Ratio of girls to boys in primary & secondary school (%)	98	102	100
HIV prevalence rate (% of population ages 15–49)	..	..	0.2
Environment			
Forests (1,000 sq. km)	250	380	460
Deforestation (average annual %, 1990–2005)			-4.1
Freshwater use (% of internal resources)	..	0.1	..
Access to improved water source (% of total pop.)	100	100	100
Access to improved sanitation facilities (% of total pop.)	100	100	100
Energy use per capita (kilograms of oil equivalent)	8,524	11,544	12,219
Carbon dioxide emissions per capita (metric tons)	7.9	7.7	7.6
Electricity use per capita (kilowatt-hours)	16,150	26,221	27,987
Economy			
GDP ($ billions)	6.4	8.7	16.3
GDP growth (annual %)	1.2	4.3	2.6
GDP implicit price deflator (annual % growth)	15.2	3.6	8.9
Value added in agriculture (% of GDP)	11	9	6
Value added in industry (% of GDP)	30	26	24
Value added in services (% of GDP)	59	65	70
Exports of goods and services (% of GDP)	34	34	33
Imports of goods and services (% of GDP)	32	41	50
Gross capital formation (% of GDP)	19	23	33
Central government revenue (% of GDP)	..	33.4	36.1
Central government cash surplus/deficit (% of GDP)	..	2.7	6.1
States and markets			
Starting a business (days)			5
Stock market capitalization (% of GDP)	..	51.2	221.9
Military expenditures (% of GDP)	0.0	0.0	0.0
Fixed-line and mobile subscribers (per 100 people)	55	146	173
Internet users (per 100 people)	0.0	44.5	64.3
Paved roads (% of total)	20	30	35
High-technology exports (% of manufactured exports)	10	12	38
Global links			
Merchandise trade (% of GDP)	51.3	51.8	58.2
Net barter terms of trade (2000 = 100)	..	..	..
Total external debt ($ billions)	..	..	..
Short-term debt ($ billions)	..	..	..
Total debt service (% of exports)	..	..	..
Foreign direct investment, net inflows ($ billions)	0.0	0.2	4.0
Remittances received ($ millions)	62	88	87
Aid ($ billions)	..	..	..

India

South Asia			**Low income**
Population (millions)	1,110	Population growth (%)	1.4
Surface area (1,000 sq. km)	3,287	National poverty rate (% of pop.)	29
GNI ($ billions)	909.1	GNI per capita ($)	820
GNI, PPP ($ billions)	2726.2	GNI per capita, PPP ($)	2,460

	1990	2000	2006
People			
Share of poorest 20% in nat'l consumption/income (%)	..	..	8.1
Life expectancy at birth (years)	59	63	64
Total fertility (births per woman)	3.8	3.1	2.5
Adolescent fertility (births per 1,000 women 15–19)	..	81	63
Contraceptive prevalence (% of married women 15–49)	43	47	56
Births attended by skilled health staff (% of total)	..	43	47
Under-five mortality rate (per 1,000)	115	89	76
Child malnutrition, underweight (% of under age 5)	..	44.4	43.5
Child immunization, measles (% of ages 12–23 mos.)	56	52	59
Primary completion rate, total (% of relevant age group)	64	72	85
Gross secondary enrollment, total (% of relevant age group)	42	46	54
Ratio of girls to boys in primary & secondary school (%)	70	79	91
HIV prevalence rate (% of population ages 15–49)	..	..	0.9
Environment			
Forests (1,000 sq. km)	639	676	677
Deforestation (average annual %, 1990–2005)			–0.4
Freshwater use (% of internal resources)	..	51.2	..
Access to improved water source (% of total pop.)	70	82	86
Access to improved sanitation facilities (% of total pop.)	14	28	33
Energy use per capita (kilograms of oil equivalent)	377	452	491
Carbon dioxide emissions per capita (metric tons)	0.8	1.1	1.2
Electricity use per capita (kilowatt-hours)	276	402	480
Economy			
GDP ($ billions)	317.5	460.2	911.8
GDP growth (annual %)	5.5	4.0	9.2
GDP implicit price deflator (annual % growth)	10.7	3.5	5.9
Value added in agriculture (% of GDP)	29	23	18
Value added in industry (% of GDP)	27	26	28
Value added in services (% of GDP)	44	50	55
Exports of goods and services (% of GDP)	7	13	23
Imports of goods and services (% of GDP)	9	14	26
Gross capital formation (% of GDP)	24	25	34
Central government revenue (% of GDP)	12.6	11.9	12.7
Central government cash surplus/deficit (% of GDP)	–3.4	–3.9	–2.8
States and markets			
Starting a business (days)			33
Stock market capitalization (% of GDP)	12.2	32.2	89.8
Military expenditures (% of GDP)	3.2	3.1	2.7
Fixed-line and mobile subscribers (per 100 people)	1	4	19
Internet users (per 100 people)	0.0	0.5	5.5
Paved roads (% of total)	47	47	..
High-technology exports (% of manufactured exports)	2	5	5
Global links			
Merchandise trade (% of GDP)	13.1	20.4	32.4
Net barter terms of trade (2000 = 100)	85	100	105
Total external debt ($ billions)	84	99	153
Short-term debt ($ billions)	8.5	3.5	12.0
Total debt service (% of exports)	31.9	14.5	7.7
Foreign direct investment, net inflows ($ billions)	0.2	3.6	17.5
Remittances received ($ billions)	2.4	12.9	25.4
Aid ($ billions)	1.4	1.5	1.4

Indonesia

East Asia & Pacific		**Lower middle income**

Population (millions)	223	Population growth (%)	1.1
Surface area (1,000 sq. km)	1,905	National poverty rate (% of pop.)	17
GNI ($ billions)	315.8	GNI per capita ($)	1,420
GNI, PPP ($ billions)	737.2	GNI per capita, PPP ($)	3,310

	1990	2000	2006
People			
Share of poorest 20% in nat'l consumption/income (%)	..	9.2	7.1
Life expectancy at birth (years)	62	66	68
Total fertility (births per woman)	3.1	2.4	2.2
Adolescent fertility (births per 1,000 women 15–19)	..	49	41
Contraceptive prevalence (% of married women 15–49)	50	..	57
Births attended by skilled health staff (% of total)	32	64	72
Under-five mortality rate (per 1,000)	91	48	34
Child malnutrition, underweight (% of under age 5)	29.8	24.8	24.4
Child immunization, measles (% of ages 12–23 mos.)	58	72	72
Primary completion rate, total (% of relevant age group)	94	95	99
Gross secondary enrollment, total (% of relevant age group)	45	55	62
Ratio of girls to boys in primary & secondary school (%)	93	96	97
HIV prevalence rate (% of population ages 15–49)	..	..	0.1
Environment			
Forests (1,000 sq. km)	1,166	979	885
Deforestation (average annual %, 1990–2005)			1.8
Freshwater use (% of internal resources)	..	2.9	..
Access to improved water source (% of total pop.)	72	76	77
Access to improved sanitation facilities (% of total pop.)	46	52	55
Energy use per capita (kilograms of oil equivalent)	579	740	814
Carbon dioxide emissions per capita (metric tons)	1.2	1.8	1.7
Electricity use per capita (kilowatt-hours)	161	400	509
Economy			
GDP ($ billions)	114.4	165.0	364.8
GDP growth (annual %)	9.0	4.9	5.5
GDP implicit price deflator (annual % growth)	7.7	20.4	13.6
Value added in agriculture (% of GDP)	19	16	13
Value added in industry (% of GDP)	39	46	47
Value added in services (% of GDP)	41	38	40
Exports of goods and services (% of GDP)	25	41	31
Imports of goods and services (% of GDP)	24	30	26
Gross capital formation (% of GDP)	31	22	25
Central government revenue (% of GDP)	18.8	18.7	18.4
Central government cash surplus/deficit (% of GDP)	0.4	–0.3	–1.1
States and markets			
Starting a business (days)			105
Stock market capitalization (% of GDP)	7.1	16.3	38.1
Military expenditures (% of GDP)	1.8	1.0	1.2
Fixed-line and mobile subscribers (per 100 people)	1	5	35
Internet users (per 100 people)	0.0	0.9	7.3
Paved roads (% of total)	45	57	55
High-technology exports (% of manufactured exports)	1	16	13
Global links			
Merchandise trade (% of GDP)	41.5	66.1	50.4
Net barter terms of trade (2000 = 100)	95	100	101
Total external debt ($ billions)	70	144	131
Short-term debt ($ billions)	11	23	33
Total debt service (% of exports)	33.3	22.4	16.6
Foreign direct investment, net inflows ($ billions)	1.1	–4.6	5.6
Remittances received ($ billions)	0.2	1.2	5.7
Aid ($ billions)	1.7	1.7	1.4

Iran, Islamic Rep.

Middle East & North Africa		Lower middle income

Population (millions)	70	Population growth (%)	1.5
Surface area (1,000 sq. km)	1,745	National poverty rate (% of pop.)	..
GNI ($ billions)	205.0	GNI per capita ($)	2,930
GNI, PPP ($ billions)	686.9	GNI per capita, PPP ($)	9,800

	1990	2000	2006
People			
Share of poorest 20% in nat'l consumption/income (%)	5.2	5.1	6.5
Life expectancy at birth (years)	65	69	71
Total fertility (births per woman)	4.8	2.3	2.1
Adolescent fertility (births per 1,000 women 15–19)	..	33	21
Contraceptive prevalence (% of married women 15–49)	49	74	..
Births attended by skilled health staff (% of total)	..	90	..
Under-five mortality rate (per 1,000)	72	44	34
Child malnutrition, underweight (% of under age 5)	..	..	..
Child immunization, measles (% of ages 12–23 mos.)	85	99	99
Primary completion rate, total (% of relevant age group)	87	90	101
Gross secondary enrollment, total (% of relevant age group)	57	79	81
Ratio of girls to boys in primary & secondary school (%)	85	95	105
HIV prevalence rate (% of population ages 15–49)	..	..	0.2
Environment			
Forests (1,000 sq. km)	111	111	111
Deforestation (average annual %, 1990–2005)			0.00
Freshwater use (% of internal resources)	..	56.7	..
Access to improved water source (% of total pop.)	92	94	94
Access to improved sanitation facilities (% of total pop.)	83	83	..
Energy use per capita (kilograms of oil equivalent)	1,264	1,856	2,352
Carbon dioxide emissions per capita (metric tons)	4.0	5.5	6.4
Electricity use per capita (kilowatt-hours)	975	1,586	2,117
Economy			
GDP ($ billions)	116.0	101.3	217.9
GDP growth (annual %)	13.7	5.1	4.6
GDP implicit price deflator (annual % growth)	20.6	26.4	11.0
Value added in agriculture (% of GDP)	19	14	10
Value added in industry (% of GDP)	29	37	45
Value added in services (% of GDP)	52	50	45
Exports of goods and services (% of GDP)	15	23	42
Imports of goods and services (% of GDP)	23	17	34
Gross capital formation (% of GDP)	37	33	34
Central government revenue (% of GDP)	18.7	23.4	36.2
Central government cash surplus/deficit (% of GDP)	–1.9	1.8	3.3
States and markets			
Starting a business (days)			47
Stock market capitalization (% of GDP)	..	7.3	17.4
Military expenditures (% of GDP)	2.9	5.4	4.8
Fixed-line and mobile subscribers (per 100 people)	4	16	51
Internet users (per 100 people)	0.0	1.0	25.7
Paved roads (% of total)	..	65	..
High-technology exports (% of manufactured exports)	..	2	6
Global links			
Merchandise trade (% of GDP)	34.2	42.1	57.3
Net barter terms of trade (2000 = 100)	..	100	155
Total external debt ($ billions)	9.0	8.0	20.1
Short-term debt ($ billions)	7.2	3.0	9.0
Total debt service (% of exports)	3.2	10.7	..
Foreign direct investment, net inflows ($ millions)	–362	39	901
Remittances received ($ billions)	1.2	0.5	1.0
Aid ($ millions)	105	130	121

Iraq

Middle East & North Africa		Lower middle income

Population (millions)	..	Population growth (%)	..
Surface area (1,000 sq. km)	438	National poverty rate (% of pop.)	..
GNI ($ billions)	..	GNI per capita ($)	..
GNI, PPP ($ billions)	..	GNI per capita, PPP ($)	..

	1990	2000	2006
People			
Share of poorest 20% in nat'l consumption/income (%)	..	..	..
Life expectancy at birth (years)	62	..	..
Total fertility (births per woman)	5.9	..	..
Adolescent fertility (births per 1,000 women 15-19)	..	..	..
Contraceptive prevalence (% of married women 15-49)	14	..	..
Births attended by skilled health staff (% of total)	54	..	..
Under-five mortality rate (per 1,000)	53	..	..
Child malnutrition, underweight (% of under age 5)	..	..	..
Child immunization, measles (% of ages 12-23 mos.)	75	..	..
Primary completion rate, total (% of relevant age group)	58	..	..
Gross secondary enrollment, total (% of relevant age group)	44	..	..
Ratio of girls to boys in primary & secondary school (%)	78	..	..
HIV prevalence rate (% of population ages 15-49)	..	..	..
Environment			
Forests (1,000 sq. km)	8.0	8.2	8.2
Deforestation (average annual %, 1990-2005)			-0.1
Freshwater use (% of internal resources)	..	121.3	..
Access to improved water source (% of total pop.)	83	..	..
Access to improved sanitation facilities (% of total pop.)	81	..	..
Energy use per capita (kilograms of oil equivalent)	1,029	..	..
Carbon dioxide emissions per capita (metric tons)	2.6	..	..
Electricity use per capita (kilowatt-hours)	1,231	..	..
Economy			
GDP ($ billions)	48.4	25.9	..
GDP growth (annual %)	..	-4.3	46.5
GDP implicit price deflator (annual % growth)	..	47.4	..
Value added in agriculture (% of GDP)	..	5	..
Value added in industry (% of GDP)	..	84	..
Value added in services (% of GDP)	..	10	..
Exports of goods and services (% of GDP)	..	..	..
Imports of goods and services (% of GDP)	..	..	..
Gross capital formation (% of GDP)	..	..	..
Central government revenue (% of GDP)	..	..	..
Central government cash surplus/deficit (% of GDP)	..	..	..
States and markets			
Starting a business (days)			77
Stock market capitalization (% of GDP)	..	..	..
Military expenditures (% of GDP)	..	..	..
Fixed-line and mobile subscribers (per 100 people)	4	..	..
Internet users (per 100 people)	0.0	..	..
Paved roads (% of total)	78	84	..
High-technology exports (% of manufactured exports)	..	..	..
Global links			
Merchandise trade (% of GDP)	55.4	131.4	..
Net barter terms of trade (2000 = 100)	..	..	..
Total external debt ($ billions)	..	..	..
Short-term debt ($ billions)	..	..	..
Total debt service (% of exports)	..	..	..
Foreign direct investment, net inflows ($ billions)	..	..	..
Remittances received ($ billions)	..	..	..
Aid ($ billions)	0.1	0.1	8.7

Ireland

Population (millions)	4.3	Population growth (%)	2.6
Surface area (1,000 sq. km)	70	National poverty rate (% of pop.)	..
GNI ($ billions)	191.3	GNI per capita ($)	44,830
GNI, PPP ($ billions)	148.2	GNI per capita, PPP ($)	34,730

	1990	2000	2006
People			
Share of poorest 20% in nat'l consumption/income (%)	..	7.4	..
Life expectancy at birth (years)	75	76	79
Total fertility (births per woman)	2.1	1.9	1.9
Adolescent fertility (births per 1,000 women 15–19)	..	19	17
Contraceptive prevalence (% of married women 15–49)	60	..	..
Births attended by skilled health staff (% of total)	..	100	..
Under-five mortality rate (per 1,000)	9	7	5
Child malnutrition, underweight (% of under age 5)	..	..	..
Child immunization, measles (% of ages 12–23 mos.)	78	79	86
Primary completion rate, total (% of relevant age group)	..	97	97
Gross secondary enrollment, total (% of relevant age group)	100	108	112
Ratio of girls to boys in primary & secondary school (%)	104	103	103
HIV prevalence rate (% of population ages 15–49)	..	..	0.2
Environment			
Forests (1,000 sq. km)	4.4	6.1	6.7
Deforestation (average annual %, 1990–2005)			–2.8
Freshwater use (% of internal resources)	..	2.3	..
Access to improved water source (% of total pop.)	..	..	..
Access to improved sanitation facilities (% of total pop.)	..	..	..
Energy use per capita (kilograms of oil equivalent)	2,957	3,753	3,676
Carbon dioxide emissions per capita (metric tons)	8.7	10.9	10.4
Electricity use per capita (kilowatt-hours)	3,776	5,796	6,234
Economy			
GDP ($ billions)	47.9	96.3	220.1
GDP growth (annual %)	8.5	9.4	5.7
GDP implicit price deflator (annual % growth)	-0.7	5.5	3.0
Value added in agriculture (% of GDP)	9	3	2
Value added in industry (% of GDP)	35	43	36
Value added in services (% of GDP)	57	54	62
Exports of goods and services (% of GDP)	57	98	81
Imports of goods and services (% of GDP)	52	85	69
Gross capital formation (% of GDP)	21	25	27
Central government revenue (% of GDP)	..	32.5	34.2
Central government cash surplus/deficit (% of GDP)	..	4.9	2.7
States and markets			
Starting a business (days)			13
Stock market capitalization (% of GDP)	..	85.0	74.2
Military expenditures (% of GDP)	1.2	0.7	0.5
Fixed-line and mobile subscribers (per 100 people)	29	113	159
Internet users (per 100 people)	0.0	17.8	33.7
Paved roads (% of total)	94	100	..
High-technology exports (% of manufactured exports)	41	48	34
Global links			
Merchandise trade (% of GDP)	92.8	133.4	83.5
Net barter terms of trade (2000 = 100)	106	100	94
Total external debt ($ billions)	..	..	..
Short-term debt ($ billions)	..	..	..
Total debt service (% of exports)	..	..	..
Foreign direct investment, net inflows ($ billions)	0.6	25.5	-0.9
Remittances received ($ millions)	286	252	532
Aid ($ billions)	..	..	..

Isle of Man

Population (thousands)	77	Population growth (%)	0.9
Surface area (sq. km)	570	National poverty rate (% of pop.)	..
GNI ($ billions)	3.1	GNI per capita ($)	40,600
GNI, PPP ($ billions)	..	GNI per capita, PPP ($)	..

	1990	2000	2006
People			
Share of poorest 20% in nat'l consumption/income (%)	..	..	..
Life expectancy at birth (years)	..	78	..
Total fertility (births per woman)	1.9	1.7	..
Adolescent fertility (births per 1,000 women 15–19)	..	..	..
Contraceptive prevalence (% of married women 15–49)	..	..	..
Births attended by skilled health staff (% of total)	..	..	..
Under-five mortality rate (per 1,000)	..	..	..
Child malnutrition, underweight (% of under age 5)	..	..	..
Child immunization, measles (% of ages 12–23 mos.)	..	..	..
Primary completion rate, total (% of relevant age group)	..	..	..
Gross secondary enrollment, total (% of relevant age group)	..	..	..
Ratio of girls to boys in primary & secondary school (%)	..	..	..
HIV prevalence rate (% of population ages 15–49)	..	..	..
Environment			
Forests (sq. km)	30	30	30
Deforestation (average annual %, 1990–2005)			0.00
Freshwater use (% of internal resources)	..		..
Access to improved water source (% of total pop.)	..		..
Access to improved sanitation facilities (% of total pop.)	..		..
Energy use per capita (kilograms of oil equivalent)	..	..	..
Carbon dioxide emissions per capita (metric tons)	..	..	..
Electricity use per capita (kilowatt-hours)	..	..	..
Economy			
GDP ($ billions)	..	1,564	2,916
GDP growth (annual %)	4.2	5.3	5.9
GDP implicit price deflator (annual % growth)	9.0	3.3	3.2
Value added in agriculture (% of GDP)	..	..	..
Value added in industry (% of GDP)	..	..	..
Value added in services (% of GDP)	..	..	..
Exports of goods and services (% of GDP)	..	..	..
Imports of goods and services (% of GDP)	..	..	..
Gross capital formation (% of GDP)	..	..	..
Central government revenue (% of GDP)	..	..	..
Central government cash surplus/deficit (% of GDP)	..	..	..
States and markets			
Starting a business (days)			..
Stock market capitalization (% of GDP)	..	..	..
Military expenditures (% of GDP)	..	..	..
Fixed-line and mobile subscribers (per 100 people)	..	..	..
Internet users (per 100 people)	..	..	..
Paved roads (% of total)	..	..	..
High-technology exports (% of manufactured exports)	..	..	..
Global links			
Merchandise trade (% of GDP)	..	..	..
Net barter terms of trade (2000 = 100)	..	..	..
Total external debt ($ billions)	..	..	..
Short-term debt ($ billions)	..	..	..
Total debt service (% of exports)	..	..	..
Foreign direct investment, net inflows ($ billions)	..	..	..
Remittances received ($ billions)	..	..	..
Aid ($ billions)	..	..	..

Israel

Population (millions)	7.0	Population growth (%)	1.8
Surface area (1,000 sq. km)	22	National poverty rate (% of pop.)	..
GNI ($ billions)	142.2	GNI per capita ($)	20,170
GNI, PPP ($ billions)	168.1	GNI per capita, PPP ($)	23,840

	1990	2000	2006
People			
Share of poorest 20% in nat'l consumption/income (%)	..	5.7	..
Life expectancy at birth (years)	77	79	80
Total fertility (births per woman)	2.8	3.0	2.7
Adolescent fertility (births per 1,000 women 15–19)	..	17	14
Contraceptive prevalence (% of married women 15–49)	68	..	..
Births attended by skilled health staff (% of total)	..	..	..
Under-five mortality rate (per 1,000)	12	7	5
Child malnutrition, underweight (% of under age 5)	..	..	..
Child immunization, measles (% of ages 12–23 mos.)	91	97	95
Primary completion rate, total (% of relevant age group)	..	104	101
Gross secondary enrollment, total (% of relevant age group)	88	92	93
Ratio of girls to boys in primary & secondary school (%)	105	100	100
HIV prevalence rate (% of population ages 15–49)	..	..	0.2
Environment			
Forests (1,000 sq. km)	1.5	1.6	1.7
Deforestation (average annual %, 1990–2005)			–0.7
Freshwater use (% of internal resources)	..	256.3	..
Access to improved water source (% of total pop.)	100	100	100
Access to improved sanitation facilities (% of total pop.)	..	..	..
Energy use per capita (kilograms of oil equivalent)	2,599	3,057	2,816
Carbon dioxide emissions per capita (metric tons)	7.1	10.2	10.5
Electricity use per capita (kilowatt-hours)	4,176	6,372	6,759
Economy			
GDP ($ billions)	52.5	121.0	140.5
GDP growth (annual %)	6.8	8.7	5.1
GDP implicit price deflator (annual % growth)	15.9	1.3	2.3
Value added in agriculture (% of GDP)	..	..	..
Value added in industry (% of GDP)	..	..	..
Value added in services (% of GDP)	..	..	..
Exports of goods and services (% of GDP)	35	38	45
Imports of goods and services (% of GDP)	45	38	44
Gross capital formation (% of GDP)	25	21	18
Central government revenue (% of GDP)	..	40.6	39.9
Central government cash surplus/deficit (% of GDP)	..	–2.1	–1.6
States and markets			
Starting a business (days)			34
Stock market capitalization (% of GDP)	6.3	53.0	123.4
Military expenditures (% of GDP)	12.4	8.0	8.4
Fixed-line and mobile subscribers (per 100 people)	35	117	162
Internet users (per 100 people)	0.1	20.2	26.9
Paved roads (% of total)	100	100	100
High-technology exports (% of manufactured exports)	10	25	14
Global links			
Merchandise trade (% of GDP)	55.0	57.1	68.7
Net barter terms of trade (2000 = 100)	89	100	94
Total external debt ($ billions)	..	..	..
Short-term debt ($ billions)	..	..	..
Total debt service (% of exports)	..	..	..
Foreign direct investment, net inflows ($ billions)	0.2	5.1	14.3
Remittances received ($ billions)	0.8	0.3	1.1
Aid ($ billions)	1.4	0.8	..

Italy

Population (millions)	59	Population growth (%)	0.4
Surface area (1,000 sq. km)	301	National poverty rate (% of pop.)	..
GNI ($ billions)	1,882.5	GNI per capita ($)	31,990
GNI, PPP ($ billions)	1,704.9	GNI per capita, PPP ($)	28,970

	1990	2000	2006
People			
Share of poorest 20% in nat'l consumption/income (%)	..	6.5	..
Life expectancy at birth (years)	77	80	81
Total fertility (births per woman)	1.3	1.2	1.4
Adolescent fertility (births per 1,000 women 15–19)	..	7	6
Contraceptive prevalence (% of married women 15–49)	..	..	..
Births attended by skilled health staff (% of total)	..	..	..
Under-five mortality rate (per 1,000)	9	5	4
Child malnutrition, underweight (% of under age 5)	..	..	..
Child immunization, measles (% of ages 12–23 mos.)	43	73	87
Primary completion rate, total (% of relevant age group)	105	100	100
Gross secondary enrollment, total (% of relevant age group)	83	93	99
Ratio of girls to boys in primary & secondary school (%)	100	98	99
HIV prevalence rate (% of population ages 15–49)	..	..	0.5
Environment			
Forests (1,000 sq. km)	84	94	100
Deforestation (average annual %, 1990–2005)			-1.2
Freshwater use (% of internal resources)	..	24.3	..
Access to improved water source (% of total pop.)	..	..	..
Access to improved sanitation facilities (% of total pop.)	..	..	..
Energy use per capita (kilograms of oil equivalent)	2,609	3,040	3,160
Carbon dioxide emissions per capita (metric tons)	6.9	7.5	7.7
Electricity use per capita (kilowatt-hours)	4,145	5,299	5,669
Economy			
GDP ($ billions)	1,133.4	1,097.3	1,851.0
GDP growth (annual %)	2.1	3.6	1.9
GDP implicit price deflator (annual % growth)	8.4	2.0	1.8
Value added in agriculture (% of GDP)	3	3	2
Value added in industry (% of GDP)	32	28	27
Value added in services (% of GDP)	64	69	71
Exports of goods and services (% of GDP)	19	27	28
Imports of goods and services (% of GDP)	19	26	29
Gross capital formation (% of GDP)	22	21	21
Central government revenue (% of GDP)	..	37.2	37.2
Central government cash surplus/deficit (% of GDP)	..	-0.7	-3.3
States and markets			
Starting a business (days)			13
Stock market capitalization (% of GDP)	13.1	70.0	55.5
Military expenditures (% of GDP)	2.1	2.0	1.7
Fixed-line and mobile subscribers (per 100 people)	40	122	165
Internet users (per 100 people)	0.0	23.2	49.0
Paved roads (% of total)	100	100	..
High-technology exports (% of manufactured exports)	8	9	7
Global links			
Merchandise trade (% of GDP)	31.1	43.7	45.8
Net barter terms of trade (2000 = 100)	94	100	98
Total external debt ($ billions)	..	..	..
Short-term debt ($ billions)	..	..	..
Total debt service (% of exports)	..	..	..
Foreign direct investment, net inflows ($ billions)	6.4	13.2	38.9
Remittances received ($ billions)	5.1	1.9	2.6
Aid ($ billions)	..	..	..

Jamaica

Latin America & Caribbean **Lower middle income**

Population (millions)	2.7	Population growth (%)		0.5
Surface area (1,000 sq. km)	11	National poverty rate (% of pop.)		19
GNI ($ billions)	9.5	GNI per capita ($)		3,560
GNI, PPP ($ billions)	18.8	GNI per capita, PPP ($)		7,050

	1990	2000	2006
People			
Share of poorest 20% in nat'l consumption/income (%)	5.8	5.9	5.3
Life expectancy at birth (years)	71	71	71
Total fertility (births per woman)	2.9	2.5	2.3
Adolescent fertility (births per 1,000 women 15–19)	..	90	80
Contraceptive prevalence (% of married women 15–49)	55	69	..
Births attended by skilled health staff (% of total)	79	97	97
Under-five mortality rate (per 1,000)	33	32	31
Child malnutrition, underweight (% of under age 5)	..	3.8	3.1
Child immunization, measles (% of ages 12–23 mos.)	74	88	87
Primary completion rate, total (% of relevant age group)	91	87	82
Gross secondary enrollment, total (% of relevant age group)	65	86	87
Ratio of girls to boys in primary & secondary school (%)	102	101	101
HIV prevalence rate (% of population ages 15–49)	..	..	1.5
Environment			
Forests (1,000 sq. km)	3.5	3.4	3.4
Deforestation (average annual %, 1990–2005)			0.1
Freshwater use (% of internal resources)	..	4.4	..
Access to improved water source (% of total pop.)	92	93	93
Access to improved sanitation facilities (% of total pop.)	75	79	80
Energy use per capita (kilograms of oil equivalent)	1,231	1,514	1,445
Carbon dioxide emissions per capita (metric tons)	3.3	4.0	4.0
Electricity use per capita (kilowatt-hours)	879	2,321	2,474
Economy			
GDP ($ billions)	4.6	8.0	10.0
GDP growth (annual %)	4.2	0.6	2.5
GDP implicit price deflator (annual % growth)	25.1	11.5	6.3
Value added in agriculture (% of GDP)	..	7	6
Value added in industry (% of GDP)	..	31	33
Value added in services (% of GDP)	..	62	61
Exports of goods and services (% of GDP)	48	43	46
Imports of goods and services (% of GDP)	52	54	63
Gross capital formation (% of GDP)	26	27	33
Central government revenue (% of GDP)	..	33.2	39.2
Central government cash surplus/deficit (% of GDP)	..	-2.6	0.3
States and markets			
Starting a business (days)			8
Stock market capitalization (% of GDP)	19.8	44.6	122.5
Military expenditures (% of GDP)	0.6	0.5	0.6
Fixed-line and mobile subscribers (per 100 people)	4	33	118
Internet users (per 100 people)	0.0	3.1	46.4
Paved roads (% of total)	64	70	74
High-technology exports (% of manufactured exports)	0	0	0
Global links			
Merchandise trade (% of GDP)	67.2	57.7	76.1
Net barter terms of trade (2000 = 100)	..	100	192
Total external debt ($ billions)	4.8	4.7	8.0
Short-term debt ($ billions)	0.3	0.8	1.2
Total debt service (% of exports)	26.9	15.4	11.9
Foreign direct investment, net inflows ($ millions)	138	468	882
Remittances received ($ billions)	0.2	0.9	1.9
Aid ($ millions)	270.6	10.0	36.7

Japan

High income

Population (millions)	128	Population growth (%)	0.0
Surface area (1,000 sq. km)	378	National poverty rate (% of pop.)	..
GNI ($ billions)	4,934.7	GNI per capita ($)	38,630
GNI, PPP ($ billions)	4,195.9	GNI per capita, PPP ($)	32,840

	1990	2000	2006
People			
Share of poorest 20% in nat'l consumption/income (%)	..	..	..
Life expectancy at birth (years)	79	81	82
Total fertility (births per woman)	1.5	1.4	1.3
Adolescent fertility (births per 1,000 women 15–19)	..	4	3
Contraceptive prevalence (% of married women 15–49)	58	56	..
Births attended by skilled health staff (% of total)	100	..	100
Under-five mortality rate (per 1,000)	6	5	4
Child malnutrition, underweight (% of under age 5)	..	..	..
Child immunization, measles (% of ages 12–23 mos.)	73	96	99
Primary completion rate, total (% of relevant age group)	100	..	..
Gross secondary enrollment, total (% of relevant age group)	97	102	102
Ratio of girls to boys in primary & secondary school (%)	101	101	100
HIV prevalence rate (% of population ages 15–49)	..	..	0.1
Environment			
Forests (1,000 sq. km)	250	249	249
Deforestation (average annual %, 1990–2005)			0.02
Freshwater use (% of internal resources)	..	20.6	..
Access to improved water source (% of total pop.)	100	100	100
Access to improved sanitation facilities (% of total pop.)	100	100	100
Energy use per capita (kilograms of oil equivalent)	3,598	4,158	4,152
Carbon dioxide emissions per capita (metric tons)	8.7	9.5	9.8
Electricity use per capita (kilowatt-hours)	6,496	7,992	8,233
Economy			
GDP ($ billions)	3,018.3	4,667.4	4,368.4
GDP growth (annual %)	5.2	2.9	2.2
GDP implicit price deflator (annual % growth)	2.4	-1.7	-0.9
Value added in agriculture (% of GDP)	3	2	2
Value added in industry (% of GDP)	40	32	30
Value added in services (% of GDP)	58	66	69
Exports of goods and services (% of GDP)	10	11	14
Imports of goods and services (% of GDP)	10	10	13
Gross capital formation (% of GDP)	33	25	23
Central government revenue (% of GDP)	14.2	..	..
Central government cash surplus/deficit (% of GDP)	-1.2	..	..
States and markets			
Starting a business (days)			23
Stock market capitalization (% of GDP)	96.7	67.6	108.2
Military expenditures (% of GDP)	0.9	1.0	0.9
Fixed-line and mobile subscribers (per 100 people)	45	101	123
Internet users (per 100 people)	0.0	30.0	68.5
Paved roads (% of total)	69	77	..
High-technology exports (% of manufactured exports)	24	28	22
Global links			
Merchandise trade (% of GDP)	17.3	18.4	28.1
Net barter terms of trade (2000 = 100)	77	100	92
Total external debt ($ billions)	..	..	..
Short-term debt ($ billions)	..	..	..
Total debt service (% of exports)	..	..	..
Foreign direct investment, net inflows ($ billions)	1.8	8.2	-6.8
Remittances received ($ billions)	0.5	1.4	1.4
Aid ($ billions)	..	..	..

Jordan

Population (millions)	5.5	Population growth (%)		2.3
Surface area (1,000 sq. km)	89	National poverty rate (% of pop.)		14
GNI ($ billions)	14.7	GNI per capita ($)		2,650
GNI, PPP ($ billions)	26.7	GNI per capita, PPP ($)		4,820

	1990	2000	2006
People			
Share of poorest 20% in nat'l consumption/income (%)	5.9	6.7	..
Life expectancy at birth (years)	68	71	72
Total fertility (births per woman)	5.4	3.8	3.2
Adolescent fertility (births per 1,000 women 15–19)	..	32	25
Contraceptive prevalence (% of married women 15–49)	40	56	..
Births attended by skilled health staff (% of total)	87	100	..
Under-five mortality rate (per 1,000)	40	30	25
Child malnutrition, underweight (% of under age 5)	..	3.6	..
Child immunization, measles (% of ages 12–23 mos.)	87	94	99
Primary completion rate, total (% of relevant age group)	98	97	100
Gross secondary enrollment, total (% of relevant age group)	63	89	89
Ratio of girls to boys in primary & secondary school (%)	101	101	102
HIV prevalence rate (% of population ages 15–49)	..	..	0.2
Environment			
Forests (1,000 sq. km)	830	830	830
Deforestation (average annual %, 1990–2005)			0.00
Freshwater use (% of internal resources)	..	144.3	..
Access to improved water source (% of total pop.)	97	97	97
Access to improved sanitation facilities (% of total pop.)	93	93	93
Energy use per capita (kilograms of oil equivalent)	1,103	1,082	1,311
Carbon dioxide emissions per capita (metric tons)	3.2	3.2	3.1
Electricity use per capita (kilowatt-hours)	1,050	1,377	1,676
Economy			
GDP ($ billions)	4.0	8.5	14.1
GDP growth (annual %)	1.0	4.2	5.7
GDP implicit price deflator (annual % growth)	11.4	-0.4	5.8
Value added in agriculture (% of GDP)	8	2	3
Value added in industry (% of GDP)	28	26	30
Value added in services (% of GDP)	64	72	67
Exports of goods and services (% of GDP)	62	42	55
Imports of goods and services (% of GDP)	93	68	92
Gross capital formation (% of GDP)	32	22	27
Central government revenue (% of GDP)	26.1	25.1	31.7
Central government cash surplus/deficit (% of GDP)	-3.5	-2.0	-3.9
States and markets			
Starting a business (days)			14
Stock market capitalization (% of GDP)	49.7	58.4	210.8
Military expenditures (% of GDP)	7.1	5.5	4.9
Fixed-line and mobile subscribers (per 100 people)	8	21	90
Internet users (per 100 people)	0.0	2.7	14.4
Paved roads (% of total)	100	100	100
High-technology exports (% of manufactured exports)	1	8	1
Global links			
Merchandise trade (% of GDP)	91.1	76.7	117.9
Net barter terms of trade (2000 = 100)	94	100	84
Total external debt ($ billions)	8.3	7.4	8.0
Short-term debt ($ billions)	1.0	0.7	0.7
Total debt service (% of exports)	20.4	12.6	6.1
Foreign direct investment, net inflows ($ billions)	0.0	0.8	3.2
Remittances received ($ billions)	0.5	1.8	2.9
Aid ($ millions)	886	552	580

Kazakhstan

Europe & Central Asia		Upper middle income	
Population (millions)	15	Population growth (%)	1.1
Surface area (1,000 sq. km)	2,725	National poverty rate (% of pop.)	15
GNI ($ billions)	59.2	GNI per capita ($)	3,870
GNI, PPP ($ billions)	133.2	GNI per capita, PPP ($)	8,700

	1990	2000	2006
People			
Share of poorest 20% in nat'l consumption/income (%)	9.5	8.1	..
Life expectancy at birth (years)	68	66	66
Total fertility (births per woman)	2.7	1.8	2.1
Adolescent fertility (births per 1,000 women 15-19)	..	33	30
Contraceptive prevalence (% of married women 15-49)	..	66	51
Births attended by skilled health staff (% of total)	..	99	100
Under-five mortality rate (per 1,000)	60	43	29
Child malnutrition, underweight (% of under age 5)	..	3.8	..
Child immunization, measles (% of ages 12-23 mos.)	89	99	99
Primary completion rate, total (% of relevant age group)	..	94	104
Gross secondary enrollment, total (% of relevant age group)	100	93	95
Ratio of girls to boys in primary & secondary school (%)	102	102	99
HIV prevalence rate (% of population ages 15-49)	..	..	0.1
Environment			
Forests (1,000 sq. km)	34	34	33
Deforestation (average annual %, 1990-2005)			0.2
Freshwater use (% of internal resources)	..	46.4	..
Access to improved water source (% of total pop.)	87	86	86
Access to improved sanitation facilities (% of total pop.)	72	72	72
Energy use per capita (kilograms of oil equivalent)	4,506	2,596	3,462
Carbon dioxide emissions per capita (metric tons)	17.6	9.4	13.3
Electricity use per capita (kilowatt-hours)	5,905	2,650	3,206
Economy			
GDP ($ billions)	26.9	18.3	81.0
GDP growth (annual %)	-11.0	9.8	10.7
GDP implicit price deflator (annual % growth)	96.4	17.4	21.6
Value added in agriculture (% of GDP)	27	9	6
Value added in industry (% of GDP)	45	40	42
Value added in services (% of GDP)	29	51	52
Exports of goods and services (% of GDP)	74	57	51
Imports of goods and services (% of GDP)	75	49	40
Gross capital formation (% of GDP)	32	18	33
Central government revenue (% of GDP)	..	11.3	16.8
Central government cash surplus/deficit (% of GDP)	..	0.1	1.6
States and markets			
Starting a business (days)			21
Stock market capitalization (% of GDP)	..	7.3	53.9
Military expenditures (% of GDP)	..	0.8	0.9
Fixed-line and mobile subscribers (per 100 people)	8	14	70
Internet users (per 100 people)	0.0	0.7	8.1
Paved roads (% of total)	55	87	84
High-technology exports (% of manufactured exports)	..	4	21
Global links			
Merchandise trade (% of GDP)	..	75.7	80.8
Net barter terms of trade (2000 = 100)	..	..	..
Total external debt ($ billions)	0.0	12.4	74.1
Short-term debt ($ billions)	0.0	1.0	12.6
Total debt service (% of exports)	..	32.0	33.7
Foreign direct investment, net inflows ($ billions)	0.1	1.3	6.1
Remittances received ($ millions)	..	122.0	187.5
Aid ($ millions)	112	189	172

Kenya

Sub-Saharan Africa | | **Low income**

Population (millions)	37	Population growth (%)	2.6
Surface area (1,000 sq. km)	580	National poverty rate (% of pop.)	..
GNI ($ billions)	21.3	GNI per capita ($)	580
GNI, PPP ($ billions)	53.8	GNI per capita, PPP ($)	1,470

	1990	2000	2006
People			
Share of poorest 20% in nat'l consumption/income (%)	3.4	..	..
Life expectancy at birth (years)	59	52	53
Total fertility (births per woman)	5.8	5.0	5.0
Adolescent fertility (births per 1,000 women 15–19)	..	104	104
Contraceptive prevalence (% of married women 15–49)	27	39	..
Births attended by skilled health staff (% of total)	50	44	..
Under-five mortality rate (per 1,000)	97	117	121
Child malnutrition, underweight (% of under age 5)	..	17.5	..
Child immunization, measles (% of ages 12–23 mos.)	78	75	77
Primary completion rate, total (% of relevant age group)	..	..	93
Gross secondary enrollment, total (% of relevant age group)	28	39	48
Ratio of girls to boys in primary & secondary school (%)	94	98	96
HIV prevalence rate (% of population ages 15–49)	..	..	6.1
Environment			
Forests (1,000 sq. km)	37	36	35
Deforestation (average annual %, 1990–2005)			0.3
Freshwater use (% of internal resources)	..	7.6	..
Access to improved water source (% of total pop.)	45	57	61
Access to improved sanitation facilities (% of total pop.)	40	43	43
Energy use per capita (kilograms of oil equivalent)	532	481	484
Carbon dioxide emissions per capita (metric tons)	0.2	0.3	0.3
Electricity use per capita (kilowatt-hours)	116	110	138
Economy			
GDP ($ billions)	8.6	12.7	22.8
GDP growth (annual %)	4.2	0.6	6.1
GDP implicit price deflator (annual % growth)	10.6	6.1	7.1
Value added in agriculture (% of GDP)	30	32	27
Value added in industry (% of GDP)	19	17	19
Value added in services (% of GDP)	51	51	54
Exports of goods and services (% of GDP)	26	22	26
Imports of goods and services (% of GDP)	31	30	36
Gross capital formation (% of GDP)	24	17	19
Central government revenue (% of GDP)	19.5	19.7	19.8
Central government cash surplus/deficit (% of GDP)	–2.8	2.0	1.5
States and markets			
Starting a business (days)			44
Stock market capitalization (% of GDP)	5.3	10.1	49.9
Military expenditures (% of GDP)	2.9	1.3	1.6
Fixed-line and mobile subscribers (per 100 people)	1	1	19
Internet users (per 100 people)	0.0	0.3	7.6
Paved roads (% of total)	13	12	14
High-technology exports (% of manufactured exports)	4	4	3
Global links			
Merchandise trade (% of GDP)	37.9	38.1	47.2
Net barter terms of trade (2000 = 100)	70	100	91
Total external debt ($ billions)	7.1	6.1	6.5
Short-term debt ($ millions)	934	798	574
Total debt service (% of exports)	35.4	20.9	6.5
Foreign direct investment, net inflows ($ millions)	57	111	51
Remittances received ($ billions)	0.1	0.5	1.1
Aid ($ billions)	1.2	0.5	0.9

Kiribati

East Asia & Pacific | | **Lower middle income**

Population (thousands)	100	Population growth (%)	1.2
Surface area (sq. km)	810	National poverty rate (% of pop.)	..
GNI ($ millions)	124	GNI per capita ($)	1,240
GNI, PPP ($ millions)	624	GNI per capita, PPP ($)	6,230

	1990	2000	2006
People			
Share of poorest 20% in nat'l consumption/income (%)	..	..	..
Life expectancy at birth (years)	57	62	..
Total fertility (births per woman)	4.0	3.8	..
Adolescent fertility (births per 1,000 women 15–19)	..	..	..
Contraceptive prevalence (% of married women 15–49)	..	21	..
Births attended by skilled health staff (% of total)	..	89	..
Under-five mortality rate (per 1,000)	88	70	64
Child malnutrition, underweight (% of under age 5)	..	..	..
Child immunization, measles (% of ages 12–23 mos.)	75	80	61
Primary completion rate, total (% of relevant age group)	..	99	125
Gross secondary enrollment, total (% of relevant age group)	..	99	88
Ratio of girls to boys in primary & secondary school (%)	..	122	107
HIV prevalence rate (% of population ages 15–49)	..	..	..
Environment			
Forests (sq. km)	20	20	20
Deforestation (average annual %, 1990–2005)			0.00
Freshwater use (% of internal resources)	..	..	..
Access to improved water source (% of total pop.)	49	62	65
Access to improved sanitation facilities (% of total pop.)	25	36	40
Energy use per capita (kilograms of oil equivalent)	..	..	..
Carbon dioxide emissions per capita (metric tons)	0.3	0.4	0.3
Electricity use per capita (kilowatt-hours)	..	..	..
Economy			
GDP ($ millions)	28	49	71
GDP growth (annual %)	2.1	1.9	5.8
GDP implicit price deflator (annual % growth)	-4.7	-0.4	2.2
Value added in agriculture (% of GDP)	19	7	7
Value added in industry (% of GDP)	8	10	7
Value added in services (% of GDP)	74	83	86
Exports of goods and services (% of GDP)	12	10	15
Imports of goods and services (% of GDP)	147	65	119
Gross capital formation (% of GDP)	93	..	..
Central government revenue (% of GDP)	..	..	..
Central government cash surplus/deficit (% of GDP)	..	..	..
States and markets			
Starting a business (days)			21
Stock market capitalization (% of GDP)	..	..	..
Military expenditures (% of GDP)	..	..	..
Fixed-line and mobile subscribers (per 100 people)	2	4	..
Internet users (per 100 people)	0.0	1.7	2.0
Paved roads (% of total)	..	..	..
High-technology exports (% of manufactured exports)	..	..	..
Global links			
Merchandise trade (% of GDP)	104.8	88.9	98.6
Net barter terms of trade (2000 = 100)	..	..	..
Total external debt ($ billions)	..	..	..
Short-term debt ($ billions)	..	..	..
Total debt service (% of exports)	..	..	..
Foreign direct investment, net inflows ($ billions)	..	..	..
Remittances received ($ millions)	5.0	7.0	7.0
Aid ($ millions)	20	18	-45

Korea, Dem. Rep.

East Asia & Pacific		**Low income**
Population (millions)	24	Population growth (%)	0.4
Surface area (1,000 sq. km)	121	National poverty rate (% of pop.)	..
GNI ($ billions)	..	GNI per capita ($)	..
GNI, PPP ($ billions)	..	GNI per capita, PPP ($)	..

	1990	2000	2006
People			
Share of poorest 20% in nat'l consumption/income (%)	..	..	..
Life expectancy at birth (years)	70	67	67
Total fertility (births per woman)	2.4	2.0	1.9
Adolescent fertility (births per 1,000 women 15–19)	..	2	1
Contraceptive prevalence (% of married women 15–49)	62	..	..
Births attended by skilled health staff (% of total)	..	97	97
Under-five mortality rate (per 1,000)	55	55	55
Child malnutrition, underweight (% of under age 5)	..	17.8	..
Child immunization, measles (% of ages 12–23 mos.)	98	78	96
Primary completion rate, total (% of relevant age group)	..	..	..
Gross secondary enrollment, total (% of relevant age group)	..	..	..
Ratio of girls to boys in primary & secondary school (%)	..	..	..
HIV prevalence rate (% of population ages 15–49)	..	..	0.2
Environment			
Forests (1,000 sq. km)	82	68	62
Deforestation (average annual %, 1990–2005)			1.9
Freshwater use (% of internal resources)	..	13.5	..
Access to improved water source (% of total pop.)	100	100	100
Access to improved sanitation facilities (% of total pop.)	..	59	59
Energy use per capita (kilograms of oil equivalent)	1,632	861	898
Carbon dioxide emissions per capita (metric tons)	12.1	3.4	3.4
Electricity use per capita (kilowatt-hours)	1,247	712	817
Economy			
GDP ($ billions)	..	..	..
GDP growth (annual %)	..	..	..
GDP implicit price deflator (annual % growth)	..	..	..
Value added in agriculture (% of GDP)	..	..	..
Value added in industry (% of GDP)	..	..	..
Value added in services (% of GDP)	..	..	..
Exports of goods and services (% of GDP)	..	..	..
Imports of goods and services (% of GDP)	..	..	..
Gross capital formation (% of GDP)	..	..	..
Central government revenue (% of GDP)	..	..	..
Central government cash surplus/deficit (% of GDP)	..	..	..
States and markets			
Starting a business (days)			..
Stock market capitalization (% of GDP)	..	..	..
Military expenditures (% of GDP)			..
Fixed-line and mobile subscribers (per 100 people)	2	2	..
Internet users (per 100 people)	0.0	0.0	..
Paved roads (% of total)	6	6	..
High-technology exports (% of manufactured exports)	..	..	..
Global links			
Merchandise trade (% of GDP)	..	..	..
Net barter terms of trade (2000 = 100)	..	..	..
Total external debt ($ billions)	..	..	..
Short-term debt ($ billions)	..	..	..
Total debt service (% of exports)	..	..	..
Foreign direct investment, net inflows ($ billions)	..	..	..
Remittances received ($ billions)	..	..	..
Aid ($ millions)	7.7	73.3	54.5

Korea, Rep.

High income

Population (millions)	48	Population growth (%)		0.3
Surface area (1,000 sq. km)	99	National poverty rate (% of pop.)		..
GNI ($ billions)	856.6	GNI per capita ($)		17,690
GNI, PPP ($ billions)	1,113.0	GNI per capita, PPP ($)		22,990

	1990	2000	2006
People			
Share of poorest 20% in nat'l consumption/income (%)	..	7.9	..
Life expectancy at birth (years)	71	76	78
Total fertility (births per woman)	1.6	1.5	1.1
Adolescent fertility (births per 1,000 women 15–19)	..	3	4
Contraceptive prevalence (% of married women 15–49)	79	..	..
Births attended by skilled health staff (% of total)	98	100	..
Under-five mortality rate (per 1,000)	9	5	5
Child malnutrition, underweight (% of under age 5)	..	..	..
Child immunization, measles (% of ages 12–23 mos.)	93	95	99
Primary completion rate, total (% of relevant age group)	97	95	101
Gross secondary enrollment, total (% of relevant age group)	90	98	96
Ratio of girls to boys in primary & secondary school (%)	99	98	96
HIV prevalence rate (% of population ages 15–49)	..	..	0.1
Environment			
Forests (1,000 sq. km)	64	63	63
Deforestation (average annual %, 1990–2005)			0.1
Freshwater use (% of internal resources)	..	28.6	..
Access to improved water source (% of total pop.)	..	92	92
Access to improved sanitation facilities (% of total pop.)	..	..	..
Energy use per capita (kilograms of oil equivalent)	2,178	4,045	4,426
Carbon dioxide emissions per capita (metric tons)	5.6	9.2	9.7
Electricity use per capita (kilowatt-hours)	2,373	5,264	7,779
Economy			
GDP ($ billions)	263.8	511.7	888.0
GDP growth (annual %)	9.2	8.5	5.0
GDP implicit price deflator (annual % growth)	10.5	0.7	-0.4
Value added in agriculture (% of GDP)	9	5	3
Value added in industry (% of GDP)	42	41	40
Value added in services (% of GDP)	49	54	57
Exports of goods and services (% of GDP)	28	41	43
Imports of goods and services (% of GDP)	29	38	42
Gross capital formation (% of GDP)	38	31	30
Central government revenue (% of GDP)	16.8	23.3	23.3
Central government cash surplus/deficit (% of GDP)	1.7	4.6	0.7
States and markets			
Starting a business (days)			17
Stock market capitalization (% of GDP)	42.1	33.5	94.1
Military expenditures (% of GDP)	3.6	2.5	2.7
Fixed-line and mobile subscribers (per 100 people)	31	112	139
Internet users (per 100 people)	0.0	40.5	70.5
Paved roads (% of total)	72	75	77
High-technology exports (% of manufactured exports)	18	35	32
Global links			
Merchandise trade (% of GDP)	51.1	65.0	71.5
Net barter terms of trade (2000 = 100)	133	100	73
Total external debt ($ billions)	..	..	..
Short-term debt ($ billions)	..	..	..
Total debt service (% of exports)	..	..	..
Foreign direct investment, net inflows ($ billions)	0.8	9.3	3.6
Remittances received ($ billions)	1.0	0.7	0.9
Aid ($ millions)	52	-198	..

Kuwait

High income

Population (millions)	2.6	Population growth (%)		2.5
Surface area (1,000 sq. km)	18	National poverty rate (% of pop.)		..
GNI ($ billions)	77.7	GNI per capita ($)		30,630
GNI, PPP ($ billions)	122.5	GNI per capita, PPP ($)		48,310

	1990	2000	2006
People			
Share of poorest 20% in nat'l consumption/income (%)	..	..	..
Life expectancy at birth (years)	75	77	78
Total fertility (births per woman)	3.5	2.6	2.3
Adolescent fertility (births per 1,000 women 15–19)	..	17	13
Contraceptive prevalence (% of married women 15–49)	..	..	..
Births attended by skilled health staff (% of total)	..	100	..
Under-five mortality rate (per 1,000)	16	11	11
Child malnutrition, underweight (% of under age 5)	..	..	..
Child immunization, measles (% of ages 12–23 mos.)	66	99	99
Primary completion rate, total (% of relevant age group)	..	96	91
Gross secondary enrollment, total (% of relevant age group)	43	94	89
Ratio of girls to boys in primary & secondary school (%)	97	103	102
HIV prevalence rate (% of population ages 15–49)	..	..	0.2
Environment			
Forests (sq. km)	30	50	60
Deforestation (average annual %, 1990–2005)			-4.7
Freshwater use (% of internal resources)			..
Access to improved water source (% of total pop.)	..	..	..
Access to improved sanitation facilities (% of total pop.)	..	..	..
Energy use per capita (kilograms of oil equivalent)	3,984	9,320	11,100
Carbon dioxide emissions per capita (metric tons)	20.4	37.7	40.4
Electricity use per capita (kilowatt-hours)	8,108	13,378	15,345
Economy			
GDP ($ billions)	18.4	37.7	80.8
GDP growth (annual %)	25.9	4.7	8.5
GDP implicit price deflator (annual % growth)	-1.7	20.5	24.5
Value added in agriculture (% of GDP)	1	0	..
Value added in industry (% of GDP)	52	59	..
Value added in services (% of GDP)	47	40	..
Exports of goods and services (% of GDP)	45	56	68
Imports of goods and services (% of GDP)	58	30	30
Gross capital formation (% of GDP)	18	11	20
Central government revenue (% of GDP)	58.7	45.3	37.2
Central government cash surplus/deficit (% of GDP)	3.7	1.4	8.2
States and markets			
Starting a business (days)			35
Stock market capitalization (% of GDP)	40.8	55.1	161.0
Military expenditures (% of GDP)	48.7	7.1	4.8
Fixed-line and mobile subscribers (per 100 people)	17	43	114
Internet users (per 100 people)	0.0	6.8	31.4
Paved roads (% of total)	73	81	85
High-technology exports (% of manufactured exports)	3	1	..
Global links			
Merchandise trade (% of GDP)	59.8	70.5	75.1
Net barter terms of trade (2000 = 100)	..	100	195
Total external debt ($ billions)	..	..	..
Short-term debt ($ billions)	..	..	..
Total debt service (% of exports)	..	..	..
Foreign direct investment, net inflows ($ millions)	..	16.3	109.6
Remittances received ($ billions)	..	..	..
Aid ($ millions)	5.7	2.8	..

Kyrgyz Republic

Europe & Central Asia		Low income
Population (millions)	5.2	Population growth (%)	0.9
Surface area (1,000 sq. km)	200	National poverty rate (% of pop.)	43
GNI ($ billions)	2.6	GNI per capita ($)	500
GNI, PPP ($ billions)	9.3	GNI per capita, PPP ($)	1,790

	1990	2000	2006
People			
Share of poorest 20% in nat'l consumption/income (%)	10.6	8.7	..
Life expectancy at birth (years)	68	69	68
Total fertility (births per woman)	3.7	2.4	2.4
Adolescent fertility (births per 1,000 women 15–19)	..	34	31
Contraceptive prevalence (% of married women 15–49)	..	..	48
Births attended by skilled health staff (% of total)	..	99	98
Under-five mortality rate (per 1,000)	75	51	41
Child malnutrition, underweight (% of under age 5)	..	..	..
Child immunization, measles (% of ages 12–23 mos.)	94	98	97
Primary completion rate, total (% of relevant age group)	..	95	99
Gross secondary enrollment, total (% of relevant age group)	100	84	86
Ratio of girls to boys in primary & secondary school (%)	..	101	100
HIV prevalence rate (% of population ages 15–49)	..	..	0.1
Environment			
Forests (1,000 sq. km)	8.4	8.6	8.7
Deforestation (average annual %, 1990–2005)			-0.3
Freshwater use (% of internal resources)	..	21.7	..
Access to improved water source (% of total pop.)	78	77	77
Access to improved sanitation facilities (% of total pop.)	60	59	59
Energy use per capita (kilograms of oil equivalent)	1,723	498	544
Carbon dioxide emissions per capita (metric tons)	2.8	0.9	1.1
Electricity use per capita (kilowatt-hours)	2,314	1,904	1,842
Economy			
GDP ($ billions)	2.7	1.4	2.8
GDP growth (annual %)	5.7	5.4	2.7
GDP implicit price deflator (annual % growth)	7.9	27.2	9.2
Value added in agriculture (% of GDP)	34	37	33
Value added in industry (% of GDP)	36	31	20
Value added in services (% of GDP)	30	32	47
Exports of goods and services (% of GDP)	29	42	39
Imports of goods and services (% of GDP)	50	48	76
Gross capital formation (% of GDP)	24	20	17
Central government revenue (% of GDP)	..	..	18.5
Central government cash surplus/deficit (% of GDP)	..	..	-0.6
States and markets			
Starting a business (days)			21
Stock market capitalization (% of GDP)	..	0.3	3.3
Military expenditures (% of GDP)	1.6	2.9	3.1
Fixed-line and mobile subscribers (per 100 people)	7	8	19
Internet users (per 100 people)	0.0	1.0	5.7
Paved roads (% of total)	90	91	..
High-technology exports (% of manufactured exports)	..	18	3
Global links			
Merchandise trade (% of GDP)	..	77.3	89.2
Net barter terms of trade (2000 = 100)	..	..	..
Total external debt ($ billions)	0.0	1.8	2.4
Short-term debt ($ millions)	0.0	129.0	107.9
Total debt service (% of exports)	..	29.3	5.7
Foreign direct investment, net inflows ($ millions)	..	-2.4	182.0
Remittances received ($ millions)	..	9.0	481.2
Aid ($ millions)	24	215	311

Lao PDR

Low income

Population (millions)	5.8	Population growth (%)		1.7
Surface area (1,000 sq. km)	237	National poverty rate (% of pop.)		33
GNI ($ billions)	2.9	GNI per capita ($)		500
GNI, PPP ($ billions)	10.0	GNI per capita, PPP ($)		1,740

	1990	2000	2006
People			
Share of poorest 20% in nat'l consumption/income (%)	9.6	8.1	..
Life expectancy at birth (years)	55	61	64
Total fertility (births per woman)	6.1	4.0	3.3
Adolescent fertility (births per 1,000 women 15-19)	..	89	75
Contraceptive prevalence (% of married women 15-49)	..	32	..
Births attended by skilled health staff (% of total)	..	19	..
Under-five mortality rate (per 1,000)	163	101	75
Child malnutrition, underweight (% of under age 5)	..	36.4	..
Child immunization, measles (% of ages 12–23 mos.)	32	42	48
Primary completion rate, total (% of relevant age group)	46	68	75
Gross secondary enrollment, total (% of relevant age group)	23	35	43
Ratio of girls to boys in primary & secondary school (%)	76	81	85
HIV prevalence rate (% of population ages 15–49)	..	..	0.1
Environment			
Forests (1,000 sq. km)	173	165	161
Deforestation (average annual %, 1990-2005)			0.5
Freshwater use (% of internal resources)	..	1.6	..
Access to improved water source (% of total pop.)	..	50	51
Access to improved sanitation facilities (% of total pop.)	..	29	30
Energy use per capita (kilograms of oil equivalent)	..	..	..
Carbon dioxide emissions per capita (metric tons)	0.1	0.2	0.2
Electricity use per capita (kilowatt-hours)	..	..	..
Economy			
GDP ($ millions)	866	1,735	3,437
GDP growth (annual %)	6.7	5.8	7.6
GDP implicit price deflator (annual % growth)	38.0	25.1	4.7
Value added in agriculture (% of GDP)	61	53	42
Value added in industry (% of GDP)	15	23	32
Value added in services (% of GDP)	24	25	26
Exports of goods and services (% of GDP)	11	30	36
Imports of goods and services (% of GDP)	25	34	42
Gross capital formation (% of GDP)	14	21	32
Central government revenue (% of GDP)	..	..	..
Central government cash surplus/deficit (% of GDP)	..	..	..
States and markets			
Starting a business (days)			103
Stock market capitalization (% of GDP)	..	..	..
Military expenditures (% of GDP)	..	2.0	..
Fixed-line and mobile subscribers (per 100 people)	0	1	13
Internet users (per 100 people)	0.0	0.1	0.4
Paved roads (% of total)	24	14	..
High-technology exports (% of manufactured exports)	..	..	..
Global links			
Merchandise trade (% of GDP)	30.5	49.8	56.3
Net barter terms of trade (2000 = 100)	..	100	118
Total external debt ($ billions)	1.8	2.5	3.0
Short-term debt ($ millions)	2.2	7.1	5.0
Total debt service (% of exports)	8.7	7.9	..
Foreign direct investment, net inflows ($ millions)	6.0	33.9	187.4
Remittances received ($ millions)	11.0	1.0	1.0
Aid ($ millions)	149	282	364

Latvia

Europe & Central Asia		Upper middle income	

Population (millions)	2.3	Population growth (%)	-0.6
Surface area (1,000 sq. km)	65	National poverty rate (% of pop.)	6
GNI ($ billions)	18.5	GNI per capita ($)	8,100
GNI, PPP ($ billions)	33.9	GNI per capita, PPP ($)	14,840

	1990	2000	2006
People			
Share of poorest 20% in nat'l consumption/income (%)	10.3	6.9	6.8
Life expectancy at birth (years)	69	70	71
Total fertility (births per woman)	2.0	1.2	1.4
Adolescent fertility (births per 1,000 women 15–19)	..	19	15
Contraceptive prevalence (% of married women 15–49)	..	..	..
Births attended by skilled health staff (% of total)	..	100	100
Under-five mortality rate (per 1,000)	18	13	9
Child malnutrition, underweight (% of under age 5)	..	..	..
Child immunization, measles (% of ages 12–23 mos.)	95	97	95
Primary completion rate, total (% of relevant age group)	..	97	92
Gross secondary enrollment, total (% of relevant age group)	92	90	99
Ratio of girls to boys in primary & secondary school (%)	101	101	99
HIV prevalence rate (% of population ages 15–49)	..	..	0.8
Environment			
Forests (1,000 sq. km)	28	29	29
Deforestation (average annual %, 1990–2005)			-0.4
Freshwater use (% of internal resources)	..	1.8	..
Access to improved water source (% of total pop.)	99	99	99
Access to improved sanitation facilities (% of total pop.)	..	78	78
Energy use per capita (kilograms of oil equivalent)	2,916	1,644	2,050
Carbon dioxide emissions per capita (metric tons)	5.4	2.5	3.1
Electricity use per capita (kilowatt-hours)	3,387	2,078	2,702
Economy			
GDP ($ billions)	7.4	7.8	20.1
GDP growth (annual %)	-7.9	6.9	11.9
GDP implicit price deflator (annual % growth)	24.1	4.2	11.1
Value added in agriculture (% of GDP)	22	5	4
Value added in industry (% of GDP)	46	24	21
Value added in services (% of GDP)	32	72	75
Exports of goods and services (% of GDP)	48	42	44
Imports of goods and services (% of GDP)	49	49	64
Gross capital formation (% of GDP)	40	24	38
Central government revenue (% of GDP)	..	26.1	27.0
Central government cash surplus/deficit (% of GDP)	..	-2.2	-0.5
States and markets			
Starting a business (days)			16
Stock market capitalization (% of GDP)	..	7.2	13.4
Military expenditures (% of GDP)	..	0.9	1.6
Fixed-line and mobile subscribers (per 100 people)	23	48	124
Internet users (per 100 people)	0.0	6.3	46.8
Paved roads (% of total)	13	100	100
High-technology exports (% of manufactured exports)	..	4	7
Global links			
Merchandise trade (% of GDP)	..	64.7	87.8
Net barter terms of trade (2000 = 100)	..	..	..
Total external debt ($ billions)	0.1	4.9	22.8
Short-term debt ($ billions)	0.0	2.8	10.5
Total debt service (% of exports)	0.0	17.4	33.3
Foreign direct investment, net inflows ($ billions)	0.0	0.4	1.7
Remittances received ($ millions)	..	72.0	482.1
Aid ($ millions)	3.4	91.0	..

Lebanon

Middle East & North Africa		Upper middle income	
Population (millions)	4.1	Population growth (%)	1.1
Surface area (1,000 sq. km)	10	National poverty rate (% of pop.)	..
GNI ($ billions)	22.6	GNI per capita ($)	5,580
GNI, PPP ($ billions)	38.9	GNI per capita, PPP ($)	9,600

	1990	2000	2006
People			
Share of poorest 20% in nat'l consumption/income (%)	..	..	..
Life expectancy at birth (years)	69	71	72
Total fertility (births per woman)	3.1	2.5	2.2
Adolescent fertility (births per 1,000 women 15–19)	..	29	25
Contraceptive prevalence (% of married women 15–49)	..	63	58
Births attended by skilled health staff (% of total)	..	93	98
Under-five mortality rate (per 1,000)	37	32	30
Child malnutrition, underweight (% of under age 5)	..	..	..
Child immunization, measles (% of ages 12–23 mos.)	61	90	96
Primary completion rate, total (% of relevant age group)	..	91	80
Gross secondary enrollment, total (% of relevant age group)	..	76	81
Ratio of girls to boys in primary & secondary school (%)	..	102	103
HIV prevalence rate (% of population ages 15–49)	..	..	0.1
Environment			
Forests (1,000 sq. km)	1.2	1.3	1.4
Deforestation (average annual %, 1990–2005)			–0.8
Freshwater use (% of internal resources)	..	28.8	..
Access to improved water source (% of total pop.)	100	100	100
Access to improved sanitation facilities (% of total pop.)	..	98	98
Energy use per capita (kilograms of oil equivalent)	776	1,341	1,391
Carbon dioxide emissions per capita (metric tons)	3.1	4.1	4.1
Electricity use per capita (kilowatt-hours)	471	2,081	2,242
Economy			
GDP ($ billions)	2.8	16.8	22.7
GDP growth (annual %)	26.5	1.5	0.0
GDP implicit price deflator (annual % growth)	15.5	–2.6	5.6
Value added in agriculture (% of GDP)	..	7	7
Value added in industry (% of GDP)	..	24	24
Value added in services (% of GDP)	..	69	70
Exports of goods and services (% of GDP)	18	14	24
Imports of goods and services (% of GDP)	100	37	40
Gross capital formation (% of GDP)	18	20	12
Central government revenue (% of GDP)	..	16.4	21.6
Central government cash surplus/deficit (% of GDP)	..	–18.9	–8.5
States and markets			
Starting a business (days)			46
Stock market capitalization (% of GDP)	..	9.4	36.4
Military expenditures (% of GDP)	7.6	4.3	4.1
Fixed-line and mobile subscribers (per 100 people)	13	35	44
Internet users (per 100 people)	0.0	8.0	23.4
Paved roads (% of total)	95	85	..
High-technology exports (% of manufactured exports)	..	2	2
Global links			
Merchandise trade (% of GDP)	106.5	41.3	54.8
Net barter terms of trade (2000 = 100)	..	100	101
Total external debt ($ billions)	1.8	9.9	24.0
Short-term debt ($ billions)	1.4	2.5	4.2
Total debt service (% of exports)	..	25.5	21.0
Foreign direct investment, net inflows ($ billions)	0.0	1.0	2.8
Remittances received ($ billions)	1.8	1.6	5.2
Aid ($ millions)	252	199	707

Lesotho

Sub-Saharan Africa	Lower middle income

Population (millions)	2.0	Population growth (%)	0.7
Surface area (1,000 sq. km)	30	National poverty rate (% of pop.)	..
GNI ($ billions)	2.0	GNI per capita ($)	980
GNI, PPP ($ billions)	3.6	GNI per capita, PPP ($)	1,810

	1990	2000	2006
People			
Share of poorest 20% in nat'l consumption/income (%)	..	..	..
Life expectancy at birth (years)	59	49	43
Total fertility (births per woman)	4.9	4.0	3.5
Adolescent fertility (births per 1,000 women 15–19)	..	91	77
Contraceptive prevalence (% of married women 15–49)	23	30	37
Births attended by skilled health staff (% of total)	..	60	55
Under-five mortality rate (per 1,000)	101	108	132
Child malnutrition, underweight (% of under age 5)	..	15.0	16.6
Child immunization, measles (% of ages 12–23 mos.)	80	74	85
Primary completion rate, total (% of relevant age group)	56	60	78
Gross secondary enrollment, total (% of relevant age group)	24	30	37
Ratio of girls to boys in primary & secondary school (%)	123	107	104
HIV prevalence rate (% of population ages 15–49)	..	..	23.2
Environment			
Forests (sq. km)	50	70	80
Deforestation (average annual %, 1990–2005)			–3.2
Freshwater use (% of internal resources)	..	1.0	..
Access to improved water source (% of total pop.)	..	79	79
Access to improved sanitation facilities (% of total pop.)	37	37	37
Energy use per capita (kilograms of oil equivalent)	..	..	..
Carbon dioxide emissions per capita (metric tons)	..	..	..
Electricity use per capita (kilowatt-hours)	..	..	..
Economy			
GDP ($ millions)	615	853	1,494
GDP growth (annual %)	6.4	2.6	7.2
GDP implicit price deflator (annual % growth)	8.7	4.5	4.2
Value added in agriculture (% of GDP)	24	18	16
Value added in industry (% of GDP)	33	41	43
Value added in services (% of GDP)	43	41	40
Exports of goods and services (% of GDP)	17	30	51
Imports of goods and services (% of GDP)	122	93	99
Gross capital formation (% of GDP)	53	43	33
Central government revenue (% of GDP)	39.4	44.3	50.0
Central government cash surplus/deficit (% of GDP)	–0.5	–2.6	4.1
States and markets			
Starting a business (days)			73
Stock market capitalization (% of GDP)	..	..	..
Military expenditures (% of GDP)	4.5	3.6	2.4
Fixed-line and mobile subscribers (per 100 people)	1	2	15
Internet users (per 100 people)	0.0	0.2	2.6
Paved roads (% of total)	18	18	..
High-technology exports (% of manufactured exports)	..	0	..
Global links			
Merchandise trade (% of GDP)	119.3	120.6	144.5
Net barter terms of trade (2000 = 100)	100	100	81
Total external debt ($ millions)	396	672	670
Short-term debt ($ millions)	2.8	4.0	0.1
Total debt service (% of exports)	4.2	11.3	4.0
Foreign direct investment, net inflows ($ millions)	17	118	78
Remittances received ($ millions)	428	252	361
Aid ($ millions)	139	37	72

Liberia

Sub-Saharan Africa   **Low income**

Population (millions)	3.6	Population growth (%)		3.9
Surface area (1,000 sq. km)	111	National poverty rate (% of pop.)		..
GNI ($ millions)	469	GNI per capita ($)		130
GNI, PPP ($ millions)	935	GNI per capita, PPP ($)		260

	1990	2000	2006
People			
Share of poorest 20% in nat'l consumption/income (%)	..	..	..
Life expectancy at birth (years)	43	43	45
Total fertility (births per woman)	6.9	6.8	6.8
Adolescent fertility (births per 1,000 women 15–19)	..	227	220
Contraceptive prevalence (% of married women 15–49)	..	10	..
Births attended by skilled health staff (% of total)	..	51	..
Under-five mortality rate (per 1,000)	235	235	235
Child malnutrition, underweight (% of under age 5)	..	22.8	..
Child immunization, measles (% of ages 12–23 mos.)	..	52	94
Primary completion rate, total (% of relevant age group)	..	..	63
Gross secondary enrollment, total (% of relevant age group)	..	32	..
Ratio of girls to boys in primary & secondary school (%)	..	73	..
HIV prevalence rate (% of population ages 15–49)	..	..	..
Environment			
Forests (1,000 sq. km)	41	35	32
Deforestation (average annual %, 1990–2005)			1.7
Freshwater use (% of internal resources)	..	0.1	..
Access to improved water source (% of total pop.)	55	61	61
Access to improved sanitation facilities (% of total pop.)	39	28	27
Energy use per capita (kilograms of oil equivalent)	..	..	..
Carbon dioxide emissions per capita (metric tons)	0.2	0.1	0.1
Electricity use per capita (kilowatt-hours)	..	..	..
Economy			
GDP ($ millions)	384	561	631
GDP growth (annual %)	–51.0	25.7	7.8
GDP implicit price deflator (annual % growth)	–0.2	–1.3	12.4
Value added in agriculture (% of GDP)	54	72	66
Value added in industry (% of GDP)	17	12	16
Value added in services (% of GDP)	29	16	18
Exports of goods and services (% of GDP)	..	21	28
Imports of goods and services (% of GDP)	..	26	72
Gross capital formation (% of GDP)	..	5	16
Central government revenue (% of GDP)	..	..	..
Central government cash surplus/deficit (% of GDP)	..	..	..
States and markets			
Starting a business (days)			99
Stock market capitalization (% of GDP)	..	..	..
Military expenditures (% of GDP)	7.4	7.5	..
Fixed-line and mobile subscribers (per 100 people)	0	0	..
Internet users (per 100 people)	0.0	0.0	..
Paved roads (% of total)	6	6	..
High-technology exports (% of manufactured exports)	..	..	..
Global links			
Merchandise trade (% of GDP)	374.1	177.8	99.0
Net barter terms of trade (2000 = 100)			
Total external debt ($ billions)	1.8	2.0	2.7
Short-term debt ($ billions)	0.4	0.7	1.2
Total debt service (% of exports)	..	..	..
Foreign direct investment, net inflows ($ millions)	225	21	–82
Remittances received ($ billions)	..	..	..
Aid ($ millions)	114	67	269

Libya

Middle East & North Africa		Upper middle income	
Population (millions)	6.0	Population growth (%)	2.0
Surface area (1,000 sq. km)	1,760	National poverty rate (% of pop.)	..
GNI ($ billions)	44.0	GNI per capita ($)	7,290
GNI, PPP ($ billions)	70.2	GNI per capita, PPP ($)	11,630

	1990	2000	2006
People			
Share of poorest 20% in nat'l consumption/income (%)	..	..	..
Life expectancy at birth (years)	68	73	74
Total fertility (births per woman)	4.7	3.2	2.8
Adolescent fertility (births per 1,000 women 15–19)	..	4	3
Contraceptive prevalence (% of married women 15–49)	..	..	..
Births attended by skilled health staff (% of total)	..	99	..
Under-five mortality rate (per 1,000)	41	22	18
Child malnutrition, underweight (% of under age 5)	..	..	..
Child immunization, measles (% of ages 12–23 mos.)	89	92	98
Primary completion rate, total (% of relevant age group)	..	..	..
Gross secondary enrollment, total (% of relevant age group)	80	108	111
Ratio of girls to boys in primary & secondary school (%)	..	103	105
HIV prevalence rate (% of population ages 15–49)	..	..	0.2
Environment			
Forests (1,000 sq. km)	2.2	2.2	2.2
Deforestation (average annual %, 1990–2005)			0.00
Freshwater use (% of internal resources)	..	711.3	..
Access to improved water source (% of total pop.)	71	71	..
Access to improved sanitation facilities (% of total pop.)	97	97	97
Energy use per capita (kilograms of oil equivalent)	2,645	3,184	3,218
Carbon dioxide emissions per capita (metric tons)	8.7	10.3	10.3
Electricity use per capita (kilowatt-hours)	1,603	2,227	3,299
Economy			
GDP ($ billions)	28.9	34.5	50.3
GDP growth (annual %)	..	1.1	5.6
GDP implicit price deflator (annual % growth)	..	23.5	14.9
Value added in agriculture (% of GDP)	..	..	..
Value added in industry (% of GDP)	..	..	..
Value added in services (% of GDP)	..	..	..
Exports of goods and services (% of GDP)	40	35	..
Imports of goods and services (% of GDP)	31	15	..
Gross capital formation (% of GDP)	19	13	..
Central government revenue (% of GDP)	..	..	..
Central government cash surplus/deficit (% of GDP)	..	..	..
States and markets			
Starting a business (days)			..
Stock market capitalization (% of GDP)	..	..	..
Military expenditures (% of GDP)	..	3.1	1.5
Fixed-line and mobile subscribers (per 100 people)	5	12	73
Internet users (per 100 people)	0.0	0.2	3.9
Paved roads (% of total)	52	57	..
High-technology exports (% of manufactured exports)	..	..	..
Global links			
Merchandise trade (% of GDP)	64.2	49.6	92.3
Net barter terms of trade (2000 = 100)	..	100	172
Total external debt ($ billions)	..	..	..
Short-term debt ($ billions)	..	..	..
Total debt service (% of exports)	..	..	..
Foreign direct investment, net inflows ($ billions)	..	..	..
Remittances received ($ millions)	..	9.0	16.0
Aid ($ millions)	8.3	13.8	37.3

Liechtenstein

Population (thousands)	35	Population growth (%)		0.4
Surface area (sq. km)	160	National poverty rate (% of pop.)		..
GNI ($ billions)	..	GNI per capita ($)		..
GNI, PPP ($ billions)	..	GNI per capita, PPP ($)		..

	1990	2000	2006
People			
Share of poorest 20% in nat'l consumption/income (%)	..	..	..
Life expectancy at birth (years)	..	..	..
Total fertility (births per woman)	..	..	..
Adolescent fertility (births per 1,000 women 15–19)	..	..	..
Contraceptive prevalence (% of married women 15–49)	..	..	..
Births attended by skilled health staff (% of total)	..	..	..
Under-five mortality rate (per 1,000)	10	6	3
Child malnutrition, underweight (% of under age 5)	..	..	..
Child immunization, measles (% of ages 12–23 mos.)	..	..	..
Primary completion rate, total (% of relevant age group)	..	..	98
Gross secondary enrollment, total (% of relevant age group)	..	..	112
Ratio of girls to boys in primary & secondary school (%)	..	..	92
HIV prevalence rate (% of population ages 15–49)	..	..	..
Environment			
Forests (sq. km)	60	70	70
Deforestation (average annual %, 1990–2005)			–1.0
Freshwater use (% of internal resources)	..	..	..
Access to improved water source (% of total pop.)	..	..	..
Access to improved sanitation facilities (% of total pop.)	..	..	..
Energy use per capita (kilograms of oil equivalent)	..	..	..
Carbon dioxide emissions per capita (metric tons)	..	..	..
Electricity use per capita (kilowatt-hours)	..	..	..
Economy			
GDP ($ billions)	..	..	..
GDP growth (annual %)	..	..	..
GDP implicit price deflator (annual % growth)	..	..	..
Value added in agriculture (% of GDP)	..	..	..
Value added in industry (% of GDP)	..	..	..
Value added in services (% of GDP)	..	..	..
Exports of goods and services (% of GDP)	..	..	..
Imports of goods and services (% of GDP)	..	..	..
Gross capital formation (% of GDP)	..	..	..
Central government revenue (% of GDP)	..	..	..
Central government cash surplus/deficit (% of GDP)	..	..	..
States and markets			
Starting a business (days)			..
Stock market capitalization (% of GDP)	..	..	..
Military expenditures (% of GDP)	..	..	..
Fixed-line and mobile subscribers (per 100 people)	..	..	140
Internet users (per 100 people)	..	..	63.0
Paved roads (% of total)	..	..	..
High-technology exports (% of manufactured exports)	..	..	..
Global links			
Merchandise trade (% of GDP)	..	..	..
Net barter terms of trade (2000 = 100)	..	..	..
Total external debt ($ billions)	..	..	..
Short-term debt ($ billions)	..	..	..
Total debt service (% of exports)	..	..	..
Foreign direct investment, net inflows ($ billions)	..	..	..
Remittances received ($ billions)	..	..	..
Aid ($ billions)	..	..	..

Lithuania

Europe & Central Asia		Upper middle income	
Population (millions)	3.4	Population growth (%)	-0.6
Surface area (1,000 sq. km)	65	National poverty rate (% of pop.)	..
GNI ($ billions)	26.9	GNI per capita ($)	7,930
GNI, PPP ($ billions)	49.4	GNI per capita, PPP ($)	14,550

	1990	2000	2006
People			
Share of poorest 20% in nat'l consumption/income (%)	10.5	7.9	6.8
Life expectancy at birth (years)	71	72	71
Total fertility (births per woman)	2.0	1.4	1.3
Adolescent fertility (births per 1,000 women 15–19)	..	26	19
Contraceptive prevalence (% of married women 15–49)	..	..	..
Births attended by skilled health staff (% of total)	..	100	100
Under-five mortality rate (per 1,000)	13	11	8
Child malnutrition, underweight (% of under age 5)	..	..	..
Child immunization, measles (% of ages 12–23 mos.)	89	97	97
Primary completion rate, total (% of relevant age group)	..	99	91
Gross secondary enrollment, total (% of relevant age group)	92	98	100
Ratio of girls to boys in primary & secondary school (%)	..	99	100
HIV prevalence rate (% of population ages 15–49)	..	..	0.2
Environment			
Forests (1,000 sq. km)	19	20	21
Deforestation (average annual %, 1990–2005)			-0.5
Freshwater use (% of internal resources)		1.7	..
Access to improved water source (% of total pop.)	..	..	..
Access to improved sanitation facilities (% of total pop.)	..	..	..
Energy use per capita (kilograms of oil equivalent)	4,377	2,034	2,515
Carbon dioxide emissions per capita (metric tons)	6.6	3.4	3.9
Electricity use per capita (kilowatt-hours)	4,023	2,517	3,104
Economy			
GDP ($ billions)	10.5	11.4	29.8
GDP growth (annual %)	-5.7	3.9	7.7
GDP implicit price deflator (annual % growth)	228.3	0.7	6.6
Value added in agriculture (% of GDP)	27	8	5
Value added in industry (% of GDP)	31	30	35
Value added in services (% of GDP)	42	62	59
Exports of goods and services (% of GDP)	52	45	60
Imports of goods and services (% of GDP)	61	51	70
Gross capital formation (% of GDP)	33	20	27
Central government revenue (% of GDP)	..	26.0	29.0
Central government cash surplus/deficit (% of GDP)	..	-2.8	-0.2
States and markets			
Starting a business (days)			26
Stock market capitalization (% of GDP)	..	13.9	34.2
Military expenditures (% of GDP)	..	1.4	1.2
Fixed-line and mobile subscribers (per 100 people)	21	49	162
Internet users (per 100 people)	0.0	6.4	31.9
Paved roads (% of total)	82	91	78
High-technology exports (% of manufactured exports)	0	4	8
Global links			
Merchandise trade (% of GDP)	..	81.2	112.3
Net barter terms of trade (2000 = 100)	..	..	..
Total external debt ($ billions)	0.1	4.7	19.0
Short-term debt ($ billions)	0.0	1.1	7.7
Total debt service (% of exports)	..	20.9	22.1
Foreign direct investment, net inflows ($ billions)	0.0	0.4	1.8
Remittances received ($ millions)	..	50.0	994.1
Aid ($ millions)	4.0	99.1	..

Luxembourg

High income

Population (thousands)	462	Population growth (%)	1.1
Surface area (1,000 sq. km)	2.6	National poverty rate (% of pop.)	..
GNI ($ billions)	32.9	GNI per capita ($)	71,240
GNI, PPP ($ billions)	28.1	GNI per capita, PPP ($)	60,870

	1990	2000	2006
People			
Share of poorest 20% in nat'l consumption/income (%)	..	8.4	..
Life expectancy at birth (years)	75	78	79
Total fertility (births per woman)	1.6	1.8	1.7
Adolescent fertility (births per 1,000 women 15–19)	..	11	10
Contraceptive prevalence (% of married women 15–49)	..	..	..
Births attended by skilled health staff (% of total)	..	100	..
Under-five mortality rate (per 1,000)	9	6	4
Child malnutrition, underweight (% of under age 5)	..	..	..
Child immunization, measles (% of ages 12–23 mos.)	80	91	95
Primary completion rate, total (% of relevant age group)	..	82	81
Gross secondary enrollment, total (% of relevant age group)	75	98	96
Ratio of girls to boys in primary & secondary school (%)	..	104	103
HIV prevalence rate (% of population ages 15–49)	..	..	0.2
Environment			
Forests (sq. km)	860	870	870
Deforestation (average annual %, 1990–2005)			–0.1
Freshwater use (% of internal resources)	..	..	..
Access to improved water source (% of total pop.)	100	100	100
Access to improved sanitation facilities (% of total pop.)	..	..	..
Energy use per capita (kilograms of oil equivalent)	9,351	8,409	10,457
Carbon dioxide emissions per capita (metric tons)	25.9	18.8	24.9
Electricity use per capita (kilowatt-hours)	13,666	15,425	15,971
Economy			
GDP ($ billions)	12.7	20.3	41.5
GDP growth (annual %)	5.3	8.4	6.2
GDP implicit price deflator (annual % growth)	2.5	2.0	5.9
Value added in agriculture (% of GDP)	1	1	0
Value added in industry (% of GDP)	27	18	15
Value added in services (% of GDP)	71	81	85
Exports of goods and services (% of GDP)	102	150	177
Imports of goods and services (% of GDP)	88	129	149
Gross capital formation (% of GDP)	26	23	18
Central government revenue (% of GDP)	..	39.8	37.9
Central government cash surplus/deficit (% of GDP)	..	5.5	0.9
States and markets			
Starting a business (days)			26
Stock market capitalization (% of GDP)	82.9	167.8	191.8
Military expenditures (% of GDP)	0.8	0.6	0.8
Fixed-line and mobile subscribers (per 100 people)	48	126	208
Internet users (per 100 people)	0.0	22.8	73.4
Paved roads (% of total)	99	100	100
High-technology exports (% of manufactured exports)	..	17	12
Global links			
Merchandise trade (% of GDP)	..	97.0	119.4
Net barter terms of trade (2000 = 100)	..	..	..
Total external debt ($ billions)	..	..	..
Short-term debt ($ billions)	..	..	..
Total debt service (% of exports)	..	..	..
Foreign direct investment, net inflows ($ billions)	..	118.3	126.5
Remittances received ($ billions)	..	0.6	1.3
Aid ($ billions)	..	..	..

Macao, China

High income

Population (thousands)	478	Population growth (%)	0.9
Surface area (sq. km)	28	National poverty rate (% of pop.)	..
GNI ($ billions)	..	GNI per capita ($)	..
GNI, PPP ($ billions)	..	GNI per capita, PPP ($)	..

	1990	2000	2006
People			
Share of poorest 20% in nat'l consumption/income (%)	..	..	..
Life expectancy at birth (years)	77	79	80
Total fertility (births per woman)	1.8	1.0	0.9
Adolescent fertility (births per 1,000 women 15-19)		5	5
Contraceptive prevalence (% of married women 15-49)	..	..	..
Births attended by skilled health staff (% of total)	..	..	100
Under-five mortality rate (per 1,000)	..	..	..
Child malnutrition, underweight (% of under age 5)	..	..	..
Child immunization, measles (% of ages 12-23 mos.)	..	..	..
Primary completion rate, total (% of relevant age group)	97	97	104
Gross secondary enrollment, total (% of relevant age group)	65	79	98
Ratio of girls to boys in primary & secondary school (%)	100	99	97
HIV prevalence rate (% of population ages 15-49)	..	..	..
Environment			
Forests (1,000 sq. km)	..	..	..
Deforestation (average annual %, 1990-2005)			..
Freshwater use (% of internal resources)	..		..
Access to improved water source (% of total pop.)	..	..	..
Access to improved sanitation facilities (% of total pop.)	..	..	..
Energy use per capita (kilograms of oil equivalent)	..	..	..
Carbon dioxide emissions per capita (metric tons)	2.8	3.7	4.7
Electricity use per capita (kilowatt-hours)	..	..	..
Economy			
GDP ($ billions)	3.0	5.9	14.2
GDP growth (annual %)	9.8	5.7	16.6
GDP implicit price deflator (annual % growth)	9.7	-1.0	6.0
Value added in agriculture (% of GDP)	..	0	0
Value added in industry (% of GDP)	..	16	19
Value added in services (% of GDP)	..	90	85
Exports of goods and services (% of GDP)	110	104	92
Imports of goods and services (% of GDP)	84	67	58
Gross capital formation (% of GDP)	25	12	34
Central government revenue (% of GDP)	..	20.7	25.6
Central government cash surplus/deficit (% of GDP)	..	1.7	10.2
States and markets			
Starting a business (days)			..
Stock market capitalization (% of GDP)	..	..	4.2
Military expenditures (% of GDP)	..	..	..
Fixed-line and mobile subscribers (per 100 people)	26	72	170
Internet users (per 100 people)	0.0	13.6	41.9
Paved roads (% of total)	100	100	100
High-technology exports (% of manufactured exports)	2	1	1
Global links			
Merchandise trade (% of GDP)	108.4	81.6	50.2
Net barter terms of trade (2000 = 100)	..	100	94
Total external debt ($ billions)	..	..	..
Short-term debt ($ billions)	..	..	..
Total debt service (% of exports)	..	..	..
Foreign direct investment, net inflows ($ billions)	..	0.4	2.7
Remittances received ($ millions)	..	..	511.5
Aid ($ millions)	0.2	0.7	13.7

Macedonia, FYR

Europe & Central Asia		Lower middle income	
Population (millions)	2.0	Population growth (%)	0.1
Surface area (1,000 sq. km)	26	National poverty rate (% of pop.)	22
GNI ($ billions)	6.3	GNI per capita ($)	3,070
GNI, PPP ($ billions)	16.0	GNI per capita, PPP ($)	7,850

	1990	2000	2006
People			
Share of poorest 20% in nat'l consumption/income (%)	..	6.7	..
Life expectancy at birth (years)	71	73	74
Total fertility (births per woman)	2.0	1.6	1.5
Adolescent fertility (births per 1,000 women 15-19)	..	28	22
Contraceptive prevalence (% of married women 15-49)	..	..	14
Births attended by skilled health staff (% of total)	..	..	98
Under-five mortality rate (per 1,000)	38	16	17
Child malnutrition, underweight (% of under age 5)	..	1.9	1.2
Child immunization, measles (% of ages 12-23 mos.)	..	97	94
Primary completion rate, total (% of relevant age group)	..	99	97
Gross secondary enrollment, total (% of relevant age group)	56	84	84
Ratio of girls to boys in primary & secondary school (%)	99	98	99
HIV prevalence rate (% of population ages 15-49)	..	..	0.1
Environment			
Forests (1,000 sq. km)	9.1	9.1	9.1
Deforestation (average annual %, 1990-2005)			0.00
Freshwater use (% of internal resources)	..	..	..
Access to improved water source (% of total pop.)	..	..	..
Access to improved sanitation facilities (% of total pop.)	..	..	..
Energy use per capita (kilograms of oil equivalent)	1,421	1,349	1,346
Carbon dioxide emissions per capita (metric tons)	8.1	5.7	5.1
Electricity use per capita (kilowatt-hours)	2,789	2,932	3,417
Economy			
GDP ($ billions)	4.5	3.6	6.2
GDP growth (annual %)	-6.2	4.5	3.0
GDP implicit price deflator (annual % growth)	93.7	8.2	2.7
Value added in agriculture (% of GDP)	9	12	13
Value added in industry (% of GDP)	44	34	29
Value added in services (% of GDP)	47	54	58
Exports of goods and services (% of GDP)	26	49	50
Imports of goods and services (% of GDP)	36	64	68
Gross capital formation (% of GDP)	19	22	21
Central government revenue (% of GDP)	..	..	..
Central government cash surplus/deficit (% of GDP)	..	..	..
States and markets			
Starting a business (days)			15
Stock market capitalization (% of GDP)	..	0.2	17.7
Military expenditures (% of GDP)	..	1.9	2.0
Fixed-line and mobile subscribers (per 100 people)	15	31	94
Internet users (per 100 people)	0.0	2.5	13.2
Paved roads (% of total)	59	64	..
High-technology exports (% of manufactured exports)	..	1	1
Global links			
Merchandise trade (% of GDP)	103.8	95.3	99.1
Net barter terms of trade (2000 = 100)	..	..	..
Total external debt ($ billions)	..	1.5	2.7
Short-term debt ($ millions)	..	55.1	302.6
Total debt service (% of exports)	..	7.9	15.7
Foreign direct investment, net inflows ($ millions)	0.0	174.5	350.5
Remittances received ($ millions)	..	81.0	266.6
Aid ($ millions)	..	251.1	199.8

Madagascar

Sub-Saharan Africa		Low income	
Population (millions)	19	Population growth (%)	2.7
Surface area (1,000 sq. km)	587	National poverty rate (% of pop.)	..
GNI ($ billions)	5.3	GNI per capita ($)	280
GNI, PPP ($ billions)	16.6	GNI per capita, PPP ($)	870

	1990	2000	2006
People			
Share of poorest 20% in nat'l consumption/income (%)	..	4.9	..
Life expectancy at birth (years)	51	56	59
Total fertility (births per woman)	6.2	5.5	4.9
Adolescent fertility (births per 1,000 women 15–19)	..	152	136
Contraceptive prevalence (% of married women 15–49)	17	19	27
Births attended by skilled health staff (% of total)	57	46	51
Under-five mortality rate (per 1,000)	168	137	115
Child malnutrition, underweight (% of under age 5)	35.5	..	36.8
Child immunization, measles (% of ages 12–23 mos.)	47	56	59
Primary completion rate, total (% of relevant age group)	35	36	57
Gross secondary enrollment, total (% of relevant age group)	17	14	24
Ratio of girls to boys in primary & secondary school (%)	98	97	96
HIV prevalence rate (% of population ages 15–49)	..	..	0.5
Environment			
Forests (1,000 sq. km)	137	130	128
Deforestation (average annual %, 1990–2005)			0.4
Freshwater use (% of internal resources)	..	4.4	..
Access to improved water source (% of total pop.)	40	45	46
Access to improved sanitation facilities (% of total pop.)	14	27	32
Energy use per capita (kilograms of oil equivalent)	..	..	..
Carbon dioxide emissions per capita (metric tons)	0.1	0.1	0.2
Electricity use per capita (kilowatt-hours)	..	..	..
Economy			
GDP ($ billions)	3.1	3.9	5.5
GDP growth (annual %)	3.1	4.8	4.9
GDP implicit price deflator (annual % growth)	11.5	7.2	11.3
Value added in agriculture (% of GDP)	29	29	28
Value added in industry (% of GDP)	13	14	15
Value added in services (% of GDP)	59	57	57
Exports of goods and services (% of GDP)	17	31	30
Imports of goods and services (% of GDP)	28	38	41
Gross capital formation (% of GDP)	17	15	25
Central government revenue (% of GDP)	..	11.7	11.7
Central government cash surplus/deficit (% of GDP)	..	-2.0	9.9
States and markets			
Starting a business (days)			7
Stock market capitalization (% of GDP)	..	..	..
Military expenditures (% of GDP)	1.2	1.2	1.0
Fixed-line and mobile subscribers (per 100 people)	0	1	6
Internet users (per 100 people)	0.0	0.2	0.6
Paved roads (% of total)	15	12	..
High-technology exports (% of manufactured exports)	8	1	1
Global links			
Merchandise trade (% of GDP)	31.5	47.0	44.4
Net barter terms of trade (2000 = 100)	81	100	77
Total external debt ($ billions)	3.7	4.7	1.5
Short-term debt ($ millions)	225	301	189
Total debt service (% of exports)	45.5	9.6	5.7
Foreign direct investment, net inflows ($ millions)	22	83	230
Remittances received ($ millions)	8.0	11.0	11.0
Aid ($ millions)	397	322	754

Malawi

Sub-Saharan Africa   **Low income**

Population (millions)	14	Population growth (%)	2.6
Surface area (1,000 sq. km)	118	National poverty rate (% of pop.)	..
GNI ($ billions)	3.1	GNI per capita ($)	230
GNI, PPP ($ billions)	9.4	GNI per capita, PPP ($)	690

	1990	2000	2006
People			
Share of poorest 20% in nat'l consumption/income (%)	..	..	7.0
Life expectancy at birth (years)	49	46	48
Total fertility (births per woman)	6.9	6.2	5.7
Adolescent fertility (births per 1,000 women 15-19)	..	160	140
Contraceptive prevalence (% of married women 15-49)	13	31	42
Births attended by skilled health staff (% of total)	55	56	54
Under-five mortality rate (per 1,000)	221	155	120
Child malnutrition, underweight (% of under age 5)	24.4	21.5	18.4
Child immunization, measles (% of ages 12-23 mos.)	81	73	85
Primary completion rate, total (% of relevant age group)	29	66	55
Gross secondary enrollment, total (% of relevant age group)	8	31	29
Ratio of girls to boys in primary & secondary school (%)	81	93	100
HIV prevalence rate (% of population ages 15-49)	..	..	14.1
Environment			
Forests (1,000 sq. km)	39	36	34
Deforestation (average annual %, 1990-2005)			0.9
Freshwater use (% of internal resources)	..	6.3	..
Access to improved water source (% of total pop.)	40	64	73
Access to improved sanitation facilities (% of total pop.)	47	58	61
Energy use per capita (kilograms of oil equivalent)	..	..	..
Carbon dioxide emissions per capita (metric tons)	0.1	0.1	0.1
Electricity use per capita (kilowatt-hours)	..	..	..
Economy			
GDP ($ billions)	1.9	1.7	3.2
GDP growth (annual %)	5.7	1.6	7.4
GDP implicit price deflator (annual % growth)	10.7	30.5	18.5
Value added in agriculture (% of GDP)	45	40	34
Value added in industry (% of GDP)	29	18	20
Value added in services (% of GDP)	26	43	46
Exports of goods and services (% of GDP)	24	26	17
Imports of goods and services (% of GDP)	33	35	29
Gross capital formation (% of GDP)	23	14	24
Central government revenue (% of GDP)	..	..	..
Central government cash surplus/deficit (% of GDP)	..	..	
States and markets			
Starting a business (days)			37
Stock market capitalization (% of GDP)	..	..	18.6
Military expenditures (% of GDP)	1.3	0.7	..
Fixed-line and mobile subscribers (per 100 people)	0	1	4
Internet users (per 100 people)	0.0	0.1	0.4
Paved roads (% of total)	22	..	..
High-technology exports (% of manufactured exports)	0	2	11
Global links			
Merchandise trade (% of GDP)	52.7	52.3	55.3
Net barter terms of trade (2000 = 100)	148	100	84
Total external debt ($ billions)	1.6	2.7	0.9
Short-term debt ($ millions)	58	78	64
Total debt service (% of exports)	29.3	13.3	..
Foreign direct investment, net inflows ($ millions)	23	26	30
Remittances received ($ millions)	..	1.0	1.0
Aid ($ millions)	500	446	669

Malaysia

East Asia & Pacific		Upper middle income	
Population (millions)	26	Population growth (%)	1.8
Surface area (1,000 sq. km)	330	National poverty rate (% of pop.)	..
GNI ($ billions)	146.8	GNI per capita ($)	5,620
GNI, PPP ($ billions)	317.4	GNI per capita, PPP ($)	12,160

	1990	2000	2006
People			
Share of poorest 20% in nat'l consumption/income (%)	4.6	..	..
Life expectancy at birth (years)	70	73	74
Total fertility (births per woman)	3.7	3.0	2.7
Adolescent fertility (births per 1,000 women 15–19)	..	15	13
Contraceptive prevalence (% of married women 15–49)	50	..	..
Births attended by skilled health staff (% of total)	..	97	98
Under-five mortality rate (per 1,000)	22	14	12
Child malnutrition, underweight (% of under age 5)	..	..	..
Child immunization, measles (% of ages 12–23 mos.)	70	88	90
Primary completion rate, total (% of relevant age group)	92	92	95
Gross secondary enrollment, total (% of relevant age group)	57	65	72
Ratio of girls to boys in primary & secondary school (%)	101	103	105
HIV prevalence rate (% of population ages 15–49)	..	..	0.5
Environment			
Forests (1,000 sq. km)	224	216	209
Deforestation (average annual %, 1990–2005)			0.5
Freshwater use (% of internal resources)	..	1.6	..
Access to improved water source (% of total pop.)	98	98	99
Access to improved sanitation facilities (% of total pop.)	..	94	94
Energy use per capita (kilograms of oil equivalent)	1,288	2,202	2,389
Carbon dioxide emissions per capita (metric tons)	3.1	5.4	7.0
Electricity use per capita (kilowatt-hours)	1,178	2,743	3,262
Economy			
GDP ($ billions)	44.0	90.3	150.7
GDP growth (annual %)	9.0	8.9	5.9
GDP implicit price deflator (annual % growth)	3.8	4.8	4.1
Value added in agriculture (% of GDP)	15	9	9
Value added in industry (% of GDP)	42	51	50
Value added in services (% of GDP)	43	40	41
Exports of goods and services (% of GDP)	75	124	117
Imports of goods and services (% of GDP)	72	104	100
Gross capital formation (% of GDP)	32	27	21
Central government revenue (% of GDP)	26.4	19.2	..
Central government cash surplus/deficit (% of GDP)	-2.9	-3.1	..
States and markets			
Starting a business (days)			24
Stock market capitalization (% of GDP)	110.4	129.5	156.2
Military expenditures (% of GDP)	2.6	1.7	2.0
Fixed-line and mobile subscribers (per 100 people)	9	42	91
Internet users (per 100 people)	0.0	21.4	43.2
Paved roads (% of total)	70	75	81
High-technology exports (% of manufactured exports)	38	60	54
Global links			
Merchandise trade (% of GDP)	133.4	199.5	193.7
Net barter terms of trade (2000 = 100)	103	100	99
Total external debt ($ billions)	15	42	53
Short-term debt ($ billions)	1.9	4.6	11.8
Total debt service (% of exports)	12.6	5.6	4.0
Foreign direct investment, net inflows ($ billions)	2.3	3.8	6.1
Remittances received ($ billions)	0.3	1.0	1.5
Aid ($ millions)	468	45	240

Maldives

South Asia   **Lower middle income**

Population (millions)	300	Population growth (%)	1.7
Surface area (sq. km)	300	National poverty rate (% of pop.)	..
GNI ($ millions)	903	GNI per capita ($)	3,010
GNI, PPP ($ billions)	1.4	GNI per capita, PPP ($)	4,740

	1990	2000	2006
People			
Share of poorest 20% in nat'l consumption/income (%)	..	..	..
Life expectancy at birth (years)	61	65	68
Total fertility (births per woman)	6.0	3.2	2.7
Adolescent fertility (births per 1,000 women 15–19)	..	34	24
Contraceptive prevalence (% of married women 15–49)	..	42	39
Births attended by skilled health staff (% of total)	..	70	84
Under-five mortality rate (per 1,000)	111	54	30
Child malnutrition, underweight (% of under age 5)	..	25.7	..
Child immunization, measles (% of ages 12–23 mos.)	96	99	97
Primary completion rate, total (% of relevant age group)	..	..	129
Gross secondary enrollment, total (% of relevant age group)	..	55	80
Ratio of girls to boys in primary & secondary school (%)	..	101	102
HIV prevalence rate (% of population ages 15–49)	..	..	0.2
Environment			
Forests (1,000 sq. km)	10	10	10
Deforestation (average annual %, 1990–2005)			0.00
Freshwater use (% of internal resources)	..	..	..
Access to improved water source (% of total pop.)	96	87	83
Access to improved sanitation facilities (% of total pop.)	..	58	59
Energy use per capita (kilograms of oil equivalent)	..	..	..
Carbon dioxide emissions per capita (metric tons)	0.7	1.8	2.5
Electricity use per capita (kilowatt-hours)	..	..	..
Economy			
GDP ($ billions)	215	624	927
GDP growth (annual %)	..	4.4	23.5
GDP implicit price deflator (annual % growth)	..	1.5	0.1
Value added in agriculture (% of GDP)	..	..	..
Value added in industry (% of GDP)	..	..	..
Value added in services (% of GDP)	..	..	..
Exports of goods and services (% of GDP)	..	89	95
Imports of goods and services (% of GDP)	..	72	83
Gross capital formation (% of GDP)	..	26	36
Central government revenue (% of GDP)	22.1	30.0	43.6
Central government cash surplus/deficit (% of GDP)	-7.5	-5.0	-7.7
States and markets			
Starting a business (days)			9
Stock market capitalization (% of GDP)	..	..	..
Military expenditures (% of GDP)	..	..	..
Fixed-line and mobile subscribers (per 100 people)	3	12	98
Internet users (per 100 people)	0.0	2.2	6.8
Paved roads (% of total)	..	..	..
High-technology exports (% of manufactured exports)	..	0	0
Global links			
Merchandise trade (% of GDP)	100.4	79.7	124.2
Net barter terms of trade (2000 = 100)	..	100	119
Total external debt ($ millions)	78	206	459
Short-term debt ($ millions)	14	21	93
Total debt service (% of exports)	4.8	4.3	4.9
Foreign direct investment, net inflows ($ millions)	5.6	13.0	13.9
Remittances received ($ millions)	2.0	2.0	2.3
Aid ($ millions)	21	19	39

Mali

Sub-Saharan Africa		**Low income**
Population (millions)	12	Population growth (%)	3.0
Surface area (1,000 sq. km)	1,240	National poverty rate (% of pop.)	..
GNI ($ billions)	5.5	GNI per capita ($)	460
GNI, PPP ($ billions)	11.9	GNI per capita, PPP ($)	1,000

	1990	2000	2006
People			
Share of poorest 20% in nat'l consumption/income (%)	6.9	6.1	..
Life expectancy at birth (years)	48	51	54
Total fertility (births per woman)	7.4	6.9	6.6
Adolescent fertility (births per 1,000 women 15–19)	..	202	183
Contraceptive prevalence (% of married women 15–49)	..	8	..
Births attended by skilled health staff (% of total)	..	41	..
Under-five mortality rate (per 1,000)	250	224	217
Child malnutrition, underweight (% of under age 5)	..	30.1	..
Child immunization, measles (% of ages 12–23 mos.)	43	49	86
Primary completion rate, total (% of relevant age group)	10	33	49
Gross secondary enrollment, total (% of relevant age group)	8	19	28
Ratio of girls to boys in primary & secondary school (%)	57	68	74
HIV prevalence rate (% of population ages 15–49)	..	1.8	1.7
Environment			
Forests (1,000 sq. km)	141	131	126
Deforestation (average annual %, 1990–2005)			0.7
Freshwater use (% of internal resources)	..	10.9	..
Access to improved water source (% of total pop.)	34	45	50
Access to improved sanitation facilities (% of total pop.)	36	43	46
Energy use per capita (kilograms of oil equivalent)	..	..	..
Carbon dioxide emissions per capita (metric tons)	0.1	0.1	0.1
Electricity use per capita (kilowatt-hours)	..	..	..
Economy			
GDP ($ billions)	2.4	2.4	5.9
GDP growth (annual %)	-1.9	3.2	5.3
GDP implicit price deflator (annual % growth)	4.9	5.6	4.1
Value added in agriculture (% of GDP)	46	42	37
Value added in industry (% of GDP)	16	21	24
Value added in services (% of GDP)	39	38	39
Exports of goods and services (% of GDP)	17	27	32
Imports of goods and services (% of GDP)	34	39	40
Gross capital formation (% of GDP)	23	25	23
Central government revenue (% of GDP)	..	13.4	16.7
Central government cash surplus/deficit (% of GDP)	..	-3.4	32.1
States and markets			
Starting a business (days)			26
Stock market capitalization (% of GDP)	..	..	..
Military expenditures (% of GDP)	2.2	2.4	2.2
Fixed-line and mobile subscribers (per 100 people)	0	0	13
Internet users (per 100 people)	0.0	0.1	0.6
Paved roads (% of total)	11	12	18
High-technology exports (% of manufactured exports)	0	15	4
Global links			
Merchandise trade (% of GDP)	39.7	55.8	54.7
Net barter terms of trade (2000 = 100)	135	100	107
Total external debt ($ billions)	2.5	3.0	1.4
Short-term debt ($ millions)	62	134	17
Total debt service (% of exports)	12.3	12.8	5.6
Foreign direct investment, net inflows ($ millions)	5.7	82.4	185.0
Remittances received ($ millions)	107	73	177
Aid ($ millions)	479	359	825

Malta

High income

Population (thousands)	406	Population growth (%)	0.6
Surface area (sq. km)	320	National poverty rate (% of pop.)	..
GNI ($ billions)	6.2	GNI per capita ($)	15,310
GNI, PPP ($ billions)	8.5	GNI per capita, PPP ($)	20,990

	1990	2000	2006
People			
Share of poorest 20% in nat'l consumption/income (%)	..	..	..
Life expectancy at birth (years)	75	78	79
Total fertility (births per woman)	2.1	1.7	1.4
Adolescent fertility (births per 1,000 women 15–19)	..	16	13
Contraceptive prevalence (% of married women 15–49)	..	..	..
Births attended by skilled health staff (% of total)	..	..	100
Under-five mortality rate (per 1,000)	11	7	6
Child malnutrition, underweight (% of under age 5)	..	..	..
Child immunization, measles (% of ages 12–23 mos.)	80	74	94
Primary completion rate, total (% of relevant age group)	102	107	96
Gross secondary enrollment, total (% of relevant age group)	83	89	101
Ratio of girls to boys in primary & secondary school (%)	95	100	99
HIV prevalence rate (% of population ages 15–49)	..	..	0.1
Environment			
Forests (1,000 sq. km)	..	..	..
Deforestation (average annual %, 1990–2005)			..
Freshwater use (% of internal resources)	..	50.5	..
Access to improved water source (% of total pop.)	100	100	100
Access to improved sanitation facilities (% of total pop.)	..	..	..
Energy use per capita (kilograms of oil equivalent)	2,150	2,013	2,352
Carbon dioxide emissions per capita (metric tons)	6.2	5.4	6.1
Electricity use per capita (kilowatt-hours)	2,778	4,313	4,917
Economy			
GDP ($ billions)	2.3	3.9	6.4
GDP growth (annual %)	6.3	6.3	3.4
GDP implicit price deflator (annual % growth)	3.2	10.2	2.8
Value added in agriculture (% of GDP)	3	..	..
Value added in industry (% of GDP)	39	..	..
Value added in services (% of GDP)	58	..	..
Exports of goods and services (% of GDP)	85	92	88
Imports of goods and services (% of GDP)	99	103	92
Gross capital formation (% of GDP)	33	26	20
Central government revenue (% of GDP)	..	..	38.0
Central government cash surplus/deficit (% of GDP)	..	..	-2.5
States and markets			
Starting a business (days)			..
Stock market capitalization (% of GDP)	..	52.6	70.6
Military expenditures (% of GDP)	0.9	0.7	0.6
Fixed-line and mobile subscribers (per 100 people)	36	82	135
Internet users (per 100 people)	0.0	13.1	31.5
Paved roads (% of total)	..	88	88
High-technology exports (% of manufactured exports)	45	72	57
Global links			
Merchandise trade (% of GDP)	133.9	150.7	104.2
Net barter terms of trade (2000 = 100)	123	100	85
Total external debt ($ billions)	..	..	..
Short-term debt ($ billions)	..	..	..
Total debt service (% of exports)	..	..	..
Foreign direct investment, net inflows ($ billions)	0.0	0.6	1.8
Remittances received ($ millions)	58	14	35
Aid ($ millions)	5.3	21.2	6.2

Marshall Islands

East Asia & Pacific		Lower middle income	
Population (thousands)	65	Population growth (%)	3.3
Surface area (sq. km)	180	National poverty rate (% of pop.)	..
GNI ($ millions)	195	GNI per capita ($)	2,980
GNI, PPP ($ millions)	525	GNI per capita, PPP ($)	8,040

	1990	2000	2006
People			
Share of poorest 20% in nat'l consumption/income (%)	..	..	..
Life expectancy at birth (years)	..	65	..
Total fertility (births per woman)	5.9	5.7	..
Adolescent fertility (births per 1,000 women 15-19)	..	..	..
Contraceptive prevalence (% of married women 15-49)		34	
Births attended by skilled health staff (% of total)	..	95	..
Under-five mortality rate (per 1,000)	92	68	56
Child malnutrition, underweight (% of under age 5)	..	..	..
Child immunization, measles (% of ages 12-23 mos.)	52	94	96
Primary completion rate, total (% of relevant age group)	..	125	..
Gross secondary enrollment, total (% of relevant age group)	..	87	76
Ratio of girls to boys in primary & secondary school (%)	..	98	100
HIV prevalence rate (% of population ages 15-49)	..	..	..
Environment			
Forests (1,000 sq. km)	..	..	..
Deforestation (average annual %, 1990-2005)			..
Freshwater use (% of internal resources)	..	..	..
Access to improved water source (% of total pop.)	96	87	87
Access to improved sanitation facilities (% of total pop.)	74	81	82
Energy use per capita (kilograms of oil equivalent)	..	..	..
Carbon dioxide emissions per capita (metric tons)	..	..	..
Electricity use per capita (kilowatt-hours)	..	..	..
Economy			
GDP ($ millions)	69	111	155
GDP growth (annual %)	7.0	0.9	3.0
GDP implicit price deflator (annual % growth)	0.7	15.4	3.9
Value added in agriculture (% of GDP)	15	9	..
Value added in industry (% of GDP)	14	19	..
Value added in services (% of GDP)	71	72	..
Exports of goods and services (% of GDP)	..	..	..
Imports of goods and services (% of GDP)	..	..	..
Gross capital formation (% of GDP)	..	..	..
Central government revenue (% of GDP)	..	..	..
Central government cash surplus/deficit (% of GDP)	..	..	..
States and markets			
Starting a business (days)			17
Stock market capitalization (% of GDP)	..	..	..
Military expenditures (% of GDP)	..	..	..
Fixed-line and mobile subscribers (per 100 people)	1	8	..
Internet users (per 100 people)	0.0	1.5	3.4
Paved roads (% of total)	..	..	..
High-technology exports (% of manufactured exports)	..	..	..
Global links			
Merchandise trade (% of GDP)	..	57.5	85.4
Net barter terms of trade (2000 = 100)	..	..	..
Total external debt ($ billions)	..	..	..
Short-term debt ($ billions)	..	..	..
Total debt service (% of exports)	..	..	..
Foreign direct investment, net inflows ($ billions)	..	..	..
Remittances received ($ billions)	..	..	..
Aid ($ millions)	0.3	57.2	55.0

Mauritania

Population (millions)	3.0	Population growth (%)	2.7
Surface area (1,000 sq. km)	1,031	National poverty rate (% of pop.)	46
GNI ($ billions)	2.3	GNI per capita ($)	760
GNI, PPP ($ billions)	6.0	GNI per capita, PPP ($)	1,970

	1990	2000	2006
People			
Share of poorest 20% in nat'l consumption/income (%)	..	6.2	..
Life expectancy at birth (years)	58	61	64
Total fertility (births per woman)	5.8	5.0	4.5
Adolescent fertility (births per 1,000 women 15–19)	..	99	88
Contraceptive prevalence (% of married women 15–49)	3	8	..
Births attended by skilled health staff (% of total)	40	57	..
Under-five mortality rate (per 1,000)	133	125	125
Child malnutrition, underweight (% of under age 5)	..	30.4	..
Child immunization, measles (% of ages 12–23 mos.)	38	62	62
Primary completion rate, total (% of relevant age group)	29	53	47
Gross secondary enrollment, total (% of relevant age group)	14	19	22
Ratio of girls to boys in primary & secondary school (%)	71	95	102
HIV prevalence rate (% of population ages 15–49)	..	..	0.7
Environment			
Forests (1,000 sq. km)	4.2	3.2	2.7
Deforestation (average annual %, 1990–2005)			2.9
Freshwater use (% of internal resources)	..	425.0	..
Access to improved water source (% of total pop.)	38	47	53
Access to improved sanitation facilities (% of total pop.)	31	33	34
Energy use per capita (kilograms of oil equivalent)	..	..	..
Carbon dioxide emissions per capita (metric tons)	1.4	1.0	0.9
Electricity use per capita (kilowatt-hours)	..	..	..
Economy			
GDP ($ billions)	1.0	1.1	2.7
GDP growth (annual %)	-1.8	1.9	11.7
GDP implicit price deflator (annual % growth)	2.6	1.3	29.8
Value added in agriculture (% of GDP)	30	28	13
Value added in industry (% of GDP)	29	30	48
Value added in services (% of GDP)	42	43	39
Exports of goods and services (% of GDP)	46	46	55
Imports of goods and services (% of GDP)	61	74	59
Gross capital formation (% of GDP)	20	19	23
Central government revenue (% of GDP)	..	..	..
Central government cash surplus/deficit (% of GDP)	..	..	..
States and markets			
Starting a business (days)			65
Stock market capitalization (% of GDP)	..	97.2	..
Military expenditures (% of GDP)	3.9	2.6	2.5
Fixed-line and mobile subscribers (per 100 people)	0	1	36
Internet users (per 100 people)	0.0	0.2	3.3
Paved roads (% of total)	11	11	..
High-technology exports (% of manufactured exports)	..	..	..
Global links			
Merchandise trade (% of GDP)	84.1	62.0	85.0
Net barter terms of trade (2000 = 100)	97	100	170
Total external debt ($ billions)	2.1	2.4	1.6
Short-term debt ($ millions)	238	251	229
Total debt service (% of exports)	29.8	27.7	..
Foreign direct investment, net inflows ($ millions)	6.7	40.1	-3.4
Remittances received ($ millions)	14.0	2.0	2.0
Aid ($ millions)	236	211	188

Mauritius

Upper middle income

Population (millions)	1.3	Population growth (%)	0.8
Surface area (1,000 sq. km)	2.0	National poverty rate (% of pop.)	..
GNI ($ billions)	6.8	GNI per capita ($)	5,430
GNI, PPP ($ billions)	13.3	GNI per capita, PPP ($)	10,640

	1990	2000	2006
People			
Share of poorest 20% in nat'l consumption/income (%)	..	..	..
Life expectancy at birth (years)	69	72	73
Total fertility (births per woman)	2.3	2.0	2.0
Adolescent fertility (births per 1,000 women 15–19)	..	39	41
Contraceptive prevalence (% of married women 15–49)	75	76	..
Births attended by skilled health staff (% of total)	91	100	99
Under-five mortality rate (per 1,000)	23	18	14
Child malnutrition, underweight (% of under age 5)	..	..	..
Child immunization, measles (% of ages 12–23 mos.)	76	84	99
Primary completion rate, total (% of relevant age group)	64	105	92
Gross secondary enrollment, total (% of relevant age group)	55	78	86
Ratio of girls to boys in primary & secondary school (%)	102	98	103
HIV prevalence rate (% of population ages 15–49)	..	..	0.6
Environment			
Forests (sq. km)	390	380	370
Deforestation (average annual %, 1990–2005)			0.4
Freshwater use (% of internal resources)	..	21.8	..
Access to improved water source (% of total pop.)	100	100	100
Access to improved sanitation facilities (% of total pop.)	..	94	94
Energy use per capita (kilograms of oil equivalent)	..	..	..
Carbon dioxide emissions per capita (metric tons)	1.4	2.3	2.6
Electricity use per capita (kilowatt-hours)	..	..	..
Economy			
GDP ($ billions)	2.4	4.5	6.3
GDP growth (annual %)	5.8	4.0	3.5
GDP implicit price deflator (annual % growth)	10.6	3.7	4.1
Value added in agriculture (% of GDP)	13	6	6
Value added in industry (% of GDP)	33	31	27
Value added in services (% of GDP)	54	63	68
Exports of goods and services (% of GDP)	64	63	60
Imports of goods and services (% of GDP)	71	65	67
Gross capital formation (% of GDP)	31	26	25
Central government revenue (% of GDP)	24.3	22.0	21.5
Central government cash surplus/deficit (% of GDP)	0.3	-1.1	-3.0
States and markets			
Starting a business (days)			7
Stock market capitalization (% of GDP)	11.2	29.8	56.7
Military expenditures (% of GDP)	0.4	0.2	0.2
Fixed-line and mobile subscribers (per 100 people)	5	39	90
Internet users (per 100 people)	0.0	7.3	14.5
Paved roads (% of total)	93	97	100
High-technology exports (% of manufactured exports)	1	1	24
Global links			
Merchandise trade (% of GDP)	118.0	81.7	91.4
Net barter terms of trade (2000 = 100)	93	100	115
Total external debt ($ billions)	1.0	1.7	2.0
Short-term debt ($ billions)	0.1	0.8	1.4
Total debt service (% of exports)	8.8	18.1	7.1
Foreign direct investment, net inflows ($ millions)	41	266	107
Remittances received ($ millions)	..	177.0	215.0
Aid ($ millions)	88	20	19

Mayotte

Sub-Saharan Africa		Upper middle income	
Population (thousands)	187	Population growth (%)	3.6
Surface area (sq. km)	374	National poverty rate (% of pop.)	..
GNI ($ billions)	..	GNI per capita ($)	..
GNI, PPP ($ billions)	..	GNI per capita, PPP ($)	..

	1990	2000	2006
People			
Share of poorest 20% in nat'l consumption/income (%)	..	..	..
Life expectancy at birth (years)	..	..	..
Total fertility (births per woman)	..	..	..
Adolescent fertility (births per 1,000 women 15–19)	..	..	..
Contraceptive prevalence (% of married women 15–49)	..	..	..
Births attended by skilled health staff (% of total)	..	..	..
Under-five mortality rate (per 1,000)	..	..	..
Child malnutrition, underweight (% of under age 5)	..	..	..
Child immunization, measles (% of ages 12–23 mos.)	..	..	..
Primary completion rate, total (% of relevant age group)	..	..	..
Gross secondary enrollment, total (% of relevant age group)	..	..	..
Ratio of girls to boys in primary & secondary school (%)	..	..	..
HIV prevalence rate (% of population ages 15–49)	..	..	..
Environment			
Forests (sq. km)	60	60	50
Deforestation (average annual %, 1990–2005)			1.2
Freshwater use (% of internal resources)	..	..	..
Access to improved water source (% of total pop.)	..	..	..
Access to improved sanitation facilities (% of total pop.)	..	..	..
Energy use per capita (kilograms of oil equivalent)	..	..	..
Carbon dioxide emissions per capita (metric tons)	..	..	..
Electricity use per capita (kilowatt-hours)	..	..	..
Economy			
GDP ($ billions)	..	..	..
GDP growth (annual %)	..	..	..
GDP implicit price deflator (annual % growth)	..	..	..
Value added in agriculture (% of GDP)	..	..	..
Value added in industry (% of GDP)	..	..	..
Value added in services (% of GDP)	..	..	..
Exports of goods and services (% of GDP)	..	..	..
Imports of goods and services (% of GDP)	..	..	..
Gross capital formation (% of GDP)	..	..	..
Central government revenue (% of GDP)	..	..	..
Central government cash surplus/deficit (% of GDP)	..	..	..
States and markets			
Starting a business (days)			..
Stock market capitalization (% of GDP)	..	..	..
Military expenditures (% of GDP)	..	..	..
Fixed-line and mobile subscribers (per 100 people)	..	..	..
Internet users (per 100 people)	..	..	..
Paved roads (% of total)	..	..	..
High-technology exports (% of manufactured exports)	..	..	..
Global links			
Merchandise trade (% of GDP)	..	..	..
Net barter terms of trade (2000 = 100)	..	..	..
Total external debt ($ billions)	..	..	..
Short-term debt ($ billions)	..	..	..
Total debt service (% of exports)	..	..	..
Foreign direct investment, net inflows ($ billions)	..	..	..
Remittances received ($ millions)	82.0	..	..
Aid ($ millions)	61	103	338

Mexico

Latin America & Caribbean		Upper middle income	
Population (millions)	104	Population growth (%)	1.1
Surface area (1,000 sq. km)	1,964	National poverty rate (% of pop.)	18
GNI ($ billions)	815.7	GNI per capita ($)	7,830
GNI, PPP ($ billions)	1,249.2	GNI per capita, PPP ($)	11,990

	1990	2000	2006
People			
Share of poorest 20% in nat'l consumption/income (%)	3.9	3.9	4.3
Life expectancy at birth (years)	71	74	74
Total fertility (births per woman)	3.4	2.7	2.2
Adolescent fertility (births per 1,000 women 15–19)	..	73	66
Contraceptive prevalence (% of married women 15–49)	..	70	71
Births attended by skilled health staff (% of total)	..	..	83
Under-five mortality rate (per 1,000)	53	39	35
Child malnutrition, underweight (% of under age 5)	13.9	6.0	3.4
Child immunization, measles (% of ages 12–23 mos.)	75	96	96
Primary completion rate, total (% of relevant age group)	86	99	103
Gross secondary enrollment, total (% of relevant age group)	53	72	85
Ratio of girls to boys in primary & secondary school (%)	97	99	99
HIV prevalence rate (% of population ages 15–49)	..	..	0.3
Environment			
Forests (1,000 sq. km)	690	655	642
Deforestation (average annual %, 1990–2005)		0.5	
Freshwater use (% of internal resources)	..	19.1	..
Access to improved water source (% of total pop.)	82	93	97
Access to improved sanitation facilities (% of total pop.)	58	75	79
Energy use per capita (kilograms of oil equivalent)	1,494	1,534	1,712
Carbon dioxide emissions per capita (metric tons)	5.0	4.3	4.3
Electricity use per capita (kilowatt-hours)	1,295	1,795	1,899
Economy			
GDP ($ billions)	262.7	581.4	839.2
GDP growth (annual %)	5.1	6.6	4.8
GDP implicit price deflator (annual % growth)	28.1	12.1	4.5
Value added in agriculture (% of GDP)	8	4	4
Value added in industry (% of GDP)	28	28	27
Value added in services (% of GDP)	64	68	69
Exports of goods and services (% of GDP)	19	31	32
Imports of goods and services (% of GDP)	20	33	33
Gross capital formation (% of GDP)	23	24	22
Central government revenue (% of GDP)	15.3	14.7	..
Central government cash surplus/deficit (% of GDP)	-2.5	-1.2	..
States and markets			
Starting a business (days)			27
Stock market capitalization (% of GDP)	12.4	21.5	41.5
Military expenditures (% of GDP)	0.4	0.5	0.4
Fixed-line and mobile subscribers (per 100 people)	7	27	74
Internet users (per 100 people)	0.0	5.2	17.5
Paved roads (% of total)	35	33	37
High-technology exports (% of manufactured exports)	8	22	19
Global links			
Merchandise trade (% of GDP)	32.1	60.0	61.8
Net barter terms of trade (2000 = 100)	102	100	104
Total external debt ($ billions)	104	151	161
Short-term debt ($ billions)	16.1	18.9	7.3
Total debt service (% of exports)	20.7	30.4	18.9
Foreign direct investment, net inflows ($ billions)	2.5	17.9	19.2
Remittances received ($ billions)	3.1	7.5	25.1
Aid ($ millions)	156	-56	247

Micronesia, Fed. Sts.

East Asia & Pacific		Lower middle income	
Population (thousands)	111	Population growth (%)	0.5
Surface area (sq. km)	700	National poverty rate (% of pop.)	..
GNI ($ millions)	264	GNI per capita ($)	2,390
GNI, PPP ($ millions)	672	GNI per capita, PPP ($)	6,070

	1990	2000	2006
People			
Share of poorest 20% in nat'l consumption/income (%)	..	..	..
Life expectancy at birth (years)	66	67	68
Total fertility (births per woman)	5.0	4.3	3.8
Adolescent fertility (births per 1,000 women 15–19)	..	39	28
Contraceptive prevalence (% of married women 15–49)	..	45	..
Births attended by skilled health staff (% of total)	..	88	..
Under-five mortality rate (per 1,000)	58	47	41
Child malnutrition, underweight (% of under age 5)	..	..	..
Child immunization, measles (% of ages 12–23 mos.)	81	85	83
Primary completion rate, total (% of relevant age group)	..	..	..
Gross secondary enrollment, total (% of relevant age group)	..	..	83
Ratio of girls to boys in primary & secondary school (%)	..	..	102
HIV prevalence rate (% of population ages 15–49)	..	..	..
Environment			
Forests (sq. km)	630	630	630
Deforestation (average annual %, 1990–2005)			0.00
Freshwater use (% of internal resources)	..	..	..
Access to improved water source (% of total pop.)	88	93	94
Access to improved sanitation facilities (% of total pop.)	29	28	28
Energy use per capita (kilograms of oil equivalent)	..	..	..
Carbon dioxide emissions per capita (metric tons)	..	..	..
Electricity use per capita (kilowatt-hours)	..	..	..
Economy			
GDP ($ millions)	147	216	245
GDP growth (annual %)	3.7	8.4	-0.7
GDP implicit price deflator (annual % growth)	4.9	2.0	4.0
Value added in agriculture (% of GDP)	..	..	..
Value added in industry (% of GDP)	..	..	..
Value added in services (% of GDP)	..	..	..
Exports of goods and services (% of GDP)	..	..	..
Imports of goods and services (% of GDP)	..	..	..
Gross capital formation (% of GDP)	..	..	..
Central government revenue (% of GDP)	..	..	..
Central government cash surplus/deficit (% of GDP)	..	..	..
States and markets			
Starting a business (days)			16
Stock market capitalization (% of GDP)	..	..	..
Military expenditures (% of GDP)	..	..	..
Fixed-line and mobile subscribers (per 100 people)	3	9	24
Internet users (per 100 people)	0.0	3.7	14.5
Paved roads (% of total)	16	18	..
High-technology exports (% of manufactured exports)	..	..	..
Global links			
Merchandise trade (% of GDP)	..	59.5	54.1
Net barter terms of trade (2000 = 100)	..	100	100
Total external debt ($ billions)	..	..	..
Short-term debt ($ billions)	..	..	..
Total debt service (% of exports)	..	..	..
Foreign direct investment, net inflows ($ billions)	..	..	..
Remittances received ($ billions)	..	..	..
Aid ($ millions)	0.5	101.5	108.5

Moldova

Europe & Central Asia		Lower middle income	

Population (millions)	3.8	Population growth (%)	-1.1
Surface area (1,000 sq. km)	34	National poverty rate (% of pop.)	49
GNI ($ billions)	3.6	GNI per capita ($)	1,080
GNI, PPP ($ billions)	10.2	GNI per capita, PPP ($)	2,660

	1990	2000	2006
People			
Share of poorest 20% in nat'l consumption/income (%)	6.9	7.1	..
Life expectancy at birth (years)	67	67	69
Total fertility (births per woman)	2.3	1.6	1.2
Adolescent fertility (births per 1,000 women 15-19)	..	46	33
Contraceptive prevalence (% of married women 15-49)	..	62	68
Births attended by skilled health staff (% of total)	..	..	100
Under-five mortality rate (per 1,000)	37	24	19
Child malnutrition, underweight (% of under age 5)	..	..	3.2
Child immunization, measles (% of ages 12-23 mos.)	92	87	96
Primary completion rate, total (% of relevant age group)	..	90	90
Gross secondary enrollment, total (% of relevant age group)	79	83	82
Ratio of girls to boys in primary & secondary school (%)	106	99	102
HIV prevalence rate (% of population ages 15-49)	..	..	1.1
Environment			
Forests (1,000 sq. km)	3.2	3.3	3.3
Deforestation (average annual %, 1990-2005)			-0.2
Freshwater use (% of internal resources)	..	231.0	..
Access to improved water source (% of total pop.)	..	92	92
Access to improved sanitation facilities (% of total pop.)	..	68	68
Energy use per capita (kilograms of oil equivalent)	2,277	692	917
Carbon dioxide emissions per capita (metric tons)	5.4	1.6	2.0
Electricity use per capita (kilowatt-hours)	2,553	871	1,428
Economy			
GDP ($ billions)	3.6	1.3	3.4
GDP growth (annual %)	-2.4	2.1	4.0
GDP implicit price deflator (annual % growth)	13.5	27.3	12.6
Value added in agriculture (% of GDP)	36	29	18
Value added in industry (% of GDP)	37	22	15
Value added in services (% of GDP)	27	49	67
Exports of goods and services (% of GDP)	48	50	46
Imports of goods and services (% of GDP)	51	75	93
Gross capital formation (% of GDP)	25	24	34
Central government revenue (% of GDP)	..	24.5	33.8
Central government cash surplus/deficit (% of GDP)	..	-1.5	0.2
States and markets			
Starting a business (days)			23
Stock market capitalization (% of GDP)	..	30.4	22.1
Military expenditures (% of GDP)	..	0.4	0.3
Fixed-line and mobile subscribers (per 100 people)	11	17	62
Internet users (per 100 people)	0.0	1.3	19.0
Paved roads (% of total)	87	86	86
High-technology exports (% of manufactured exports)	..	3	5
Global links			
Merchandise trade (% of GDP)	..	96.9	111.6
Net barter terms of trade (2000 = 100)	..	..	..
Total external debt ($ billions)	0.0	1.7	2.4
Short-term debt ($ millions)	0.0	488.6	821.6
Total debt service (% of exports)	..	18.1	12.2
Foreign direct investment, net inflows ($ millions)	17	128	242
Remittances received ($ billions)	..	0.2	1.2
Aid ($ millions)	9.7	122.6	228.2

Monaco

High income

Population (thousands)	33	Population growth (%)	0.3
Surface area (sq. km)	2.0	National poverty rate (% of pop.)	..
GNI ($ billions)	..	GNI per capita ($)	..
GNI, PPP ($ billions)	..	GNI per capita, PPP ($)	..

	1990	2000	2006
People			
Share of poorest 20% in nat'l consumption/income (%)	..	..	..
Life expectancy at birth (years)	..	..	..
Total fertility (births per woman)	..	..	..
Adolescent fertility (births per 1,000 women 15-19)	..	..	..
Contraceptive prevalence (% of married women 15-49)	..	..	..
Births attended by skilled health staff (% of total)	..	..	..
Under-five mortality rate (per 1,000)	9	6	4
Child malnutrition, underweight (% of under age 5)	..	..	..
Child immunization, measles (% of ages 12-23 mos.)	99	99	99
Primary completion rate, total (% of relevant age group)	..	..	..
Gross secondary enrollment, total (% of relevant age group)	..	..	..
Ratio of girls to boys in primary & secondary school (%)	..	..	..
HIV prevalence rate (% of population ages 15-49)	..	..	..
Environment			
Forests (sq. km)	0.0	0.0	0.0
Deforestation (average annual %, 1990-2005)			..
Freshwater use (% of internal resources)	..	..	..
Access to improved water source (% of total pop.)	100	100	100
Access to improved sanitation facilities (% of total pop.)	100	100	100
Energy use per capita (kilograms of oil equivalent)	..	..	..
Carbon dioxide emissions per capita (metric tons)	..	..	..
Electricity use per capita (kilowatt-hours)	..	..	..
Economy			
GDP ($ millions)	..	..	..
GDP growth (annual %)	..	..	..
GDP implicit price deflator (annual % growth)	..	..	..
Value added in agriculture (% of GDP)	..	..	..
Value added in industry (% of GDP)	..	..	..
Value added in services (% of GDP)	..	..	..
Exports of goods and services (% of GDP)	..	..	..
Imports of goods and services (% of GDP)	..	..	..
Gross capital formation (% of GDP)	..	..	..
Central government revenue (% of GDP)	..	..	..
Central government cash surplus/deficit (% of GDP)	..	..	..
States and markets			
Starting a business (days)			..
Stock market capitalization (% of GDP)	..	..	..
Military expenditures (% of GDP)	..	..	..
Fixed-line and mobile subscribers (per 100 people)	..	..	..
Internet users (per 100 people)	..	..	..
Paved roads (% of total)	100	100	..
High-technology exports (% of manufactured exports)	..	..	..
Global links			
Merchandise trade (% of GDP)	..	..	..
Net barter terms of trade (2000 = 100)	..	..	..
Total external debt ($ billions)	..	..	..
Short-term debt ($ billions)	..	..	..
Total debt service (% of exports)	..	..	..
Foreign direct investment, net inflows ($ billions)	..	..	..
Remittances received ($ billions)	..	..	..
Aid ($ billions)	..	..	..

Mongolia

East Asia & Pacific				Low income
Population (millions)	2.6	Population growth (%)		1.2
Surface area (1,000 sq. km)	1,567	National poverty rate (% of pop.)		36
GNI ($ billions)	2.6	GNI per capita ($)		1,000
GNI, PPP ($ billions)	7.3	GNI per capita, PPP ($)		2,810

	1990	2000	2006
People			
Share of poorest 20% in nat'l consumption/income (%)	..	7.5	..
Life expectancy at birth (years)	63	65	67
Total fertility (births per woman)	4.0	2.6	2.3
Adolescent fertility (births per 1,000 women 15–19)	..	46	46
Contraceptive prevalence (% of married women 15–49)	..	67	66
Births attended by skilled health staff (% of total)	..	97	99
Under-five mortality rate (per 1,000)	109	62	43
Child malnutrition, underweight (% of under age 5)	..	11.6	4.8
Child immunization, measles (% of ages 12–23 mos.)	92	94	99
Primary completion rate, total (% of relevant age group)	..	87	109
Gross secondary enrollment, total (% of relevant age group)	82	63	89
Ratio of girls to boys in primary & secondary school (%)	109	112	108
HIV prevalence rate (% of population ages 15–49)	..	..	0.1
Environment			
Forests (1,000 sq. km)	115	107	103
Deforestation (average annual %, 1990–2005)			0.8
Freshwater use (% of internal resources)	..	1.3	..
Access to improved water source (% of total pop.)	63	62	62
Access to improved sanitation facilities (% of total pop.)	..	59	59
Energy use per capita (kilograms of oil equivalent)	..	..	..
Carbon dioxide emissions per capita (metric tons)	4.7	3.1	3.4
Electricity use per capita (kilowatt-hours)	..	..	..
Economy			
GDP ($ billions)	2.1	1.1	3.1
GDP growth (annual %)	-2.5	0.5	8.6
GDP implicit price deflator (annual % growth)	0.0	26.1	23.1
Value added in agriculture (% of GDP)	15	33	22
Value added in industry (% of GDP)	41	20	42
Value added in services (% of GDP)	44	47	36
Exports of goods and services (% of GDP)	22	56	65
Imports of goods and services (% of GDP)	49	71	60
Gross capital formation (% of GDP)	36	29	35
Central government revenue (% of GDP)	..	..	..
Central government cash surplus/deficit (% of GDP)	..	..	..
States and markets			
Starting a business (days)			20
Stock market capitalization (% of GDP)	..	3.4	3.6
Military expenditures (% of GDP)	5.7	2.2	1.3
Fixed-line and mobile subscribers (per 100 people)	3	11	28
Internet users (per 100 people)	0.0	1.3	10.5
Paved roads (% of total)	10	4	..
High-technology exports (% of manufactured exports)	..	0	2
Global links			
Merchandise trade (% of GDP)	75.7	105.7	96.7
Net barter terms of trade (2000 = 100)	..	100	162
Total external debt ($ billions)	0.4	0.9	1.4
Short-term debt ($ millions)	59	13	50
Total debt service (% of exports)	17.3	6.1	2.2
Foreign direct investment, net inflows ($ millions)	11	54	344
Remittances received ($ millions)	..	12.0	181.4
Aid ($ millions)	13	217	203

Montenegro

Europe & Central Asia		Upper middle income	
Population (thousands)	601	Population growth (%)	–1.1
Surface area (1,000 sq. km)	14	National poverty rate (% of pop.)	..
GNI ($ billions)	2.5	GNI per capita ($)	4,130
GNI, PPP ($ billions)	5.4	GNI per capita, PPP ($)	8,930

	1990	2000	2006
People			
Share of poorest 20% in nat'l consumption/income (%)	..	..	..
Life expectancy at birth (years)	75	75	74
Total fertility (births per woman)	2.0	1.8	1.6
Adolescent fertility (births per 1,000 women 15–19)	..	20	17
Contraceptive prevalence (% of married women 15–49)	..	..	..
Births attended by skilled health staff (% of total)	..	..	99
Under-five mortality rate (per 1,000)	16	13	10
Child malnutrition, underweight (% of under age 5)	..	..	..
Child immunization, measles (% of ages 12–23 mos.)	..	..	90
Primary completion rate, total (% of relevant age group)	..	..	..
Gross secondary enrollment, total (% of relevant age group)	..	..	..
Ratio of girls to boys in primary & secondary school (%)	..	..	..
HIV prevalence rate (% of population ages 15–49)	..	..	..
Environment			
Forests (1,000 sq. km)		..	..
Deforestation (average annual %, 1990–2005)			..
Freshwater use (% of internal resources)	..	..	..
Access to improved water source (% of total pop.)	..	..	..
Access to improved sanitation facilities (% of total pop.)	..	..	..
Energy use per capita (kilograms of oil equivalent)	..	..	..
Carbon dioxide emissions per capita (metric tons)	..	..	..
Electricity use per capita (kilowatt-hours)	..	..	..
Economy			
GDP ($ millions)	..	944	2,491
GDP growth (annual %)	..	3.1	16.2
GDP implicit price deflator (annual % growth)	..	22.0	2.6
Value added in agriculture (% of GDP)	..	13	8
Value added in industry (% of GDP)	..	25	18
Value added in services (% of GDP)	..	62	75
Exports of goods and services (% of GDP)	..	38	48
Imports of goods and services (% of GDP)	..	53	81
Gross capital formation (% of GDP)	..	21	32
Central government revenue (% of GDP)	..	..	..
Central government cash surplus/deficit (% of GDP)	..	..	..
States and markets			
Starting a business (days)			24
Stock market capitalization (% of GDP)	..	..	70.4
Military expenditures (% of GDP)	..	..	..
Fixed-line and mobile subscribers (per 100 people)	..	..	..
Internet users (per 100 people)	..	..	..
Paved roads (% of total)	..	..	..
High-technology exports (% of manufactured exports)	..	..	..
Global links			
Merchandise trade (% of GDP)	..	..	97.4
Net barter terms of trade (2000 = 100)	..	..	..
Total external debt ($ millions)	..	..	924.0
Short-term debt ($ millions)	..	..	0.0
Total debt service (% of exports)	..	..	..
Foreign direct investment, net inflows ($ billions)	..	..	..
Remittances received ($ billions)	..	..	..
Aid ($ millions)	..	..	95.9

Morocco

Middle East & North Africa   **Lower middle income**

Population (millions)	30	Population growth (%)	1.2
Surface area (1,000 sq. km)	447	National poverty rate (% of pop.)	..
GNI ($ billions)	65.8	GNI per capita ($)	2,160
GNI, PPP ($ billions)	117.7	GNI per capita, PPP ($)	3,860

	1990	2000	2006
People			
Share of poorest 20% in nat'l consumption/income (%)	6.6	6.5	..
Life expectancy at birth (years)	64	69	71
Total fertility (births per woman)	4.0	2.6	2.4
Adolescent fertility (births per 1,000 women 15–19)	..	25	19
Contraceptive prevalence (% of married women 15–49)	42	..	63
Births attended by skilled health staff (% of total)	31	..	63
Under-five mortality rate (per 1,000)	89	54	37
Child malnutrition, underweight (% of under age 5)	8.1	..	9.9
Child immunization, measles (% of ages 12–23 mos.)	79	93	95
Primary completion rate, total (% of relevant age group)	48	57	84
Gross secondary enrollment, total (% of relevant age group)	36	38	52
Ratio of girls to boys in primary & secondary school (%)	70	82	87
HIV prevalence rate (% of population ages 15–49)	..	..	0.1
Environment			
Forests (1,000 sq. km)	43	43	44
Deforestation (average annual %, 1990–2005)			-0.1
Freshwater use (% of internal resources)	..	43.4	..
Access to improved water source (% of total pop.)	75	79	81
Access to improved sanitation facilities (% of total pop.)	56	69	73
Energy use per capita (kilograms of oil equivalent)	278	350	458
Carbon dioxide emissions per capita (metric tons)	1.0	1.2	1.4
Electricity use per capita (kilowatt-hours)	369	489	644
Economy			
GDP ($ billions)	25.8	37.1	65.4
GDP growth (annual %)	4.0	1.8	8.0
GDP implicit price deflator (annual % growth)	5.5	-0.8	1.9
Value added in agriculture (% of GDP)	18	15	16
Value added in industry (% of GDP)	33	29	28
Value added in services (% of GDP)	48	56	57
Exports of goods and services (% of GDP)	26	28	33
Imports of goods and services (% of GDP)	32	33	38
Gross capital formation (% of GDP)	25	26	32
Central government revenue (% of GDP)	..	23.9	25.1
Central government cash surplus/deficit (% of GDP)	..	-4.9	-1.8
States and markets			
Starting a business (days)			12
Stock market capitalization (% of GDP)	3.7	29.4	75.5
Military expenditures (% of GDP)	5.0	4.2	3.7
Fixed-line and mobile subscribers (per 100 people)	2	13	57
Internet users (per 100 people)	0.0	0.7	20.0
Paved roads (% of total)	49	56	62
High-technology exports (% of manufactured exports)	0	11	10
Global links			
Merchandise trade (% of GDP)	43.3	51.2	55.5
Net barter terms of trade (2000 = 100)	85	100	86
Total external debt ($ billions)	25	21	18
Short-term debt ($ billions)	0.4	1.6	1.8
Total debt service (% of exports)	21.5	21.0	12.2
Foreign direct investment, net inflows ($ billions)	0.2	0.2	2.7
Remittances received ($ billions)	2.0	2.2	5.5
Aid ($ billions)	1.0	0.4	1.0

Mozambique

Sub-Saharan Africa		Low income	
Population (millions)	21	Population growth (%)	2.1
Surface area (1,000 sq. km)	799	National poverty rate (% of pop.)	54
GNI ($ billions)	6.5	GNI per capita ($)	310
GNI, PPP ($ billions)	13.9	GNI per capita, PPP ($)	660

	1990	2000	2006
People			
Share of poorest 20% in nat'l consumption/income (%)	..	5.4	..
Life expectancy at birth (years)	44	45	42
Total fertility (births per woman)	6.2	5.7	5.2
Adolescent fertility (births per 1,000 women 15–19)	..	153	155
Contraceptive prevalence (% of married women 15–49)	..	..	17
Births attended by skilled health staff (% of total)	..	..	..
Under-five mortality rate (per 1,000)	235	178	138
Child malnutrition, underweight (% of under age 5)	..	..	..
Child immunization, measles (% of ages 12–23 mos.)	59	71	77
Primary completion rate, total (% of relevant age group)	26	16	42
Gross secondary enrollment, total (% of relevant age group)	7	6	16
Ratio of girls to boys in primary & secondary school (%)	71	75	85
HIV prevalence rate (% of population ages 15–49)	..	..	16.1
Environment			
Forests (1,000 sq. km)	200	195	193
Deforestation (average annual %, 1990–2005)			0.3
Freshwater use (% of internal resources)	..	0.6	..
Access to improved water source (% of total pop.)	36	42	43
Access to improved sanitation facilities (% of total pop.)	20	27	32
Energy use per capita (kilograms of oil equivalent)	532	476	497
Carbon dioxide emissions per capita (metric tons)	0.1	0.1	0.1
Electricity use per capita (kilowatt-hours)	40	122	450
Economy			
GDP ($ billions)	2.5	4.2	6.8
GDP growth (annual %)	1.0	1.1	8.0
GDP implicit price deflator (annual % growth)	34.1	12.0	6.0
Value added in agriculture (% of GDP)	37	23	28
Value added in industry (% of GDP)	18	23	26
Value added in services (% of GDP)	44	54	46
Exports of goods and services (% of GDP)	8	18	41
Imports of goods and services (% of GDP)	36	37	47
Gross capital formation (% of GDP)	22	31	19
Central government revenue (% of GDP)	..	..	..
Central government cash surplus/deficit (% of GDP)	..	..	..
States and markets			
Starting a business (days)			29
Stock market capitalization (% of GDP)	..	..	..
Military expenditures (% of GDP)	0.0	0.0	0.0
Fixed-line and mobile subscribers (per 100 people)	0	1	11
Internet users (per 100 people)	0.0	0.1	0.9
Paved roads (% of total)	17	19	..
High-technology exports (% of manufactured exports)	..	9	2
Global links			
Merchandise trade (% of GDP)	40.8	35.8	76.2
Net barter terms of trade (2000 = 100)	175	100	131
Total external debt ($ billions)	4.6	7.3	3.3
Short-term debt ($ millions)	345	578	744
Total debt service (% of exports)	26.2	12.5	1.9
Foreign direct investment, net inflows ($ millions)	9.2	139.2	153.7
Remittances received ($ millions)	70	37	80
Aid ($ billions)	1.0	0.9	1.6

Myanmar

Population (millions)	48	Population growth (%)		0.9
Surface area (1,000 sq. km)	677	National poverty rate (% of pop.)		..
GNI ($ billions)	..	GNI per capita ($)		..
GNI, PPP ($ billions)	..	GNI per capita, PPP ($)		..

	1990	2000	2006
People			
Share of poorest 20% in nat'l consumption/income (%)	..	..	..
Life expectancy at birth (years)	59	60	62
Total fertility (births per woman)	3.4	2.4	2.1
Adolescent fertility (births per 1,000 women 15–19)	..	21	17
Contraceptive prevalence (% of married women 15-49)	17	37	..
Births attended by skilled health staff (% of total)	..	57	..
Under-five mortality rate (per 1,000)	130	110	104
Child malnutrition, underweight (% of under age 5)	..	30.1	..
Child immunization, measles (% of ages 12-23 mos.)	90	84	78
Primary completion rate, total (% of relevant age group)	..	81	95
Gross secondary enrollment, total (% of relevant age group)	23	39	49
Ratio of girls to boys in primary & secondary school (%)	97	102	101
HIV prevalence rate (% of population ages 15–49)	..	..	1.3
Environment			
Forests (1,000 sq. km)	392	346	322
Deforestation (average annual %, 1990–2005)			1.3
Freshwater use (% of internal resources)	..	3.8	..
Access to improved water source (% of total pop.)	57	71	78
Access to improved sanitation facilities (% of total pop.)	24	58	77
Energy use per capita (kilograms of oil equivalent)	266	274	307
Carbon dioxide emissions per capita (metric tons)	0.1	0.2	0.2
Electricity use per capita (kilowatt-hours)	45	77	82
Economy			
GDP ($ billions)	..	..	..
GDP growth (annual %)	2.8	9.8	5.0
GDP implicit price deflator (annual % growth)	18.5	6.1	17.6
Value added in agriculture (% of GDP)	57	57	..
Value added in industry (% of GDP)	11	10	..
Value added in services (% of GDP)	32	33	..
Exports of goods and services (% of GDP)	3	0	..
Imports of goods and services (% of GDP)	5	1	..
Gross capital formation (% of GDP)	13	12	..
Central government revenue (% of GDP)	10.5	5.3	8.0
Central government cash surplus/deficit (% of GDP)	..	..	-1.8
States and markets			
Starting a business (days)			..
Stock market capitalization (% of GDP)	..	..	..
Military expenditures (% of GDP)	3.4	2.3	..
Fixed-line and mobile subscribers (per 100 people)	0	1	1
Internet users (per 100 people)	0.0	0.0	0.2
Paved roads (% of total)	11	11	..
High-technology exports (% of manufactured exports)	0	..	..
Global links			
Merchandise trade (% of GDP)	..	..	..
Net barter terms of trade (2000 = 100)	252	100	111
Total external debt ($ billions)	4.7	5.9	6.8
Short-term debt ($ billions)	0.2	0.7	1.6
Total debt service (% of exports)	18.4	3.9	1.7
Foreign direct investment, net inflows ($ millions)	163	258	279
Remittances received ($ millions)	6.0	104.0	116.4
Aid ($ millions)	161	106	147

Namibia

Sub-Saharan Africa   **Lower middle income**

Population (millions)	2.0	Population growth (%)	1.3
Surface area (1,000 sq. km)	824	National poverty rate (% of pop.)	..
GNI ($ billions)	6.6	GNI per capita ($)	3,210
GNI, PPP ($ billions)	9.8	GNI per capita, PPP ($)	4,770

	1990	2000	2006
People			
Share of poorest 20% in nat'l consumption/income (%)	..	..	..
Life expectancy at birth (years)	62	54	52
Total fertility (births per woman)	5.7	3.9	3.3
Adolescent fertility (births per 1,000 women 15–19)	..	79	61
Contraceptive prevalence (% of married women 15–49)	29	44	..
Births attended by skilled health staff (% of total)	68	76	..
Under-five mortality rate (per 1,000)	86	69	61
Child malnutrition, underweight (% of under age 5)	..	20.3	..
Child immunization, measles (% of ages 12–23 mos.)	57	69	63
Primary completion rate, total (% of relevant age group)	..	82	76
Gross secondary enrollment, total (% of relevant age group)	45	57	57
Ratio of girls to boys in primary & secondary school (%)	106	103	104
HIV prevalence rate (% of population ages 15–49)	..	..	19.6
Environment			
Forests (1,000 sq. km)	88	80	77
Deforestation (average annual %, 1990–2005)			0.9
Freshwater use (% of internal resources)	..	4.8	..
Access to improved water source (% of total pop.)	57	80	87
Access to improved sanitation facilities (% of total pop.)	24	25	25
Energy use per capita (kilograms of oil equivalent)	0	549	683
Carbon dioxide emissions per capita (metric tons)	0.01	0.93	1.24
Electricity use per capita (kilowatt-hours)	1,047	1,270	1,428
Economy			
GDP ($ billions)	2.4	3.4	6.6
GDP growth (annual %)	2.5	3.5	2.9
GDP implicit price deflator (annual % growth)	4.3	10.7	9.1
Value added in agriculture (% of GDP)	12	11	11
Value added in industry (% of GDP)	38	28	31
Value added in services (% of GDP)	50	61	58
Exports of goods and services (% of GDP)	52	46	54
Imports of goods and services (% of GDP)	67	51	55
Gross capital formation (% of GDP)	34	20	29
Central government revenue (% of GDP)	31.3	32.8	..
Central government cash surplus/deficit (% of GDP)	-2.6	-3.0	..
States and markets			
Starting a business (days)			99
Stock market capitalization (% of GDP)	0.7	9.1	8.3
Military expenditures (% of GDP)	5.8	2.7	2.9
Fixed-line and mobile subscribers (per 100 people)	4	10	31
Internet users (per 100 people)	0.0	1.6	4.0
Paved roads (% of total)	11	13	..
High-technology exports (% of manufactured exports)	..	2	7
Global links			
Merchandise trade (% of GDP)	95.6	84.1	84.8
Net barter terms of trade (2000 = 100)	93	100	127
Total external debt ($ billions)	..	..	..
Short-term debt ($ billions)	..	..	..
Total debt service (% of exports)	..	..	..
Foreign direct investment, net inflows ($ billions)	..	..	..
Remittances received ($ millions)	13.0	9.0	16.9
Aid ($ millions)	120	152	145

Nepal

South Asia				Low income
Population (millions)	28	Population growth (%)		2.0
Surface area (1,000 sq. km)	147	National poverty rate (% of pop.)		31
GNI ($ billions)	8.8	GNI per capita ($)		320
GNI, PPP ($ billions)	27.8	GNI per capita, PPP ($)		1,010

	1990	2000	2006
People			
Share of poorest 20% in nat'l consumption/income (%)	..	..	..
Life expectancy at birth (years)	54	61	63
Total fertility (births per woman)	5.1	4.0	3.1
Adolescent fertility (births per 1,000 women 15–19)	..	124	116
Contraceptive prevalence (% of married women 15–49)	23	37	48
Births attended by skilled health staff (% of total)	7	12	19
Under-five mortality rate (per 1,000)	142	86	59
Child malnutrition, underweight (% of under age 5)	..	43.0	38.8
Child immunization, measles (% of ages 12–23 mos.)	57	71	85
Primary completion rate, total (% of relevant age group)	51	66	76
Gross secondary enrollment, total (% of relevant age group)	34	35	43
Ratio of girls to boys in primary & secondary school (%)	59	77	93
HIV prevalence rate (% of population ages 15–49)	..	..	0.5
Environment			
Forests (1,000 sq. km)	48	39	36
Deforestation (average annual %, 1990–2005)			1.9
Freshwater use (% of internal resources)	..	5.1	..
Access to improved water source (% of total pop.)	70	85	90
Access to improved sanitation facilities (% of total pop.)	11	28	35
Energy use per capita (kilograms of oil equivalent)	304	334	338
Carbon dioxide emissions per capita (metric tons)	0.03	0.13	0.11
Electricity use per capita (kilowatt-hours)	35	58	70
Economy			
GDP ($ billions)	3.6	5.5	8.9
GDP growth (annual %)	4.5	6.1	2.8
GDP implicit price deflator (annual % growth)	10.9	4.6	6.7
Value added in agriculture (% of GDP)	52	41	34
Value added in industry (% of GDP)	16	22	16
Value added in services (% of GDP)	32	37	49
Exports of goods and services (% of GDP)	11	23	14
Imports of goods and services (% of GDP)	22	32	32
Gross capital formation (% of GDP)	18	24	26
Central government revenue (% of GDP)	8.4	10.6	10.9
Central government cash surplus/deficit (% of GDP)	..	..	-1.6
States and markets			
Starting a business (days)			31
Stock market capitalization (% of GDP)	..	14.4	20.2
Military expenditures (% of GDP)	1.1	1.0	1.9
Fixed-line and mobile subscribers (per 100 people)	0	1	6
Internet users (per 100 people)	0.0	0.2	0.9
Paved roads (% of total)	38	31	57
High-technology exports (% of manufactured exports)	0	0	..
Global links			
Merchandise trade (% of GDP)	24.1	43.3	32.0
Net barter terms of trade (2000 = 100)	..	100	79
Total external debt ($ billions)	1.6	2.9	3.4
Short-term debt ($ millions)	24	29	81
Total debt service (% of exports)	15.2	6.9	5.1
Foreign direct investment, net inflows ($ millions)	5.9	-0.5	-6.6
Remittances received ($ billions)	0.0	0.1	1.5
Aid ($ millions)	423	387	514

Netherlands

Population (millions)	16	Population growth (%)	0.1
Surface area (1,000 sq. km)	42	National poverty rate (% of pop.)	..
GNI ($ billions)	703.5	GNI per capita ($)	43,050
GNI, PPP ($ billions)	620.0	GNI per capita, PPP ($)	37,940

	1990	2000	2006
People			
Share of poorest 20% in nat'l consumption/income (%)	..	7.6	..
Life expectancy at birth (years)	77	78	80
Total fertility (births per woman)	1.6	1.7	1.7
Adolescent fertility (births per 1,000 women 15–19)	..	5	5
Contraceptive prevalence (% of married women 15–49)	76	75	..
Births attended by skilled health staff (% of total)	..	100	..
Under-five mortality rate (per 1,000)	9	6	5
Child malnutrition, underweight (% of under age 5)	..	..	..
Child immunization, measles (% of ages 12–23 mos.)	94	96	96
Primary completion rate, total (% of relevant age group)	..	97	..
Gross secondary enrollment, total (% of relevant age group)	120	123	118
Ratio of girls to boys in primary & secondary school (%)	97	97	98
HIV prevalence rate (% of population ages 15–49)	..	..	0.2
Environment			
Forests (1,000 sq. km)	3.5	3.6	3.7
Deforestation (average annual %, 1990–2005)			–0.4
Freshwater use (% of internal resources)	..	72.2	..
Access to improved water source (% of total pop.)	100	100	100
Access to improved sanitation facilities (% of total pop.)	100	100	100
Energy use per capita (kilograms of oil equivalent)	4,464	4,764	5,015
Carbon dioxide emissions per capita (metric tons)	9.4	8.9	8.7
Electricity use per capita (kilowatt-hours)	5,218	6,560	6,988
Economy			
GDP ($ billions)	294.9	385.1	662.3
GDP growth (annual %)	4.2	3.9	2.9
GDP implicit price deflator (annual % growth)	1.6	4.1	1.5
Value added in agriculture (% of GDP)	4	3	2
Value added in industry (% of GDP)	29	25	25
Value added in services (% of GDP)	66	72	73
Exports of goods and services (% of GDP)	56	70	74
Imports of goods and services (% of GDP)	53	65	66
Gross capital formation (% of GDP)	23	22	20
Central government revenue (% of GDP)	..	40.7	42.2
Central government cash surplus/deficit (% of GDP)	..	2.0	0.5
States and markets			
Starting a business (days)			10
Stock market capitalization (% of GDP)	40.7	166.3	117.7
Military expenditures (% of GDP)	2.5	1.6	1.5
Fixed-line and mobile subscribers (per 100 people)	47	130	144
Internet users (per 100 people)	0.3	44.0	89.0
Paved roads (% of total)	88	90	..
High-technology exports (% of manufactured exports)	16	35	28
Global links			
Merchandise trade (% of GDP)	87.5	117.2	132.7
Net barter terms of trade (2000 = 100)	101	100	101
Total external debt ($ billions)	..	..	..
Short-term debt ($ billions)	..	..	..
Total debt service (% of exports)	..	..	..
Foreign direct investment, net inflows ($ billions)	10.7	63.1	7.2
Remittances received ($ billions)	0.7	1.2	2.4
Aid ($ billions)	..	..	..

Netherlands Antilles

High income

Population (thousands)	189	Population growth (%)		1.3
Surface area (sq. km)	800	National poverty rate (% of pop.)		..
GNI ($ billions)	..	GNI per capita ($)		..
GNI, PPP ($ billions)	..	GNI per capita, PPP ($)		..

	1990	2000	2006
People			
Share of poorest 20% in nat'l consumption/income (%)	..	..	..
Life expectancy at birth (years)	74	75	75
Total fertility (births per woman)	2.3	2.1	1.9
Adolescent fertility (births per 1,000 women 15–19)	..	39	31
Contraceptive prevalence (% of married women 15–49)	..	..	..
Births attended by skilled health staff (% of total)	..	..	..
Under-five mortality rate (per 1,000)	..	..	..
Child malnutrition, underweight (% of under age 5)	..	..	..
Child immunization, measles (% of ages 12–23 mos.)	..	..	..
Primary completion rate, total (% of relevant age group)	..	108	..
Gross secondary enrollment, total (% of relevant age group)	93	87	..
Ratio of girls to boys in primary & secondary school (%)	..	101	..
HIV prevalence rate (% of population ages 15–49)	..	..	..
Environment			
Forests (sq. km)	10	10	10
Deforestation (average annual %, 1990–2005)			0.00
Freshwater use (% of internal resources)	..	..	..
Access to improved water source (% of total pop.)	..	..	..
Access to improved sanitation facilities (% of total pop.)	..	..	..
Energy use per capita (kilograms of oil equivalent)	7,832	7,688	8,890
Carbon dioxide emissions per capita (metric tons)	6.3	18.2	22.2
Electricity use per capita (kilowatt-hours)	3,557	5,402	5,172
Economy			
GDP ($ billions)	..	..	..
GDP growth (annual %)	..	..	..
GDP implicit price deflator (annual % growth)	..	..	..
Value added in agriculture (% of GDP)	..	..	..
Value added in industry (% of GDP)	..	..	..
Value added in services (% of GDP)	..	..	..
Exports of goods and services (% of GDP)	..	..	..
Imports of goods and services (% of GDP)	..	..	..
Gross capital formation (% of GDP)	..	..	..
Central government revenue (% of GDP)	..	..	..
Central government cash surplus/deficit (% of GDP)	..	..	..
States and markets			
Starting a business (days)			..
Stock market capitalization (% of GDP)	..	..	..
Military expenditures (% of GDP)	..	..	..
Fixed-line and mobile subscribers (per 100 people)	25	60	..
Internet users (per 100 people)	0.0	1.1	..
Paved roads (% of total)	..	..	..
High-technology exports (% of manufactured exports)	..	..	..
Global links			
Merchandise trade (% of GDP)	..	..	..
Net barter terms of trade (2000 = 100)	..	100	141
Total external debt ($ billions)	..	..	..
Short-term debt ($ billions)	..	..	..
Total debt service (% of exports)	..	..	..
Foreign direct investment, net inflows ($ millions)	8.1	-12.7	73.5
Remittances received ($ millions)	5.0	12.0	8.1
Aid ($ millions)	58	177	21

New Caledonia

High income

Population (thousands)	238	Population growth (%)		1.5
Surface area (1,000 sq. km)	19	National poverty rate (% of pop.)		..
GNI ($ billions)	..	GNI per capita ($)		..
GNI, PPP ($ billions)	..	GNI per capita, PPP ($)		..

	1990	2000	2006
People			
Share of poorest 20% in nat'l consumption/income (%)	..	..	..
Life expectancy at birth (years)	70	73	75
Total fertility (births per woman)	3.2	2.6	2.3
Adolescent fertility (births per 1,000 women 15–19)	..	30	27
Contraceptive prevalence (% of married women 15–49)	..	..	..
Births attended by skilled health staff (% of total)	..	..	..
Under-five mortality rate (per 1,000)	..	..	..
Child malnutrition, underweight (% of under age 5)	..	..	..
Child immunization, measles (% of ages 12–23 mos.)	..	..	..
Primary completion rate, total (% of relevant age group)	..	..	..
Gross secondary enrollment, total (% of relevant age group)	..	..	..
Ratio of girls to boys in primary & secondary school (%)	..	..	..
HIV prevalence rate (% of population ages 15–49)	..	..	..
Environment			
Forests (1,000 sq. km)	7.2	7.2	7.2
Deforestation (average annual %, 1990–2005)			0.00
Freshwater use (% of internal resources)	..	..	..
Access to improved water source (% of total pop.)	..	..	..
Access to improved sanitation facilities (% of total pop.)	..	..	..
Energy use per capita (kilograms of oil equivalent)	..	..	..
Carbon dioxide emissions per capita (metric tons)	9.6	10.6	11.2
Electricity use per capita (kilowatt-hours)	..	..	..
Economy			
GDP ($ billions)	2.5	2.7	..
GDP growth (annual %)	3.6	2.1	..
GDP implicit price deflator (annual % growth)	-4.6	-0.6	..
Value added in agriculture (% of GDP)	4	..	..
Value added in industry (% of GDP)	23	..	..
Value added in services (% of GDP)	73	..	..
Exports of goods and services (% of GDP)	18	13	..
Imports of goods and services (% of GDP)	35	33	..
Gross capital formation (% of GDP)	31	..	..
Central government revenue (% of GDP)	..	..	..
Central government cash surplus/deficit (% of GDP)	..	..	..
States and markets			
Starting a business (days)			..
Stock market capitalization (% of GDP)	..	..	..
Military expenditures (% of GDP)	..	..	..
Fixed-line and mobile subscribers (per 100 people)	17	47	81
Internet users (per 100 people)	0.0	14.1	33.6
Paved roads (% of total)	..	..	..
High-technology exports (% of manufactured exports)	..	1	1
Global links			
Merchandise trade (% of GDP)	52.7	57.0	..
Net barter terms of trade (2000 = 100)	..	100	169
Total external debt ($ billions)	..	..	..
Short-term debt ($ billions)	..	..	..
Total debt service (% of exports)	..	..	..
Foreign direct investment, net inflows ($ millions)	..	59.1	749.1
Remittances received ($ millions)	..	..	535.1
Aid ($ millions)	302	350	524

New Zealand

			High income
Population (millions)	4.2	Population growth (%)	1.2
Surface area (1,000 sq. km)	268	National poverty rate (% of pop.)	..
GNI ($ billions)	112.0	GNI per capita ($)	26,750
GNI, PPP ($ billions)	107.7	GNI per capita, PPP ($)	25,750

	1990	2000	2006
People			
Share of poorest 20% in nat'l consumption/income (%)	..	..	..
Life expectancy at birth (years)	75	79	80
Total fertility (births per woman)	2.2	2.0	2.1
Adolescent fertility (births per 1,000 women 15–19)	..	29	23
Contraceptive prevalence (% of married women 15–49)	..	..	..
Births attended by skilled health staff (% of total)	..	97	..
Under-five mortality rate (per 1,000)	11	8	6
Child malnutrition, underweight (% of under age 5)	..	..	..
Child immunization, measles (% of ages 12–23 mos.)	90	85	82
Primary completion rate, total (% of relevant age group)	98	..	..
Gross secondary enrollment, total (% of relevant age group)	90	112	121
Ratio of girls to boys in primary & secondary school (%)	100	103	104
HIV prevalence rate (% of population ages 15–49)	..	..	0.1
Environment			
Forests (1,000 sq. km)	77	82	83
Deforestation (average annual %, 1990–2005)			-0.5
Freshwater use (% of internal resources)	..	0.6	..
Access to improved water source (% of total pop.)	97	..	..
Access to improved sanitation facilities (% of total pop.)	..	..	..
Energy use per capita (kilograms of oil equivalent)	3,990	4,654	4,090
Carbon dioxide emissions per capita (metric tons)	6.6	8.4	7.7
Electricity use per capita (kilowatt-hours)	8,298	9,076	9,656
Economy			
GDP ($ billions)	43.9	52.7	104.5
GDP growth (annual %)	0.0	2.1	1.9
GDP implicit price deflator (annual % growth)	2.5	3.5	1.3
Value added in agriculture (% of GDP)	7	9	..
Value added in industry (% of GDP)	28	25	..
Value added in services (% of GDP)	65	66	..
Exports of goods and services (% of GDP)	27	35	28
Imports of goods and services (% of GDP)	27	34	30
Gross capital formation (% of GDP)	20	22	25
Central government revenue (% of GDP)	..	34.2	39.6
Central government cash surplus/deficit (% of GDP)	..	1.7	4.7
States and markets			
Starting a business (days)			12
Stock market capitalization (% of GDP)	20.1	35.8	43.0
Military expenditures (% of GDP)	1.8	1.2	1.0
Fixed-line and mobile subscribers (per 100 people)	44	87	127
Internet users (per 100 people)	0.0	39.3	76.5
Paved roads (% of total)	57	63	65
High-technology exports (% of manufactured exports)	4	10	11
Global links			
Merchandise trade (% of GDP)	43.0	51.6	46.8
Net barter terms of trade (2000 = 100)	105	100	112
Total external debt ($ billions)	..	..	..
Short-term debt ($ billions)	..	..	..
Total debt service (% of exports)	..	..	..
Foreign direct investment, net inflows ($ billions)	1.7	3.9	7.9
Remittances received ($ millions)	762	452	650
Aid ($ billions)	..	..	..

Nicaragua

Latin America & Caribbean   **Lower middle income**

Population (millions)	5.5	Population growth (%)		1.3
Surface area (1,000 sq. km)	130	National poverty rate (% of pop.)		..
GNI ($ billions)	5.2	GNI per capita ($)		930
GNI, PPP ($ billions)	15.1	GNI per capita, PPP ($)		2,720

	1990	2000	2006
People			
Share of poorest 20% in nat'l consumption/income (%)	..	5.6	..
Life expectancy at birth (years)	64	70	72
Total fertility (births per woman)	4.7	3.2	2.8
Adolescent fertility (births per 1,000 women 15–19)	..	125	114
Contraceptive prevalence (% of married women 15–49)	..	69	..
Births attended by skilled health staff (% of total)	..	67	..
Under-five mortality rate (per 1,000)	68	43	36
Child malnutrition, underweight (% of under age 5)	..	7.8	..
Child immunization, measles (% of ages 12–23 mos.)	82	86	99
Primary completion rate, total (% of relevant age group)	44	66	73
Gross secondary enrollment, total (% of relevant age group)	42	53	66
Ratio of girls to boys in primary & secondary school (%)	109	105	102
HIV prevalence rate (% of population ages 15–49)	..	..	0.2
Environment			
Forests (1,000 sq. km)	65	55	52
Deforestation (average annual %, 1990–2005)			1.5
Freshwater use (% of internal resources)	..	0.7	
Access to improved water source (% of total pop.)	70	76	79
Access to improved sanitation facilities (% of total pop.)	45	46	47
Energy use per capita (kilograms of oil equivalent)	512	538	611
Carbon dioxide emissions per capita (metric tons)	0.6	0.7	0.7
Electricity use per capita (kilowatt-hours)	295	337	414
Economy			
GDP ($ billions)	1.0	3.9	5.3
GDP growth (annual %)	–0.1	4.1	3.7
GDP implicit price deflator (annual % growth)	5,018.1	8.6	10.6
Value added in agriculture (% of GDP)	..	21	20
Value added in industry (% of GDP)	..	28	30
Value added in services (% of GDP)	..	51	51
Exports of goods and services (% of GDP)	25	24	31
Imports of goods and services (% of GDP)	46	51	61
Gross capital formation (% of GDP)	19	30	29
Central government revenue (% of GDP)	30.0	15.1	18.8
Central government cash surplus/deficit (% of GDP)	–34.2	–3.6	0.1
States and markets			
Starting a business (days)			39
Stock market capitalization (% of GDP)	..	..	..
Military expenditures (% of GDP)	102.9	0.8	0.7
Fixed-line and mobile subscribers (per 100 people)	1	5	38
Internet users (per 100 people)	0.0	1.0	2.8
Paved roads (% of total)	11	11	..
High-technology exports (% of manufactured exports)	0	5	7
Global links			
Merchandise trade (% of GDP)	95.9	62.2	75.8
Net barter terms of trade (2000 = 100)	155	100	79
Total external debt ($ billions)	10.7	6.9	4.4
Short-term debt ($ billions)	2.4	0.9	0.6
Total debt service (% of exports)	3.9	19.7	4.1
Foreign direct investment, net inflows ($ millions)	0.7	266.9	282.3
Remittances received ($ millions)	0.0	320.0	655.5
Aid ($ millions)	330	561	733

Niger

Sub-Saharan Africa		Low income	
Population (millions)	14	Population growth (%)	3.5
Surface area (1,000 sq. km)	1,267	National poverty rate (% of pop.)	..
GNI ($ billions)	3.7	GNI per capita ($)	270
GNI, PPP ($ billions)	8.6	GNI per capita, PPP ($)	630

	1990	2000	2006
People			
Share of poorest 20% in nat'l consumption/income (%)	7.5	..	..
Life expectancy at birth (years)	47	53	56
Total fertility (births per woman)	7.9	7.5	7.0
Adolescent fertility (births per 1,000 women 15–19)	..	224	201
Contraceptive prevalence (% of married women 15–49)	4	14	11
Births attended by skilled health staff (% of total)	15	16	18
Under-five mortality rate (per 1,000)	320	270	253
Child malnutrition, underweight (% of under age 5)	41.0	43.6	39.9
Child immunization, measles (% of ages 12–23 mos.)	25	34	47
Primary completion rate, total (% of relevant age group)	15	18	33
Gross secondary enrollment, total (% of relevant age group)	7	7	11
Ratio of girls to boys in primary & secondary school (%)	53	66	70
HIV prevalence rate (% of population ages 15–49)	..	..	1.1
Environment			
Forests (1,000 sq. km)	19	13	13
Deforestation (average annual %, 1990–2005)			2.8
Freshwater use (% of internal resources)	..	62.3	..
Access to improved water source (% of total pop.)	39	44	46
Access to improved sanitation facilities (% of total pop.)	7	11	13
Energy use per capita (kilograms of oil equivalent)	..	..	..
Carbon dioxide emissions per capita (metric tons)	0.1	0.1	0.1
Electricity use per capita (kilowatt-hours)	..	..	..
Economy			
GDP ($ billions)	2.5	1.8	3.7
GDP growth (annual %)	-1.3	-1.4	4.8
GDP implicit price deflator (annual % growth)	-1.6	4.5	1.0
Value added in agriculture (% of GDP)	35	38	..
Value added in industry (% of GDP)	16	18	..
Value added in services (% of GDP)	49	44	..
Exports of goods and services (% of GDP)	15	18	15
Imports of goods and services (% of GDP)	22	26	24
Gross capital formation (% of GDP)	8	11	18
Central government revenue (% of GDP)	..	..	..
Central government cash surplus/deficit (% of GDP)	..	..	..
States and markets			
Starting a business (days)			23
Stock market capitalization (% of GDP)	..	..	..
Military expenditures (% of GDP)	..	1.1	1.1
Fixed-line and mobile subscribers (per 100 people)	0	0	3
Internet users (per 100 people)	0.0	0.0	0.3
Paved roads (% of total)	29	26	21
High-technology exports (% of manufactured exports)	..	15	11
Global links			
Merchandise trade (% of GDP)	27.0	37.7	40.7
Net barter terms of trade (2000 = 100)	165	100	164
Total external debt ($ billions)	1.7	1.7	0.8
Short-term debt ($ millions)	154	72	49
Total debt service (% of exports)	17.4	7.7	5.9
Foreign direct investment, net inflows ($ millions)	40.8	8.4	20.5
Remittances received ($ millions)	14	14	66
Aid ($ millions)	388	208	401

Nigeria

Sub-Saharan Africa		Low income	
Population (millions)	145	Population growth (%)	2.4
Surface area (1,000 sq. km)	924	National poverty rate (% of pop.)	..
GNI ($ billions)	90.0	GNI per capita ($)	620
GNI, PPP ($ billions)	203.7	GNI per capita, PPP ($)	1,410

	1990	2000	2006
People			
Share of poorest 20% in nat'l consumption/income (%)	..	..	..
Life expectancy at birth (years)	47	47	47
Total fertility (births per woman)	6.7	6.0	5.4
Adolescent fertility (births per 1,000 women 15–19)	..	158	131
Contraceptive prevalence (% of married women 15–49)	6	15	..
Births attended by skilled health staff (% of total)	33	42	..
Under-five mortality rate (per 1,000)	230	207	191
Child malnutrition, underweight (% of under age 5)	35.1	..	..
Child immunization, measles (% of ages 12–23 mos.)	54	35	62
Primary completion rate, total (% of relevant age group)	..	..	76
Gross secondary enrollment, total (% of relevant age group)	24	23	32
Ratio of girls to boys in primary & secondary school (%)	77	81	83
HIV prevalence rate (% of population ages 15–49)	..	..	3.9
Environment			
Forests (1,000 sq. km)	172	131	111
Deforestation (average annual %, 1990–2005)			2.9
Freshwater use (% of internal resources)	..	3.6	..
Access to improved water source (% of total pop.)	49	49	48
Access to improved sanitation facilities (% of total pop.)	39	42	44
Energy use per capita (kilograms of oil equivalent)	751	715	734
Carbon dioxide emissions per capita (metric tons)	0.5	0.7	0.8
Electricity use per capita (kilowatt-hours)	88	73	127
Economy			
GDP ($ billions)	28.5	46.0	115.3
GDP growth (annual %)	8.2	5.4	5.2
GDP implicit price deflator (annual % growth)	7.2	38.2	7.9
Value added in agriculture (% of GDP)	33	26	23
Value added in industry (% of GDP)	41	53	57
Value added in services (% of GDP)	26	21	20
Exports of goods and services (% of GDP)	43	54	56
Imports of goods and services (% of GDP)	29	32	35
Gross capital formation (% of GDP)	15	20	22
Central government revenue (% of GDP)	..	..	..
Central government cash surplus/deficit (% of GDP)	..	..	..
States and markets			
Starting a business (days)			34
Stock market capitalization (% of GDP)	4.8	9.2	28.5
Military expenditures (% of GDP)	0.9	0.8	0.7
Fixed-line and mobile subscribers (per 100 people)	0	0	24
Internet users (per 100 people)	0.0	0.1	5.5
Paved roads (% of total)	30	31	15
High-technology exports (% of manufactured exports)	0	0	..
Global links			
Merchandise trade (% of GDP)	67.5	64.6	64.0
Net barter terms of trade (2000 = 100)	89	100	161
Total external debt ($ billions)	33.4	31.4	7.7
Short-term debt ($ billions)	1.5	1.1	3.9
Total debt service (% of exports)	22.6	8.2	15.8
Foreign direct investment, net inflows ($ billions)	0.6	1.1	5.4
Remittances received ($ billions)	0.0	1.4	3.3
Aid ($ billions)	0.3	0.2	11.4

Northern Mariana Islands

East Asia & Pacific   **Upper middle income**

Population (thousands)	82	Population growth (%)	2.2
Surface area (sq. km)	460	National poverty rate (% of pop.)	..
GNI ($ billions)	..	GNI per capita ($)	..
GNI, PPP ($ billions)	..	GNI per capita, PPP ($)	..

	1990	2000	2006
People			
Share of poorest 20% in nat'l consumption/income (%)	..	..	..
Life expectancy at birth (years)	..	..	..
Total fertility (births per woman)	..	..	..
Adolescent fertility (births per 1,000 women 15–19)	..	..	..
Contraceptive prevalence (% of married women 15–49)	..	..	..
Births attended by skilled health staff (% of total)	..	100	..
Under-five mortality rate (per 1,000)	..	..	..
Child malnutrition, underweight (% of under age 5)	..	..	..
Child immunization, measles (% of ages 12–23 mos.)	..	..	..
Primary completion rate, total (% of relevant age group)	..	..	..
Gross secondary enrollment, total (% of relevant age group)	..	..	..
Ratio of girls to boys in primary & secondary school (%)	..	..	..
HIV prevalence rate (% of population ages 15–49)	..	..	..
Environment			
Forests (sq. km)	350	340	330
Deforestation (average annual %, 1990–2005)			0.4
Freshwater use (% of internal resources)	..	..	..
Access to improved water source (% of total pop.)	98	99	99
Access to improved sanitation facilities (% of total pop.)	84	93	95
Energy use per capita (kilograms of oil equivalent)	..	..	..
Carbon dioxide emissions per capita (metric tons)	..	..	..
Electricity use per capita (kilowatt-hours)	..	..	..
Economy			
GDP ($ billions)	..	..	..
GDP growth (annual %)	..	..	..
GDP implicit price deflator (annual % growth)	..	..	..
Value added in agriculture (% of GDP)	..	..	..
Value added in industry (% of GDP)	..	..	..
Value added in services (% of GDP)	..	..	..
Exports of goods and services (% of GDP)	..	..	..
Imports of goods and services (% of GDP)	..	..	..
Gross capital formation (% of GDP)	..	..	..
Central government revenue (% of GDP)	..	..	..
Central government cash surplus/deficit (% of GDP)	..	..	..
States and markets			
Starting a business (days)			..
Stock market capitalization (% of GDP)	..	..	..
Military expenditures (% of GDP)	..	..	..
Fixed-line and mobile subscribers (per 100 people)	..	..	..
Internet users (per 100 people)	..	..	..
Paved roads (% of total)	..	..	..
High-technology exports (% of manufactured exports)	..	..	..
Global links			
Merchandise trade (% of GDP)	..	..	..
Net barter terms of trade (2000 = 100)	..	..	..
Total external debt ($ billions)	..	..	..
Short-term debt ($ billions)	..	..	..
Total debt service (% of exports)	..	..	..
Foreign direct investment, net inflows ($ billions)	..	..	..
Remittances received ($ billions)	..	..	..
Aid ($ millions)	63.1	0.2	..

Norway

High income

Population (millions)	4.7	Population growth (%)	0.8
Surface area (1,000 sq. km)	324	National poverty rate (% of pop.)	..
GNI ($ billions)	318.9	GNI per capita ($)	68,440
GNI, PPP ($ billions)	233.3	GNI per capita, PPP ($)	50,070

	1990	2000	2006
People			
Share of poorest 20% in nat'l consumption/income (%)	..	9.6	..
Life expectancy at birth (years)	77	79	80
Total fertility (births per woman)	1.9	1.9	1.9
Adolescent fertility (births per 1,000 women 15–19)	..	11	9
Contraceptive prevalence (% of married women 15–49)	74	..	..
Births attended by skilled health staff (% of total)	100	..	..
Under-five mortality rate (per 1,000)	9	5	4
Child malnutrition, underweight (% of under age 5)	..	..	..
Child immunization, measles (% of ages 12–23 mos.)	87	88	91
Primary completion rate, total (% of relevant age group)	100	98	99
Gross secondary enrollment, total (% of relevant age group)	103	116	113
Ratio of girls to boys in primary & secondary school (%)	102	101	101
HIV prevalence rate (% of population ages 15–49)	..	..	0.1
Environment			
Forests (1,000 sq. km)	91	93	94
Deforestation (average annual %, 1990–2005)			-0.2
Freshwater use (% of internal resources)	..	0.6	..
Access to improved water source (% of total pop.)	100	100	100
Access to improved sanitation facilities (% of total pop.)	..	..	..
Energy use per capita (kilograms of oil equivalent)	5,072	5,747	6,948
Carbon dioxide emissions per capita (metric tons)	7.8	9.9	19.1
Electricity use per capita (kilowatt-hours)	23,354	24,994	25,137
Economy			
GDP ($ billions)	117.6	168.3	334.9
GDP growth (annual %)	1.9	3.3	2.9
GDP implicit price deflator (annual % growth)	3.8	15.7	7.4
Value added in agriculture (% of GDP)	3	2	2
Value added in industry (% of GDP)	34	42	45
Value added in services (% of GDP)	63	56	54
Exports of goods and services (% of GDP)	40	47	46
Imports of goods and services (% of GDP)	34	29	29
Gross capital formation (% of GDP)	23	20	22
Central government revenue (% of GDP)	..	48.4	50.4
Central government cash surplus/deficit (% of GDP)	..	15.7	17.9
States and markets			
Starting a business (days)			10
Stock market capitalization (% of GDP)	22.2	38.6	83.9
Military expenditures (% of GDP)	2.9	1.7	1.5
Fixed-line and mobile subscribers (per 100 people)	55	125	152
Internet users (per 100 people)	0.7	26.7	87.4
Paved roads (% of total)	69	76	..
High-technology exports (% of manufactured exports)	12	17	19
Global links			
Merchandise trade (% of GDP)	52.1	56.1	55.4
Net barter terms of trade (2000 = 100)	67	100	139
Total external debt ($ millions)	..	..	..
Short-term debt ($ millions)	..	..	..
Total debt service (% of exports)	..	..	..
Foreign direct investment, net inflows ($ billions)	1.0	7.0	4.7
Remittances received ($ millions)	158	246	524
Aid ($ millions)	..	..	..

Oman

Middle East & North Africa		**Upper middle income**

Population (millions)	2.5	Population growth (%)	1.6
Surface area (1,000 sq. km)	310	National poverty rate (% of pop.)	..
GNI ($ billions)	27.9	GNI per capita ($)	11,120
GNI, PPP ($ billions)	49.5	GNI per capita, PPP ($)	19,740

	1990	2000	2006
People			
Share of poorest 20% in nat'l consumption/income (%)	..	..	..
Life expectancy at birth (years)	70	74	76
Total fertility (births per woman)	6.5	4.3	3.1
Adolescent fertility (births per 1,000 women 15–19)	..	26	11
Contraceptive prevalence (% of married women 15–49)	9	32	..
Births attended by skilled health staff (% of total)	..	95	98
Under-five mortality rate (per 1,000)	32	15	12
Child malnutrition, underweight (% of under age 5)	..	13.1	..
Child immunization, measles (% of ages 12–23 mos.)	98	99	96
Primary completion rate, total (% of relevant age group)	65	81	94
Gross secondary enrollment, total (% of relevant age group)	45	78	89
Ratio of girls to boys in primary & secondary school (%)	89	98	98
HIV prevalence rate (% of population ages 15–49)	..	..	0.2
Environment			
Forests (sq. km)	20	20	20
Deforestation (average annual %, 1990–2005)			0.00
Freshwater use (% of internal resources)	..	136.0	..
Access to improved water source (% of total pop.)	80	82	..
Access to improved sanitation facilities (% of total pop.)	83	88	..
Energy use per capita (kilograms of oil equivalent)	2,475	4,026	5,570
Carbon dioxide emissions per capita (metric tons)	5.6	9.2	12.5
Electricity use per capita (kilowatt-hours)	2,150	3,140	3,757
Economy			
GDP ($ billions)	11.7	19.9	30.8
GDP growth (annual %)	-0.1	5.4	5.7
GDP implicit price deflator (annual % growth)	24.8	20.0	17.8
Value added in agriculture (% of GDP)	3	2	2
Value added in industry (% of GDP)	54	57	55
Value added in services (% of GDP)	43	41	43
Exports of goods and services (% of GDP)	47	59	63
Imports of goods and services (% of GDP)	28	31	36
Gross capital formation (% of GDP)	12	12	18
Central government revenue (% of GDP)	35.0	23.9	..
Central government cash surplus/deficit (% of GDP)	-0.3	-4.4	..
States and markets			
Starting a business (days)			34
Stock market capitalization (% of GDP)	8.5	17.4	49.5
Military expenditures (% of GDP)	16.5	10.6	11.8
Fixed-line and mobile subscribers (per 100 people)	6	16	82
Internet users (per 100 people)	0.0	3.7	12.5
Paved roads (% of total)	21	30	..
High-technology exports (% of manufactured exports)	2	3	1
Global links			
Merchandise trade (% of GDP)	71.1	82.8	89.2
Net barter terms of trade (2000 = 100)	..	100	182
Total external debt ($ billions)	2.7	6.6	4.8
Short-term debt ($ billions)	0.3	1.3	2.0
Total debt service (% of exports)	12.3	7.2	1.3
Foreign direct investment, net inflows ($ millions)	142	82	952
Remittances received ($ millions)	39	39	39
Aid ($ millions)	61	45	35

Pakistan

Low income

Population (millions)	159	Population growth (%)		2.1
Surface area (1,000 sq. km)	796	National poverty rate (% of pop.)		..
GNI ($ billions)	126.7	GNI per capita ($)		800
GNI, PPP ($ billions)	382.8	GNI per capita, PPP ($)		2,410

	1990	2000	2006
People			
Share of poorest 20% in nat'l consumption/income (%)	8.1	9.4	9.1
Life expectancy at birth (years)	59	63	65
Total fertility (births per woman)	5.8	4.7	3.9
Adolescent fertility (births per 1,000 women 15–19)	..	41	33
Contraceptive prevalence (% of married women 15–49)	15	28	..
Births attended by skilled health staff (% of total)	19	23	31
Under-five mortality rate (per 1,000)	130	108	97
Child malnutrition, underweight (% of under age 5)	39.0	31.3	..
Child immunization, measles (% of ages 12–23 mos.)	50	56	80
Primary completion rate, total (% of relevant age group)	..	..	62
Gross secondary enrollment, total (% of relevant age group)	25	..	30
Ratio of girls to boys in primary & secondary school (%)	..	..	78
HIV prevalence rate (% of population ages 15–49)	..	..	0.1
Environment			
Forests (1,000 sq. km)	25	21	19
Deforestation (average annual %, 1990–2005)			1.9
Freshwater use (% of internal resources)	..	323.3	..
Access to improved water source (% of total pop.)	83	89	91
Access to improved sanitation facilities (% of total pop.)	37	52	59
Energy use per capita (kilograms of oil equivalent)	402	463	490
Carbon dioxide emissions per capita (metric tons)	0.6	0.8	0.8
Electricity use per capita (kilowatt-hours)	277	374	456
Economy			
GDP ($ billions)	40.0	74.0	126.8
GDP growth (annual %)	4.5	4.3	6.9
GDP implicit price deflator (annual % growth)	6.5	24.9	9.3
Value added in agriculture (% of GDP)	26	26	19
Value added in industry (% of GDP)	25	23	27
Value added in services (% of GDP)	49	51	53
Exports of goods and services (% of GDP)	16	13	15
Imports of goods and services (% of GDP)	23	15	23
Gross capital formation (% of GDP)	19	17	22
Central government revenue (% of GDP)	19.1	13.9	13.5
Central government cash surplus/deficit (% of GDP)	-2.5	-4.1	-4.2
States and markets			
Starting a business (days)			24
Stock market capitalization (% of GDP)	7.1	8.9	35.9
Military expenditures (% of GDP)	6.8	4.0	3.8
Fixed-line and mobile subscribers (per 100 people)	1	2	25
Internet users (per 100 people)	0.0	0.2	7.5
Paved roads (% of total)	54	56	65
High-technology exports (% of manufactured exports)	0	0	1
Global links			
Merchandise trade (% of GDP)	32.6	26.9	36.9
Net barter terms of trade (2000 = 100)	109	100	76
Total external debt ($ billions)	21	33	36
Short-term debt ($ billions)	3.2	1.5	1.2
Total debt service (% of exports)	21.3	25.2	8.6
Foreign direct investment, net inflows ($ billions)	0.2	0.3	4.3
Remittances received ($ billions)	2.0	1.1	5.1
Aid ($ billions)	1.1	0.7	2.1

Palau

East Asia & Pacific		**Upper middle income**	
Population (thousands)	20	Population growth (%)	0.5
Surface area (sq. km)	460	National poverty rate (% of pop.)	..
GNI ($ millions)	161	GNI per capita ($)	7,990
GNI, PPP ($ millions)	290	GNI per capita, PPP ($)	14,340

	1990	2000	2006
People			
Share of poorest 20% in nat'l consumption/income (%)	..	..	..
Life expectancy at birth (years)	..	..	..
Total fertility (births per woman)	..	..	..
Adolescent fertility (births per 1,000 women 15–19)		..	..
Contraceptive prevalence (% of married women 15–49)	47	17	..
Births attended by skilled health staff (% of total)	99	100	..
Under-five mortality rate (per 1,000)	21	14	11
Child malnutrition, underweight (% of under age 5)	..	..	..
Child immunization, measles (% of ages 12–23 mos.)	98	83	98
Primary completion rate, total (% of relevant age group)	..	99	119
Gross secondary enrollment, total (% of relevant age group)		86	102
Ratio of girls to boys in primary & secondary school (%)	..	100	102
HIV prevalence rate (% of population ages 15–49)	..	..	..
Environment			
Forests (sq. km)	380	400	400
Deforestation (average annual %, 1990–2005)			–0.3
Freshwater use (% of internal resources)	..	..	..
Access to improved water source (% of total pop.)	80	84	85
Access to improved sanitation facilities (% of total pop.)	67	79	80
Energy use per capita (kilograms of oil equivalent)	..	..	..
Carbon dioxide emissions per capita (metric tons)	..	..	11.9
Electricity use per capita (kilowatt-hours)	..	..	..
Economy			
GDP ($ millions)	77	120	157
GDP growth (annual %)	–6.4	0.3	5.7
GDP implicit price deflator (annual % growth)	5.0	5.3	2.8
Value added in agriculture (% of GDP)	26	4	3
Value added in industry (% of GDP)	13	15	19
Value added in services (% of GDP)	59	80	77
Exports of goods and services (% of GDP)	20	10	72
Imports of goods and services (% of GDP)	39	106	82
Gross capital formation (% of GDP)	..	..	..
Central government revenue (% of GDP)	..	..	..
Central government cash surplus/deficit (% of GDP)	..	..	..
States and markets			
Starting a business (days)			28
Stock market capitalization (% of GDP)	..	..	..
Military expenditures (% of GDP)	..	..	..
Fixed-line and mobile subscribers (per 100 people)	..	..	78
Internet users (per 100 people)	..	..	27.0
Paved roads (% of total)	..	..	..
High-technology exports (% of manufactured exports)	..	..	..
Global links			
Merchandise trade (% of GDP)	..	112.8	75.0
Net barter terms of trade (2000 = 100)	..	100	117
Total external debt ($ billions)	..	..	..
Short-term debt ($ billions)	..	..	..
Total debt service (% of exports)	..	..	..
Foreign direct investment, net inflows ($ billions)	..	..	..
Remittances received ($ billions)	..	..	..
Aid ($ millions)	0.0	39.1	37.3

Panama

Latin America & Caribbean   **Upper middle income**

Population (millions)	3.3	Population growth (%)	1.7
Surface area (1,000 sq. km)	76	National poverty rate (% of pop.)	..
GNI ($ billions)	16.4	GNI per capita ($)	5,000
GNI, PPP ($ billions)	28.6	GNI per capita, PPP ($)	8,690

	1990	2000	2006
People			
Share of poorest 20% in nat'l consumption/income (%)	2.1	2.4	..
Life expectancy at birth (years)	72	74	75
Total fertility (births per woman)	3.0	2.7	2.6
Adolescent fertility (births per 1,000 women 15–19)	..	91	84
Contraceptive prevalence (% of married women 15–49)	..	..	..
Births attended by skilled health staff (% of total)	..	90	91
Under-five mortality rate (per 1,000)	34	26	23
Child malnutrition, underweight (% of under age 5)	..	..	..
Child immunization, measles (% of ages 12–23 mos.)	73	97	94
Primary completion rate, total (% of relevant age group)	86	94	94
Gross secondary enrollment, total (% of relevant age group)	62	67	70
Ratio of girls to boys in primary & secondary school (%)	..	100	101
HIV prevalence rate (% of population ages 15–49)	..	..	0.9
Environment			
Forests (1,000 sq. km)	44	43	43
Deforestation (average annual %, 1990–2005)			0.1
Freshwater use (% of internal resources)	..	0.6	..
Access to improved water source (% of total pop.)	90	90	90
Access to improved sanitation facilities (% of total pop.)	71	72	73
Energy use per capita (kilograms of oil equivalent)	618	875	804
Carbon dioxide emissions per capita (metric tons)	1.3	1.9	1.8
Electricity use per capita (kilowatt-hours)	854	1,301	1,500
Economy			
GDP ($ billions)	5.3	11.6	17.1
GDP growth (annual %)	8.1	2.7	8.1
GDP implicit price deflator (annual % growth)	0.6	-1.2	2.1
Value added in agriculture (% of GDP)	10	7	8
Value added in industry (% of GDP)	15	19	19
Value added in services (% of GDP)	75	74	73
Exports of goods and services (% of GDP)	87	73	73
Imports of goods and services (% of GDP)	79	70	71
Gross capital formation (% of GDP)	17	24	20
Central government revenue (% of GDP)	25.6	23.1	..
Central government cash surplus/deficit (% of GDP)	2.0	-0.8	..
States and markets			
Starting a business (days)			19
Stock market capitalization (% of GDP)	3.4	24.0	33.4
Military expenditures (% of GDP)	1.4	1.0	..
Fixed-line and mobile subscribers (per 100 people)	9	28	67
Internet users (per 100 people)	0.0	3.6	6.7
Paved roads (% of total)	32	35	..
High-technology exports (% of manufactured exports)	0	0	0
Global links			
Merchandise trade (% of GDP)	35.4	36.5	34.6
Net barter terms of trade (2000 = 100)	69	100	91
Total external debt ($ billions)	6.5	7.0	10.0
Short-term debt ($ billions)	2.4	0.5	0.5
Total debt service (% of exports)	6.2	9.7	24.7
Foreign direct investment, net inflows ($ billions)	0.1	0.6	2.6
Remittances received ($ millions)	110	16	149
Aid ($ millions)	99	16	30

Papua New Guinea

East Asia & Pacific | | **Low income**

Population (millions)	6.2	Population growth (%)	2.2
Surface area (1,000 sq. km)	463	National poverty rate (% of pop.)	..
GNI ($ billions)	4.6	GNI per capita ($)	740
GNI, PPP ($ billions)	10.1	GNI per capita, PPP ($)	1,630

	1990	2000	2006
People			
Share of poorest 20% in nat'l consumption/income (%)	..	..	..
Life expectancy at birth (years)	55	57	57
Total fertility (births per woman)	4.8	4.4	3.9
Adolescent fertility (births per 1,000 women 15–19)	..	78	55
Contraceptive prevalence (% of married women 15–49)	..	..	..
Births attended by skilled health staff (% of total)	..	41	42
Under-five mortality rate (per 1,000)	94	80	73
Child malnutrition, underweight (% of under age 5)	..	..	..
Child immunization, measles (% of ages 12–23 mos.)	67	62	65
Primary completion rate, total (% of relevant age group)	51	..	..
Gross secondary enrollment, total (% of relevant age group)	12	..	..
Ratio of girls to boys in primary & secondary school (%)	80	..	..
HIV prevalence rate (% of population ages 15–49)	..	..	1.8
Environment			
Forests (1,000 sq. km)	315	301	294
Deforestation (average annual %, 1990–2005)			0.5
Freshwater use (% of internal resources)	..	..	..
Access to improved water source (% of total pop.)	39	39	39
Access to improved sanitation facilities (% of total pop.)	44	44	44
Energy use per capita (kilograms of oil equivalent)	..	..	..
Carbon dioxide emissions per capita (metric tons)	0.6	0.5	0.4
Electricity use per capita (kilowatt-hours)	..	..	..
Economy			
GDP ($ billions)	3.2	3.4	5.7
GDP growth (annual %)	–3.0	–1.2	2.6
GDP implicit price deflator (annual % growth)	4.1	9.7	9.7
Value added in agriculture (% of GDP)	32	28	42
Value added in industry (% of GDP)	34	44	39
Value added in services (% of GDP)	45	28	19
Exports of goods and services (% of GDP)	41	72	..
Imports of goods and services (% of GDP)	49	63	..
Gross capital formation (% of GDP)	24	16	..
Central government revenue (% of GDP)	25.2	24.8	..
Central government cash surplus/deficit (% of GDP)	–2.2	–1.9	..
States and markets			
Starting a business (days)			56
Stock market capitalization (% of GDP)	..	49.6	117.3
Military expenditures (% of GDP)	2.1	0.9	0.5
Fixed-line and mobile subscribers (per 100 people)	1	1	2
Internet users (per 100 people)	0.0	0.8	1.8
Paved roads (% of total)	3	4	..
High-technology exports (% of manufactured exports)	0	19	..
Global links			
Merchandise trade (% of GDP)	73.6	94.9	112.7
Net barter terms of trade (2000 = 100)	..	100	160
Total external debt ($ billions)	2.6	2.6	1.7
Short-term debt ($ millions)	72	49	167
Total debt service (% of exports)	37.2	12.9	10.8
Foreign direct investment, net inflows ($ millions)	155	96	32
Remittances received ($ millions)	5.0	7.0	13.3
Aid ($ millions)	412	275	279

Paraguay

Latin America & Caribbean   **Lower middle income**

Population (millions)	6.0	Population growth (%)	2.0
Surface area (1,000 sq. km)	407	National poverty rate (% of pop.)	..
GNI ($ billions)	8.5	GNI per capita ($)	1,410
GNI, PPP ($ billions)	24.3	GNI per capita, PPP ($)	4,040

	1990	2000	2006
People			
Share of poorest 20% in nat'l consumption/income (%)	5.8	2.2	..
Life expectancy at birth (years)	68	70	72
Total fertility (births per woman)	4.7	3.6	3.2
Adolescent fertility (births per 1,000 women 15–19)	..	86	74
Contraceptive prevalence (% of married women 15–49)	48	57	73
Births attended by skilled health staff (% of total)	66	61	77
Under-five mortality rate (per 1,000)	41	27	22
Child malnutrition, underweight (% of under age 5)	2.8	..	..
Child immunization, measles (% of ages 12–23 mos.)	69	92	88
Primary completion rate, total (% of relevant age group)	64	92	94
Gross secondary enrollment, total (% of relevant age group)	31	61	67
Ratio of girls to boys in primary & secondary school (%)	98	98	99
HIV prevalence rate (% of population ages 15–49)	..	..	0.4
Environment			
Forests (1,000 sq. km)	212	194	185
Deforestation (average annual %, 1990–2005)			0.9
Freshwater use (% of internal resources)	..	0.5	..
Access to improved water source (% of total pop.)	62	80	86
Access to improved sanitation facilities (% of total pop.)	58	74	80
Energy use per capita (kilograms of oil equivalent)	731	723	674
Carbon dioxide emissions per capita (metric tons)	0.5	0.7	0.7
Electricity use per capita (kilowatt-hours)	505	880	849
Economy			
GDP ($ billions)	5.3	7.1	9.3
GDP growth (annual %)	3.1	–3.3	4.3
GDP implicit price deflator (annual % growth)	36.3	12.1	10.7
Value added in agriculture (% of GDP)	28	17	21
Value added in industry (% of GDP)	25	22	18
Value added in services (% of GDP)	47	61	61
Exports of goods and services (% of GDP)	33	38	49
Imports of goods and services (% of GDP)	39	49	66
Gross capital formation (% of GDP)	23	19	21
Central government revenue (% of GDP)	..	..	21.3
Central government cash surplus/deficit (% of GDP)	..	..	1.2
States and markets			
Starting a business (days)			35
Stock market capitalization (% of GDP)	..	3.5	4.4
Military expenditures (% of GDP)	1.0	1.1	0.8
Fixed-line and mobile subscribers (per 100 people)	3	21	59
Internet users (per 100 people)	0.0	0.7	4.3
Paved roads (% of total)	..	51	..
High-technology exports (% of manufactured exports)	0	3	8
Global links			
Merchandise trade (% of GDP)	43.9	43.3	83.9
Net barter terms of trade (2000 = 100)	103	100	96
Total external debt ($ billions)	2.1	3.1	3.4
Short-term debt ($ millions)	373	580	711
Total debt service (% of exports)	12.4	10.6	6.8
Foreign direct investment, net inflows ($ millions)	77	104	189
Remittances received ($ millions)	34	278	432
Aid ($ millions)	57	82	56

Peru

Latin America & Caribbean		Lower middle income	
Population (millions)	28	Population growth (%)	1.1
Surface area (1,000 sq. km)	1,285	National poverty rate (% of pop.)	53
GNI ($ billions)	82.2	GNI per capita ($)	2,980
GNI, PPP ($ billions)	179.2	GNI per capita, PPP ($)	6,490

	1990	2000	2006
People			
Share of poorest 20% in nat'l consumption/income (%)	5.6	3.0	..
Life expectancy at birth (years)	66	69	71
Total fertility (births per woman)	3.9	2.9	2.6
Adolescent fertility (births per 1,000 women 15–19)	..	70	61
Contraceptive prevalence (% of married women 15–49)	59	69	46
Births attended by skilled health staff (% of total)	80	59	87
Under-five mortality rate (per 1,000)	78	41	25
Child malnutrition, underweight (% of under age 5)	8.8	5.2	..
Child immunization, measles (% of ages 12–23 mos.)	64	97	99
Primary completion rate, total (% of relevant age group)	..	103	100
Gross secondary enrollment, total (% of relevant age group)	67	87	92
Ratio of girls to boys in primary & secondary school (%)	96	97	101
HIV prevalence rate (% of population ages 15–49)	..	..	0.6
Environment			
Forests (1,000 sq. km)	702	692	687
Deforestation (average annual %, 1990–2005)			0.1
Freshwater use (% of internal resources)	..	1.2	..
Access to improved water source (% of total pop.)	74	81	83
Access to improved sanitation facilities (% of total pop.)	52	61	63
Energy use per capita (kilograms of oil equivalent)	457	488	506
Carbon dioxide emissions per capita (metric tons)	1.0	1.1	1.2
Electricity use per capita (kilowatt-hours)	548	687	848
Economy			
GDP ($ billions)	26.3	53.3	92.4
GDP growth (annual %)	-5.1	3.0	7.7
GDP implicit price deflator (annual % growth)	6,836.9	3.7	7.3
Value added in agriculture (% of GDP)	9	8	7
Value added in industry (% of GDP)	27	30	38
Value added in services (% of GDP)	64	62	55
Exports of goods and services (% of GDP)	16	16	29
Imports of goods and services (% of GDP)	14	18	20
Gross capital formation (% of GDP)	16	20	20
Central government revenue (% of GDP)	12.5	17.4	17.6
Central government cash surplus/deficit (% of GDP)	-8.1	-2.1	-0.8
States and markets			
Starting a business (days)			72
Stock market capitalization (% of GDP)	3.1	19.8	64.6
Military expenditures (% of GDP)	0.1	1.7	1.2
Fixed-line and mobile subscribers (per 100 people)	3	12	39
Internet users (per 100 people)	0.0	3.1	22.1
Paved roads (% of total)	10	13	14
High-technology exports (% of manufactured exports)	0	4	2
Global links			
Merchandise trade (% of GDP)	22.3	27.1	41.9
Net barter terms of trade (2000 = 100)	114	100	151
Total external debt ($ billions)	20	29	28
Short-term debt ($ billions)	5.3	3.9	3.0
Total debt service (% of exports)	10.8	25.8	12.9
Foreign direct investment, net inflows ($ billions)	0.0	0.8	3.5
Remittances received ($ billions)	0.1	0.7	1.8
Aid ($ millions)	397	398	468

Philippines

East Asia & Pacific   **Lower middle income**

Population (millions)	86	Population growth (%)	2.0
Surface area (1,000 sq. km)	300	National poverty rate (% of pop.)	..
GNI ($ billions)	120.2	GNI per capita ($)	1,390
GNI, PPP ($ billions)	296.2	GNI per capita, PPP ($)	3,430

	1990	2000	2006
People			
Share of poorest 20% in nat'l consumption/income (%)	5.9	5.4	..
Life expectancy at birth (years)	66	70	71
Total fertility (births per woman)	4.3	3.6	3.3
Adolescent fertility (births per 1,000 women 15–19)	..	50	48
Contraceptive prevalence (% of married women 15–49)	36	47	..
Births attended by skilled health staff (% of total)	..	58	..
Under-five mortality rate (per 1,000)	62	40	32
Child malnutrition, underweight (% of under age 5)	..	..	..
Child immunization, measles (% of ages 12–23 mos.)	85	81	92
Primary completion rate, total (% of relevant age group)	86	104	96
Gross secondary enrollment, total (% of relevant age group)	71	77	85
Ratio of girls to boys in primary & secondary school (%)	100	103	103
HIV prevalence rate (% of population ages 15–49)	..	..	0.1
Environment			
Forests (1,000 sq. km)	106	79	72
Deforestation (average annual %, 1990–2005)			2.6
Freshwater use (% of internal resources)	..	6.0	..
Access to improved water source (% of total pop.)	87	86	85
Access to improved sanitation facilities (% of total pop.)	57	68	72
Energy use per capita (kilograms of oil equivalent)	427	557	528
Carbon dioxide emissions per capita (metric tons)	0.7	1.0	1.0
Electricity use per capita (kilowatt-hours)	360	511	588
Economy			
GDP ($ billions)	44.3	75.9	117.6
GDP growth (annual %)	3.0	6.0	5.4
GDP implicit price deflator (annual % growth)	13.0	6.3	5.2
Value added in agriculture (% of GDP)	22	16	14
Value added in industry (% of GDP)	34	32	32
Value added in services (% of GDP)	44	52	54
Exports of goods and services (% of GDP)	28	55	46
Imports of goods and services (% of GDP)	33	53	48
Gross capital formation (% of GDP)	24	21	14
Central government revenue (% of GDP)	16.2	15.2	16.2
Central government cash surplus/deficit (% of GDP)	-2.8	-3.9	-1.3
States and markets			
Starting a business (days)			58
Stock market capitalization (% of GDP)	13.4	34.2	58.2
Military expenditures (% of GDP)	1.4	1.1	0.9
Fixed-line and mobile subscribers (per 100 people)	1	12	54
Internet users (per 100 people)	0.0	2.0	5.5
Paved roads (% of total)	..	10	..
High-technology exports (% of manufactured exports)	0	73	68
Global links			
Merchandise trade (% of GDP)	47.8	101.2	83.8
Net barter terms of trade (2000 = 100)	87	100	84
Total external debt ($ billions)	31	58	60
Short-term debt ($ billions)	4.4	5.5	5.0
Total debt service (% of exports)	27.0	14.3	19.6
Foreign direct investment, net inflows ($ billions)	0.5	2.2	2.3
Remittances received ($ billions)	1.5	6.2	15.3
Aid ($ billions)	1.3	0.6	0.6

Poland

Europe & Central Asia	Upper middle income

Population (millions)	38	Population growth (%)	–0.1
Surface area (1,000 sq. km)	313	National poverty rate (% of pop.)	..
GNI ($ billions)	313.0	GNI per capita ($)	8,210
GNI, PPP ($ billions)	543.4	GNI per capita, PPP ($)	14,250

	1990	2000	2006
People			
Share of poorest 20% in nat'l consumption/income (%)	9.1	7.9	7.4
Life expectancy at birth (years)	71	74	75
Total fertility (births per woman)	2.0	1.3	1.3
Adolescent fertility (births per 1,000 women 15–19)	..	17	13
Contraceptive prevalence (% of married women 15–49)	49	..	..
Births attended by skilled health staff (% of total)	..	100	100
Under-five mortality rate (per 1,000)	18	9	7
Child malnutrition, underweight (% of under age 5)	..	..	..
Child immunization, measles (% of ages 12–23 mos.)	95	97	99
Primary completion rate, total (% of relevant age group)	101	95	97
Gross secondary enrollment, total (% of relevant age group)	81	100	100
Ratio of girls to boys in primary & secondary school (%)	101	98	99
HIV prevalence rate (% of population ages 15–49)	..	..	0.1
Environment			
Forests (1,000 sq. km)	89	91	92
Deforestation (average annual %, 1990–2005)			–0.2
Freshwater use (% of internal resources)	..	30.2	..
Access to improved water source (% of total pop.)	..	..	..
Access to improved sanitation facilities (% of total pop.)	..	..	..
Energy use per capita (kilograms of oil equivalent)	2,620	2,326	2,436
Carbon dioxide emissions per capita (metric tons)	9.1	7.8	8.0
Electricity use per capita (kilowatt-hours)	3,272	3,240	3,437
Economy			
GDP ($ billions)	59.0	171.3	338.7
GDP growth (annual %)	–7.0	4.3	6.1
GDP implicit price deflator (annual % growth)	55.2	7.2	1.0
Value added in agriculture (% of GDP)	8	5	5
Value added in industry (% of GDP)	50	32	32
Value added in services (% of GDP)	42	63	64
Exports of goods and services (% of GDP)	29	27	41
Imports of goods and services (% of GDP)	22	34	41
Gross capital formation (% of GDP)	26	25	20
Central government revenue (% of GDP)	..	31.6	32.2
Central government cash surplus/deficit (% of GDP)	..	–2.8	–3.6
States and markets			
Starting a business (days)			31
Stock market capitalization (% of GDP)	0.2	18.3	44.0
Military expenditures (% of GDP)	2.8	1.8	2.0
Fixed-line and mobile subscribers (per 100 people)	9	46	126
Internet users (per 100 people)	0.0	7.3	28.8
Paved roads (% of total)	62	68	..
High-technology exports (% of manufactured exports)	0	3	4
Global links			
Merchandise trade (% of GDP)	43.9	47.1	69.8
Net barter terms of trade (2000 = 100)	95	100	107
Total external debt ($ billions)	49	65	126
Short-term debt ($ billions)	9.6	9.7	21.4
Total debt service (% of exports)	4.9	20.3	24.7
Foreign direct investment, net inflows ($ billions)	0.1	9.3	19.2
Remittances received ($ billions)	..	1.7	4.4
Aid ($ billions)	1.3	1.4	..

Portugal

High income

Population (millions)	11	Population growth (%)	0.4
Surface area (1,000 sq. km)	92	National poverty rate (% of pop.)	..
GNI ($ billions)	189.0	GNI per capita ($)	17,850
GNI, PPP ($ billions)	211.3	GNI per capita, PPP ($)	19,960

	1990	2000	2006
People			
Share of poorest 20% in nat'l consumption/income (%)	..	..	..
Life expectancy at birth (years)	74	77	78
Total fertility (births per woman)	1.4	1.5	1.4
Adolescent fertility (births per 1,000 women 15–19)	..	17	14
Contraceptive prevalence (% of married women 15–49)	..	..	..
Births attended by skilled health staff (% of total)	98	100	..
Under-five mortality rate (per 1,000)	14	8	5
Child malnutrition, underweight (% of under age 5)	..	..	..
Child immunization, measles (% of ages 12–23 mos.)	85	87	93
Primary completion rate, total (% of relevant age group)	93	..	104
Gross secondary enrollment, total (% of relevant age group)	66	108	97
Ratio of girls to boys in primary & secondary school (%)	103	101	102
HIV prevalence rate (% of population ages 15–49)	..	..	0.4
Environment			
Forests (1,000 sq. km)	31	36	38
Deforestation (average annual %, 1990–2005)			–1.3
Freshwater use (% of internal resources)	..	29.6	..
Access to improved water source (% of total pop.)	..	..	..
Access to improved sanitation facilities (% of total pop.)	..	..	..
Energy use per capita (kilograms of oil equivalent)	1,793	2,473	2,575
Carbon dioxide emissions per capita (metric tons)	4.3	5.8	5.6
Electricity use per capita (kilowatt-hours)	2,564	4,014	4,663
Economy			
GDP ($ billions)	75.3	112.6	194.7
GDP growth (annual %)	4.0	3.9	1.3
GDP implicit price deflator (annual % growth)	13.1	3.0	2.9
Value added in agriculture (% of GDP)	9	4	3
Value added in industry (% of GDP)	29	28	25
Value added in services (% of GDP)	62	69	72
Exports of goods and services (% of GDP)	31	30	31
Imports of goods and services (% of GDP)	38	41	39
Gross capital formation (% of GDP)	27	28	22
Central government revenue (% of GDP)	..	36.2	38.6
Central government cash surplus/deficit (% of GDP)	..	–2.4	–3.9
States and markets			
Starting a business (days)			7
Stock market capitalization (% of GDP)	12.2	53.9	53.5
Military expenditures (% of GDP)	2.5	2.0	2.1
Fixed-line and mobile subscribers (per 100 people)	24	107	155
Internet users (per 100 people)	0.0	16.4	30.3
Paved roads (% of total)	..	86	86
High-technology exports (% of manufactured exports)	4	6	9
Global links			
Merchandise trade (% of GDP)	55.4	57.1	56.5
Net barter terms of trade (2000 = 100)	103	100	..
Total external debt ($ billions)	..	..	..
Short-term debt ($ billions)	..	..	..
Total debt service (% of exports)	..	..	..
Foreign direct investment, net inflows ($ billions)	2.6	6.7	7.4
Remittances received ($ billions)	4.5	3.4	3.3
Aid ($ billions)	..	..	..

Puerto Rico

		High income	
Population (millions)	3.9	Population growth (%)	0.4
Surface area (1,000 sq. km)	9.0	National poverty rate (% of pop.)	..
GNI ($ billions)	..	GNI per capita ($)	..
GNI, PPP ($ billions)	..	GNI per capita, PPP ($)	..

	1990	2000	2006
People			
Share of poorest 20% in nat'l consumption/income (%)	..	..	..
Life expectancy at birth (years)	75	77	78
Total fertility (births per woman)	2.2	2.0	1.8
Adolescent fertility (births per 1,000 women 15–19)	..	66	50
Contraceptive prevalence (% of married women 15–49)	..	..	..
Births attended by skilled health staff (% of total)	..	..	100
Under-five mortality rate (per 1,000)	..	..	..
Child malnutrition, underweight (% of under age 5)	..	..	..
Child immunization, measles (% of ages 12–23 mos.)	..	..	..
Primary completion rate, total (% of relevant age group)	..	..	..
Gross secondary enrollment, total (% of relevant age group)	..	..	..
Ratio of girls to boys in primary & secondary school (%)	..	..	..
HIV prevalence rate (% of population ages 15–49)	..	..	..
Environment			
Forests (1,000 sq. km)	4.0	4.1	4.1
Deforestation (average annual %, 1990–2005)			-0.1
Freshwater use (% of internal resources)	..	..	..
Access to improved water source (% of total pop.)	..	..	..
Access to improved sanitation facilities (% of total pop.)	..	..	..
Energy use per capita (kilograms of oil equivalent)	..	..	..
Carbon dioxide emissions per capita (metric tons)	3.32	2.61	..
Electricity use per capita (kilowatt-hours)	..	..	..
Economy			
GDP ($ billions)	30.6	61.0	..
GDP growth (annual %)	3.8	2.4	..
GDP implicit price deflator (annual % growth)	4.3	3.1	..
Value added in agriculture (% of GDP)	1	1	..
Value added in industry (% of GDP)	42	41	..
Value added in services (% of GDP)	57	58	..
Exports of goods and services (% of GDP)	77	75	..
Imports of goods and services (% of GDP)	101	98	..
Gross capital formation (% of GDP)	17	..	..
Central government revenue (% of GDP)	..	..	..
Central government cash surplus/deficit (% of GDP)	..	..	..
States and markets			
Starting a business (days)			7
Stock market capitalization (% of GDP)	..	..	..
Military expenditures (% of GDP)	..	..	..
Fixed-line and mobile subscribers (per 100 people)	28	58	112
Internet users (per 100 people)	0.0	10.5	23.4
Paved roads (% of total)	..	94	95
High-technology exports (% of manufactured exports)	..	..	..
Global links			
Merchandise trade (% of GDP)	..	..	..
Net barter terms of trade (2000 = 100)	..	..	..
Total external debt ($ billions)	..	..	..
Short-term debt ($ billions)	..	..	..
Total debt service (% of exports)	..	..	..
Foreign direct investment, net inflows ($ billions)	..	..	..
Remittances received ($ billions)	..	..	..
Aid ($ billions)	..	..	..

Qatar

High income

Population (thousands)	821	Population growth (%)	3.1
Surface area (1,000 sq. km)	11	National poverty rate (% of pop.)	..
GNI ($ billions)	..	GNI per capita ($)	..
GNI, PPP ($ billions)	..	GNI per capita, PPP ($)	..

	1990	2000	2006
People			
Share of poorest 20% in nat'l consumption/income (%)	..	..	..
Life expectancy at birth (years)	70	74	75
Total fertility (births per woman)	4.3	3.1	2.7
Adolescent fertility (births per 1,000 women 15-19)	..	21	18
Contraceptive prevalence (% of married women 15-49)	..	43	..
Births attended by skilled health staff (% of total)	..	100	..
Under-five mortality rate (per 1,000)	26	23	21
Child malnutrition, underweight (% of under age 5)	..	..	..
Child immunization, measles (% of ages 12-23 mos.)	79	91	99
Primary completion rate, total (% of relevant age group)	70	89	94
Gross secondary enrollment, total (% of relevant age group)	84	88	101
Ratio of girls to boys in primary & secondary school (%)	98	101	98
HIV prevalence rate (% of population ages 15-49)	..	..	0.2
Environment			
Forests (1,000 sq. km)	..	..	..
Deforestation (average annual %, 1990-2005)	..	..	..
Freshwater use (% of internal resources)	..	290.0	..
Access to improved water source (% of total pop.)	100	100	100
Access to improved sanitation facilities (% of total pop.)	100	100	100
Energy use per capita (kilograms of oil equivalent)	13,542	19,245	19,877
Carbon dioxide emissions per capita (metric tons)	26.1	58.9	69.2
Electricity use per capita (kilowatt-hours)	9,773	13,784	16,801
Economy			
GDP ($ billions)	7.4	17.8	42.5
GDP growth (annual %)	..	7.1	6.1
GDP implicit price deflator (annual % growth)	..	3.1	26.2
Value added in agriculture (% of GDP)	..	..	..
Value added in industry (% of GDP)	..	..	..
Value added in services (% of GDP)	..	..	..
Exports of goods and services (% of GDP)	..	67	68
Imports of goods and services (% of GDP)	..	22	33
Gross capital formation (% of GDP)	..	20	35
Central government revenue (% of GDP)	..	..	42.0
Central government cash surplus/deficit (% of GDP)	..	..	9.7
States and markets			
Starting a business (days)	..	..	..
Stock market capitalization (% of GDP)	..	29.0	205.6
Military expenditures (% of GDP)	..	..	..
Fixed-line and mobile subscribers (per 100 people)	21	46	140
Internet users (per 100 people)	0.0	4.9	35.3
Paved roads (% of total)	86	90	..
High-technology exports (% of manufactured exports)	0	0	0
Global links			
Merchandise trade (% of GDP)	75.9	83.6	84.4
Net barter terms of trade (2000 = 100)	..	100	165
Total external debt ($ billions)	..	..	..
Short-term debt ($ billions)	..	..	..
Total debt service (% of exports)	..	..	..
Foreign direct investment, net inflows ($ billions)	..	..	..
Remittances received ($ billions)	..	..	..
Aid ($ millions)	1.5	0.5	2.2

Romania

Europe & Central Asia   **Upper middle income**

Population (millions)	22	Population growth (%)	-0.2
Surface area (1,000 sq. km)	238	National poverty rate (% of pop.)	..
GNI ($ billions)	104.4	GNI per capita ($)	4,830
GNI, PPP ($ billions)	219.2	GNI per capita, PPP ($)	10,150

	1990	2000	2006
People			
Share of poorest 20% in nat'l consumption/income (%)	9.2	8.2	8.2
Life expectancy at birth (years)	70	71	72
Total fertility (births per woman)	1.8	1.3	1.3
Adolescent fertility (births per 1,000 women 15–19)	..	38	33
Contraceptive prevalence (% of married women 15–49)	..	64	70
Births attended by skilled health staff (% of total)	..	99	98
Under-five mortality rate (per 1,000)	31	22	18
Child malnutrition, underweight (% of under age 5)	..	3.7	..
Child immunization, measles (% of ages 12–23 mos.)	92	98	95
Primary completion rate, total (% of relevant age group)	96	102	99
Gross secondary enrollment, total (% of relevant age group)	92	81	86
Ratio of girls to boys in primary & secondary school (%)	99	100	100
HIV prevalence rate (% of population ages 15–49)	..	..	0.1
Environment			
Forests (1,000 sq. km)	64	64	64
Deforestation (average annual %, 1990–2005)			0.00
Freshwater use (% of internal resources)	..	54.8	..
Access to improved water source (% of total pop.)	..	57	57
Access to improved sanitation facilities (% of total pop.)	..		
Energy use per capita (kilograms of oil equivalent)	2,689	1,616	1,772
Carbon dioxide emissions per capita (metric tons)	6.7	3.9	4.2
Electricity use per capita (kilowatt-hours)	2,924	1,988	2,342
Economy			
GDP ($ billions)	38.3	37.1	121.6
GDP growth (annual %)	-5.6	2.1	7.7
GDP implicit price deflator (annual % growth)	13.6	44.3	10.1
Value added in agriculture (% of GDP)	24	13	11
Value added in industry (% of GDP)	50	36	38
Value added in services (% of GDP)	26	51	52
Exports of goods and services (% of GDP)	17	33	34
Imports of goods and services (% of GDP)	26	38	44
Gross capital formation (% of GDP)	30	20	24
Central government revenue (% of GDP)	..	25.8	24.5
Central government cash surplus/deficit (% of GDP)	..	-2.0	-1.0
States and markets			
Starting a business (days)			14
Stock market capitalization (% of GDP)	..	2.9	27.0
Military expenditures (% of GDP)	4.5	2.5	1.9
Fixed-line and mobile subscribers (per 100 people)	10	29	100
Internet users (per 100 people)	0.0	3.6	32.4
Paved roads (% of total)	51	50	30
High-technology exports (% of manufactured exports)	2	6	4
Global links			
Merchandise trade (% of GDP)	32.8	63.2	68.6
Net barter terms of trade (2000 = 100)	..	..	..
Total external debt ($ billions)	1.1	11.2	55.1
Short-term debt ($ billions)	0.9	0.8	17.7
Total debt service (% of exports)	0.3	20.1	18.4
Foreign direct investment, net inflows ($ billions)	0.0	1.0	11.4
Remittances received ($ billions)	..	0.1	6.7
Aid ($ millions)	243	432	..

Russian Federation

Europe & Central Asia		Upper middle income	
Population (millions)	143	Population growth (%)	-0.5
Surface area (1,000 sq. km)	17,098	National poverty rate (% of pop.)	20
GNI ($ billions)	822.3	GNI per capita ($)	5,770
GNI, PPP ($ billions)	1,814.9	GNI per capita, PPP ($)	12,740

	1990	2000	2006
People			
Share of poorest 20% in nat'l consumption/income (%)	10.0	4.9	..
Life expectancy at birth (years)	69	65	66
Total fertility (births per woman)	1.9	1.2	1.3
Adolescent fertility (births per 1,000 women 15–19)	..	32	28
Contraceptive prevalence (% of married women 15–49)	34	73	..
Births attended by skilled health staff (% of total)	..	99	99
Under-five mortality rate (per 1,000)	27	24	16
Child malnutrition, underweight (% of under age 5)	..	..	..
Child immunization, measles (% of ages 12–23 mos.)	83	97	99
Primary completion rate, total (% of relevant age group)	..	94	94
Gross secondary enrollment, total (% of relevant age group)	93	..	91
Ratio of girls to boys in primary & secondary school (%)	104	..	99
HIV prevalence rate (% of population ages 15–49)	..	..	1.1
Environment			
Forests (1,000 sq. km)	8,090	8,093	8,088
Deforestation (average annual %, 1990–2005)			0.00
Freshwater use (% of internal resources)	..	1.8	..
Access to improved water source (% of total pop.)	94	96	97
Access to improved sanitation facilities (% of total pop.)	87	87	87
Energy use per capita (kilograms of oil equivalent)	5,923	4,196	4,517
Carbon dioxide emissions per capita (metric tons)	15.3	10.0	10.6
Electricity use per capita (kilowatt-hours)	6,673	5,209	5,785
Economy			
GDP ($ billions)	516.8	259.7	986.9
GDP growth (annual %)	-3.0	10.0	6.7
GDP implicit price deflator (annual % growth)	15.9	37.7	16.1
Value added in agriculture (% of GDP)	17	6	5
Value added in industry (% of GDP)	48	38	39
Value added in services (% of GDP)	35	56	56
Exports of goods and services (% of GDP)	18	44	34
Imports of goods and services (% of GDP)	18	24	21
Gross capital formation (% of GDP)	30	19	20
Central government revenue (% of GDP)	..	24.6	28.8
Central government cash surplus/deficit (% of GDP)	..	2.5	8.1
States and markets			
Starting a business (days)			29
Stock market capitalization (% of GDP)	0.0	15.0	107.1
Military expenditures (% of GDP)	15.5	3.7	4.0
Fixed-line and mobile subscribers (per 100 people)	14	24	112
Internet users (per 100 people)	0.0	2.0	18.0
Paved roads (% of total)	74	67	..
High-technology exports (% of manufactured exports)	..	14	9
Global links			
Merchandise trade (% of GDP)	..	57.8	47.5
Net barter terms of trade (2000 = 100)	..	..	..
Total external debt ($ billions)	78	160	251
Short-term debt ($ billions)	13	16	40
Total debt service (% of exports)	..	9.9	13.8
Foreign direct investment, net inflows ($ billions)	1.2	2.7	30.8
Remittances received ($ billions)	..	1.3	3.1
Aid ($ billions)	0.3	1.6	..

Rwanda

Sub-Saharan Africa		Low income

Population (millions)	9.5	Population growth (%)	2.5
Surface area (1,000 sq. km)	26	National poverty rate (% of pop.)	60
GNI ($ billions)	2.3	GNI per capita ($)	250
GNI, PPP ($ billions)	6.9	GNI per capita, PPP ($)	730

	1990	2000	2006
People			
Share of poorest 20% in nat'l consumption/income (%)	..	5.3	..
Life expectancy at birth (years)	32	40	46
Total fertility (births per woman)	7.4	6.0	5.9
Adolescent fertility (births per 1,000 women 15–19)	..	50	41
Contraceptive prevalence (% of married women 15–49)	21	13	17
Births attended by skilled health staff (% of total)	26	31	39
Under-five mortality rate (per 1,000)	176	183	160
Child malnutrition, underweight (% of under age 5)	24.3	20.3	18.0
Child immunization, measles (% of ages 12–23 mos.)	83	74	95
Primary completion rate, total (% of relevant age group)	45	21	35
Gross secondary enrollment, total (% of relevant age group)	9	10	13
Ratio of girls to boys in primary & secondary school (%)	92	96	102
HIV prevalence rate (% of population ages 15–49)	..	..	3.0
Environment			
Forests (1,000 sq. km)	3.2	3.4	4.8
Deforestation (average annual %, 1990–2005)			–2.8
Freshwater use (% of internal resources)	..	1.6	..
Access to improved water source (% of total pop.)	59	70	74
Access to improved sanitation facilities (% of total pop.)	37	40	42
Energy use per capita (kilograms of oil equivalent)	..	..	..
Carbon dioxide emissions per capita (metric tons)	0.1	0.1	0.1
Electricity use per capita (kilowatt-hours)	..	..	..
Economy			
GDP ($ billions)	2.6	1.8	2.5
GDP growth (annual %)	–2.4	6.0	5.3
GDP implicit price deflator (annual % growth)	13.5	3.3	9.1
Value added in agriculture (% of GDP)	33	41	41
Value added in industry (% of GDP)	25	20	21
Value added in services (% of GDP)	43	38	38
Exports of goods and services (% of GDP)	6	8	12
Imports of goods and services (% of GDP)	14	25	32
Gross capital formation (% of GDP)	15	18	21
Central government revenue (% of GDP)	10.8	..	..
Central government cash surplus/deficit (% of GDP)	–5.4	..	..
States and markets			
Starting a business (days)			16
Stock market capitalization (% of GDP)	..	..	..
Military expenditures (% of GDP)	3.7	3.4	2.7
Fixed-line and mobile subscribers (per 100 people)	0	1	3
Internet users (per 100 people)	0.0	0.1	0.7
Paved roads (% of total)	9	8	19
High-technology exports (% of manufactured exports)	..	0	..
Global links			
Merchandise trade (% of GDP)	15.4	14.5	25.6
Net barter terms of trade (2000 = 100)	40	100	129
Total external debt ($ billions)	0.7	1.3	0.4
Short-term debt ($ millions)	47	38	25
Total debt service (% of exports)	13.4	24.1	9.6
Foreign direct investment, net inflows ($ millions)	7.6	8.3	11.2
Remittances received ($ millions)	3.0	7.0	21.2
Aid ($ millions)	288	321	585

Samoa

East Asia & Pacific		Lower middle income		
Population (thousands)	185	Population growth (%)		0.8
Surface area (1,000 sq. km)	2.8	National poverty rate (% of pop.)		..
GNI ($ millions)	421	GNI per capita ($)		2,270
GNI, PPP ($ millions)	943	GNI per capita, PPP ($)		5,090

	1990	2000	2006
People			
Share of poorest 20% in nat'l consumption/income (%)	..	..	..
Life expectancy at birth (years)	65	70	71
Total fertility (births per woman)	4.7	4.5	4.0
Adolescent fertility (births per 1,000 women 15–19)	..	40	29
Contraceptive prevalence (% of married women 15–49)	..	..	..
Births attended by skilled health staff (% of total)	76	100	100
Under-five mortality rate (per 1,000)	50	34	28
Child malnutrition, underweight (% of under age 5)	..	..	..
Child immunization, measles (% of ages 12–23 mos.)	89	93	54
Primary completion rate, total (% of relevant age group)	..	95	96
Gross secondary enrollment, total (% of relevant age group)	33	78	81
Ratio of girls to boys in primary & secondary school (%)	118	106	105
HIV prevalence rate (% of population ages 15–49)	..	..	..
Environment			
Forests (1,000 sq. km)	1.3	1.7	1.7
Deforestation (average annual %, 1990–2005)			–1.8
Freshwater use (% of internal resources)	..	..	..
Access to improved water source (% of total pop.)	91	89	88
Access to improved sanitation facilities (% of total pop.)	98	100	100
Energy use per capita (kilograms of oil equivalent)	..	..	..
Carbon dioxide emissions per capita (metric tons)	0.8	0.8	0.8
Electricity use per capita (kilowatt-hours)	..	..	..
Economy			
GDP ($ millions)	112	232	424
GDP growth (annual %)	–4.4	7.0	2.3
GDP implicit price deflator (annual % growth)	9.0	2.8	5.2
Value added in agriculture (% of GDP)	..	17	12
Value added in industry (% of GDP)	..	26	27
Value added in services (% of GDP)	..	57	60
Exports of goods and services (% of GDP)	..	34	..
Imports of goods and services (% of GDP)	..	57	..
Gross capital formation (% of GDP)	..	..	..
Central government revenue (% of GDP)	..	..	..
Central government cash surplus/deficit (% of GDP)	..	..	..
States and markets			
Starting a business (days)			35
Stock market capitalization (% of GDP)	..	..	..
Military expenditures (% of GDP)	..	..	..
Fixed-line and mobile subscribers (per 100 people)	3	6	24
Internet users (per 100 people)	0.0	0.6	4.3
Paved roads (% of total)	..	14	..
High-technology exports (% of manufactured exports)	0	1	0
Global links			
Merchandise trade (% of GDP)	80.3	51.8	54.1
Net barter terms of trade (2000 = 100)	..	100	91
Total external debt ($ millions)	92	197	858
Short-term debt ($ millions)	0.2	50.1	652.0
Total debt service (% of exports)	5.8	5.1	19.9
Foreign direct investment, net inflows ($ millions)	6.6	–1.5	20.7
Remittances received ($ millions)	43.0	45.0	0.8
Aid ($ millions)	48	27	47

San Marino

Population (thousands)	29	Population growth (%)		1.4
Surface area (sq. km)	60	National poverty rate (% of pop.)		..
GNI ($ billions)	1.3	GNI per capita ($)		45,130
GNI, PPP ($ billions)	..	GNI per capita, PPP ($)		..

	1990	2000	2006
People			
Share of poorest 20% in nat'l consumption/income (%)	..	..	..
Life expectancy at birth (years)	..	..	82
Total fertility (births per woman)	..	..	..
Adolescent fertility (births per 1,000 women 15–19)	..	..	..
Contraceptive prevalence (% of married women 15–49)	..	..	..
Births attended by skilled health staff (% of total)	..	..	..
Under-five mortality rate (per 1,000)	14	6	3
Child malnutrition, underweight (% of under age 5)	..	..	..
Child immunization, measles (% of ages 12–23 mos.)	99	74	94
Primary completion rate, total (% of relevant age group)	..	..	..
Gross secondary enrollment, total (% of relevant age group)	..	..	..
Ratio of girls to boys in primary & secondary school (%)	..	..	..
HIV prevalence rate (% of population ages 15–49)	..	..	..
Environment			
Forests (1,000 sq. km)	..	..	..
Deforestation (average annual %, 1990–2005)			..
Freshwater use (% of internal resources)	..	..	..
Access to improved water source (% of total pop.)	..	..	..
Access to improved sanitation facilities (% of total pop.)	..	..	..
Energy use per capita (kilograms of oil equivalent)	..	..	..
Carbon dioxide emissions per capita (metric tons)	..	..	..
Electricity use per capita (kilowatt-hours)	..	..	..
Economy			
GDP ($ millions)	..	774	1,690
GDP growth (annual %)	..	2.2	5.0
GDP implicit price deflator (annual % growth)	..	2.5	..
Value added in agriculture (% of GDP)	..	..	..
Value added in industry (% of GDP)	..	..	..
Value added in services (% of GDP)	..	..	..
Exports of goods and services (% of GDP)	..	..	..
Imports of goods and services (% of GDP)	..	..	..
Gross capital formation (% of GDP)	..	..	..
Central government revenue (% of GDP)	..	46.4	44.1
Central government cash surplus/deficit (% of GDP)	..	1.3	5.2
States and markets			
Starting a business (days)			..
Stock market capitalization (% of GDP)	..	..	..
Military expenditures (% of GDP)	..	..	..
Fixed-line and mobile subscribers (per 100 people)	..	..	134
Internet users (per 100 people)	..	..	53.8
Paved roads (% of total)	..	..	..
High-technology exports (% of manufactured exports)	..	..	..
Global links			
Merchandise trade (% of GDP)	..	..	..
Net barter terms of trade (2000 = 100)	..	..	..
Total external debt ($ billions)	..	..	..
Short-term debt ($ billions)	..	..	..
Total debt service (% of exports)	..	..	..
Foreign direct investment, net inflows ($ billions)	..	..	..
Remittances received ($ billions)	..	..	..
Aid ($ billions)	..	..	..

São Tomé and Principe

Sub-Saharan Africa   **Low income**

Population (thousands)	155	Population growth (%)	1.6
Surface area (sq. km)	960	National poverty rate (% of pop.)	..
GNI ($ millions)	124	GNI per capita ($)	800
GNI, PPP ($ millions)	231	GNI per capita, PPP ($)	1,490

	1990	2000	2006
People			
Share of poorest 20% in nat'l consumption/income (%)	..	..	..
Life expectancy at birth (years)	62	64	65
Total fertility (births per woman)	5.4	4.5	4.0
Adolescent fertility (births per 1,000 women 15–19)	..	86	69
Contraceptive prevalence (% of married women 15–49)	..	29	30
Births attended by skilled health staff (% of total)	..	79	81
Under-five mortality rate (per 1,000)	100	97	96
Child malnutrition, underweight (% of under age 5)	..	10.1	..
Child immunization, measles (% of ages 12–23 mos.)	71	69	85
Primary completion rate, total (% of relevant age group)	..	62	74
Gross secondary enrollment, total (% of relevant age group)	..	40	45
Ratio of girls to boys in primary & secondary school (%)	..	93	99
HIV prevalence rate (% of population ages 15–49)	..	..	..
Environment			
Forests (sq. km)	270	270	270
Deforestation (average annual %, 1990–2005)			0.00
Freshwater use (% of internal resources)	..	..	..
Access to improved water source (% of total pop.)	..	79	79
Access to improved sanitation facilities (% of total pop.)	..	24	25
Energy use per capita (kilograms of oil equivalent)	..	..	..
Carbon dioxide emissions per capita (metric tons)	0.6	0.6	0.6
Electricity use per capita (kilowatt-hours)	..	..	..
Economy			
GDP ($ millions)	..	76	123
GDP growth (annual %)	..	11.6	7.0
GDP implicit price deflator (annual % growth)	..	10.7	20.0
Value added in agriculture (% of GDP)	..	20	17
Value added in industry (% of GDP)	..	17	21
Value added in services (% of GDP)	..	63	62
Exports of goods and services (% of GDP)	..	..	..
Imports of goods and services (% of GDP)	..	..	..
Gross capital formation (% of GDP)	..	..	..
Central government revenue (% of GDP)	..	..	..
Central government cash surplus/deficit (% of GDP)	..	..	..
States and markets			
Starting a business (days)			144
Stock market capitalization (% of GDP)	..	..	..
Military expenditures (% of GDP)	..	..	..
Fixed-line and mobile subscribers (per 100 people)	2	3	17
Internet users (per 100 people)	0.0	4.6	18.7
Paved roads (% of total)	62	68	..
High-technology exports (% of manufactured exports)	..	0	1
Global links			
Merchandise trade (% of GDP)	..	40.7	60.9
Net barter terms of trade (2000 = 100)	..	..	..
Total external debt ($ millions)	150	310	355
Short-term debt ($ millions)	16	23	15
Total debt service (% of exports)	34.4	25.8	..
Foreign direct investment, net inflows ($ millions)	–0.1	3.8	–0.4
Remittances received ($ millions)	..	1.0	1.0
Aid ($ millions)	54	35	22

Saudi Arabia

			High income
Population (millions)	24	Population growth (%)	2.4
Surface area (1,000 sq. km)	2,000	National poverty rate (% of pop.)	..
GNI ($ billions)	331.0	GNI per capita ($)	13,980
GNI, PPP ($ billions)	528.0	GNI per capita, PPP ($)	22,300

	1990	2000	2006
People			
Share of poorest 20% in nat'l consumption/income (%)	..	..	..
Life expectancy at birth (years)	68	71	73
Total fertility (births per woman)	5.9	4.1	3.4
Adolescent fertility (births per 1,000 women 15-19)	..	35	29
Contraceptive prevalence (% of married women 15-49)	..	21	..
Births attended by skilled health staff (% of total)	..	93	96
Under-five mortality rate (per 1,000)	44	29	25
Child malnutrition, underweight (% of under age 5)	..	..	..
Child immunization, measles (% of ages 12-23 mos.)	88	94	95
Primary completion rate, total (% of relevant age group)	53	..	93
Gross secondary enrollment, total (% of relevant age group)	44	..	96
Ratio of girls to boys in primary & secondary school (%)	84	..	95
HIV prevalence rate (% of population ages 15-49)	..	..	0.2
Environment			
Forests (1,000 sq. km)	27	27	27
Deforestation (average annual %, 1990-2005)			0.00
Freshwater use (% of internal resources)	..	721.7	..
Access to improved water source (% of total pop.)	94	92	96
Access to improved sanitation facilities (% of total pop.)	91	..	99
Energy use per capita (kilograms of oil equivalent)	3,744	5,169	6,068
Carbon dioxide emissions per capita (metric tons)	15.6	13.2	13.7
Electricity use per capita (kilowatt-hours)	3,982	5,666	6,813
Economy			
GDP ($ billions)	116.8	188.4	349.1
GDP growth (annual %)	8.3	4.9	4.3
GDP implicit price deflator (annual % growth)	13.1	11.6	6.0
Value added in agriculture (% of GDP)	6	5	3
Value added in industry (% of GDP)	49	54	65
Value added in services (% of GDP)	45	41	32
Exports of goods and services (% of GDP)	41	44	62
Imports of goods and services (% of GDP)	32	25	31
Gross capital formation (% of GDP)	15	19	18
Central government revenue (% of GDP)	..	..	..
Central government cash surplus/deficit (% of GDP)	..	..	..
States and markets			
Starting a business (days)			15
Stock market capitalization (% of GDP)	36.7	35.6	93.6
Military expenditures (% of GDP)	14.0	10.6	8.5
Fixed-line and mobile subscribers (per 100 people)	8	21	100
Internet users (per 100 people)	0.0	2.2	19.8
Paved roads (% of total)	41	30	..
High-technology exports (% of manufactured exports)	0	0	1
Global links			
Merchandise trade (% of GDP)	58.6	57.2	79.0
Net barter terms of trade (2000 = 100)	..	100	205
Total external debt ($ billions)	..	..	..
Short-term debt ($ billions)	..	..	..
Total debt service (% of exports)	..	..	..
Foreign direct investment, net inflows ($ billions)	1.9	-1.9	0.7
Remittances received ($ billions)	..	..	..
Aid ($ billions)	15	22	25

Senegal

Sub-Saharan Africa		Low income	
Population (millions)	12	Population growth (%)	2.5
Surface area (1,000 sq. km)	197	National poverty rate (% of pop.)	..
GNI ($ billions)	9.1	GNI per capita ($)	760
GNI, PPP ($ billions)	18.8	GNI per capita, PPP ($)	1,560

	1990	2000	2006
People			
Share of poorest 20% in nat'l consumption/income (%)	3.5	6.6	..
Life expectancy at birth (years)	57	61	63
Total fertility (births per woman)	6.5	5.4	5.3
Adolescent fertility (births per 1,000 women 15–19)	..	107	91
Contraceptive prevalence (% of married women 15–49)	..	11	12
Births attended by skilled health staff (% of total)	..	60	52
Under-five mortality rate (per 1,000)	149	133	116
Child malnutrition, underweight (% of under age 5)	..	20.3	14.5
Child immunization, measles (% of ages 12–23 mos.)	51	48	80
Primary completion rate, total (% of relevant age group)	42	38	49
Gross secondary enrollment, total (% of relevant age group)	15	16	22
Ratio of girls to boys in primary & secondary school (%)	69	82	91
HIV prevalence rate (% of population ages 15–49)	..	..	0.7
Environment			
Forests (1,000 sq. km)	93	89	87
Deforestation (average annual %, 1990–2005)			0.5
Freshwater use (% of internal resources)	..	8.6	..
Access to improved water source (% of total pop.)	65	73	76
Access to improved sanitation facilities (% of total pop.)	33	50	57
Energy use per capita (kilograms of oil equivalent)	283	257	258
Carbon dioxide emissions per capita (metric tons)	0.4	0.4	0.4
Electricity use per capita (kilowatt-hours)	99	97	151
Economy			
GDP ($ billions)	5.7	4.7	9.2
GDP growth (annual %)	-0.7	3.2	2.3
GDP implicit price deflator (annual % growth)	0.0	1.9	2.9
Value added in agriculture (% of GDP)	20	19	16
Value added in industry (% of GDP)	22	23	23
Value added in services (% of GDP)	58	58	61
Exports of goods and services (% of GDP)	25	28	26
Imports of goods and services (% of GDP)	32	37	44
Gross capital formation (% of GDP)	9	20	29
Central government revenue (% of GDP)	..	16.9	..
Central government cash surplus/deficit (% of GDP)	..	-0.9	..
States and markets			
Starting a business (days)			58
Stock market capitalization (% of GDP)	..	..	..
Military expenditures (% of GDP)	2.0	1.3	1.6
Fixed-line and mobile subscribers (per 100 people)	1	4	27
Internet users (per 100 people)	0.0	0.4	5.4
Paved roads (% of total)	27	29	..
High-technology exports (% of manufactured exports)	0	8	6
Global links			
Merchandise trade (% of GDP)	34.6	52.0	54.3
Net barter terms of trade (2000 = 100)	172	100	102
Total external debt ($ billions)	3.7	3.6	2.0
Short-term debt ($ millions)	421	146	95
Total debt service (% of exports)	19.9	14.3	11.8
Foreign direct investment, net inflows ($ millions)	57	63	58
Remittances received ($ millions)	142	233	633
Aid ($ millions)	812	423	825

Serbia

Europe & Central Asia		Upper middle income	
Population (millions)	7.4	Population growth (%)	0.0
Surface area (1,000 sq. km)	88	National poverty rate (% of pop.)	..
GNI ($ billions)	30.0	GNI per capita ($)	4,030
GNI, PPP ($ billions)	69.3	GNI per capita, PPP ($)	9,320

	1990	2000	2006
People			
Share of poorest 20% in nat'l consumption/income (%)	..	..	..
Life expectancy at birth (years)	71	72	73
Total fertility (births per woman)	1.8	1.5	1.4
Adolescent fertility (births per 1,000 women 15–19)	..	27	25
Contraceptive prevalence (% of married women 15–49)	..	..	41
Births attended by skilled health staff (% of total)	..	..	99
Under-five mortality rate (per 1,000)	..	13	8
Child malnutrition, underweight (% of under age 5)	..	..	..
Child immunization, measles (% of ages 12–23 mos.)	83	89	88
Primary completion rate, total (% of relevant age group)	..	..	..
Gross secondary enrollment, total (% of relevant age group)	..	..	..
Ratio of girls to boys in primary & secondary school (%)	..	..	..
HIV prevalence rate (% of population ages 15–49)	..	..	..
Environment			
Forests (1,000 sq. km)	..	..	..
Deforestation (average annual %, 1990–2005)			..
Freshwater use (% of internal resources)		..	..
Access to improved water source (% of total pop.)	..	..	..
Access to improved sanitation facilities (% of total pop.)	..	..	..
Energy use per capita (kilograms of oil equivalent)	..	..	..
Carbon dioxide emissions per capita (metric tons)	..	..	..
Electricity use per capita (kilowatt-hours)	..	..	..
Economy			
GDP ($ millions)	..	8,963	31,989
GDP growth (annual %)	..	4.5	5.7
GDP implicit price deflator (annual % growth)	..	81.0	15.6
Value added in agriculture (% of GDP)	..	19	13
Value added in industry (% of GDP)	..	30	26
Value added in services (% of GDP)	..	51	62
Exports of goods and services (% of GDP)	..	23	27
Imports of goods and services (% of GDP)	..	39	47
Gross capital formation (% of GDP)	..	8	21
Central government revenue (% of GDP)	..	..	..
Central government cash surplus/deficit (% of GDP)	..	..	..
States and markets			
Starting a business (days)			23
Stock market capitalization (% of GDP)	..	4.6	34.3
Military expenditures (% of GDP)	..	5.4	2.1
Fixed-line and mobile subscribers (per 100 people)	22	49	99
Internet users (per 100 people)	0.0	5.3	20.3
Paved roads (% of total)	..	63	..
High-technology exports (% of manufactured exports)	4	3	4
Global links			
Merchandise trade (% of GDP)	..	..	61.3
Net barter terms of trade (2000 = 100)	..	..	..
Total external debt ($ billions)	18	11	14
Short-term debt ($ billions)	0.5	4.6	1.8
Total debt service (% of exports)	..	3.2	..
Foreign direct investment, net inflows ($ billions)	0.1	0.0	5.1
Remittances received ($ billions)	..	1.1	4.7
Aid ($ billions)	..	1.1	1.6

Seychelles

Sub-Saharan Africa   **Upper middle income**

Population (thousands)	85	Population growth (%)		2.0
Surface area (sq. km)	460	National poverty rate (% of pop.)		..
GNI ($ millions)	751	GNI per capita ($)		8,870
GNI, PPP ($ billions)	1.2	GNI per capita, PPP ($)		14,360

	1990	2000	2006
People			
Share of poorest 20% in nat'l consumption/income (%)	..	..	..
Life expectancy at birth (years)	70	72	72
Total fertility (births per woman)	2.8	2.1	2.0
Adolescent fertility (births per 1,000 women 15–19)	..	..	..
Contraceptive prevalence (% of married women 15–49)	..	..	..
Births attended by skilled health staff (% of total)	..	..	..
Under-five mortality rate (per 1,000)	19	15	13
Child malnutrition, underweight (% of under age 5)	..	..	..
Child immunization, measles (% of ages 12–23 mos.)	86	97	99
Primary completion rate, total (% of relevant age group)	..	113	115
Gross secondary enrollment, total (% of relevant age group)	..	113	105
Ratio of girls to boys in primary & secondary school (%)	..	101	100
HIV prevalence rate (% of population ages 15–49)	..	..	..
Environment			
Forests (sq. km)	400	400	400
Deforestation (average annual %, 1990–2005)			0.00
Freshwater use (% of internal resources)	..	..	..
Access to improved water source (% of total pop.)	88	87	88
Access to improved sanitation facilities (% of total pop.)	..	..	..
Energy use per capita (kilograms of oil equivalent)	..	..	..
Carbon dioxide emissions per capita (metric tons)	1.6	7.0	6.6
Electricity use per capita (kilowatt-hours)	..	..	..
Economy			
GDP ($ millions)	369	615	775
GDP growth (annual %)	7.0	4.3	5.3
GDP implicit price deflator (annual % growth)	5.6	1.3	2.2
Value added in agriculture (% of GDP)	5	3	3
Value added in industry (% of GDP)	16	29	26
Value added in services (% of GDP)	79	68	71
Exports of goods and services (% of GDP)	62	78	111
Imports of goods and services (% of GDP)	67	81	133
Gross capital formation (% of GDP)	25	25	33
Central government revenue (% of GDP)	..	38.7	57.2
Central government cash surplus/deficit (% of GDP)	..	-13.9	-2.6
States and markets			
Starting a business (days)			38
Stock market capitalization (% of GDP)	..	..	..
Military expenditures (% of GDP)	4.0	1.7	1.8
Fixed-line and mobile subscribers (per 100 people)	12	57	108
Internet users (per 100 people)	0.0	7.4	34.3
Paved roads (% of total)	57	..	..
High-technology exports (% of manufactured exports)	0	0	3
Global links			
Merchandise trade (% of GDP)	65.7	87.2	153.2
Net barter terms of trade (2000 = 100)	78	100	102
Total external debt ($ millions)	181	304	905
Short-term debt ($ millions)	46	84	606
Total debt service (% of exports)	8.9	4.2	20.6
Foreign direct investment, net inflows ($ millions)	20	24	146
Remittances received ($ millions)	8.0	2.0	14.0
Aid ($ millions)	36	18	14

Sierra Leone

Sub-Saharan Africa		Low income

Population (millions)	5.7	Population growth (%)	2.8
Surface area (1,000 sq. km)	72	National poverty rate (% of pop.)	70
GNI ($ billions)	1.4	GNI per capita ($)	240
GNI, PPP ($ billions)	3.5	GNI per capita, PPP ($)	610

	1990	2000	2006
People			
Share of poorest 20% in nat'l consumption/income (%)	1.1	..	..
Life expectancy at birth (years)	39	41	42
Total fertility (births per woman)	6.5	6.5	6.5
Adolescent fertility (births per 1,000 women 15–19)	..	192	166
Contraceptive prevalence (% of married women 15–49)	..	4	5
Births attended by skilled health staff (% of total)	..	42	43
Under-five mortality rate (per 1,000)	290	277	270
Child malnutrition, underweight (% of under age 5)	..	24.7	..
Child immunization, measles (% of ages 12–23 mos.)	..	37	67
Primary completion rate, total (% of relevant age group)	..	..	..
Gross secondary enrollment, total (% of relevant age group)	17	26	..
Ratio of girls to boys in primary & secondary school (%)	67	71	..
HIV prevalence rate (% of population ages 15–49)	..	..	1.6
Environment			
Forests (1,000 sq. km)	30	29	28
Deforestation (average annual %, 1990–2005)			0.7
Freshwater use (% of internal resources)	..	0.2	..
Access to improved water source (% of total pop.)	..	57	57
Access to improved sanitation facilities (% of total pop.)	..	38	39
Energy use per capita (kilograms of oil equivalent)	..	..	..
Carbon dioxide emissions per capita (metric tons)	0.1	0.1	0.2
Electricity use per capita (kilowatt-hours)	..	..	..
Economy			
GDP ($ millions)	650	634	1,450
GDP growth (annual %)	3.3	3.8	7.4
GDP implicit price deflator (annual % growth)	70.6	6.1	14.1
Value added in agriculture (% of GDP)	47	58	46
Value added in industry (% of GDP)	19	28	25
Value added in services (% of GDP)	34	13	29
Exports of goods and services (% of GDP)	22	18	23
Imports of goods and services (% of GDP)	24	39	36
Gross capital formation (% of GDP)	10	8	15
Central government revenue (% of GDP)	5.6	11.4	12.3
Central government cash surplus/deficit (% of GDP)	..	-9.3	-2.5
States and markets			
Starting a business (days)			26
Stock market capitalization (% of GDP)	..	..	..
Military expenditures (% of GDP)	1.4	4.1	1.0
Fixed-line and mobile subscribers (per 100 people)	0	1	..
Internet users (per 100 people)	0.0	0.1	0.2
Paved roads (% of total)	11	8	..
High-technology exports (% of manufactured exports)	..	31	..
Global links			
Merchandise trade (% of GDP)	44.2	25.6	41.7
Net barter terms of trade (2000 = 100)	..	..	..
Total external debt ($ billions)	1.2	1.2	1.4
Short-term debt ($ millions)	148	46	70
Total debt service (% of exports)	10.1	67.1	9.6
Foreign direct investment, net inflows ($ millions)	32	39	59
Remittances received ($ millions)	..	7.0	33.1
Aid ($ millions)	59	181	364

Singapore

High income

Population (millions)	4.5	Population growth (%)		3.2
Surface area (sq. km)	699	National poverty rate (% of pop.)		..
GNI ($ billions)	128.8	GNI per capita ($)		28,730
GNI, PPP ($ billions)	194.1	GNI per capita, PPP ($)		43,300

	1990	2000	2006
People			
Share of poorest 20% in nat'l consumption/income (%)	..	5.0	..
Life expectancy at birth (years)	74	78	80
Total fertility (births per woman)	1.9	1.4	1.3
Adolescent fertility (births per 1,000 women 15–19)	..	6	5
Contraceptive prevalence (% of married women 15–49)	65	..	..
Births attended by skilled health staff (% of total)	..	100	100
Under-five mortality rate (per 1,000)	8	4	3
Child malnutrition, underweight (% of under age 5)	..	3.3	..
Child immunization, measles (% of ages 12–23 mos.)	84	96	93
Primary completion rate, total (% of relevant age group)	..	..	..
Gross secondary enrollment, total (% of relevant age group)	67	64	63
Ratio of girls to boys in primary & secondary school (%)	95	101	101
HIV prevalence rate (% of population ages 15–49)	..	..	0.3
Environment			
Forests (sq. km)	20	20	20
Deforestation (average annual %, 1990–2005)			0.00
Freshwater use (% of internal resources)	..	..	..
Access to improved water source (% of total pop.)	100	100	100
Access to improved sanitation facilities (% of total pop.)	100	100	100
Energy use per capita (kilograms of oil equivalent)	4,384	5,524	6,933
Carbon dioxide emissions per capita (metric tons)	14.8	14.0	12.3
Electricity use per capita (kilowatt-hours)	4,860	7,575	8,358
Economy			
GDP ($ billions)	36.8	92.7	132.2
GDP growth (annual %)	9.2	10.1	7.9
GDP implicit price deflator (annual % growth)	4.1	3.7	0.2
Value added in agriculture (% of GDP)	0	0	0
Value added in industry (% of GDP)	35	36	35
Value added in services (% of GDP)	65	64	65
Exports of goods and services (% of GDP)	..	192	253
Imports of goods and services (% of GDP)	..	177	221
Gross capital formation (% of GDP)	37	33	19
Central government revenue (% of GDP)	26.8	26.6	19.9
Central government cash surplus/deficit (% of GDP)	11.1	11.4	7.0
States and markets			
Starting a business (days)			5
Stock market capitalization (% of GDP)	93.1	164.8	209.1
Military expenditures (% of GDP)	4.9	4.7	4.7
Fixed-line and mobile subscribers (per 100 people)	36	117	148
Internet users (per 100 people)	0.0	32.3	38.3
Paved roads (% of total)	97	100	100
High-technology exports (% of manufactured exports)	40	63	58
Global links			
Merchandise trade (% of GDP)	308.1	293.7	386.2
Net barter terms of trade (2000 = 100)	116	100	86
Total external debt ($ millions)	..	..	..
Short-term debt ($ millions)	..	..	..
Total debt service (% of exports)	..	..	..
Foreign direct investment, net inflows ($ billions)	5.6	16.5	24.2
Remittances received ($ billions)	..	..	..
Aid ($ millions)	–3.1	1.1	..

Slovak Republic

Europe & Central Asia　　　　　　　　　　**Upper middle income**

Population (millions)	5.4	Population growth (%)	0.1
Surface area (1,000 sq. km)	49	National poverty rate (% of pop.)	..
GNI ($ billions)	51.8	GNI per capita ($)	9,610
GNI, PPP ($ billions)	91.9	GNI per capita, PPP ($)	17,060

	1990	2000	2006
People			
Share of poorest 20% in nat'l consumption/income (%)	11.6	..	..
Life expectancy at birth (years)	71	73	74
Total fertility (births per woman)	2.1	1.3	1.2
Adolescent fertility (births per 1,000 women 15–19)	..	24	20
Contraceptive prevalence (% of married women 15–49)	74	..	..
Births attended by skilled health staff (% of total)	..	99	100
Under-five mortality rate (per 1,000)	14	10	8
Child malnutrition, underweight (% of under age 5)	..	..	..
Child immunization, measles (% of ages 12–23 mos.)	..	98	98
Primary completion rate, total (% of relevant age group)	..	98	94
Gross secondary enrollment, total (% of relevant age group)	..	87	96
Ratio of girls to boys in primary & secondary school (%)	..	101	100
HIV prevalence rate (% of population ages 15–49)	..	..	0.1
Environment			
Forests (1,000 sq. km)	19	19	19
Deforestation (average annual %, 1990–2005)			–0.02
Freshwater use (% of internal resources)	..	..	..
Access to improved water source (% of total pop.)	100	100	100
Access to improved sanitation facilities (% of total pop.)	99	99	99
Energy use per capita (kilograms of oil equivalent)	4,035	3,292	3,496
Carbon dioxide emissions per capita (metric tons)	9.7	6.6	6.7
Electricity use per capita (kilowatt-hours)	5,559	4,956	4,920
Economy			
GDP ($ billions)	15.5	20.4	55.0
GDP growth (annual %)	–2.7	0.7	8.3
GDP implicit price deflator (annual % growth)	6.9	9.7	2.7
Value added in agriculture (% of GDP)	7	4	4
Value added in industry (% of GDP)	59	32	32
Value added in services (% of GDP)	33	64	65
Exports of goods and services (% of GDP)	27	70	86
Imports of goods and services (% of GDP)	36	73	90
Gross capital formation (% of GDP)	33	26	29
Central government revenue (% of GDP)	..	..	30.5
Central government cash surplus/deficit (% of GDP)	..	..	–3.4
States and markets			
Starting a business (days)			25
Stock market capitalization (% of GDP)	..	6.0	10.1
Military expenditures (% of GDP)	..	1.7	1.7
Fixed-line and mobile subscribers (per 100 people)	13	55	112
Internet users (per 100 people)	0.0	9.4	41.8
Paved roads (% of total)	..	87	87
High-technology exports (% of manufactured exports)	..	4	6
Global links			
Merchandise trade (% of GDP)	110.8	120.7	159.1
Net barter terms of trade (2000 = 100)	..	..	..
Total external debt ($ billions)	..	12.1	27.1
Short-term debt ($ billions)	..	2.4	15.6
Total debt service (% of exports)	..	19.4	..
Foreign direct investment, net inflows ($ billions)	0.1	1.9	4.2
Remittances received ($ millions)	..	18.0	424.0
Aid ($ millions)	6.8	113.0	..

Slovenia

High income

Population (millions)	2.0	Population growth (%)	0.3
Surface area (1,000 sq. km)	20	National poverty rate (% of pop.)	..
GNI ($ billions)	37.4	GNI per capita ($)	18,660
GNI, PPP ($ billions)	48.1	GNI per capita, PPP ($)	23,970

	1990	2000	2006
People			
Share of poorest 20% in nat'l consumption/income (%)	..	9.1	8.3
Life expectancy at birth (years)	73	76	78
Total fertility (births per woman)	1.5	1.3	1.3
Adolescent fertility (births per 1,000 women 15–19)		8	7
Contraceptive prevalence (% of married women 15–49)	..	..	..
Births attended by skilled health staff (% of total)	100	100	100
Under-five mortality rate (per 1,000)	10	6	4
Child malnutrition, underweight (% of under age 5)	..	..	..
Child immunization, measles (% of ages 12–23 mos.)	90	95	96
Primary completion rate, total (% of relevant age group)	..	96	..
Gross secondary enrollment, total (% of relevant age group)	89	101	96
Ratio of girls to boys in primary & secondary school (%)	..	103	100
HIV prevalence rate (% of population ages 15–49)	..	..	0.1
Environment			
Forests (1,000 sq. km)	12	12	13
Deforestation (average annual %, 1990–2005)			-0.4
Freshwater use (% of internal resources)	..	..	..
Access to improved water source (% of total pop.)	..	..	..
Access to improved sanitation facilities (% of total pop.)	..	..	..
Energy use per capita (kilograms of oil equivalent)	2,801	3,260	3,657
Carbon dioxide emissions per capita (metric tons)	9.0	7.2	8.1
Electricity use per capita (kilowatt-hours)	5,091	5,778	6,918
Economy			
GDP ($ billions)	17.4	19.3	37.3
GDP growth (annual %)	-8.9	4.1	5.2
GDP implicit price deflator (annual % growth)	94.9	5.4	2.3
Value added in agriculture (% of GDP)	6	3	2
Value added in industry (% of GDP)	42	36	35
Value added in services (% of GDP)	52	61	63
Exports of goods and services (% of GDP)	91	56	69
Imports of goods and services (% of GDP)	79	59	70
Gross capital formation (% of GDP)	17	27	27
Central government revenue (% of GDP)	39.8	40.2	40.2
Central government cash surplus/deficit (% of GDP)	3.2	-1.1	-0.8
States and markets			
Starting a business (days)			60
Stock market capitalization (% of GDP)	..	13.2	40.7
Military expenditures (% of GDP)	2.2	1.2	1.7
Fixed-line and mobile subscribers (per 100 people)	21	101	132
Internet users (per 100 people)	0.0	15.1	62.3
Paved roads (% of total)	72	100	100
High-technology exports (% of manufactured exports)	3	5	5
Global links			
Merchandise trade (% of GDP)	102.4	98.0	127.0
Net barter terms of trade (2000 = 100)	..	..	..
Total external debt ($ billions)	..	..	..
Short-term debt ($ billions)	..	..	..
Total debt service (% of exports)	..	..	..
Foreign direct investment, net inflows ($ millions)	111	136	649
Remittances received ($ millions)	38	205	282
Aid ($ millions)	..	60.9	..

Solomon Islands

East Asia & Pacific   **Low income**

Population (thousands)	484	Population growth (%)	2.4
Surface area (1,000 sq. km)	29	National poverty rate (% of pop.)	..
GNI ($ millions)	333	GNI per capita ($)	690
GNI, PPP ($ millions)	896	GNI per capita, PPP ($)	1,850

	1990	2000	2006
People			
Share of poorest 20% in nat'l consumption/income (%)	..	..	..
Life expectancy at birth (years)	57	62	63
Total fertility (births per woman)	5.8	4.6	4.0
Adolescent fertility (births per 1,000 women 15–19)	..	56	43
Contraceptive prevalence (% of married women 15–49)	..	7	..
Births attended by skilled health staff (% of total)	..	85	..
Under-five mortality rate (per 1,000)	121	88	73
Child malnutrition, underweight (% of under age 5)	16.3	..	..
Child immunization, measles (% of ages 12–23 mos.)	70	87	84
Primary completion rate, total (% of relevant age group)	72	..	..
Gross secondary enrollment, total (% of relevant age group)	15	20	30
Ratio of girls to boys in primary & secondary school (%)	84	90	93
HIV prevalence rate (% of population ages 15–49)	..	..	..
Environment			
Forests (1,000 sq. km)	28	24	22
Deforestation (average annual %, 1990–2005)			1.6
Freshwater use (% of internal resources)	..	..	..
Access to improved water source (% of total pop.)	..	69	70
Access to improved sanitation facilities (% of total pop.)	..	31	31
Energy use per capita (kilograms of oil equivalent)	..	..	..
Carbon dioxide emissions per capita (metric tons)	0.5	0.4	0.4
Electricity use per capita (kilowatt-hours)	..	..	..
Economy			
GDP ($ millions)	211	299	336
GDP growth (annual %)	1.8	-14.3	6.1
GDP implicit price deflator (annual % growth)	0.1	10.7	6.8
Value added in agriculture (% of GDP)	..	..	..
Value added in industry (% of GDP)	..	..	..
Value added in services (% of GDP)	..	..	..
Exports of goods and services (% of GDP)	47	40	48
Imports of goods and services (% of GDP)	73	59	54
Gross capital formation (% of GDP)	29	22	35
Central government revenue (% of GDP)	..	..	..
Central government cash surplus/deficit (% of GDP)	..	..	..
States and markets			
Starting a business (days)			57
Stock market capitalization (% of GDP)	..	..	..
Military expenditures (% of GDP)	..	..	..
Fixed-line and mobile subscribers (per 100 people)	1	2	3
Internet users (per 100 people)	0.0	0.5	1.7
Paved roads (% of total)	2	2	..
High-technology exports (% of manufactured exports)	..	..	..
Global links			
Merchandise trade (% of GDP)	76.2	53.8	95.2
Net barter terms of trade (2000 = 100)	85	100	92
Total external debt ($ millions)	120	155	173
Short-term debt ($ millions)	16.6	3.2	15.6
Total debt service (% of exports)	11.8	7.1	2.0
Foreign direct investment, net inflows ($ millions)	10	13	19
Remittances received ($ millions)	..	2.0	20.4
Aid ($ millions)	46	68	205

Somalia

Sub-Saharan Africa **Low income**

Population (millions)	8.4	Population growth (%)	3.0
Surface area (1,000 sq. km)	638	National poverty rate (% of pop.)	..
GNI ($ billions)	..	GNI per capita ($)	..
GNI, PPP ($ billions)	..	GNI per capita, PPP ($)	..

	1990	2000	2006
People			
Share of poorest 20% in nat'l consumption/income (%)	..	..	..
Life expectancy at birth (years)	42	45	48
Total fertility (births per woman)	6.8	6.6	6.1
Adolescent fertility (births per 1,000 women 15–19)	..	73	67
Contraceptive prevalence (% of married women 15–49)	1	8	15
Births attended by skilled health staff (% of total)	..	25	33
Under-five mortality rate (per 1,000)	203	165	145
Child malnutrition, underweight (% of under age 5)	..	..	..
Child immunization, measles (% of ages 12–23 mos.)	30	38	35
Primary completion rate, total (% of relevant age group)	..	..	..
Gross secondary enrollment, total (% of relevant age group)	..	..	..
Ratio of girls to boys in primary & secondary school (%)	..	55	..
HIV prevalence rate (% of population ages 15–49)	..	..	0.9
Environment			
Forests (1,000 sq. km)	83	75	71
Deforestation (average annual %, 1990–2005)			1.0
Freshwater use (% of internal resources)	..	54.8	
Access to improved water source (% of total pop.)	..	29	29
Access to improved sanitation facilities (% of total pop.)	..	25	26
Energy use per capita (kilograms of oil equivalent)	..	..	..
Carbon dioxide emissions per capita (metric tons)	0.00	..	..
Electricity use per capita (kilowatt-hours)	..	..	..
Economy			
GDP ($ millions)	917.0	..	..
GDP growth (annual %)	–1.5	..	..
GDP implicit price deflator (annual % growth)	215.5	..	..
Value added in agriculture (% of GDP)	65	..	..
Value added in industry (% of GDP)	..	..	..
Value added in services (% of GDP)	..	..	..
Exports of goods and services (% of GDP)	10	..	..
Imports of goods and services (% of GDP)	38	..	..
Gross capital formation (% of GDP)	16	..	..
Central government revenue (% of GDP)	..	..	..
Central government cash surplus/deficit (% of GDP)	..	..	..
States and markets			
Starting a business (days)			..
Stock market capitalization (% of GDP)	..	..	..
Military expenditures (% of GDP)	..	..	..
Fixed-line and mobile subscribers (per 100 people)	0	1	7
Internet users (per 100 people)	0.0	0.2	1.1
Paved roads (% of total)	11	12	..
High-technology exports (% of manufactured exports)	..	..	..
Global links			
Merchandise trade (% of GDP)	..	..	..
Net barter terms of trade (2000 = 100)	..	..	..
Total external debt ($ billions)	2.4	2.6	2.8
Short-term debt ($ millions)	285	591	745
Total debt service (% of exports)	47.6	..	..
Foreign direct investment, net inflows ($ millions)	5.6	0.3	96.0
Remittances received ($ billions)	..	..	..
Aid ($ millions)	491	101	392

South Africa

Sub-Saharan Africa		Upper middle income	
Population (millions)	47	Population growth (%)	1.1
Surface area (1,000 sq. km)	1,219	National poverty rate (% of pop.)	..
GNI ($ billions)	255.4	GNI per capita ($)	5,390
GNI, PPP ($ billions)	421.7	GNI per capita, PPP ($)	8,900

	1990	2000	2006
People			
Share of poorest 20% in nat'l consumption/income (%)	..	3.5	..
Life expectancy at birth (years)	62	49	51
Total fertility (births per woman)	3.3	2.9	2.7
Adolescent fertility (births per 1,000 women 15–19)	..	75	63
Contraceptive prevalence (% of married women 15–49)	57	56	..
Births attended by skilled health staff (% of total)	..	84	..
Under-five mortality rate (per 1,000)	60	63	69
Child malnutrition, underweight (% of under age 5)	..	..	..
Child immunization, measles (% of ages 12–23 mos.)	79	77	85
Primary completion rate, total (% of relevant age group)	76	90	100
Gross secondary enrollment, total (% of relevant age group)	69	86	95
Ratio of girls to boys in primary & secondary school (%)	104	100	100
HIV prevalence rate (% of population ages 15–49)	..	15.6	18.8
Environment			
Forests (1,000 sq. km)	92	92	92
Deforestation (average annual %, 1990–2005)			0.00
Freshwater use (% of internal resources)	..	27.9	..
Access to improved water source (% of total pop.)	83	87	88
Access to improved sanitation facilities (% of total pop.)	69	66	65
Energy use per capita (kilograms of oil equivalent)	2,592	2,525	2,722
Carbon dioxide emissions per capita (metric tons)	9.4	9.0	9.4
Electricity use per capita (kilowatt-hours)	4,431	4,417	4,847
Economy			
GDP ($ billions)	112.0	132.9	255.2
GDP growth (annual %)	-0.3	4.2	5.0
GDP implicit price deflator (annual % growth)	15.5	8.8	6.8
Value added in agriculture (% of GDP)	5	3	3
Value added in industry (% of GDP)	40	32	31
Value added in services (% of GDP)	55	65	66
Exports of goods and services (% of GDP)	24	28	30
Imports of goods and services (% of GDP)	19	25	33
Gross capital formation (% of GDP)	18	16	20
Central government revenue (% of GDP)	..	26.3	31.8
Central government cash surplus/deficit (% of GDP)	..	-2.0	1.2
States and markets			
Starting a business (days)			31
Stock market capitalization (% of GDP)	123.2	154.2	280.2
Military expenditures (% of GDP)	3.8	1.4	1.4
Fixed-line and mobile subscribers (per 100 people)	9	30	83
Internet users (per 100 people)	0.0	5.5	10.9
Paved roads (% of total)	30	20	..
High-technology exports (% of manufactured exports)	7	7	6
Global links			
Merchandise trade (% of GDP)	37.4	44.9	53.2
Net barter terms of trade (2000 = 100)	104	100	125
Total external debt ($ billions)	..	24.9	35.5
Short-term debt ($ billions)	..	9.6	15.3
Total debt service (% of exports)	..	9.8	6.7
Foreign direct investment, net inflows ($ millions)	-76	969	-120
Remittances received ($ millions)	136	344	734
Aid ($ millions)	..	487.3	717.8

Spain

Population (millions)	44	Population growth (%)		1.7
Surface area (1,000 sq. km)	505	National poverty rate (% of pop.)		..
GNI ($ billions)	1,206.2	GNI per capita ($)		27,340
GNI, PPP ($ billions)	1,244.2	GNI per capita, PPP ($)		28,200

	1990	2000	2006
People			
Share of poorest 20% in nat'l consumption/income (%)	..	7.0	..
Life expectancy at birth (years)	77	79	81
Total fertility (births per woman)	1.3	1.2	1.4
Adolescent fertility (births per 1,000 women 15–19)	..	9	9
Contraceptive prevalence (% of married women 15–49)	..	..	..
Births attended by skilled health staff (% of total)	..	..	..
Under-five mortality rate (per 1,000)	9	6	4
Child malnutrition, underweight (% of under age 5)	..	..	..
Child immunization, measles (% of ages 12–23 mos.)	99	94	97
Primary completion rate, total (% of relevant age group)	..	..	103
Gross secondary enrollment, total (% of relevant age group)	105	111	118
Ratio of girls to boys in primary & secondary school (%)	104	103	103
HIV prevalence rate (% of population ages 15–49)	..	..	0.6
Environment			
Forests (1,000 sq. km)	135	164	179
Deforestation (average annual %, 1990–2005)			-1.9
Freshwater use (% of internal resources)	..	32.0	..
Access to improved water source (% of total pop.)	100	100	100
Access to improved sanitation facilities (% of total pop.)	100	100	100
Energy use per capita (kilograms of oil equivalent)	2,345	3,097	3,346
Carbon dioxide emissions per capita (metric tons)	5.5	7.0	7.7
Electricity use per capita (kilowatt-hours)	3,540	5,207	6,147
Economy			
GDP ($ billions)	521.0	580.7	1,224.7
GDP growth (annual %)	3.8	5.0	3.9
GDP implicit price deflator (annual % growth)	7.3	3.5	3.8
Value added in agriculture (% of GDP)	6	4	3
Value added in industry (% of GDP)	34	29	30
Value added in services (% of GDP)	61	66	67
Exports of goods and services (% of GDP)	16	29	26
Imports of goods and services (% of GDP)	19	32	32
Gross capital formation (% of GDP)	26	26	31
Central government revenue (% of GDP)	..	31.1	27.2
Central government cash surplus/deficit (% of GDP)	..	-0.5	1.9
States and markets			
Starting a business (days)			47
Stock market capitalization (% of GDP)	21.3	86.8	108.0
Military expenditures (% of GDP)	1.7	1.2	1.0
Fixed-line and mobile subscribers (per 100 people)	33	103	146
Internet users (per 100 people)	0.0	13.6	42.1
Paved roads (% of total)	99	99	..
High-technology exports (% of manufactured exports)	6	8	6
Global links			
Merchandise trade (% of GDP)	27.5	46.7	42.6
Net barter terms of trade (2000 = 100)	100	100	104
Total external debt ($ billions)	..	..	..
Short-term debt ($ billions)	..	..	..
Total debt service (% of exports)	..	..	..
Foreign direct investment, net inflows ($ billions)	14	39	20
Remittances received ($ billions)	2.2	4.5	8.9
Aid ($ billions)	..	..	..

Sri Lanka

South Asia　　　　　　　　　　　**Lower middle income**

Population (millions)	20	Population growth (%)	1.1
Surface area (1,000 sq. km)	66	National poverty rate (% of pop.)	23
GNI ($ billions)	26.0	GNI per capita ($)	1,310
GNI, PPP ($ billions)	74.2	GNI per capita, PPP ($)	3,730

	1990	2000	2006
People			
Share of poorest 20% in nat'l consumption/income (%)	9.0	8.3	..
Life expectancy at birth (years)	71	74	75
Total fertility (births per woman)	2.5	1.9	1.9
Adolescent fertility (births per 1,000 women 15–19)	..	29	26
Contraceptive prevalence (% of married women 15–49)	..	70	..
Births attended by skilled health staff (% of total)	..	96	..
Under-five mortality rate (per 1,000)	32	19	13
Child malnutrition, underweight (% of under age 5)	..	22.8	..
Child immunization, measles (% of ages 12–23 mos.)	80	99	99
Primary completion rate, total (% of relevant age group)	92	..	108
Gross secondary enrollment, total (% of relevant age group)	71	86	87
Ratio of girls to boys in primary & secondary school (%)	102	103	..
HIV prevalence rate (% of population ages 15–49)	..	..	0.1
Environment			
Forests (1,000 sq. km)	24	21	19
Deforestation (average annual %, 1990–2005)			1.3
Freshwater use (% of internal resources)	..	25.2	..
Access to improved water source (% of total pop.)	68	76	79
Access to improved sanitation facilities (% of total pop.)	69	87	91
Energy use per capita (kilograms of oil equivalent)	324	418	477
Carbon dioxide emissions per capita (metric tons)	0.2	0.5	0.6
Electricity use per capita (kilowatt-hours)	154	288	378
Economy			
GDP ($ billions)	8.0	16.3	27.0
GDP growth (annual %)	6.4	6.0	7.4
GDP implicit price deflator (annual % growth)	20.1	7.3	10.3
Value added in agriculture (% of GDP)	26	20	16
Value added in industry (% of GDP)	26	27	27
Value added in services (% of GDP)	48	53	56
Exports of goods and services (% of GDP)	30	39	32
Imports of goods and services (% of GDP)	38	50	43
Gross capital formation (% of GDP)	22	28	29
Central government revenue (% of GDP)	21.0	16.8	17.0
Central government cash surplus/deficit (% of GDP)	−5.2	−8.4	−7.2
States and markets			
Starting a business (days)			39
Stock market capitalization (% of GDP)	11.4	6.6	28.8
Military expenditures (% of GDP)	2.1	4.5	2.4
Fixed-line and mobile subscribers (per 100 people)	1	6	37
Internet users (per 100 people)	0.0	0.6	2.2
Paved roads (% of total)	32	86	..
High-technology exports (% of manufactured exports)	1	2	2
Global links			
Merchandise trade (% of GDP)	57.3	77.2	63.6
Net barter terms of trade (2000 = 100)	82	100	80
Total external debt ($ billions)	5.9	9.2	11.4
Short-term debt ($ millions)	405	685	855
Total debt service (% of exports)	13.8	10.3	8.6
Foreign direct investment, net inflows ($ millions)	43	173	480
Remittances received ($ billions)	0.4	1.2	2.3
Aid ($ millions)	728	276	796

St. Kitts and Nevis

Latin America & Caribbean		Upper middle income	
Population (thousands)	48	Population growth (%)	0.8
Surface area (sq. km)	260	National poverty rate (% of pop.)	..
GNI ($ millions)	406	GNI per capita ($)	8,460
GNI, PPP ($ millions)	597	GNI per capita, PPP ($)	12,440

	1990	2000	2006
People			
Share of poorest 20% in nat'l consumption/income (%)	..	..	..
Life expectancy at birth (years)	67	71	..
Total fertility (births per woman)	2.7	2.2	..
Adolescent fertility (births per 1,000 women 15-19)	..	..	..
Contraceptive prevalence (% of married women 15-49)	..	..	54
Births attended by skilled health staff (% of total)	..	99	100
Under-five mortality rate (per 1,000)	36	25	19
Child malnutrition, underweight (% of under age 5)	..	..	..
Child immunization, measles (% of ages 12-23 mos.)	99	99	99
Primary completion rate, total (% of relevant age group)	..	119	109
Gross secondary enrollment, total (% of relevant age group)	85	93	94
Ratio of girls to boys in primary & secondary school (%)	105	105	103
HIV prevalence rate (% of population ages 15-49)	..	..	..
Environment			
Forests (1,000 sq. km)	50	50	50
Deforestation (average annual %, 1990-2005)			0.00
Freshwater use (% of internal resources)	..	..	..
Access to improved water source (% of total pop.)	100	100	100
Access to improved sanitation facilities (% of total pop.)	95	95	95
Energy use per capita (kilograms of oil equivalent)	..	..	..
Carbon dioxide emissions per capita (metric tons)	1.6	2.3	2.7
Electricity use per capita (kilowatt-hours)	..	..	..
Economy			
GDP ($ millions)	159	329	477
GDP growth (annual %)	2.3	2.8	5.8
GDP implicit price deflator (annual % growth)	8.7	5.1	5.2
Value added in agriculture (% of GDP)	6	3	3
Value added in industry (% of GDP)	29	29	28
Value added in services (% of GDP)	65	68	69
Exports of goods and services (% of GDP)	52	46	47
Imports of goods and services (% of GDP)	83	76	67
Gross capital formation (% of GDP)	55	50	45
Central government revenue (% of GDP)	28.3	..	..
Central government cash surplus/deficit (% of GDP)	0.6	..	..
States and markets			
Starting a business (days)			46
Stock market capitalization (% of GDP)	..	..	63.8
Military expenditures (% of GDP)	..	..	..
Fixed-line and mobile subscribers (per 100 people)	23	52	74
Internet users (per 100 people)	0.0	6.1	..
Paved roads (% of total)	39	43	..
High-technology exports (% of manufactured exports)	..	1	1
Global links			
Merchandise trade (% of GDP)	86.7	69.6	65.2
Net barter terms of trade (2000 = 100)	..	100	83
Total external debt ($ millions)	45	157	293
Short-term debt ($ millions)	1.0	1.8	2.4
Total debt service (% of exports)	2.9	12.9	21.6
Foreign direct investment, net inflows ($ millions)	49	96	203
Remittances received ($ millions)	19.0	4.0	3.7
Aid ($ millions)	8.1	3.9	5.2

St. Lucia

Latin America & Caribbean		Upper middle income	
Population (thousands)	166	Population growth (%)	0.7
Surface area (sq. km)	620	National poverty rate (% of pop.)	..
GNI ($ millions)	833	GNI per capita ($)	5,060
GNI, PPP ($ billions)	1.4	GNI per capita, PPP ($)	8,500

	1990	2000	2006
People			
Share of poorest 20% in nat'l consumption/income (%)	..	..	..
Life expectancy at birth (years)	71	71	74
Total fertility (births per woman)	3.3	2.0	2.1
Adolescent fertility (births per 1,000 women 15–19)	..	64	60
Contraceptive prevalence (% of married women 15–49)	47	..	..
Births attended by skilled health staff (% of total)	..	100	100
Under-five mortality rate (per 1,000)	21	16	14
Child malnutrition, underweight (% of under age 5)	..	..	..
Child immunization, measles (% of ages 12–23 mos.)	82	88	94
Primary completion rate, total (% of relevant age group)	122	101	114
Gross secondary enrollment, total (% of relevant age group)	53	75	87
Ratio of girls to boys in primary & secondary school (%)	103	109	103
HIV prevalence rate (% of population ages 15–49)	..	..	..
Environment			
Forests (sq. km)	170	170	170
Deforestation (average annual %, 1990–2005)			0.00
Freshwater use (% of internal resources)	..	..	..
Access to improved water source (% of total pop.)	98	98	98
Access to improved sanitation facilities (% of total pop.)	..	89	89
Energy use per capita (kilograms of oil equivalent)	..	..	..
Carbon dioxide emissions per capita (metric tons)	1.2	2.3	2.3
Electricity use per capita (kilowatt-hours)	..	..	..
Economy			
GDP ($ billions)	397	659	899
GDP growth (annual %)	23.5	-0.2	4.5
GDP implicit price deflator (annual % growth)	3.2	7.2	-2.5
Value added in agriculture (% of GDP)	15	7	4
Value added in industry (% of GDP)	18	18	19
Value added in services (% of GDP)	67	75	77
Exports of goods and services (% of GDP)	73	57	52
Imports of goods and services (% of GDP)	84	68	66
Gross capital formation (% of GDP)	26	28	23
Central government revenue (% of GDP)	..	..	..
Central government cash surplus/deficit (% of GDP)	..	..	..
States and markets			
Starting a business (days)			40
Stock market capitalization (% of GDP)	..	..	..
Military expenditures (% of GDP)	..	..	..
Fixed-line and mobile subscribers (per 100 people)	13	33	..
Internet users (per 100 people)	0.0	5.1	33.9
Paved roads (% of total)	..	..	..
High-technology exports (% of manufactured exports)	0	8	8
Global links			
Merchandise trade (% of GDP)	100.2	60.4	72.5
Net barter terms of trade (2000 = 100)	..	100	124
Total external debt ($ millions)	79	235	374
Short-term debt ($ millions)	7.0	67.8	117.0
Total debt service (% of exports)	2.1	8.2	6.6
Foreign direct investment, net inflows ($ millions)	45	54	119
Remittances received ($ millions)	16.0	3.0	2.6
Aid ($ millions)	12	11	18

St. Vincent & Grenadines

Latin America & Caribbean		Upper middle income	
Population (thousands)	120	Population growth (%)	0.5
Surface area (sq. km)	390	National poverty rate (% of pop.)	..
GNI ($ millions)	395	GNI per capita ($)	3,320
GNI, PPP ($ millions)	741	GNI per capita, PPP ($)	6,220

	1990	2000	2006
People			
Share of poorest 20% in nat'l consumption/income (%)	..	..	..
Life expectancy at birth (years)	69	70	71
Total fertility (births per woman)	3.0	2.3	2.2
Adolescent fertility (births per 1,000 women 15–19)	..	70	65
Contraceptive prevalence (% of married women 15–49)	58	58	48
Births attended by skilled health staff (% of total)	..	100	100
Under-five mortality rate (per 1,000)	25	23	20
Child malnutrition, underweight (% of under age 5)	..	..	..
Child immunization, measles (% of ages 12–23 mos.)	96	96	99
Primary completion rate, total (% of relevant age group)	..	74	92
Gross secondary enrollment, total (% of relevant age group)	58	69	75
Ratio of girls to boys in primary & secondary school (%)	106	105	101
HIV prevalence rate (% of population ages 15–49)	..	..	..
Environment			
Forests (sq. km)	90	100	110
Deforestation (average annual %, 1990–2005)			-1.3
Freshwater use (% of internal resources)	..	..	..
Access to improved water source (% of total pop.)	..	..	..
Access to improved sanitation facilities (% of total pop.)	..	..	..
Energy use per capita (kilograms of oil equivalent)	..	..	..
Carbon dioxide emissions per capita (metric tons)	0.7	1.3	1.7
Electricity use per capita (kilowatt-hours)	..	..	..
Economy			
GDP ($ millions)	198	335	423
GDP growth (annual %)	5.0	1.8	1.5
GDP implicit price deflator (annual % growth)	6.4	-1.0	-8.4
Value added in agriculture (% of GDP)	21	11	8
Value added in industry (% of GDP)	23	24	25
Value added in services (% of GDP)	56	65	67
Exports of goods and services (% of GDP)	66	54	48
Imports of goods and services (% of GDP)	77	60	77
Gross capital formation (% of GDP)	30	27	29
Central government revenue (% of GDP)	25.6	..	..
Central government cash surplus/deficit (% of GDP)	..	..	..
States and markets			
Starting a business (days)			12
Stock market capitalization (% of GDP)	..	..	..
Military expenditures (% of GDP)	..	..	..
Fixed-line and mobile subscribers (per 100 people)	12	24	92
Internet users (per 100 people)	0.0	3.0	8.4
Paved roads (% of total)	..	68	..
High-technology exports (% of manufactured exports)	..	0	0
Global links			
Merchandise trade (% of GDP)	110.5	62.8	69.8
Net barter terms of trade (2000 = 100)	..	100	112
Total external debt ($ millions)	62	196	300
Short-term debt ($ millions)	2.1	31.4	58.1
Total debt service (% of exports)	2.9	7.3	11.5
Foreign direct investment, net inflows ($ millions)	7.7	37.7	85.0
Remittances received ($ millions)	16.0	3.0	5.0
Aid ($ millions)	15.4	6.2	4.7

Sudan

Sub-Saharan Africa		Low income	
Population (millions)	38	Population growth (%)	2.2
Surface area (1,000 sq. km)	2,506	National poverty rate (% of pop.)	..
GNI ($ billions)	30.1	GNI per capita ($)	800
GNI, PPP ($ billions)	67.2	GNI per capita, PPP ($)	1,780

	1990	2000	2006
People			
Share of poorest 20% in nat'l consumption/income (%)	..	..	..
Life expectancy at birth (years)	53	56	58
Total fertility (births per woman)	5.9	5.1	4.3
Adolescent fertility (births per 1,000 women 15–19)	..	76	59
Contraceptive prevalence (% of married women 15–49)	9	7	8
Births attended by skilled health staff (% of total)	69	87	49
Under-five mortality rate (per 1,000)	120	97	89
Child malnutrition, underweight (% of under age 5)	..	38.4	..
Child immunization, measles (% of ages 12–23 mos.)	57	58	73
Primary completion rate, total (% of relevant age group)	42	37	47
Gross secondary enrollment, total (% of relevant age group)	21	26	34
Ratio of girls to boys in primary & secondary school (%)	77	88	89
HIV prevalence rate (% of population ages 15–49)	..	..	1.6
Environment			
Forests (1,000 sq. km)	764	705	675
Deforestation (average annual %, 1990–2005)			0.8
Freshwater use (% of internal resources)	..	124.4	..
Access to improved water source (% of total pop.)	64	69	70
Access to improved sanitation facilities (% of total pop.)	33	34	34
Energy use per capita (kilograms of oil equivalent)	410	414	499
Carbon dioxide emissions per capita (metric tons)	0.2	0.2	0.3
Electricity use per capita (kilowatt-hours)	49	62	94
Economy			
GDP ($ billions)	9.0	12.4	37.4
GDP growth (annual %)	-5.5	8.4	11.8
GDP implicit price deflator (annual % growth)	40.9	8.7	7.0
Value added in agriculture (% of GDP)	..	42	32
Value added in industry (% of GDP)	..	22	29
Value added in services (% of GDP)	..	37	39
Exports of goods and services (% of GDP)	6	15	16
Imports of goods and services (% of GDP)	10	18	27
Gross capital formation (% of GDP)	7	18	25
Central government revenue (% of GDP)	..	8.0	..
Central government cash surplus/deficit (% of GDP)	..	-0.4	..
States and markets			
Starting a business (days)			39
Stock market capitalization (% of GDP)	..	..	..
Military expenditures (% of GDP)	3.6	4.7	..
Fixed-line and mobile subscribers (per 100 people)	0	1	14
Internet users (per 100 people)	0.0	0.1	9.3
Paved roads (% of total)	34	36	..
High-technology exports (% of manufactured exports)	0	4	1
Global links			
Merchandise trade (% of GDP)	11.0	27.2	36.7
Net barter terms of trade (2000 = 100)	100	100	189
Total external debt ($ billions)	15	16	19
Short-term debt ($ billions)	4.2	4.8	6.5
Total debt service (% of exports)	8.7	9.7	4.1
Foreign direct investment, net inflows ($ billions)	0.0	0.4	3.5
Remittances received ($ billions)	0.1	0.6	1.2
Aid ($ billions)	0.8	0.2	2.1

Suriname

Latin America & Caribbean **Lower middle income**

Population (thousands)	455	Population growth (%)	0.6
Surface area (1,000 sq. km)	163	National poverty rate (% of pop.)	..
GNI ($ billions)	1.9	GNI per capita ($)	4,210
GNI, PPP ($ billions)	3.5	GNI per capita, PPP ($)	7,720

	1990	2000	2006
People			
Share of poorest 20% in nat'l consumption/income (%)	..	..	..
Life expectancy at birth (years)	68	69	70
Total fertility (births per woman)	2.8	2.7	2.5
Adolescent fertility (births per 1,000 women 15–19)	..	47	41
Contraceptive prevalence (% of married women 15–49)	..	42	..
Births attended by skilled health staff (% of total)	..	85	..
Under-five mortality rate (per 1,000)	48	41	39
Child malnutrition, underweight (% of under age 5)	..	11.4	..
Child immunization, measles (% of ages 12–23 mos.)	65	79	83
Primary completion rate, total (% of relevant age group)	81	98	97
Gross secondary enrollment, total (% of relevant age group)	58	72	77
Ratio of girls to boys in primary & secondary school (%)	107	108	114
HIV prevalence rate (% of population ages 15–49)	..	..	1.9
Environment			
Forests (1,000 sq. km)	148	148	148
Deforestation (average annual %, 1990–2005)			0.00
Freshwater use (% of internal resources)	..	0.8	..
Access to improved water source (% of total pop.)	..	92	92
Access to improved sanitation facilities (% of total pop.)	..	93	94
Energy use per capita (kilograms of oil equivalent)	..	..	..
Carbon dioxide emissions per capita (metric tons)	4.5	4.9	5.1
Electricity use per capita (kilowatt-hours)	..	..	..
Economy			
GDP ($ millions)	399	892	2,115
GDP growth (annual %)	-0.5	-0.1	5.8
GDP implicit price deflator (annual % growth)	43.9	54.8	13.0
Value added in agriculture (% of GDP)	9	11	5
Value added in industry (% of GDP)	24	25	36
Value added in services (% of GDP)	67	64	59
Exports of goods and services (% of GDP)	42	20	31
Imports of goods and services (% of GDP)	44	33	46
Gross capital formation (% of GDP)	11	12	25
Central government revenue (% of GDP)	..	..	..
Central government cash surplus/deficit (% of GDP)	..	..	..
States and markets			
Starting a business (days)			694
Stock market capitalization (% of GDP)	..	..	..
Military expenditures (% of GDP)	..	..	..
Fixed-line and mobile subscribers (per 100 people)	9	27	88
Internet users (per 100 people)	0.0	2.7	7.1
Paved roads (% of total)	24	26	..
High-technology exports (% of manufactured exports)	0	0	..
Global links			
Merchandise trade (% of GDP)	236.5	103.7	95.5
Net barter terms of trade (2000 = 100)	..	100	193
Total external debt ($ billions)	..	..	..
Short-term debt ($ billions)	..	..	..
Total debt service (% of exports)	..	..	..
Foreign direct investment, net inflows ($ billions)	..	..	..
Remittances received ($ millions)	1.0	15.0	2.1
Aid ($ millions)	61	34	64

Swaziland

Sub-Saharan Africa		Lower middle income	
Population (millions)	1.1	Population growth (%)	0.6
Surface area (1,000 sq. km)	17	National poverty rate (% of pop.)	69
GNI ($ billions)	2.7	GNI per capita ($)	2,400
GNI, PPP ($ billions)	5.3	GNI per capita, PPP ($)	4,700

	1990	2000	2006
People			
Share of poorest 20% in nat'l consumption/income (%)	..	4.3	..
Life expectancy at birth (years)	57	45	41
Total fertility (births per woman)	5.3	4.1	3.5
Adolescent fertility (births per 1,000 women 15–19)	..	41	34
Contraceptive prevalence (% of married women 15–49)	20	28	..
Births attended by skilled health staff (% of total)	..	70	..
Under-five mortality rate (per 1,000)	110	142	164
Child malnutrition, underweight (% of under age 5)	..	9.1	..
Child immunization, measles (% of ages 12–23 mos.)	85	72	57
Primary completion rate, total (% of relevant age group)	61	64	67
Gross secondary enrollment, total (% of relevant age group)	42	43	47
Ratio of girls to boys in primary & secondary school (%)	98	95	95
HIV prevalence rate (% of population ages 15–49)	..	..	33.4
Environment			
Forests (1,000 sq. km)	4.7	5.2	5.4
Deforestation (average annual %, 1990–2005)			-0.9
Freshwater use (% of internal resources)	..	40.1	..
Access to improved water source (% of total pop.)	..	62	62
Access to improved sanitation facilities (% of total pop.)	..	48	48
Energy use per capita (kilograms of oil equivalent)	..	..	..
Carbon dioxide emissions per capita (metric tons)	0.6	1.0	0.9
Electricity use per capita (kilowatt-hours)	..	..	..
Economy			
GDP ($ millions)	882	1,389	2,648
GDP growth (annual %)	8.6	2.0	2.1
GDP implicit price deflator (annual % growth)	15.0	12.3	5.7
Value added in agriculture (% of GDP)	13	16	11
Value added in industry (% of GDP)	42	45	46
Value added in services (% of GDP)	45	40	43
Exports of goods and services (% of GDP)	75	82	81
Imports of goods and services (% of GDP)	87	97	86
Gross capital formation (% of GDP)	19	19	17
Central government revenue (% of GDP)	..	..	..
Central government cash surplus/deficit (% of GDP)	..	..	..
States and markets			
Starting a business (days)			61
Stock market capitalization (% of GDP)	1.9	5.3	7.5
Military expenditures (% of GDP)	1.9	1.9	1.9
Fixed-line and mobile subscribers (per 100 people)	2	6	26
Internet users (per 100 people)	0.0	1.0	3.7
Paved roads (% of total)	54	30	..
High-technology exports (% of manufactured exports)	..	0	0
Global links			
Merchandise trade (% of GDP)	138.2	140.9	160.9
Net barter terms of trade (2000 = 100)	100	100	93
Total external debt ($ millions)	298	289	544
Short-term debt ($ millions)	4.6	1.8	50.8
Total debt service (% of exports)	5.7	2.4	1.8
Foreign direct investment, net inflows ($ millions)	30	91	36
Remittances received ($ millions)	113	74	99
Aid ($ millions)	54	13	35

Sweden

High income

Population (millions)	9.1	Population growth (%)	0.7
Surface area (1,000 sq. km)	450	National poverty rate (% of pop.)	..
GNI ($ billions)	395.4	GNI per capita ($)	43,530
GNI, PPP ($ billions)	311.7	GNI per capita, PPP ($)	34,310

	1990	2000	2006
People			
Share of poorest 20% in nat'l consumption/income (%)	..	9.1	..
Life expectancy at birth (years)	78	80	81
Total fertility (births per woman)	2.1	1.5	1.9
Adolescent fertility (births per 1,000 women 15–19)	..	5	4
Contraceptive prevalence (% of married women 15–49)	..	..	..
Births attended by skilled health staff (% of total)	..	..	..
Under-five mortality rate (per 1,000)	7	4	3
Child malnutrition, underweight (% of under age 5)	..	..	..
Child immunization, measles (% of ages 12–23 mos.)	96	91	95
Primary completion rate, total (% of relevant age group)	97	..	..
Gross secondary enrollment, total (% of relevant age group)	90	152	103
Ratio of girls to boys in primary & secondary school (%)	102	115	100
HIV prevalence rate (% of population ages 15–49)	..	..	0.2
Environment			
Forests (1,000 sq. km)	274	275	275
Deforestation (average annual %, 1990–2005)			-0.04
Freshwater use (% of internal resources)	..	1.7	..
Access to improved water source (% of total pop.)	100	100	100
Access to improved sanitation facilities (% of total pop.)	100	100	100
Energy use per capita (kilograms of oil equivalent)	5,557	5,436	5,782
Carbon dioxide emissions per capita (metric tons)	5.8	5.2	5.9
Electricity use per capita (kilowatt-hours)	15,836	15,687	15,440
Economy			
GDP ($ billions)	242.2	242.0	383.8
GDP growth (annual %)	1.0	4.3	4.2
GDP implicit price deflator (annual % growth)	8.8	1.4	1.8
Value added in agriculture (% of GDP)	3	2	1
Value added in industry (% of GDP)	31	29	29
Value added in services (% of GDP)	66	70	70
Exports of goods and services (% of GDP)	30	46	51
Imports of goods and services (% of GDP)	30	40	43
Gross capital formation (% of GDP)	23	18	18
Central government revenue (% of GDP)	..	38.9	37.9
Central government cash surplus/deficit (% of GDP)	..	3.2	1.9
States and markets			
Starting a business (days)			15
Stock market capitalization (% of GDP)	40.4	135.7	149.4
Military expenditures (% of GDP)	2.5	2.0	1.4
Fixed-line and mobile subscribers (per 100 people)	74	137	165
Internet users (per 100 people)	0.6	45.6	76.9
Paved roads (% of total)	71	78	31
High-technology exports (% of manufactured exports)	13	23	16
Global links			
Merchandise trade (% of GDP)	46.2	66.1	71.4
Net barter terms of trade (2000 = 100)	108	100	88
Total external debt ($ billions)	..	..	..
Short-term debt ($ billions)	..	..	..
Total debt service (% of exports)	..	..	..
Foreign direct investment, net inflows ($ billions)	2.0	22.1	27.3
Remittances received ($ millions)	153	510	336
Aid ($ billions)	..	..	..

Switzerland

		High income
Population (millions)	7.5	Population growth (%)	0.7
Surface area (1,000 sq. km)	41	National poverty rate (% of pop.)	..
GNI ($ billions)	434.8	GNI per capita ($)	58,050
GNI, PPP ($ billions)	305.9	GNI per capita, PPP ($)	40,840

	1990	2000	2006
People			
Share of poorest 20% in nat'l consumption/income (%)	..	7.6	..
Life expectancy at birth (years)	77	80	82
Total fertility (births per woman)	1.6	1.5	1.4
Adolescent fertility (births per 1,000 women 15-19)	..	5	4
Contraceptive prevalence (% of married women 15-49)	..	..	..
Births attended by skilled health staff (% of total)	..	..	100
Under-five mortality rate (per 1,000)	9	6	5
Child malnutrition, underweight (% of under age 5)	..	..	..
Child immunization, measles (% of ages 12-23 mos.)	90	81	86
Primary completion rate, total (% of relevant age group)	52	96	91
Gross secondary enrollment, total (% of relevant age group)	99	94	93
Ratio of girls to boys in primary & secondary school (%)	97	96	97
HIV prevalence rate (% of population ages 15-49)	..	..	0.4
Environment			
Forests (1,000 sq. km)	12	12	12
Deforestation (average annual %, 1990-2005)			-0.4
Freshwater use (% of internal resources)	..	6.4	..
Access to improved water source (% of total pop.)	100	100	100
Access to improved sanitation facilities (% of total pop.)	100	100	100
Energy use per capita (kilograms of oil equivalent)	3,723	3,641	3,651
Carbon dioxide emissions per capita (metric tons)	6.4	5.4	5.5
Electricity use per capita (kilowatt-hours)	7,507	7,847	8,305
Economy			
GDP ($ billions)	235.8	246.0	380.4
GDP growth (annual %)	3.8	3.6	3.2
GDP implicit price deflator (annual % growth)	4.4	0.8	1.4
Value added in agriculture (% of GDP)	3	2	1
Value added in industry (% of GDP)	33	29	28
Value added in services (% of GDP)	64	70	70
Exports of goods and services (% of GDP)	36	46	48
Imports of goods and services (% of GDP)	34	40	41
Gross capital formation (% of GDP)	31	23	22
Central government revenue (% of GDP)	20.2	24.7	18.6
Central government cash surplus/deficit (% of GDP)	0.0	2.2	-0.4
States and markets			
Starting a business (days)			20
Stock market capitalization (% of GDP)	67.9	322.0	318.7
Military expenditures (% of GDP)	1.8	1.1	0.9
Fixed-line and mobile subscribers (per 100 people)	61	137	166
Internet users (per 100 people)	0.6	29.2	58.2
Paved roads (% of total)	..	..	100
High-technology exports (% of manufactured exports)	12	19	22
Global links			
Merchandise trade (% of GDP)	56.6	66.3	75.9
Net barter terms of trade (2000 = 100)	..	..	..
Total external debt ($ billions)	..	..	..
Short-term debt ($ billions)	..	..	..
Total debt service (% of exports)	..	..	..
Foreign direct investment, net inflows ($ billions)	5.5	19.8	27.2
Remittances received ($ billions)	0.9	1.1	1.9
Aid ($ billions)	..	..	..

Syrian Arab Republic

Middle East & North Africa		Lower middle income	

Population (millions)	19	Population growth (%)	2.7
Surface area (1,000 sq. km)	185	National poverty rate (% of pop.)	..
GNI ($ billions)	30.3	GNI per capita ($)	1,560
GNI, PPP ($ billions)	79.7	GNI per capita, PPP ($)	4,110

	1990	2000	2006
People			
Share of poorest 20% in nat'l consumption/income (%)	..	..	..
Life expectancy at birth (years)	68	72	74
Total fertility (births per woman)	5.4	3.7	3.2
Adolescent fertility (births per 1,000 women 15–19)	..	52	38
Contraceptive prevalence (% of married women 15–49)	..	45	58
Births attended by skilled health staff (% of total)	..	70	93
Under-five mortality rate (per 1,000)	38	20	14
Child malnutrition, underweight (% of under age 5)	..	..	..
Child immunization, measles (% of ages 12–23 mos.)	87	96	98
Primary completion rate, total (% of relevant age group)	101	86	115
Gross secondary enrollment, total (% of relevant age group)	48	41	70
Ratio of girls to boys in primary & secondary school (%)	85	92	95
HIV prevalence rate (% of population ages 15–49)	..	..	0.2
Environment			
Forests (1,000 sq. km)	3.7	4.3	4.6
Deforestation (average annual %, 1990–2005)			–1.4
Freshwater use (% of internal resources)	..	285.0	..
Access to improved water source (% of total pop.)	80	88	93
Access to improved sanitation facilities (% of total pop.)	73	84	90
Energy use per capita (kilograms of oil equivalent)	918	1,064	948
Carbon dioxide emissions per capita (metric tons)	2.8	2.9	3.7
Electricity use per capita (kilowatt-hours)	674	1,058	1,411
Economy			
GDP ($ billions)	12.3	19.3	33.4
GDP growth (annual %)	7.6	2.7	5.1
GDP implicit price deflator (annual % growth)	19.3	9.7	9.1
Value added in agriculture (% of GDP)	30	24	18
Value added in industry (% of GDP)	25	38	32
Value added in services (% of GDP)	45	38	49
Exports of goods and services (% of GDP)	28	35	39
Imports of goods and services (% of GDP)	28	29	36
Gross capital formation (% of GDP)	17	17	16
Central government revenue (% of GDP)	21.9	23.9	..
Central government cash surplus/deficit (% of GDP)	..	..	..
States and markets			
Starting a business (days)			43
Stock market capitalization (% of GDP)	..	..	..
Military expenditures (% of GDP)	6.0	5.4	3.8
Fixed-line and mobile subscribers (per 100 people)	4	10	41
Internet users (per 100 people)	0.0	0.2	7.7
Paved roads (% of total)	72	20	20
High-technology exports (% of manufactured exports)	0	1	1
Global links			
Merchandise trade (% of GDP)	53.7	43.7	55.1
Net barter terms of trade (2000 = 100)	..	100	133
Total external debt ($ billions)	17.3	21.7	6.5
Short-term debt ($ billions)	2.2	5.7	0.9
Total debt service (% of exports)	21.8	4.8	1.3
Foreign direct investment, net inflows ($ millions)	71	270	600
Remittances received ($ millions)	385	180	795
Aid ($ millions)	683	158	27

Tajikistan

Europe & Central Asia			Low income
Population (millions)	6.6	Population growth (%)	1.4
Surface area (1,000 sq. km)	143	National poverty rate (% of pop.)	..
GNI ($ billions)	2.6	GNI per capita ($)	390
GNI, PPP ($ billions)	10.3	GNI per capita, PPP ($)	1,560

	1990	2000	2006
People			
Share of poorest 20% in nat'l consumption/income (%)	..	8.1	7.8
Life expectancy at birth (years)	63	65	67
Total fertility (births per woman)	5.1	4.0	3.4
Adolescent fertility (births per 1,000 women 15–19)		33	28
Contraceptive prevalence (% of married women 15–49)	..	34	38
Births attended by skilled health staff (% of total)	..	71	83
Under-five mortality rate (per 1,000)	115	93	68
Child malnutrition, underweight (% of under age 5)	..	..	..
Child immunization, measles (% of ages 12–23 mos.)	68	87	87
Primary completion rate, total (% of relevant age group)	..	95	106
Gross secondary enrollment, total (% of relevant age group)	102	74	83
Ratio of girls to boys in primary & secondary school (%)	..	89	88
HIV prevalence rate (% of population ages 15–49)	..	..	0.1
Environment			
Forests (1,000 sq. km)	4.1	4.1	4.1
Deforestation (average annual %, 1990–2005)			-0.03
Freshwater use (% of internal resources)	..	18.0	..
Access to improved water source (% of total pop.)	..	59	59
Access to improved sanitation facilities (% of total pop.)	..	51	51
Energy use per capita (kilograms of oil equivalent)	1,055	463	528
Carbon dioxide emissions per capita (metric tons)	4.4	0.6	0.8
Electricity use per capita (kilowatt-hours)	3,346	2,177	2,267
Economy			
GDP ($ billions)	2.6	1.0	2.8
GDP growth (annual %)	-0.6	8.3	7.0
GDP implicit price deflator (annual % growth)	6.2	22.7	20.2
Value added in agriculture (% of GDP)	33	27	25
Value added in industry (% of GDP)	38	39	27
Value added in services (% of GDP)	29	34	48
Exports of goods and services (% of GDP)	28	87	23
Imports of goods and services (% of GDP)	35	89	58
Gross capital formation (% of GDP)	25	11	15
Central government revenue (% of GDP)	..	10.6	13.5
Central government cash surplus/deficit (% of GDP)	..	-0.8	-6.6
States and markets			
Starting a business (days)			49
Stock market capitalization (% of GDP)	..	..	..
Military expenditures (% of GDP)	0.4	1.2	2.2
Fixed-line and mobile subscribers (per 100 people)	5	4	8
Internet users (per 100 people)	0.0	0.0	0.3
Paved roads (% of total)	72	..	..
High-technology exports (% of manufactured exports)	..	42	..
Global links			
Merchandise trade (% of GDP)	..	149.0	111.0
Net barter terms of trade (2000 = 100)	..	..	..
Total external debt ($ billions)	0.0	1.0	1.2
Short-term debt ($ billions)	0.0	77.0	94.5
Total debt service (% of exports)	..	11.3	5.1
Foreign direct investment, net inflows ($ millions)	9.0	23.5	338.6
Remittances received ($ billions)		0.1	1.0
Aid ($ millions)	12	124	240

Tanzania

Sub-Saharan Africa			Low income	

Population (millions)	39	Population growth (%)	2.5
Surface area (1,000 sq. km)	947	National poverty rate (% of pop.)	36
GNI ($ billions)	13.4	GNI per capita ($)	350
GNI, PPP ($ billions)	38.8	GNI per capita, PPP ($)	980

	1990	2000	2006
People			
Share of poorest 20% in nat'l consumption/income (%)	7.4	7.3	..
Life expectancy at birth (years)	51	49	52
Total fertility (births per woman)	6.1	5.7	5.3
Adolescent fertility (births per 1,000 women 15–19)	..	132	123
Contraceptive prevalence (% of married women 15–49)	10	25	26
Births attended by skilled health staff (% of total)	53	98	46
Under-five mortality rate (per 1,000)	161	141	118
Child malnutrition, underweight (% of under age 5)	25.1	..	16.7
Child immunization, measles (% of ages 12–23 mos.)	80	78	93
Primary completion rate, total (% of relevant age group)	46	55	74
Gross secondary enrollment, total (% of relevant age group)	5	6	..
Ratio of girls to boys in primary & secondary school (%)	97	99	..
HIV prevalence rate (% of population ages 15–49)	..	..	6.5
Environment			
Forests (1,000 sq. km)	414	373	353
Deforestation (average annual %, 1990–2005)			1.1
Freshwater use (% of internal resources)	..	6.2	..
Access to improved water source (% of total pop.)	46	58	62
Access to improved sanitation facilities (% of total pop.)	47	47	47
Energy use per capita (kilograms of oil equivalent)	385	397	530
Carbon dioxide emissions per capita (metric tons)	0.1	0.1	0.1
Electricity use per capita (kilowatt-hours)	51	58	61
Economy			
GDP ($ billions)	4.3	9.1	12.8
GDP growth (annual %)	7.0	5.1	5.9
GDP implicit price deflator (annual % growth)	22.4	7.5	6.3
Value added in agriculture (% of GDP)	46	45	45
Value added in industry (% of GDP)	18	16	17
Value added in services (% of GDP)	36	39	37
Exports of goods and services (% of GDP)	13	17	24
Imports of goods and services (% of GDP)	37	24	31
Gross capital formation (% of GDP)	26	18	19
Central government revenue (% of GDP)	..	..	..
Central government cash surplus/deficit (% of GDP)	..	..	..
States and markets			
Starting a business (days)			29
Stock market capitalization (% of GDP)	..	2.6	4.2
Military expenditures (% of GDP)	2.0	1.5	1.1
Fixed-line and mobile subscribers (per 100 people)	0	1	15
Internet users (per 100 people)	0.0	0.1	1.0
Paved roads (% of total)	37	4	..
High-technology exports (% of manufactured exports)	..	1	0
Global links			
Merchandise trade (% of GDP)	31.9	24.9	46.5
Net barter terms of trade (2000 = 100)	107	100	116
Total external debt ($ billions)	6.5	6.9	4.2
Short-term debt ($ billions)	0.5	0.8	1.3
Total debt service (% of exports)	32.9	12.8	3.4
Foreign direct investment, net inflows ($ millions)	0.0	463.4	474.5
Remittances received ($ millions)	..	8.0	14.9
Aid ($ billions)	1.2	1.0	1.8

Thailand

East Asia & Pacific		Lower middle income	
Population (millions)	63	Population growth (%)	0.7
Surface area (1,000 sq. km)	513	National poverty rate (% of pop.)	..
GNI ($ billions)	193.7	GNI per capita ($)	3,050
GNI, PPP ($ billions)	472.2	GNI per capita, PPP ($)	7,440

	1990	2000	2006
People			
Share of poorest 20% in nat'l consumption/income (%)	5.6	6.1	..
Life expectancy at birth (years)	67	68	70
Total fertility (births per woman)	2.1	1.9	1.8
Adolescent fertility (births per 1,000 women 15–19)	..	46	42
Contraceptive prevalence (% of married women 15–49)	..	79	77
Births attended by skilled health staff (% of total)	..	99	97
Under-five mortality rate (per 1,000)	31	13	8
Child malnutrition, underweight (% of under age 5)	..	..	..
Child immunization, measles (% of ages 12–23 mos.)	80	94	96
Primary completion rate, total (% of relevant age group)	..	96	..
Gross secondary enrollment, total (% of relevant age group)	33	67	78
Ratio of girls to boys in primary & secondary school (%)	97	99	104
HIV prevalence rate (% of population ages 15–49)	..	..	1.4
Environment			
Forests (1,000 sq. km)	160	148	145
Deforestation (average annual %, 1990–2005)			0.6
Freshwater use (% of internal resources)	..	41.5	..
Access to improved water source (% of total pop.)	95	99	99
Access to improved sanitation facilities (% of total pop.)	80	99	99
Energy use per capita (kilograms of oil equivalent)	808	1,229	1,588
Carbon dioxide emissions per capita (metric tons)	1.8	3.3	4.3
Electricity use per capita (kilowatt-hours)	739	1,503	1,988
Economy			
GDP ($ billions)	85.3	122.7	206.3
GDP growth (annual %)	11.2	4.8	5.0
GDP implicit price deflator (annual % growth)	5.8	1.3	5.0
Value added in agriculture (% of GDP)	12	9	11
Value added in industry (% of GDP)	37	42	45
Value added in services (% of GDP)	50	49	45
Exports of goods and services (% of GDP)	34	67	74
Imports of goods and services (% of GDP)	42	58	70
Gross capital formation (% of GDP)	41	23	28
Central government revenue (% of GDP)	..	..	20.2
Central government cash surplus/deficit (% of GDP)	..	..	1.9
States and markets			
Starting a business (days)			33
Stock market capitalization (% of GDP)	28.0	24.0	68.4
Military expenditures (% of GDP)	2.6	1.4	1.1
Fixed-line and mobile subscribers (per 100 people)	3	14	75
Internet users (per 100 people)	0.0	3.8	13.3
Paved roads (% of total)	55	99	..
High-technology exports (% of manufactured exports)	21	33	27
Global links			
Merchandise trade (% of GDP)	65.7	106.7	125.7
Net barter terms of trade (2000 = 100)	119	100	92
Total external debt ($ billions)	28	80	55
Short-term debt ($ billions)	8.3	14.9	17.8
Total debt service (% of exports)	16.9	16.3	9.4
Foreign direct investment, net inflows ($ billions)	2.4	3.4	9.0
Remittances received ($ billions)	1.0	1.7	1.3
Aid ($ millions)	796	698	–216

Timor-Leste

Population (millions)	1.0	Population growth (%)	5.4
Surface area (1,000 sq. km)	15	National poverty rate (% of pop.)	..
GNI ($ millions)	865	GNI per capita ($)	840
GNI, PPP ($ billions)	5.2	GNI per capita, PPP ($)	5,100

	1990	2000	2006
People			
Share of poorest 20% in nat'l consumption/income (%)	..	..	..
Life expectancy at birth (years)	46	54	57
Total fertility (births per woman)	4.9	6.6	7.3
Adolescent fertility (births per 1,000 women 15–19)	..	84	56
Contraceptive prevalence (% of married women 15–49)	..	8	..
Births attended by skilled health staff (% of total)	..	24	..
Under-five mortality rate (per 1,000)	177	107	55
Child malnutrition, underweight (% of under age 5)	..	40.6	..
Child immunization, measles (% of ages 12–23 mos.)	..	39	64
Primary completion rate, total (% of relevant age group)	..	..	..
Gross secondary enrollment, total (% of relevant age group)	..	35	53
Ratio of girls to boys in primary & secondary school (%)	..	..	95
HIV prevalence rate (% of population ages 15–49)	..	..	0.2
Environment			
Forests (1,000 sq. km)	9.7	8.5	8.0
Deforestation (average annual %, 1990–2005)			1.3
Freshwater use (% of internal resources)	..	..	..
Access to improved water source (% of total pop.)	..	58	58
Access to improved sanitation facilities (% of total pop.)	..	35	36
Energy use per capita (kilograms of oil equivalent)	..	..	..
Carbon dioxide emissions per capita (metric tons)	..	0.2	0.2
Electricity use per capita (kilowatt-hours)	..	..	..
Economy			
GDP ($ millions)	..	316	356
GDP growth (annual %)	..	13.7	-1.6
GDP implicit price deflator (annual % growth)	..	3.0	3.4
Value added in agriculture (% of GDP)	..	26	32
Value added in industry (% of GDP)	..	19	13
Value added in services (% of GDP)	..	56	55
Exports of goods and services (% of GDP)	..	..	..
Imports of goods and services (% of GDP)	..	..	..
Gross capital formation (% of GDP)	..	26	19
Central government revenue (% of GDP)	..	..	..
Central government cash surplus/deficit (% of GDP)	..	..	..
States and markets			
Starting a business (days)			82
Stock market capitalization (% of GDP)	..	..	..
Military expenditures (% of GDP)	..	..	..
Fixed-line and mobile subscribers (per 100 people)	..	..	..
Internet users (per 100 people)	..	..	..
Paved roads (% of total)	..	..	..
High-technology exports (% of manufactured exports)	..	..	..
Global links			
Merchandise trade (% of GDP)	..	..	..
Net barter terms of trade (2000 = 100)	..	..	..
Total external debt ($ billions)	..	..	..
Short-term debt ($ billions)	..	..	..
Total debt service (% of exports)	..	..	..
Foreign direct investment, net inflows ($ billions)	..	..	..
Remittances received ($ billions)	..	..	..
Aid ($ millions)	0.1	231.3	209.7

Togo

Sub-Saharan Africa   **Low income**

Population (millions)	6.4	Population growth (%)	2.7
Surface area (1,000 sq. km)	57	National poverty rate (% of pop.)	..
GNI ($ billions)	2.3	GNI per capita ($)	350
GNI, PPP ($ billions)	4.9	GNI per capita, PPP ($)	770

	1990	2000	2006
People			
Share of poorest 20% in nat'l consumption/income (%)	..	..	..
Life expectancy at birth (years)	58	58	58
Total fertility (births per woman)	6.4	5.5	4.9
Adolescent fertility (births per 1,000 women 15–19)	..	108	92
Contraceptive prevalence (% of married women 15–49)	34	26	17
Births attended by skilled health staff (% of total)	31	49	62
Under-five mortality rate (per 1,000)	149	124	108
Child malnutrition, underweight (% of under age 5)	21.2	23.2	..
Child immunization, measles (% of ages 12–23 mos.)	73	58	83
Primary completion rate, total (% of relevant age group)	35	61	67
Gross secondary enrollment, total (% of relevant age group)	20	30	40
Ratio of girls to boys in primary & secondary school (%)	59	69	73
HIV prevalence rate (% of population ages 15–49)	..	..	3.2
Environment			
Forests (1,000 sq. km)	6.9	4.9	3.9
Deforestation (average annual %, 1990–2005)			3.8
Freshwater use (% of internal resources)	..	1.5	..
Access to improved water source (% of total pop.)	50	51	52
Access to improved sanitation facilities (% of total pop.)	37	34	35
Energy use per capita (kilograms of oil equivalent)	365	327	320
Carbon dioxide emissions per capita (metric tons)	0.2	0.3	0.4
Electricity use per capita (kilowatt-hours)	87	86	94
Economy			
GDP ($ billions)	1.6	1.3	2.2
GDP growth (annual %)	-0.2	-0.8	4.1
GDP implicit price deflator (annual % growth)	3.0	-1.7	-0.4
Value added in agriculture (% of GDP)	34	34	44
Value added in industry (% of GDP)	23	18	24
Value added in services (% of GDP)	44	48	32
Exports of goods and services (% of GDP)	33	31	35
Imports of goods and services (% of GDP)	45	51	49
Gross capital formation (% of GDP)	27	18	18
Central government revenue (% of GDP)	..	..	17.7
Central government cash surplus/deficit (% of GDP)	..	..	-0.1
States and markets			
Starting a business (days)			53
Stock market capitalization (% of GDP)	..	..	..
Military expenditures (% of GDP)	3.1	..	1.6
Fixed-line and mobile subscribers (per 100 people)	0	2	12
Internet users (per 100 people)	0.0	1.9	5.0
Paved roads (% of total)	21	32	..
High-technology exports (% of manufactured exports)	0	1	0
Global links			
Merchandise trade (% of GDP)	52.1	69.6	77.8
Net barter terms of trade (2000 = 100)	133	100	78
Total external debt ($ billions)	1.3	1.4	1.8
Short-term debt ($ millions)	113	132	233
Total debt service (% of exports)	11.9	6.3	1.6
Foreign direct investment, net inflows ($ millions)	18	42	57
Remittances received ($ millions)	27	34	193
Aid ($ millions)	258	70	79

Tonga

East Asia & Pacific   **Lower middle income**

Population (thousands)	100	Population growth (%)	0.5
Surface area (sq. km)	750	National poverty rate (% of pop.)	..
GNI ($ millions)	225	GNI per capita ($)	2,250
GNI, PPP ($ millions)	546	GNI per capita, PPP ($)	5,470

	1990	2000	2006
People			
Share of poorest 20% in nat'l consumption/income (%)	..	..	..
Life expectancy at birth (years)	70	72	73
Total fertility (births per woman)	4.6	3.8	3.8
Adolescent fertility (births per 1,000 women 15–19)	..	17	18
Contraceptive prevalence (% of married women 15–49)	..	33	..
Births attended by skilled health staff (% of total)	92	95	98
Under-five mortality rate (per 1,000)	32	26	24
Child malnutrition, underweight (% of under age 5)	..	..	..
Child immunization, measles (% of ages 12–23 mos.)	86	95	99
Primary completion rate, total (% of relevant age group)	102	104	100
Gross secondary enrollment, total (% of relevant age group)	98	101	94
Ratio of girls to boys in primary & secondary school (%)	101	102	99
HIV prevalence rate (% of population ages 15–49)	..	..	..
Environment			
Forests (sq. km)	40	40	40
Deforestation (average annual %, 1990–2005)			0.00
Freshwater use (% of internal resources)	..	..	..
Access to improved water source (% of total pop.)	100	100	100
Access to improved sanitation facilities (% of total pop.)	96	96	96
Energy use per capita (kilograms of oil equivalent)	..	..	..
Carbon dioxide emissions per capita (metric tons)	0.8	1.2	1.2
Electricity use per capita (kilowatt-hours)	..	..	..
Economy			
GDP ($ millions)	114	147	223
GDP growth (annual %)	-2.0	5.4	1.4
GDP implicit price deflator (annual % growth)	12.2	0.2	7.0
Value added in agriculture (% of GDP)	36	30	29
Value added in industry (% of GDP)	14	17	15
Value added in services (% of GDP)	50	53	56
Exports of goods and services (% of GDP)	34	8	10
Imports of goods and services (% of GDP)	65	37	44
Gross capital formation (% of GDP)	18	19	17
Central government revenue (% of GDP)	..	..	..
Central government cash surplus/deficit (% of GDP)	..	..	..
States and markets			
Starting a business (days)			32
Stock market capitalization (% of GDP)	..	..	..
Military expenditures (% of GDP)	..	1.5	1.1
Fixed-line and mobile subscribers (per 100 people)	5	10	44
Internet users (per 100 people)	0.0	2.4	3.1
Paved roads (% of total)	..	27	..
High-technology exports (% of manufactured exports)	0	0	..
Global links			
Merchandise trade (% of GDP)	64.3	53.6	58.7
Net barter terms of trade (2000 = 100)	..	..	..
Total external debt ($ millions)	54	65	85
Short-term debt ($ millions)	9.2	0.5	1.0
Total debt service (% of exports)	2.9	2.9	2.7
Foreign direct investment, net inflows ($ millions)	0.2	4.7	-1.5
Remittances received ($ millions)	24	53	72
Aid ($ millions)	30	19	21

Trinidad and Tobago

High income

Population (millions)	1.3	Population growth (%)	0.4
Surface area (1,000 sq. km)	5.1	National poverty rate (% of pop.)	..
GNI ($ billions)	16.6	GNI per capita ($)	12,500
GNI, PPP ($ billions)	22.3	GNI per capita, PPP ($)	16,800

	1990	2000	2006
People			
Share of poorest 20% in nat'l consumption/income (%)	5.9	..	..
Life expectancy at birth (years)	70	69	70
Total fertility (births per woman)	2.4	1.7	1.6
Adolescent fertility (births per 1,000 women 15–19)	..	38	35
Contraceptive prevalence (% of married women 15–49)	..	38	43
Births attended by skilled health staff (% of total)	..	96	98
Under-five mortality rate (per 1,000)	34	34	38
Child malnutrition, underweight (% of under age 5)	..	4.4	..
Child immunization, measles (% of ages 12–23 mos.)	70	90	89
Primary completion rate, total (% of relevant age group)	101	85	88
Gross secondary enrollment, total (% of relevant age group)	82	75	76
Ratio of girls to boys in primary & secondary school (%)	101	104	101
HIV prevalence rate (% of population ages 15–49)	..	..	2.6
Environment			
Forests (1,000 sq. km)	2.4	2.3	2.3
Deforestation (average annual %, 1990–2005)			0.3
Freshwater use (% of internal resources)	..	8.2	..
Access to improved water source (% of total pop.)	92	92	91
Access to improved sanitation facilities (% of total pop.)	100	100	100
Energy use per capita (kilograms of oil equivalent)	4,934	7,578	9,599
Carbon dioxide emissions per capita (metric tons)	13.8	21.4	24.7
Electricity use per capita (kilowatt-hours)	2,679	3,891	5,038
Economy			
GDP ($ billions)	5.1	8.2	18.1
GDP growth (annual %)	1.5	6.1	12.0
GDP implicit price deflator (annual % growth)	15.5	12.9	7.5
Value added in agriculture (% of GDP)	3	1	1
Value added in industry (% of GDP)	47	49	62
Value added in services (% of GDP)	50	49	38
Exports of goods and services (% of GDP)	45	59	65
Imports of goods and services (% of GDP)	29	45	43
Gross capital formation (% of GDP)	13	20	16
Central government revenue (% of GDP)	..	27.1	32.5
Central government cash surplus/deficit (% of GDP)	..	2.0	6.1
States and markets			
Starting a business (days)			43
Stock market capitalization (% of GDP)	13.7	53.1	85.9
Military expenditures (% of GDP)	..	..	..
Fixed-line and mobile subscribers (per 100 people)	13	37	149
Internet users (per 100 people)	0.0	7.7	12.3
Paved roads (% of total)	46	51	..
High-technology exports (% of manufactured exports)	0	1	1
Global links			
Merchandise trade (% of GDP)	60.6	93.0	113.8
Net barter terms of trade (2000 = 100)	100	100	123
Total external debt ($ billions)	..	..	..
Short-term debt ($ billions)	..	..	..
Total debt service (% of exports)	..	..	..
Foreign direct investment, net inflows ($ millions)	109	680	940
Remittances received ($ millions)	3.0	38.0	92.4
Aid ($ millions)	17.8	-1.5	13.0

Tunisia

Middle East & North Africa		**Lower middle income**	
Population (millions)	10	Population growth (%)	1.0
Surface area (1,000 sq. km)	164	National poverty rate (% of pop.)	..
GNI ($ billions)	30.1	GNI per capita ($)	2,970
GNI, PPP ($ billions)	65.7	GNI per capita, PPP ($)	6,490

	1990	2000	2006
People			
Share of poorest 20% in nat'l consumption/income (%)	5.9	6.0	..
Life expectancy at birth (years)	70	73	74
Total fertility (births per woman)	3.5	2.1	2.0
Adolescent fertility (births per 1,000 women 15-19)	..	8	7
Contraceptive prevalence (% of married women 15-49)	50	66	..
Births attended by skilled health staff (% of total)	69	90	..
Under-five mortality rate (per 1,000)	52	31	23
Child malnutrition, underweight (% of under age 5)	8.5	..	..
Child immunization, measles (% of ages 12-23 mos.)	93	95	98
Primary completion rate, total (% of relevant age group)	80	87	99
Gross secondary enrollment, total (% of relevant age group)	45	75	83
Ratio of girls to boys in primary & secondary school (%)	86	100	104
HIV prevalence rate (% of population ages 15-49)	..	..	0.1
Environment			
Forests (1,000 sq. km)	6.4	9.6	10.6
Deforestation (average annual %, 1990-2005)			-3.4
Freshwater use (% of internal resources)	..	62.9	..
Access to improved water source (% of total pop.)	81	90	93
Access to improved sanitation facilities (% of total pop.)	75	83	85
Energy use per capita (kilograms of oil equivalent)	679	794	843
Carbon dioxide emissions per capita (metric tons)	1.6	2.1	2.3
Electricity use per capita (kilowatt-hours)	638	991	1,194
Economy			
GDP ($ billions)	12.3	19.4	30.3
GDP growth (annual %)	7.9	4.7	5.2
GDP implicit price deflator (annual % growth)	4.5	3.2	3.0
Value added in agriculture (% of GDP)	16	12	11
Value added in industry (% of GDP)	30	29	28
Value added in services (% of GDP)	54	59	60
Exports of goods and services (% of GDP)	44	45	54
Imports of goods and services (% of GDP)	51	48	54
Gross capital formation (% of GDP)	27	27	24
Central government revenue (% of GDP)	30.7	29.2	30.1
Central government cash surplus/deficit (% of GDP)	-3.2	-2.7	-2.8
States and markets			
Starting a business (days)			11
Stock market capitalization (% of GDP)	4.3	14.5	14.7
Military expenditures (% of GDP)	2.0	1.7	1.4
Fixed-line and mobile subscribers (per 100 people)	4	11	85
Internet users (per 100 people)	0.0	2.7	12.8
Paved roads (% of total)	76	68	66
High-technology exports (% of manufactured exports)	2	3	4
Global links			
Merchandise trade (% of GDP)	73.5	74.1	87.1
Net barter terms of trade (2000 = 100)	109	100	94
Total external debt ($ billions)	7.7	11.3	18.5
Short-term debt ($ billions)	0.6	1.6	3.3
Total debt service (% of exports)	24.5	20.1	14.4
Foreign direct investment, net inflows ($ billions)	0.1	0.8	3.3
Remittances received ($ billions)	0.6	0.8	1.5
Aid ($ millions)	391	222	432

Turkey

Europe & Central Asia		Upper middle income	
Population (millions)	73	Population growth (%)	1.3
Surface area (1,000 sq. km)	784	National poverty rate (% of pop.)	27
GNI ($ billions)	393.9	GNI per capita ($)	5,400
GNI, PPP ($ billions)	613.7	GNI per capita, PPP ($)	8,410

	1990	2000	2006
People			
Share of poorest 20% in nat'l consumption/income (%)	..	6.0	..
Life expectancy at birth (years)	66	70	71
Total fertility (births per woman)	3.0	2.6	2.2
Adolescent fertility (births per 1,000 women 15–19)	..	51	39
Contraceptive prevalence (% of married women 15–49)	63	64	..
Births attended by skilled health staff (% of total)	..	81	..
Under-five mortality rate (per 1,000)	82	44	26
Child malnutrition, underweight (% of under age 5)	..	7.0	..
Child immunization, measles (% of ages 12–23 mos.)	78	86	98
Primary completion rate, total (% of relevant age group)	90	..	86
Gross secondary enrollment, total (% of relevant age group)	48	78	74
Ratio of girls to boys in primary & secondary school (%)	81	85	89
HIV prevalence rate (% of population ages 15–49)	..	..	0.2
Environment			
Forests (1,000 sq. km)	97	101	102
Deforestation (average annual %, 1990–2005)			-0.3
Freshwater use (% of internal resources)	..	16.5	..
Access to improved water source (% of total pop.)	85	93	96
Access to improved sanitation facilities (% of total pop.)	85	87	88
Energy use per capita (kilograms of oil equivalent)	943	1,142	1,182
Carbon dioxide emissions per capita (metric tons)	2.6	3.3	3.2
Electricity use per capita (kilowatt-hours)	893	1,550	1,898
Economy			
GDP ($ billions)	150.6	199.7	402.7
GDP growth (annual %)	9.3	7.4	6.1
GDP implicit price deflator (annual % growth)	58.3	49.9	11.5
Value added in agriculture (% of GDP)	18	15	10
Value added in industry (% of GDP)	26	24	27
Value added in services (% of GDP)	55	61	63
Exports of goods and services (% of GDP)	13	24	28
Imports of goods and services (% of GDP)	18	32	36
Gross capital formation (% of GDP)	25	25	24
Central government revenue (% of GDP)	..	..	32.9
Central government cash surplus/deficit (% of GDP)	..	..	2.5
States and markets			
Starting a business (days)			6
Stock market capitalization (% of GDP)	12.7	34.9	40.3
Military expenditures (% of GDP)	3.5	5.0	2.9
Fixed-line and mobile subscribers (per 100 people)	12	51	98
Internet users (per 100 people)	0.0	3.7	16.8
Paved roads (% of total)	..	34	..
High-technology exports (% of manufactured exports)	..	..	..
Global links			
Merchandise trade (% of GDP)	23.4	41.2	55.6
Net barter terms of trade (2000 = 100)	109	100	96
Total external debt ($ billions)	49	117	208
Short-term debt ($ billions)	9.5	28.9	42.3
Total debt service (% of exports)	29.4	36.0	33.2
Foreign direct investment, net inflows ($ billions)	0.7	1.0	20.1
Remittances received ($ billions)	3.2	4.6	1.1
Aid ($ billions)	1.2	0.3	0.6

Turkmenistan

Europe & Central Asia | **Lower middle income**

Population (millions)	4.9	Population growth (%)	1.4
Surface area (1,000 sq. km)	488	National poverty rate (% of pop.)	..
GNI ($ billions)	..	GNI per capita ($)	..
GNI, PPP ($ billions)	19.3	GNI per capita, PPP ($)	3,990

	1990	2000	2006
People			
Share of poorest 20% in nat'l consumption/income (%)	10.5	6.1	..
Life expectancy at birth (years)	63	63	63
Total fertility (births per woman)	4.2	2.9	2.6
Adolescent fertility (births per 1,000 women 15-19)	..	17	16
Contraceptive prevalence (% of married women 15-49)	..	62	48
Births attended by skilled health staff (% of total)	..	97	100
Under-five mortality rate (per 1,000)	99	71	51
Child malnutrition, underweight (% of under age 5)	..	..	..
Child immunization, measles (% of ages 12-23 mos.)	76	97	99
Primary completion rate, total (% of relevant age group)	..	..	..
Gross secondary enrollment, total (% of relevant age group)	..	..	..
Ratio of girls to boys in primary & secondary school (%)	..	..	..
HIV prevalence rate (% of population ages 15-49)	..	..	0.1
Environment			
Forests (1,000 sq. km)	41	41	41
Deforestation (average annual %, 1990-2005)			0.00
Freshwater use (% of internal resources)	..	1,760.7	..
Access to improved water source (% of total pop.)	..	71	72
Access to improved sanitation facilities (% of total pop.)	..	62	62
Energy use per capita (kilograms of oil equivalent)	5,353	3,215	3,381
Carbon dioxide emissions per capita (metric tons)	8.7	8.3	8.7
Electricity use per capita (kilowatt-hours)	2,293	1,698	1,731
Economy			
GDP ($ billions)	3.2	2.9	10.5
GDP growth (annual %)	0.7	18.6	..
GDP implicit price deflator (annual % growth)	6.3	9.8	..
Value added in agriculture (% of GDP)	32	24	20
Value added in industry (% of GDP)	30	44	40
Value added in services (% of GDP)	38	31	40
Exports of goods and services (% of GDP)	..	96	72
Imports of goods and services (% of GDP)	..	81	54
Gross capital formation (% of GDP)	40	35	23
Central government revenue (% of GDP)	..	..	..
Central government cash surplus/deficit (% of GDP)	..	..	..
States and markets			
Starting a business (days)			..
Stock market capitalization (% of GDP)	..	..	..
Military expenditures (% of GDP)	..	2.9	..
Fixed-line and mobile subscribers (per 100 people)	6	8	10
Internet users (per 100 people)	0.0	0.1	1.3
Paved roads (% of total)	74	81	..
High-technology exports (% of manufactured exports)	..	5	..
Global links			
Merchandise trade (% of GDP)	..	147.8	88.8
Net barter terms of trade (2000 = 100)	..	..	..
Total external debt ($ billions)	..	2.5	0.9
Short-term debt ($ millions)	..	230.3	151.7
Total debt service (% of exports)	..	..	..
Foreign direct investment, net inflows ($ millions)	..	126.0	730.9
Remittances received ($ billions)	..	..	..
Aid ($ millions)	8.6	31.5	26.2

Uganda

Sub-Saharan Africa		Low income	

Population (millions)	30	Population growth (%)	3.2
Surface area (1,000 sq. km)	241	National poverty rate (% of pop.)	28
GNI ($ billions)	9.0	GNI per capita ($)	300
GNI, PPP ($ billions)	26.3	GNI per capita, PPP ($)	880

	1990	2000	2006
People			
Share of poorest 20% in nat'l consumption/income (%)	6.0	5.7	..
Life expectancy at birth (years)	50	46	51
Total fertility (births per woman)	7.1	6.8	6.7
Adolescent fertility (births per 1,000 women 15–19)	..	180	156
Contraceptive prevalence (% of married women 15–49)	5	23	24
Births attended by skilled health staff (% of total)	38	39	42
Under-five mortality rate (per 1,000)	160	145	134
Child malnutrition, underweight (% of under age 5)	19.7	19.0	..
Child immunization, measles (% of ages 12–23 mos.)	52	61	89
Primary completion rate, total (% of relevant age group)	..	57	54
Gross secondary enrollment, total (% of relevant age group)	11	16	18
Ratio of girls to boys in primary & secondary school (%)	82	93	98
HIV prevalence rate (% of population ages 15–49)	..	..	6.4
Environment			
Forests (1,000 sq. km)	49	41	36
Deforestation (average annual %, 1990–2005)			2.0
Freshwater use (% of internal resources)	..	0.8	..
Access to improved water source (% of total pop.)	44	55	60
Access to improved sanitation facilities (% of total pop.)	42	43	43
Energy use per capita (kilograms of oil equivalent)	..	..	..
Carbon dioxide emissions per capita (metric tons)	0.05	0.06	0.07
Electricity use per capita (kilowatt-hours)	..	..	..
Economy			
GDP ($ billions)	4.3	5.9	9.4
GDP growth (annual %)	6.5	5.6	5.4
GDP implicit price deflator (annual % growth)	44.4	3.8	7.3
Value added in agriculture (% of GDP)	57	37	32
Value added in industry (% of GDP)	11	20	18
Value added in services (% of GDP)	32	42	49
Exports of goods and services (% of GDP)	7	11	15
Imports of goods and services (% of GDP)	19	23	29
Gross capital formation (% of GDP)	13	20	23
Central government revenue (% of GDP)	..	11.3	13.5
Central government cash surplus/deficit (% of GDP)	..	-2.0	-2.0
States and markets			
Starting a business (days)			28
Stock market capitalization (% of GDP)	..	0.6	1.2
Military expenditures (% of GDP)	3.5	2.3	2.1
Fixed-line and mobile subscribers (per 100 people)	0	1	7
Internet users (per 100 people)	0.0	0.2	2.5
Paved roads (% of total)	..	..	..
High-technology exports (% of manufactured exports)	..	4	34
Global links			
Merchandise trade (% of GDP)	10.2	33.7	37.2
Net barter terms of trade (2000 = 100)	146	100	102
Total external debt ($ billions)	2.6	3.5	1.3
Short-term debt ($ millions)	146	129	148
Total debt service (% of exports)	81.4	7.8	4.8
Foreign direct investment, net inflows ($ millions)	-5.9	160.7	391.6
Remittances received ($ millions)	..	238.0	814.3
Aid ($ billions)	0.7	0.8	1.6

Ukraine

Europe & Central Asia		Lower middle income	

Population (millions)	47	Population growth (%)	-0.7
Surface area (1,000 sq. km)	604	National poverty rate (% of pop.)	20
GNI ($ billions)	90.7	GNI per capita ($)	1,940
GNI, PPP ($ billions)	286.0	GNI per capita, PPP ($)	6,110

	1990	2000	2006
People			
Share of poorest 20% in nat'l consumption/income (%)	9.4	8.9	9.0
Life expectancy at birth (years)	70	68	68
Total fertility (births per woman)	1.8	1.1	1.3
Adolescent fertility (births per 1,000 women 15-19)	..	35	28
Contraceptive prevalence (% of married women 15-49)	..	72	66
Births attended by skilled health staff (% of total)	..	100	100
Under-five mortality rate (per 1,000)	25	23	24
Child malnutrition, underweight (% of under age 5)	..	4.1	..
Child immunization, measles (% of ages 12-23 mos.)	90	99	98
Primary completion rate, total (% of relevant age group)	94	92	105
Gross secondary enrollment, total (% of relevant age group)	94	99	93
Ratio of girls to boys in primary & secondary school (%)	..	100	99
HIV prevalence rate (% of population ages 15-49)	..	..	1.4
Environment			
Forests (1,000 sq. km)	93	95	96
Deforestation (average annual %, 1990-2005)			-0.2
Freshwater use (% of internal resources)	..	70.7	..
Access to improved water source (% of total pop.)	..	96	96
Access to improved sanitation facilities (% of total pop.)	..	96	96
Energy use per capita (kilograms of oil equivalent)	4,851	2,727	3,041
Carbon dioxide emissions per capita (metric tons)	13.2	6.3	6.9
Electricity use per capita (kilowatt-hours)	4,782	2,773	3,246
Economy			
GDP ($ billions)	81.5	31.3	106.5
GDP growth (annual %)	-6.3	5.9	7.1
GDP implicit price deflator (annual % growth)	16.3	23.1	13.7
Value added in agriculture (% of GDP)	26	17	9
Value added in industry (% of GDP)	45	36	35
Value added in services (% of GDP)	30	47	57
Exports of goods and services (% of GDP)	28	62	47
Imports of goods and services (% of GDP)	29	57	50
Gross capital formation (% of GDP)	27	20	24
Central government revenue (% of GDP)	..	26.8	36.6
Central government cash surplus/deficit (% of GDP)	..	-0.6	-1.0
States and markets			
Starting a business (days)			27
Stock market capitalization (% of GDP)	..	6.0	40.3
Military expenditures (% of GDP)	..	3.6	2.1
Fixed-line and mobile subscribers (per 100 people)	14	23	131
Internet users (per 100 people)	0.0	0.7	11.9
Paved roads (% of total)	94	97	97
High-technology exports (% of manufactured exports)	..	5	3
Global links			
Merchandise trade (% of GDP)	..	91.3	78.3
Net barter terms of trade (2000 = 100)	..	..	..
Total external debt ($ billions)	0.6	12.2	49.9
Short-term debt ($ billions)	0.1	0.4	15.4
Total debt service (% of exports)	..	18.6	18.1
Foreign direct investment, net inflows ($ billions)	0.2	0.6	5.6
Remittances received ($ millions)	..	33.0	829.0
Aid ($ millions)	289	541	484

United Arab Emirates

High income

Population (millions)	4.2	Population growth (%)	3.5
Surface area (1,000 sq. km)	84	National poverty rate (% of pop.)	..
GNI ($ billions)	103.5	GNI per capita ($)	26,210
GNI, PPP ($ billions)	123.1	GNI per capita, PPP ($)	31,190

	1990	2000	2006
People			
Share of poorest 20% in nat'l consumption/income (%)	..	..	..
Life expectancy at birth (years)	73	78	79
Total fertility (births per woman)	4.3	3.0	2.3
Adolescent fertility (births per 1,000 women 15-19)	..	28	19
Contraceptive prevalence (% of married women 15-49)	..	..	..
Births attended by skilled health staff (% of total)	..	..	..
Under-five mortality rate (per 1,000)	15	10	8
Child malnutrition, underweight (% of under age 5)	..	..	..
Child immunization, measles (% of ages 12-23 mos.)	80	94	92
Primary completion rate, total (% of relevant age group)	105	80	100
Gross secondary enrollment, total (% of relevant age group)	68	75	90
Ratio of girls to boys in primary & secondary school (%)	104	100	101
HIV prevalence rate (% of population ages 15-49)	..	..	0.2
Environment			
Forests (1,000 sq. km)	2.5	3.1	3.1
Deforestation (average annual %, 1990-2005)			-1.6
Freshwater use (% of internal resources)	..	1,150.0	..
Access to improved water source (% of total pop.)	100	100	100
Access to improved sanitation facilities (% of total pop.)	97	98	98
Energy use per capita (kilograms of oil equivalent)	12,716	11,023	11,436
Carbon dioxide emissions per capita (metric tons)	30.8	49.1	37.8
Electricity use per capita (kilowatt-hours)	8,766	11,886	13,708
Economy			
GDP ($ billions)	33.7	70.6	129.7
GDP growth (annual %)	17.5	5.0	8.5
GDP implicit price deflator (annual % growth)	4.3	21.8	14.3
Value added in agriculture (% of GDP)	2	4	2
Value added in industry (% of GDP)	64	56	56
Value added in services (% of GDP)	35	41	42
Exports of goods and services (% of GDP)	66	73	94
Imports of goods and services (% of GDP)	41	55	76
Gross capital formation (% of GDP)	20	23	24
Central government revenue (% of GDP)	..	10.0	..
Central government cash surplus/deficit (% of GDP)	..	0.1	..
States and markets			
Starting a business (days)			62
Stock market capitalization (% of GDP)	..	8.1	173.9
Military expenditures (% of GDP)	6.2	3.4	2.0
Fixed-line and mobile subscribers (per 100 people)	24	75	161
Internet users (per 100 people)	0.0	23.6	40.2
Paved roads (% of total)	94	100	..
High-technology exports (% of manufactured exports)	0	1	..
Global links			
Merchandise trade (% of GDP)	103.2	120.2	155.7
Net barter terms of trade (2000 = 100)	..	100	153
Total external debt ($ billions)	..	..	..
Short-term debt ($ billions)	..	..	..
Total debt service (% of exports)	..	..	..
Foreign direct investment, net inflows ($ billions)	..	..	..
Remittances received ($ billions)	..	..	..
Aid ($ millions)	3.5	3.2	..

United Kingdom

Population (millions)	61	Population growth (%)	0.5
Surface area (1,000 sq. km)	244	National poverty rate (% of pop.)	..
GNI ($ billions)	2,455.7	GNI per capita ($)	40,560
GNI, PPP ($ billions)	2,037.2	GNI per capita, PPP ($)	33,650

	1990	2000	2006
People			
Share of poorest 20% in nat'l consumption/income (%)	..	6.1	..
Life expectancy at birth (years)	76	78	79
Total fertility (births per woman)	1.8	1.6	1.9
Adolescent fertility (births per 1,000 women 15–19)	..	28	24
Contraceptive prevalence (% of married women 15–49)	..	83	..
Births attended by skilled health staff (% of total)	..	99	..
Under-five mortality rate (per 1,000)	10	7	6
Child malnutrition, underweight (% of under age 5)	..	..	..
Child immunization, measles (% of ages 12–23 mos.)	87	88	85
Primary completion rate, total (% of relevant age group)	..	..	..
Gross secondary enrollment, total (% of relevant age group)	87	102	105
Ratio of girls to boys in primary & secondary school (%)	102	100	101
HIV prevalence rate (% of population ages 15–49)	..	..	0.2
Environment			
Forests (1,000 sq. km)	26	28	28
Deforestation (average annual %, 1990–2005)			-0.6
Freshwater use (% of internal resources)	..	6.6	..
Access to improved water source (% of total pop.)	100	100	100
Access to improved sanitation facilities (% of total pop.)	..		
Energy use per capita (kilograms of oil equivalent)	3,686	3,914	3,884
Carbon dioxide emissions per capita (metric tons)	10.1	9.7	9.8
Electricity use per capita (kilowatt-hours)	5,327	6,027	6,253
Economy			
GDP ($ billions)	991.1	1,442.3	2,377.0
GDP growth (annual %)	0.7	3.8	2.8
GDP implicit price deflator (annual % growth)	7.6	1.3	2.4
Value added in agriculture (% of GDP)	2	1	1
Value added in industry (% of GDP)	35	28	24
Value added in services (% of GDP)	63	71	75
Exports of goods and services (% of GDP)	24	28	29
Imports of goods and services (% of GDP)	27	30	33
Gross capital formation (% of GDP)	20	17	18
Central government revenue (% of GDP)	..	37.9	38.8
Central government cash surplus/deficit (% of GDP)	..	1.7	-2.8
States and markets			
Starting a business (days)			13
Stock market capitalization (% of GDP)	85.7	178.7	159.6
Military expenditures (% of GDP)	3.9	2.4	2.6
Fixed-line and mobile subscribers (per 100 people)	46	132	171
Internet users (per 100 people)	0.1	26.4	55.4
Paved roads (% of total)	100	100	100
High-technology exports (% of manufactured exports)	24	30	34
Global links			
Merchandise trade (% of GDP)	41.2	43.9	44.9
Net barter terms of trade (2000 = 100)	101	100	104
Total external debt ($ billions)	..	..	..
Short-term debt ($ billions)	..	..	..
Total debt service (% of exports)	..	..	..
Foreign direct investment, net inflows ($ billions)	34	122	140
Remittances received ($ billions)	2.1	3.6	7.0
Aid ($ billions)	..	..	..

United States

Population (millions)	299	Population growth (%)	1.0
Surface area (1,000 sq. km)	9,632	National poverty rate (% of pop.)	..
GNI ($ billions)	13,386.9	GNI per capita ($)	44,710
GNI, PPP ($ billions)	13,195.7	GNI per capita, PPP ($)	44,070

	1990	2000	2006
People			
Share of poorest 20% in nat'l consumption/income (%)	..	5.4	..
Life expectancy at birth (years)	75	77	78
Total fertility (births per woman)	2.1	2.1	2.1
Adolescent fertility (births per 1,000 women 15–19)	..	47	43
Contraceptive prevalence (% of married women 15–49)	71	64	..
Births attended by skilled health staff (% of total)	99	99	..
Under-five mortality rate (per 1,000)	11	8	8
Child malnutrition, underweight (% of under age 5)	..	1.1	..
Child immunization, measles (% of ages 12–23 mos.)	90	91	93
Primary completion rate, total (% of relevant age group)	..	..	..
Gross secondary enrollment, total (% of relevant age group)	92	94	94
Ratio of girls to boys in primary & secondary school (%)	100	99	100
HIV prevalence rate (% of population ages 15–49)	..	..	0.6
Environment			
Forests (1,000 sq. km)	2,986	3,023	3,031
Deforestation (average annual %, 1990–2005)			–0.1
Freshwater use (% of internal resources)	..	17.1	..
Access to improved water source (% of total pop.)	100	100	100
Access to improved sanitation facilities (% of total pop.)	100	100	100
Energy use per capita (kilograms of oil equivalent)	7,721	8,173	7,893
Carbon dioxide emissions per capita (metric tons)	19.3	21.1	20.6
Electricity use per capita (kilowatt-hours)	11,713	13,668	13,648
Economy			
GDP ($ billions)	5,757.2	9,764.8	13,163.9
GDP growth (annual %)	1.9	3.7	2.9
GDP implicit price deflator (annual % growth)	3.9	2.2	3.2
Value added in agriculture (% of GDP)	2	1	1
Value added in industry (% of GDP)	28	24	23
Value added in services (% of GDP)	70	75	76
Exports of goods and services (% of GDP)	10	11	11
Imports of goods and services (% of GDP)	11	15	16
Gross capital formation (% of GDP)	18	20	19
Central government revenue (% of GDP)	..	20.4	19.3
Central government cash surplus/deficit (% of GDP)	..	0.5	–2.0
States and markets			
Starting a business (days)			6
Stock market capitalization (% of GDP)	53.2	154.7	147.6
Military expenditures (% of GDP)	5.3	3.1	4.1
Fixed-line and mobile subscribers (per 100 people)	57	107	135
Internet users (per 100 people)	0.8	43.9	69.5
Paved roads (% of total)	58	59	65
High-technology exports (% of manufactured exports)	33	34	30
Global links			
Merchandise trade (% of GDP)	15.8	20.9	22.5
Net barter terms of trade (2000 = 100)	101	100	96
Total external debt ($ billions)	..	..	..
Short-term debt ($ billions)	..	..	..
Total debt service (% of exports)	..	..	..
Foreign direct investment, net inflows ($ billions)	48	321	181
Remittances received ($ billions)	1.2	2.8	2.9
Aid ($ billions)	..	..	..

Uruguay

Latin America & Caribbean   **Upper middle income**

Population (millions)	3.3	Population growth (%)		0.3
Surface area (1,000 sq. km)	176	National poverty rate (% of pop.)		..
GNI ($ billions)	17.6	GNI per capita ($)		5,310
GNI, PPP ($ billions)	32.9	GNI per capita, PPP ($)		9,940

	1990	2000	2006
People			
Share of poorest 20% in nat'l consumption/income (%)	5.4	4.8	4.5
Life expectancy at birth (years)	73	75	76
Total fertility (births per woman)	2.5	2.2	2.0
Adolescent fertility (births per 1,000 women 15–19)	..	66	62
Contraceptive prevalence (% of married women 15–49)	..	..	..
Births attended by skilled health staff (% of total)	..	99	99
Under-five mortality rate (per 1,000)	23	16	12
Child malnutrition, underweight (% of under age 5)	..	5.4	6.0
Child immunization, measles (% of ages 12–23 mos.)	97	89	94
Primary completion rate, total (% of relevant age group)	93	97	93
Gross secondary enrollment, total (% of relevant age group)	84	98	107
Ratio of girls to boys in primary & secondary school (%)	..	105	106
HIV prevalence rate (% of population ages 15–49)	..	..	0.5
Environment			
Forests (1,000 sq. km)	9.1	14.1	15.1
Deforestation (average annual %, 1990–2005)			–3.5
Freshwater use (% of internal resources)	..	5.3	..
Access to improved water source (% of total pop.)	100	100	100
Access to improved sanitation facilities (% of total pop.)	100	100	100
Energy use per capita (kilograms of oil equivalent)	725	932	875
Carbon dioxide emissions per capita (metric tons)	1.3	1.5	1.7
Electricity use per capita (kilowatt-hours)	1,246	1,990	2,007
Economy			
GDP ($ billions)	9.3	20.7	19.3
GDP growth (annual %)	0.3	–1.4	7.0
GDP implicit price deflator (annual % growth)	106.8	4.0	6.8
Value added in agriculture (% of GDP)	9	6	9
Value added in industry (% of GDP)	35	27	32
Value added in services (% of GDP)	56	67	58
Exports of goods and services (% of GDP)	24	19	30
Imports of goods and services (% of GDP)	18	21	30
Gross capital formation (% of GDP)	12	14	16
Central government revenue (% of GDP)	23.8	28.0	27.7
Central government cash surplus/deficit (% of GDP)	0.5	–3.4	–0.9
States and markets			
Starting a business (days)			44
Stock market capitalization (% of GDP)	..	0.8	0.6
Military expenditures (% of GDP)	3.1	1.6	1.2
Fixed-line and mobile subscribers (per 100 people)	13	41	100
Internet users (per 100 people)	0.0	10.6	22.8
Paved roads (% of total)	74	90	10
High-technology exports (% of manufactured exports)	0	2	3
Global links			
Merchandise trade (% of GDP)	32.7	27.9	45.1
Net barter terms of trade (2000 = 100)	116	100	89
Total external debt ($ billions)	4.4	8.1	9.8
Short-term debt ($ billions)	1.2	1.9	2.2
Total debt service (% of exports)	40.8	28.3	87.8
Foreign direct investment, net inflows ($ billions)	0.0	0.3	1.3
Remittances received ($ millions)	..	36.0	88.8
Aid ($ millions)	52	17	21

Uzbekistan

Europe & Central Asia		Low income
Population (millions)	27	Population growth (%)	1.4
Surface area (1,000 sq. km)	447	National poverty rate (% of pop.)	28
GNI ($ billions)	16.2	GNI per capita ($)	610
GNI, PPP ($ billions)	58.1	GNI per capita, PPP ($)	2,190

	1990	2000	2006
People			
Share of poorest 20% in nat'l consumption/income (%)	10.9	7.9	..
Life expectancy at birth (years)	69	68	67
Total fertility (births per woman)	4.1	2.6	2.4
Adolescent fertility (births per 1,000 women 15–19)	..	39	34
Contraceptive prevalence (% of married women 15–49)	..	67	65
Births attended by skilled health staff (% of total)	..	96	100
Under-five mortality rate (per 1,000)	74	62	43
Child malnutrition, underweight (% of under age 5)	..	..	..
Child immunization, measles (% of ages 12–23 mos.)	84	99	95
Primary completion rate, total (% of relevant age group)	..	99	..
Gross secondary enrollment, total (% of relevant age group)	99	95	100
Ratio of girls to boys in primary & secondary school (%)	94	98	97
HIV prevalence rate (% of population ages 15–49)	..	..	0.2
Environment			
Forests (1,000 sq. km)	30	32	33
Deforestation (average annual %, 1990–2005)			-0.5
Freshwater use (% of internal resources)	..	357.9	..
Access to improved water source (% of total pop.)	94	87	82
Access to improved sanitation facilities (% of total pop.)	51	61	67
Energy use per capita (kilograms of oil equivalent)	2,262	2,044	1,798
Carbon dioxide emissions per capita (metric tons)	6.3	5.2	5.3
Electricity use per capita (kilowatt-hours)	2,383	1,780	1,659
Economy			
GDP ($ billions)	13.4	13.8	17.2
GDP growth (annual %)	1.6	3.8	7.3
GDP implicit price deflator (annual % growth)	4.0	47.3	21.5
Value added in agriculture (% of GDP)	33	34	26
Value added in industry (% of GDP)	33	23	27
Value added in services (% of GDP)	34	43	46
Exports of goods and services (% of GDP)	29	25	38
Imports of goods and services (% of GDP)	48	22	26
Gross capital formation (% of GDP)	32	16	22
Central government revenue (% of GDP)	..	..	..
Central government cash surplus/deficit (% of GDP)	..	..	..
States and markets			
Starting a business (days)			15
Stock market capitalization (% of GDP)	..	0.2	4.2
Military expenditures (% of GDP)	..	0.8	..
Fixed-line and mobile subscribers (per 100 people)	7	7	10
Internet users (per 100 people)	0.0	0.5	6.4
Paved roads (% of total)	79	87	..
High-technology exports (% of manufactured exports)	..	..	..
Global links			
Merchandise trade (% of GDP)	..	40.1	56.0
Net barter terms of trade (2000 = 100)	..	..	..
Total external debt ($ billions)	0.1	4.6	3.9
Short-term debt ($ millions)	0.0	282.2	166.5
Total debt service (% of exports)	..	..	..
Foreign direct investment, net inflows ($ millions)	9.0	75.0	164.0
Remittances received ($ billions)	..	..	..
Aid ($ millions)	62	186	149

Vanuatu

East Asia & Pacific   **Lower middle income**

Population (thousands)	221	Population growth (%)	2.5
Surface area (1,000 sq. km)	12	National poverty rate (% of pop.)	..
GNI ($ millions)	373	GNI per capita ($)	1,690
GNI, PPP ($ millions)	768	GNI per capita, PPP ($)	3,480

	1990	2000	2006
People			
Share of poorest 20% in nat'l consumption/income (%)	..	..	..
Life expectancy at birth (years)	63	68	70
Total fertility (births per woman)	4.9	4.3	3.8
Adolescent fertility (births per 1,000 women 15–19)	..	56	46
Contraceptive prevalence (% of married women 15–49)	15	28	..
Births attended by skilled health staff (% of total)	..	88	..
Under-five mortality rate (per 1,000)	62	48	36
Child malnutrition, underweight (% of under age 5)	..	..	..
Child immunization, measles (% of ages 12–23 mos.)	66	94	99
Primary completion rate, total (% of relevant age group)	..	86	84
Gross secondary enrollment, total (% of relevant age group)	18	34	40
Ratio of girls to boys in primary & secondary school (%)	93	101	95
HIV prevalence rate (% of population ages 15–49)	..	..	..
Environment			
Forests (1,000 sq. km)	4.4	4.4	4.4
Deforestation (average annual %, 1990–2005)			0.00
Freshwater use (% of internal resources)	..	..	..
Access to improved water source (% of total pop.)	60	59	60
Access to improved sanitation facilities (% of total pop.)	..	50	50
Energy use per capita (kilograms of oil equivalent)	..	..	..
Carbon dioxide emissions per capita (metric tons)	0.4	0.4	0.4
Electricity use per capita (kilowatt-hours)	..	..	..
Economy			
GDP ($ millions)	151	245	388
GDP growth (annual %)	0.0	2.7	7.2
GDP implicit price deflator (annual % growth)	8.2	1.2	0.0
Value added in agriculture (% of GDP)	21	16	16
Value added in industry (% of GDP)	12	9	9
Value added in services (% of GDP)	67	75	82
Exports of goods and services (% of GDP)	49	44	40
Imports of goods and services (% of GDP)	77	59	60
Gross capital formation (% of GDP)	35	20	..
Central government revenue (% of GDP)	27.5	20.7	..
Central government cash surplus/deficit (% of GDP)	–8.2	–0.8	..
States and markets			
Starting a business (days)			39
Stock market capitalization (% of GDP)	..	..	..
Military expenditures (% of GDP)	..	..	..
Fixed-line and mobile subscribers (per 100 people)	2	4	9
Internet users (per 100 people)	0.0	2.1	3.5
Paved roads (% of total)	22	24	..
High-technology exports (% of manufactured exports)	20	1	..
Global links			
Merchandise trade (% of GDP)	76.3	46.2	49.0
Net barter terms of trade (2000 = 100)	..	..	..
Total external debt ($ millions)	38	74	86
Short-term debt ($ millions)	9.6	1.4	14.1
Total debt service (% of exports)	2.1	1.0	1.7
Foreign direct investment, net inflows ($ millions)	13	20	43
Remittances received ($ millions)	8.0	35.0	11.3
Aid ($ millions)	50	46	49

Venezuela, RB

Latin America & Caribbean		Upper middle income	
Population (millions)	27	Population growth (%)	1.7
Surface area (1,000 sq. km)	912	National poverty rate (% of pop.)	..
GNI ($ billions)	164.0	GNI per capita ($)	6,070
GNI, PPP ($ billions)	296.4	GNI per capita, PPP ($)	10,970

	1990	2000	2006
People			
Share of poorest 20% in nat'l consumption/income (%)	4.8	3.0	..
Life expectancy at birth (years)	71	73	74
Total fertility (births per woman)	3.4	2.8	2.6
Adolescent fertility (births per 1,000 women 15–19)	..	93	90
Contraceptive prevalence (% of married women 15–49)	..	77	..
Births attended by skilled health staff (% of total)	..	94	..
Under-five mortality rate (per 1,000)	33	25	21
Child malnutrition, underweight (% of under age 5)	..	..	..
Child immunization, measles (% of ages 12–23 mos.)	61	84	55
Primary completion rate, total (% of relevant age group)	79	83	96
Gross secondary enrollment, total (% of relevant age group)	34	59	78
Ratio of girls to boys in primary & secondary school (%)	105	105	103
HIV prevalence rate (% of population ages 15–49)	..	..	0.7
Environment			
Forests (1,000 sq. km)	520	492	477
Deforestation (average annual %, 1990–2005)			0.6
Freshwater use (% of internal resources)	..	1.2	..
Access to improved water source (% of total pop.)	..	83	83
Access to improved sanitation facilities (% of total pop.)	..	68	68
Energy use per capita (kilograms of oil equivalent)	2,224	2,333	2,293
Carbon dioxide emissions per capita (metric tons)	5.9	6.7	6.6
Electricity use per capita (kilowatt-hours)	2,463	2,654	2,848
Economy			
GDP ($ billions)	47.0	117.1	181.9
GDP growth (annual %)	6.5	3.7	10.3
GDP implicit price deflator (annual % growth)	41.7	29.5	16.9
Value added in agriculture (% of GDP)	5	4	4
Value added in industry (% of GDP)	61	50	55
Value added in services (% of GDP)	34	46	40
Exports of goods and services (% of GDP)	39	30	37
Imports of goods and services (% of GDP)	20	18	21
Gross capital formation (% of GDP)	10	24	25
Central government revenue (% of GDP)	24.5	21.2	28.4
Central government cash surplus/deficit (% of GDP)	3.0	-1.2	2.2
States and markets			
Starting a business (days)			141
Stock market capitalization (% of GDP)	17.8	6.9	4.5
Military expenditures (% of GDP)	1.9	1.3	1.1
Fixed-line and mobile subscribers (per 100 people)	8	33	85
Internet users (per 100 people)	0.0	3.4	15.3
Paved roads (% of total)	36	34	..
High-technology exports (% of manufactured exports)	4	3	2
Global links			
Merchandise trade (% of GDP)	52.8	42.5	54.3
Net barter terms of trade (2000 = 100)	90	100	184
Total external debt ($ billions)	33	42	45
Short-term debt ($ billions)	2.0	8.2	11.8
Total debt service (% of exports)	23.3	16.7	13.3
Foreign direct investment, net inflows ($ billions)	0.5	4.7	-0.5
Remittances received ($ millions)	1.0	17.0	165.0
Aid ($ millions)	76	76	58

Vietnam

Low income

Population (millions)	84	Population growth (%)	1.2
Surface area (1,000 sq. km)	329	National poverty rate (% of pop.)	29
GNI ($ billions)	58.5	GNI per capita ($)	700
GNI, PPP ($ billions)	194.4	GNI per capita, PPP ($)	2,310

	1990	2000	2006
People			
Share of poorest 20% in nat'l consumption/income (%)	..	7.2	7.1
Life expectancy at birth (years)	65	69	71
Total fertility (births per woman)	3.6	1.9	2.1
Adolescent fertility (births per 1,000 women 15–19)	..	23	18
Contraceptive prevalence (% of married women 15–49)	53	74	76
Births attended by skilled health staff (% of total)	..	68	88
Under-five mortality rate (per 1,000)	53	30	17
Child malnutrition, underweight (% of under age 5)	..	26.7	..
Child immunization, measles (% of ages 12–23 mos.)	88	97	93
Primary completion rate, total (% of relevant age group)	..	96	92
Gross secondary enrollment, total (% of relevant age group)	32	65	76
Ratio of girls to boys in primary & secondary school (%)	..	93	97
HIV prevalence rate (% of population ages 15–49)	..	..	0.5
Environment			
Forests (1,000 sq. km)	94	117	129
Deforestation (average annual %, 1990–2005)			-2.2
Freshwater use (% of internal resources)	..	19.5	..
Access to improved water source (% of total pop.)	65	78	85
Access to improved sanitation facilities (% of total pop.)	36	53	61
Energy use per capita (kilograms of oil equivalent)	367	482	617
Carbon dioxide emissions per capita (metric tons)	0.3	0.7	1.2
Electricity use per capita (kilowatt-hours)	98	295	573
Economy			
GDP ($ billions)	6.5	31.2	61.0
GDP growth (annual %)	5.1	6.8	8.2
GDP implicit price deflator (annual % growth)	42.1	3.4	7.3
Value added in agriculture (% of GDP)	39	25	20
Value added in industry (% of GDP)	23	37	42
Value added in services (% of GDP)	39	39	38
Exports of goods and services (% of GDP)	36	55	73
Imports of goods and services (% of GDP)	45	57	77
Gross capital formation (% of GDP)	13	30	36
Central government revenue (% of GDP)	..	..	..
Central government cash surplus/deficit (% of GDP)	..	..	..
States and markets			
Starting a business (days)			50
Stock market capitalization (% of GDP)	..	..	14.9
Military expenditures (% of GDP)	7.9	..	..
Fixed-line and mobile subscribers (per 100 people)	0	4	31
Internet users (per 100 people)	0.0	0.3	17.5
Paved roads (% of total)	24	25	..
High-technology exports (% of manufactured exports)	..	11	5
Global links			
Merchandise trade (% of GDP)	79.7	96.6	137.7
Net barter terms of trade (2000 = 100)	..	100	97
Total external debt ($ billions)	23	13	20
Short-term debt ($ billions)	1.8	0.9	2.5
Total debt service (% of exports)	..	7.5	2.6
Foreign direct investment, net inflows ($ billions)	0.2	1.3	2.3
Remittances received ($ billions)	..	2.0	4.8
Aid ($ billions)	0.2	1.7	1.8

Virgin Islands (U.S.)

High income

Population (thousands)	109	Population growth (%)	-0.1
Surface area (sq. km)	350	National poverty rate (% of pop.)	..
GNI ($ billions)	..	GNI per capita ($)	..
GNI, PPP ($ billions)	..	GNI per capita, PPP ($)	..

	1990	2000	2006
People			
Share of poorest 20% in nat'l consumption/income (%)	..	..	..
Life expectancy at birth (years)	74	78	79
Total fertility (births per woman)	2.6	2.4	2.2
Adolescent fertility (births per 1,000 women 15–19)	..	43	32
Contraceptive prevalence (% of married women 15–49)	..	..	..
Births attended by skilled health staff (% of total)	..	98	..
Under-five mortality rate (per 1,000)	..	..	..
Child malnutrition, underweight (% of under age 5)	..	..	..
Child immunization, measles (% of ages 12–23 mos.)	..	..	..
Primary completion rate, total (% of relevant age group)	..	..	..
Gross secondary enrollment, total (% of relevant age group)	..	..	..
Ratio of girls to boys in primary & secondary school (%)	..	..	..
HIV prevalence rate (% of population ages 15–49)	..	..	..
Environment			
Forests (sq. km)	120	100	100
Deforestation (average annual %, 1990–2005)			1.2
Freshwater use (% of internal resources)	..	..	..
Access to improved water source (% of total pop.)	..	..	..
Access to improved sanitation facilities (% of total pop.)	..	..	..
Energy use per capita (kilograms of oil equivalent)	..	..	..
Carbon dioxide emissions per capita (metric tons)	81.03	111.57	..
Electricity use per capita (kilowatt-hours)	..	..	..
Economy			
GDP ($ billions)	1.6	..	..
GDP growth (annual %)	7.1	..	..
GDP implicit price deflator (annual % growth)	4.1	..	..
Value added in agriculture (% of GDP)	..	..	..
Value added in industry (% of GDP)	..	..	..
Value added in services (% of GDP)	..	..	..
Exports of goods and services (% of GDP)	..	..	..
Imports of goods and services (% of GDP)	..	..	..
Gross capital formation (% of GDP)	..	..	..
Central government revenue (% of GDP)	..	..	..
Central government cash surplus/deficit (% of GDP)	..	..	..
States and markets			
Starting a business (days)			..
Stock market capitalization (% of GDP)	..	..	..
Military expenditures (% of GDP)			
Fixed-line and mobile subscribers (per 100 people)	45	95	140
Internet users (per 100 people)	0.0	13.8	27.6
Paved roads (% of total)	..	..	..
High-technology exports (% of manufactured exports)	..	..	..
Global links			
Merchandise trade (% of GDP)	..	..	..
Net barter terms of trade (2000 = 100)	..	..	..
Total external debt ($ billions)	..	..	..
Short-term debt ($ billions)	..	..	..
Total debt service (% of exports)	..	..	..
Foreign direct investment, net inflows ($ billions)	..	..	..
Remittances received ($ billions)	..	..	..
Aid ($ billions)	..	..	..

West Bank and Gaza

Middle East & North Africa		Lower middle income	
Population (millions)	3.8	Population growth (%)	4.0
Surface area (1,000 sq. km)	6.0	National poverty rate (% of pop.)	..
GNI ($ billions)	4.5	GNI per capita ($)	1,230
GNI, PPP ($ billions)	14.0	GNI per capita, PPP ($)	3,720

	1990	2000	2006
People			
Share of poorest 20% in nat'l consumption/income (%)	..	..	..
Life expectancy at birth (years)	69	72	73
Total fertility (births per woman)	6.3	5.1	4.6
Adolescent fertility (births per 1,000 women 15–19)	..	99	82
Contraceptive prevalence (% of married women 15–49)	..	..	50
Births attended by skilled health staff (% of total)	..	97	99
Under-five mortality rate (per 1,000)	40	27	22
Child malnutrition, underweight (% of under age 5)	..	..	..
Child immunization, measles (% of ages 12–23 mos.)	..	..	..
Primary completion rate, total (% of relevant age group)	..	103	89
Gross secondary enrollment, total (% of relevant age group)	..	82	94
Ratio of girls to boys in primary & secondary school (%)	..	103	104
HIV prevalence rate (% of population ages 15–49)	..	..	..
Environment			
Forests (sq. km)	90	90	90
Deforestation (average annual %, 1990–2005)			0.00
Freshwater use (% of internal resources)	..	..	..
Access to improved water source (% of total pop.)	..	92	92
Access to improved sanitation facilities (% of total pop.)	..	73	73
Energy use per capita (kilograms of oil equivalent)	..	..	..
Carbon dioxide emissions per capita (metric tons)	..	..	..
Electricity use per capita (kilowatt-hours)	..	..	..
Economy			
GDP ($ millions)	..	4,113	4,059
GDP growth (annual %)	..	–5.6	1.4
GDP implicit price deflator (annual % growth)	..	2.9	–0.3
Value added in agriculture (% of GDP)	..	..	..
Value added in industry (% of GDP)	..	..	..
Value added in services (% of GDP)	..	..	..
Exports of goods and services (% of GDP)	..	16	16
Imports of goods and services (% of GDP)	..	71	70
Gross capital formation (% of GDP)	..	33	27
Central government revenue (% of GDP)	..	..	..
Central government cash surplus/deficit (% of GDP)	..	..	..
States and markets			
Starting a business (days)			92
Stock market capitalization (% of GDP)	..	18.6	67.2
Military expenditures (% of GDP)	..	..	..
Fixed-line and mobile subscribers (per 100 people)	3	15	31
Internet users (per 100 people)	0.0	1.2	7.0
Paved roads (% of total)	..	100	100
High-technology exports (% of manufactured exports)	..	..	..
Global links			
Merchandise trade (% of GDP)	..	..	..
Net barter terms of trade (2000 = 100)	..	..	..
Total external debt ($ billions)	..	..	..
Short-term debt ($ billions)	..	..	..
Total debt service (% of exports)	..	..	..
Foreign direct investment, net inflows ($ billions)	..	..	..
Remittances received ($ millions)	..	858.8	598.0
Aid ($ billions)	..	0.6	1.4

Yemen, Rep.

Middle East & North Africa		Low income

Population (millions)	22	Population growth (%)	3.0
Surface area (1,000 sq. km)	528	National poverty rate (% of pop.)	..
GNI ($ billions)	16.4	GNI per capita ($)	760
GNI, PPP ($ billions)	45.5	GNI per capita, PPP ($)	2,090

	1990	2000	2006
People			
Share of poorest 20% in nat'l consumption/income (%)	6.1	7.4	7.2
Life expectancy at birth (years)	54	59	62
Total fertility (births per woman)	8.0	6.3	5.6
Adolescent fertility (births per 1,000 women 15–19)	..	90	73
Contraceptive prevalence (% of married women 15–49)	10	..	..
Births attended by skilled health staff (% of total)	16	..	..
Under-five mortality rate (per 1,000)	139	110	100
Child malnutrition, underweight (% of under age 5)	..	..	..
Child immunization, measles (% of ages 12–23 mos.)	69	71	80
Primary completion rate, total (% of relevant age group)	..	55	60
Gross secondary enrollment, total (% of relevant age group)	..	43	46
Ratio of girls to boys in primary & secondary school (%)	..	56	66
HIV prevalence rate (% of population ages 15–49)	..	..	0.2
Environment			
Forests (1,000 sq. km)	5.5	5.5	5.5
Deforestation (average annual %, 1990–2005)			0.00
Freshwater use (% of internal resources)	..	161.7	..
Access to improved water source (% of total pop.)	71	69	67
Access to improved sanitation facilities (% of total pop.)	32	39	43
Energy use per capita (kilograms of oil equivalent)	208	268	319
Carbon dioxide emissions per capita (metric tons)	0.8	0.9	1.0
Electricity use per capita (kilowatt-hours)	119	136	174
Economy			
GDP ($ billions)	4.8	9.4	19.1
GDP growth (annual %)	2.0	4.4	3.3
GDP implicit price deflator (annual % growth)	17.1	25.8	13.3
Value added in agriculture (% of GDP)	24	10	..
Value added in industry (% of GDP)	27	47	..
Value added in services (% of GDP)	49	43	..
Exports of goods and services (% of GDP)	14	42	..
Imports of goods and services (% of GDP)	20	37	..
Gross capital formation (% of GDP)	15	19	..
Central government revenue (% of GDP)	18.9	23.9	..
Central government cash surplus/deficit (% of GDP)	-7.8	-2.3	..
States and markets			
Starting a business (days)			63
Stock market capitalization (% of GDP)	..	..	..
Military expenditures (% of GDP)	7.7	5.0	6.0
Fixed-line and mobile subscribers (per 100 people)	1	2	14
Internet users (per 100 people)	0.0	0.1	1.2
Paved roads (% of total)	9	16	9
High-technology exports (% of manufactured exports)	0	0	5
Global links			
Merchandise trade (% of GDP)	46.9	67.8	64.1
Net barter terms of trade (2000 = 100)	..	100	150
Total external debt ($ billions)	6.4	5.1	5.6
Short-term debt ($ billions)	1.2	0.7	0.3
Total debt service (% of exports)	5.6	4.5	2.4
Foreign direct investment, net inflows ($ billions)	-0.1	0.0	1.1
Remittances received ($ billions)	1.5	1.3	1.3
Aid ($ millions)	400	263	284

Zambia

Sub-Saharan Africa | | **Low income**

Population (millions)	12	Population growth (%)	1.9
Surface area (1,000 sq. km)	753	National poverty rate (% of pop.)	68
GNI ($ billions)	7.4	GNI per capita ($)	630
GNI, PPP ($ billions)	13.4	GNI per capita, PPP ($)	1,140

	1990	2000	2006
People			
Share of poorest 20% in nat'l consumption/income (%)	3.0	3.4	3.6
Life expectancy at birth (years)	48	40	42
Total fertility (births per woman)	6.4	5.8	5.3
Adolescent fertility (births per 1,000 women 15–19)	..	144	130
Contraceptive prevalence (% of married women 15–49)	15	34	..
Births attended by skilled health staff (% of total)	51	43	..
Under-five mortality rate (per 1,000)	180	182	182
Child malnutrition, underweight (% of under age 5)	21.2	23.3	..
Child immunization, measles (% of ages 12–23 mos.)	90	85	84
Primary completion rate, total (% of relevant age group)	..	60	84
Gross secondary enrollment, total (% of relevant age group)	23	23	36
Ratio of girls to boys in primary & secondary school (%)	..	91	96
HIV prevalence rate (% of population ages 15–49)	..	15.6	17.0
Environment			
Forests (1,000 sq. km)	491	447	425
Deforestation (average annual %, 1990–2005)			1.0
Freshwater use (% of internal resources)	..	2.2	..
Access to improved water source (% of total pop.)	50	55	58
Access to improved sanitation facilities (% of total pop.)	44	51	55
Energy use per capita (kilograms of oil equivalent)	673	600	621
Carbon dioxide emissions per capita (metric tons)	0.3	0.2	0.2
Electricity use per capita (kilowatt-hours)	754	595	721
Economy			
GDP ($ billions)	3.3	3.2	10.7
GDP growth (annual %)	–0.5	3.6	6.2
GDP implicit price deflator (annual % growth)	106.4	30.0	12.2
Value added in agriculture (% of GDP)	21	22	22
Value added in industry (% of GDP)	51	25	33
Value added in services (% of GDP)	28	52	45
Exports of goods and services (% of GDP)	36	27	38
Imports of goods and services (% of GDP)	37	41	30
Gross capital formation (% of GDP)	17	17	24
Central government revenue (% of GDP)	20.4	19.7	17.7
Central government cash surplus/deficit (% of GDP)	..	1.8	–2.8
States and markets			
Starting a business (days)			33
Stock market capitalization (% of GDP)	..	7.3	11.0
Military expenditures (% of GDP)	3.7	0.8	2.3
Fixed-line and mobile subscribers (per 100 people)	1	2	15
Internet users (per 100 people)	0.0	0.2	4.3
Paved roads (% of total)	17	22	..
High-technology exports (% of manufactured exports)	..	0	2
Global links			
Merchandise trade (% of GDP)	76.9	51.2	61.6
Net barter terms of trade (2000 = 100)	207	100	187
Total external debt ($ billions)	6.9	5.7	2.3
Short-term debt ($ billions)	1.4	0.1	0.5
Total debt service (% of exports)	14.7	20.8	3.6
Foreign direct investment, net inflows ($ millions)	203	122	575
Remittances received ($ millions)	..	..	57.7
Aid ($ billions)	0.5	0.8	1.4

Zimbabwe

Sub-Saharan Africa		Low income		
Population (millions)	13	Population growth (%)		0.8
Surface area (1,000 sq. km)	391	National poverty rate (% of pop.)		..
GNI ($ billions)	4.5	GNI per capita ($)		340
GNI, PPP ($ billions)	..	GNI per capita, PPP ($)		..

	1990	2000	2006
People			
Share of poorest 20% in nat'l consumption/income (%)	4.0	..	..
Life expectancy at birth (years)	61	43	43
Total fertility (births per woman)	5.1	3.8	3.8
Adolescent fertility (births per 1,000 women 15–19)	..	85	62
Contraceptive prevalence (% of married women 15–49)	43	54	60
Births attended by skilled health staff (% of total)	70	73	80
Under-five mortality rate (per 1,000)	76	105	105
Child malnutrition, underweight (% of under age 5)	8.0	11.5	14.0
Child immunization, measles (% of ages 12–23 mos.)	87	70	90
Primary completion rate, total (% of relevant age group)	97	89	..
Gross secondary enrollment, total (% of relevant age group)	49	43	..
Ratio of girls to boys in primary & secondary school (%)	92	94	..
HIV prevalence rate (% of population ages 15–49)	..	..	18.1
Environment			
Forests (1,000 sq. km)	222	191	175
Deforestation (average annual %, 1990–2005)			1.6
Freshwater use (% of internal resources)	..	34.2	..
Access to improved water source (% of total pop.)	78	80	81
Access to improved sanitation facilities (% of total pop.)	50	52	53
Energy use per capita (kilograms of oil equivalent)	895	792	741
Carbon dioxide emissions per capita (metric tons)	1.6	1.2	0.8
Electricity use per capita (kilowatt-hours)	861	843	953
Economy			
GDP ($ billions)	8.8	7.4	3.4
GDP growth (annual %)	7.0	-7.9	-5.3
GDP implicit price deflator (annual % growth)	14.7	56.2	237.9
Value added in agriculture (% of GDP)	16	18	19
Value added in industry (% of GDP)	33	25	24
Value added in services (% of GDP)	50	57	57
Exports of goods and services (% of GDP)	23	36	57
Imports of goods and services (% of GDP)	23	36	73
Gross capital formation (% of GDP)	17	14	17
Central government revenue (% of GDP)	24.1	..	..
Central government cash surplus/deficit (% of GDP)	-2.6	..	..
States and markets			
Starting a business (days)			96
Stock market capitalization (% of GDP)	27.3	32.9	70.3
Military expenditures (% of GDP)	0.0	0.0	0.0
Fixed-line and mobile subscribers (per 100 people)	1	4	9
Internet users (per 100 people)	0.0	0.4	9.2
Paved roads (% of total)	14	19	..
High-technology exports (% of manufactured exports)	2	2	2
Global links			
Merchandise trade (% of GDP)	40.7	51.2	121.4
Net barter terms of trade (2000 = 100)	98	100	93
Total external debt ($ billions)	3.3	3.8	4.7
Short-term debt ($ billions)	0.6	0.6	1.1
Total debt service (% of exports)	23.1	..	..
Foreign direct investment, net inflows ($ millions)	-12	23	40
Remittances received ($ millions)	1.0	..	..
Aid ($ millions)	334	176	280

Glossary

Access to improved sanitation is the percentage of population with adequate access to excreta disposal facilities (private or shared, but not public) that can effectively prevent human, animal, and insect contact with excreta. Improved facilities range from simple but protected pit latrines to flush toilets with a sewerage connection. To be effective, facilities must be correctly constructed and properly maintained. (World Health Organization)

Access to improved water source is the percentage of the population with reasonable access to an adequate amount of water from an improved source, such as a piped water into a dwelling, plot, or yard; public tap or standpipe; tubewell or borehole; protected dug well or spring; or rainwater collection. Unimproved sources include an unprotected dug well or spring, cart with small tank or drum, bottled water, and tanker trucks. Reasonable access to an adequate amount means the availability of at least 20 liters a person a day from a source within 1 kilometer of the dwelling. (World Health Organization)

Adolescent fertility is the number of births per 1,000 women ages 15–19. (United Nations Population Division)

Aid is official development assistance or official aid flows (net of repayment of principal) as defined by the Development Assistance Committee (DAC) that are made to countries and territories on the DAC list of aid recipients. (Organisation for Economic Co-operation and Development)

Births attended by skilled health staff are the percentage of deliveries attended by personnel trained to give the necessary supervision, care, and advice to women during pregnancy, labor, and the postpartum period; to conduct deliveries on their own; and to care for newborns. (United Nations Children's Fund and Macro International)

Carbon dioxide emissions per capita are emissions stemming from the burning of fossil fuels and the manufacture of cement divided by midyear population. They include carbon dioxide produced during consumption of solid, liquid, and gas fuels and gas flaring. (Carbon Dioxide Information Analysis Center)

Central government cash surplus/deficit is revenue (including grants) minus expense, minus net acquisition of nonfinancial assets. Before 2005 nonfinancial assets were included under revenue and expenditure in gross terms. The concept of cash surplus or deficit is close to the earlier overall budget balance (still missing is lending minus repayments, which is brought into the balance sheet as a financing item under net acquisition of financial assets). (International Monetary Fund)

Glossary

Central government revenue is cash receipts from taxes, social contributions, and other revenues such as fines, fees, rent, and income from property or sales. Grants are also considered revenue but are excluded here. (International Monetary Fund)

Child immunization, measles, is the percentage of children ages 12–23 months at the time of the survey who received a dose of measles vaccine by age 12 months or at any time before the interview date. A child is considered adequately immunized against measles after receiving one dose of the vaccine. (World Health Organization and United Nations Children's Fund)

Child malnutrition, underweight, is the percentage of children under age five whose weight for age is more than two standard deviations below median for the international reference population ages 0–59 months. The data conform to the new Child Growth Standards released by the World Health Organization in 2006. (World Health Organization)

Contraceptive prevalence is the percentage of women married or in-union ages 15–49 who are practicing, or whose sexual partners are practicing, any form of contraception. (United Nations Children's Fund and Macro International)

Deforestation is the permanent conversion of natural forest areas to other uses, including shifting cultivation, permanent agriculture, ranching, settlements, and infrastructure development. Deforested areas do not include areas logged but intended for regeneration or areas degraded by fuelwood gathering, acid precipitation, or forest fires. Negative numbers indicate an increase in forest area. (Food and Agriculture Organization)

Electricity use per capita is the production of power plants and combined heat and power plants less transmission, distribution, and transformation losses and own use by heat and power plants plus imports less exports divided by midyear population. (International Energy Agency)

Energy use per capita is the use of primary energy before transformation to other end-use fuels, which is equal to indigenous production plus imports and stock changes, minus exports and fuels supplied to ships and aircraft engaged in international transportation, divided by midyear population. (International Energy Agency)

Exports of goods and services are the value of all goods and other market services provided to the rest of the world, including the value of merchandise, freight, insurance, transport, travel, royalties, license fees, and other services. Compensation of employees, investment income (formerly called factor services), and transfer payments are excluded. (World Bank, Organisation for Economic Co-operation and Development, and United Nations)

Fixed-line and mobile subscribers are subscribers to fixed-line telephone service (telephone lines connecting a customer's equipment to the public switched telephone network) and mobile telephone service (automatic public mobile telephone service using cellular technology that provides access to the public switched telephone network). (International Telecommunication Union)

Foreign direct investment, net inflows, are investments to acquire a lasting management interest in an enterprise operating in an economy other than that of the investor. They are the sum of inflows of equity capital, reinvestment of earnings, other long-term capital, and short-term capital as shown in the balance of payments. (World Bank and International Monetary Fund)

Forests are land under natural or planted stands of trees, whether productive or not. (Food and Agriculture Organization)

Freshwater use is total freshwater withdrawals for domestic, industrial, and agricultural use, not counting evaporation losses from storage basins. Internal resources refer to internal renewable resources only (flows of rivers and groundwater from rainfall in the country). Withdrawals can exceed 100 percent of internal renewable resources because rivers flows from other countries are not included, because extraction from nonrenewable aquifers or desalination plants is considerable, or because there is significant water reuse. (Food and Agriculture Organization and World Resources Institute)

GDP is gross domestic product at purchaser prices. It is the sum of gross value added by all resident producers in the economy plus any product taxes and minus any subsidies not included in the value of the products. It is calculated without deductions for depreciation of fabricated assets or for depletion and degradation of natural resources. (World Bank, Organisation for Economic Co-operation and Development, and United Nations)

GDP growth is the one-year rate of growth in real gross domestic product. (World Bank, Organisation for Economic Co-operation and Development, and United Nations)

GDP implicit price deflator is the one-year rate of price change in the economy as a whole. (World Bank, Organisation for Economic Co-operation and Development, and United Nations)

GNI is gross national income. It is calculated as gross domestic product (GDP) plus net receipts of primary income (employee compensation and

Glossary

investment income) from abroad. GDP is the sum of value added by all resident producers plus any product taxes (less subsidies) not included in the valuation of output. (World Bank)

GNI per capita is gross national income (GNI) converted to U.S. dollars using the *World Bank Atlas* method divided by midyear population. GNI is the sum of value added by all resident producers plus any product taxes (less subsidies) not included in the valuation of output plus net receipts of primary income (compensation of employees and property income) from abroad. GNI, calculated in national currency, is usually converted to U.S. dollars at official exchange rates for comparisons across economies. The *World Bank Atlas* method is used to smooth fluctuations in prices and exchange rates. It averages the exchange rate for a given year and the two preceding years, adjusted for differences in rates of inflation between the country and the Euro zone, Japan, the United Kingdom, and the United States. (World Bank)

GNI, PPP, is gross national income (GNI) converted to international dollars using purchasing power parities (PPP). An international dollar has the same purchasing power over GNI that a U.S. dollar has in the United States. (World Bank)

GNI per capita, PPP, is gross national income (GNI) converted to international dollars using purchasing power parities (PPP), divided by midyear population. An international dollar has the same purchasing power over GNI that a U.S. dollar has in the United States. (World Bank)

Gross capital formation is outlays on additions to the fixed assets of the economy plus net changes in the level of inventories. Fixed assets include land improvements (fences, ditches, drains, and so on); plant, machinery, and equipment purchase; and the construction of roads, railways, and the like, including schools, offices, hospitals, private residential dwellings, and commercial and industrial buildings. Inventories are stocks of goods held by firms to meet temporary or unexpected fluctuations in production or sales and work in progress. According to the 1993 System of National Accounts, net acquisitions of valuables are also considered capital formation. (World Bank, Organisation for Economic Co-operation and Development, and United Nations)

Gross secondary enrollment, total, is the ratio of total enrollment in secondary education, regardless of age, to the population of the age group that officially corresponds to secondary education. Secondary education completes the provision of basic education that begins at the primary level and aims at laying the foundations for lifelong learning and human development by offering more subject- or skill-oriented instruction using more specialized teachers. (United Nations Educational, Scientific, and Cultural Organization Institute for Statistics)

High-technology exports are products with high research and development intensity, as in aerospace, computers, pharmaceuticals, and scientific instruments. (United Nations Statistics Division's Commodity Trade database)

HIV prevalence rate is the percentage of people ages 15–49 who are infected with HIV. (Joint United Nations Programme on HIV/AIDS and World Health Organization)

Imports of goods and services are the value of all goods and other market services received from the rest of the world, including the value of merchandise, freight, insurance, transport, travel, royalties, license fees and other services. Labor and property income (formerly called factor services) and transfer payments are excluded. (World Bank, Organisation for Economic Co-operation and Development, and United Nations)

Internet users are people with access to the worldwide network. (International Telecommunication Union)

Life expectancy at birth is the number of years a newborn infant would live if prevailing patterns of mortality at the time of its birth were to stay the same throughout its life. (Eurostat, United Nations Population Division, and World Bank)

Merchandise trade is the sum of merchandise exports and imports measured in current U.S. dollars. (World Trade Organization and World Bank)

Military expenditures include all current and capital expenditures on the armed forces, including peacekeeping forces; defense ministries and other government agencies engaged in defense projects; paramilitary forces, if judged to be trained and equipped for military operations; and military space activities. Such expenditures include military and civil personnel, including retirement pensions of military personnel and social services for personnel; operation and maintenance; procurement; military research and development; and military aid (included in the military expenditures of the donor country). Excluded are civil defense and current expenditures for previous military activities, such as for veterans' benefits, demobilization, conversion, and destruction of weapons. This definition cannot be applied for all countries, however, since that would require much more detailed information than is available about what is included in military budgets and off-budget military expenditure items. (Stockholm International Peace Research Institute)

[**Note for China:** Estimate differs from official statistics of the government of China, which has published the following estimates for military expenditure: 1.6 percent in 1990 and 1.4 percent in 2005.]

Glossary

National poverty rate is the percentage of the population living below the national poverty line. National estimates are based on population-weighted subgroup estimates from household surveys. Data are for most recent estimate since 2000. Figures in italics are for years other than 2006. (World Bank)

Net barter terms of trade are the ratio of the export price index to the corresponding import price index measured relative to the base year 2000. (United Nations Conference on Trade and Development and International Monetary Fund)

Paved roads are roads surfaced with crushed stone (macadam) and hydrocarbon binder or bituminized agents, with concrete, or with cobblestones, as a percentage of all the country's roads, measured in length. (International Road Federation)

Population is the midyear estimate of all residents regardless of legal status or citizenship, except for refugees not permanently settled in the country of asylum who are generally considered part of the population of their country of origin. (Eurostat, United Nations Population Division, and World Bank)

Population growth is the exponential growth rate from the previous midyear population. (World Bank)

Primary completion rate, total, is the percentage of students completing the last year of primary school. It is calculated by dividing the total number of students in the last grade of primary school minus the number of repeaters in that grade by the total number of children of official completing age. Because of the change from International Standard Classification of Education 1976 (ISCED76) to ISCED97 in 1998, data before 1999 are not fully comparable with data from 1999 onward. (United Nations Educational, Scientific, and Cultural Organization Institute for Statistics)

Ratio of girls to boys in primary and secondary school is the ratio of the female to male gross enrollment rate in primary and secondary school. (United Nations Educational, Scientific, and Cultural Organization Institute for Statistics)

Remittances received are current transfers by migrant workers and wages and salaries earned by nonresident workers. (International Monetary Fund and World Bank)

Share of poorest 20% in national consumption or income is the share of total national income or consumption that accrues to the poorest quintile. (World Bank)

Short-term debt is debt owed to nonresidents having an original maturity of one year or less and interest in arrears on long-term debt. (World Bank)

Starting a business is the number of calendar days needed to complete the required procedures for legally operating a business. If a procedure can be expedited at additional cost, the fastest procedure, independent of cost, is chosen. (World Bank)

Stock market capitalization is the share price times the number of shares outstanding. (Standard and Poor's)

Surface area is a country's total area, including areas under inland bodies of water and some coastal waterways. (Food and Agriculture Organization)

Total debt service is the sum of principal repayments and interest actually paid on long-term debt (public and publicly guaranteed and private nonguaranteed); interest paid on short-term debt; and use of International Monetary Fund credit, expressed as a percentage of exports. Exports refer to international transactions involving a change in ownership of general merchandise, goods sent for processing and repairs, nonmonetary gold, services, receipts of employee compensation for nonresident workers, investment income, and workers' remittances. (World Bank)

Total external debt is debt owed to nonresidents repayable in foreign currency, goods, or services. It is the sum of public, publicly guaranteed, and private nonguaranted long-term debt, short-term debt, and use of International Monetary Fund credit. (World Bank)

Total fertility is the number of children that would be born to a woman if she were to live to the end of her childbearing years and bear children in accordance with current age-specific fertility rates. (Eurostat, United Nations Population Division, and World Bank)

Under-five mortality rate is the probability that a newborn baby will die before age five if subject to current age-specific mortality rates. (United Nations Children's Fund, World Health Organization, World Bank, and United Nations Population Division)

Value added in agriculture is the net output of agriculture (International Standard Industrial Classification divisions 1–5 including forestry and fishing) after totaling outputs and subtracting intermediate outputs. (World Bank, Organisation for Economic Co-operation and Development, and United Nations)

Value added in industry is the net output of industry (International Standard Industrial Classification divisions 10–45, which includes mining,

Glossary

manufacturing, construction, electricity, water, and gas) after totaling outputs and subtracting intermediate inputs. (World Bank, Organisation for Economic Co-operation and Development, and United Nations)

Value added in services is the net output of services (International Standard Industrial Classification divisions 50–99) after totaling outputs and subtracting intermediate inputs. This sector is derived as a residual and may not properly reflect the sum of services outputs, including banking and financial services. (World Bank, Organisation for Economic Co-operation and Development, and United Nations)